DAX Patterns

SECOND EDITION

The most comprehensive collection of
ready-to-use solutions in DAX for Power BI,
Analysis Services, and Power Pivot.

Alberto Ferrari
Marco Russo

Publisher / Editorial Production: SQLBI Corp., Las Vegas, NV, Unites States

Authors: Alberto Ferrari, Marco Russo
Copy Editor: Claire Costa
Technical Editors: Daniil Maslyuk, Sergio Murru
Cover Designer: Daniele Perilli

ISBN: 978-1-7353652-0-6
Library of Congress Control Number: 2020912594

All the samples and files used in this book are available on **www.daxpatterns.com**

All the code in this book has been formatted with **www.daxformatter.com**

Contents at a glance

Contents

CHAPTER 3   **Month-related calculations**   **49**

CHAPTER 4 Week-related calculations   83

CHAPTER 6	**Comparing different time periods**	**169**

CHAPTER 7	**Semi-additive calculations**	**173**

Introduction

At SQLBI we have a beautiful job: we are world-wide trainers and consultants. We meet thousands of people all over the world every year: a crowd of very diverse persons, sharing the same passion for Business Intelligence and DAX. We are asked to solve scenarios of various complexity by our students and customers.

Say a student approaches you because they need to compute the number of new customers for their report. You solve the problem once, twice, three times... And at some point, you feel that the next time you need to answer the same question, you would love to have a ready-to-use solution. This is the reason we started the daxpatterns.com website in 2013. We started collecting patterns that repeat themselves. We created a collection of DAX formulas aimed at solving the most frequently-asked questions we receive. At that time, the goal was not to write a new book. Instead, our goal was to create some sort of memory bank for the solutions we would find. We thought we would be the main users of our own website.

As is often the case, real-life does not go according to plan. This time, for the better. The website had a tremendous success. Users downloaded the samples and achieved two different goals: they found a ready-to-use solution to their problems, and they improved their DAX skills based on the formulas we authored. Because of the different file formats, we included samples for Excel 2010 and Excel 2013 – the latter still works with later versions of Excel. Eventually, we collected the content of the website into a book. That was the first edition of DAX Patterns. It was at the end of 2015. At the time, we had not yet published the first edition of The Definitive Guide to DAX. Therefore, we included a short introduction to DAX in the DAX Patterns book.

Many things changed over the following five years. DAX evolved with many useful features. Most importantly, Power BI hit the market and the number of users adopting DAX grew at an exponential rate. Today, most of the DAX users create a Power BI solution. When we published the first edition of this book, Power BI had not even been announced yet.

During these five years, the process of collecting patterns continued. We met more students, we solved more problems, we also got better and better at DAX. Plus, we now had thousands of users who were able to provide feedback on previous patterns. Studying user comments gave us a better picture of what our readers needed. In parallel, we went on to publish two editions of The Definitive Guide to DAX. At that point, there was no longer a reason to be teaching DAX in a book about patterns.

Long story short, it started to make a lot of sense to author a new version of both the DAX Patterns website and book. We rolled up our sleeves and created the book you are reading right now.

We did not use any of the content from the previous book. We wanted a fresh start. The entire library of code is rewritten from scratch, using the latest DAX and Power BI features and adapting the code to Excel 2019 when necessary.

In this new edition we made several choices:

- We greatly increased the share of the book dedicated to time intelligence calculations. Time intelligence is by far the most widely studied topic. Therefore, it made sense to increase the number of time-related calculations and patterns.

- Similarly, the New and returning customers pattern was an absolute hit. We gave that pattern a bigger share of the book as well, increasing the number of formulas and models to compute new and returning customers.

- We increased the number of patterns, adding several that – in our experience – are likely to be useful to our readers.

- We decided to cut out a few patterns. For example, the chapter about statistical calculations was useful back in 2015, because of the lack of statistical functions in DAX. Since then, DAX introduced many new functions to compute the formulas that were explained in that chapter. There is no need for that content in 2020.

- We no longer provide code snippets. In the previous book, most of the code was shown including placeholders for the columns that readers were likely to change. We no longer do that. We show code that works, because you often have to adapt the data model and other details in the formula. We felt this would make the code more readable and easier to use and to adapt to your model.

- We optimized every single formula. All the code you see in these patterns has been thoroughly reviewed for performance. This is not to say that these patterns are the very best. They are the best we could come up with. If you can make the code better and faster, let us know! The comment sections on the website are the right place to provide your feedback.

- We created a Power BI and an Excel version of each sample file. In the book, we include pictures of Power BI reports showing the results of the code, but the examples you can download are available in both formats: Power BI and Excel.

- We improved the readability of the eBook version of DAX Patterns. This meant keeping the code formatting intact regardless of the eBook reader size.

Why we published this book

If you are wondering what the differences may be between the content of this book and the content published on daxpatterns.com, we want to assure you that there are no differences. Should you buy the book to obtain extra content? No. The access to the web site is free, where you can read the same content as what you will find in this book and download the sample files for free.

That said, if you enjoy having an offline copy of the patterns, if you enjoy having a printed version, if you would like to have it in your eBook collection, then you should purchase it. This way, you help us keep the business up and running. We were surprised with the number of people who purchased the first edition. This motivated us to further invest into this new version of the website and the pattern. We hope the process will continue!

By visiting the daxpatterns.com website, you will also see that we have recorded a video for each pattern. This is where we go into more depth on how to use the patterns and how the formulas work. These videos are for sale. You can buy all of them, or just the pattern you want to study more. It is an additional service that many people have been asking for; we know some prefer the book, some prefer the video, and many people want both!

How to use this book

What will you find in this book? Each standalone chapter covers a separate pattern and can be read without having read the others. You can read the Currency conversion pattern without having ever looked at the Basket analysis, or at any of the time-related calculations.

Each chapter about a pattern starts with a brief description of the business scenario; it then goes into a more complete description of the solution, along with all the DAX code that needs to be implemented in order to solve the scenario. We kept the description of the code short, using comments in the code to document the measures where needed.

You need separate companion content for the book. At the beginning of each chapter, a short URL points to the corresponding pattern on the daxpatterns.com website. You can download the sample files for Power BI and Excel from the website.

The book is intended to be used as a reference. When you want to implement a pattern, you do not want to read long descriptions: you want to see the code and the reason for it. Therefore, we kept it as compact as possible, keeping the spotlight on the DAX code.

That said, if you want to implement a pattern we strongly suggest that you read the entire chapter before implementing any code. The reason is that we sometimes present multiple solutions and you need to choose the best for your specific scenario. For each pattern we also provide the demo files both in Power BI and Power Pivot for Excel. Sometimes the code of the two versions is slightly different. The book always presents the Power BI solution, which is using the latest features of DAX at the time of printing. Some of those features are not available in Power Pivot – like calculated tables. This is the main reason for the differences.

There is only one exception: time-related calculations. As we said, we gave the time-related calculations more space in the book: we now present four different patterns for time-related calculations. Each of these four patterns is huge. Together, they represent more than 40% of this book. This is why we created an introductory chapter to the time-related calculations, which aims to help you choose the right pattern for your scenario. If you need to implement time-related calculations, make sure to read the introduction first, and then the full chapter covering the pattern you decide to use.

Prerequisites

One word of advice to our readers: this book does not teach DAX.

You are expected to already know DAX to make the best use of these patterns. Most of the patterns show advanced DAX techniques that you are welcome to study and use in your solutions. By reading this book you will not learn DAX. But if you already know DAX, you will likely become a better DAX developer.

We suggest that you use these patterns with the latest version of Power BI or Excel, because DAX evolves and improves over time. We tested the patterns on Power BI June 2020, Excel 2019, and Excel for Microsoft 365 version 2006. Most of the patterns work with earlier versions of Power BI and Excel, but we cannot guarantee this because we did not thoroughly test for all the previous versions.

Acknowledgments

Last, but not least: the acknowledgments section.

The most important person we want to thank is you. This work was made possible by the discussions we have had over time with readers, users, customers, and students like yourself. Therefore, even without knowing it you have contributed to this content; and if you post comments in our public forums, you will be contributing further.

That said, there are some people who directly contributed to the entire writing process: Daniil Maslyuk meticulously reviewed each pattern, found all the errors we had made and provided invaluable feedback. Claire Costa reviewed our English grammar and readability, making the book more precise and enjoyable. Sergio Murru built the Excel versions of the sample files, which made the patterns available also to Power Pivot for Excel users. Daniele Perilli is the reason behind the book and the website being as beautiful as they are. We are responsible for the content and for any mistake, but if you can read accurate numbers, in good English, in both Excel and Power BI, and with a gorgeous overall presentation, it is thanks to them.

Enjoy DAX!

CHAPTER 1

Time-related calculations

This chapter introduces the four time-related calculations patterns presented in the next chapters. The goal here is to help you choose the right pattern based on your specific needs. Indeed, when it comes to time-related calculations, the choice of the pattern is hard.

First, what is a time-related calculation? A time-related calculation refers to any calculation that involves time. Examples include the set of period-to-date calculations, like year-to-date, quarter-to-date, or month-to-date. These calculations accumulate values from the beginning of a time period – year, quarter, month – and they return the aggregation of the measure from the start of the period to the date shown in the report. The definition of a time period changes depending on whether you work with the Gregorian calendar or a fiscal calendar. In Figure 1-1, you can see an example of period-to-date calculations, where YTD stands for year-to-date, and QTD for quarter-to-date.

Year	Sales Amount	Sales YTD	Sales QTD	Sales Fiscal YTD
⊞ 2007	9,008,591.74	9,008,591.74	2,731,424.16	5,616,670.71
⊟ 2008	9,927,582.99	9,927,582.99	2,797,611.46	5,373,157.05
Jan 2008	656,766.69	656,766.69	656,766.69	6,273,437.41
Feb 2008	600,080.00	1,256,846.69	1,256,846.69	6,873,517.40
Mar 2008	559,538.52	1,816,385.21	1,816,385.21	7,433,055.92
Apr 2008	999,667.17	2,816,052.38	999,667.17	8,432,723.09
May 2008	893,231.96	3,709,284.34	1,892,899.13	9,325,955.05
Jun 2008	845,141.60	4,554,425.94	2,738,040.73	10,171,096.65
Jul 2008	890,547.41	5,444,973.35	890,547.41	890,547.41
Aug 2008	721,560.95	6,166,534.30	1,612,108.36	1,612,108.36
Sep 2008	963,437.23	7,129,971.53	2,575,545.59	2,575,545.59
Oct 2008	719,792.99	7,849,764.52	719,792.99	3,295,338.58
Nov 2008	1,156,109.32	9,005,873.85	1,875,902.31	4,451,447.90
Dec 2008	921,709.14	9,927,582.99	2,797,611.46	5,373,157.05

FIGURE 1-1 Examples of period-to-date calculations.

Included in these patterns are also comparisons of a parameter over a certain period of time, with a different period of time. For example, you can compare the sales of the current month against the sales of the same month in the previous year. Another example of time-related calculations is the moving average over a time period, like a rolling average over 12 months which smoothes out line charts and removes the effect of seasonality from calculations. The four time-related patterns implement the same set of calculations.

What makes the patterns so different from one another, is the definition of what a calendar is. You can already appreciate the different definitions of a year-to-date calculation by looking at Figure 1-1.

Depending on whether you are working with the Gregorian or the fiscal calendar, the numbers are different. When talking about a calendar, things can easily become very complicated because of the definition of the calendar.

For example, you might have a week-based calendar following an ISO standard or your own definition. In a week-based calendar every month starts the same day of the week, and the same goes for the year. Therefore, a year in a week-based calendar might start in the Gregorian year before, or end in the next one. Moreover, some calendars split a year into 13 periods instead of 12 months, for accounting purposes. The calendar requirements are the main driver for the choice of the time-related pattern.

The four time-related patterns are presented in order of increasing complexity:

1. Standard time-related calculations

2. Month-related calculations

3. Week-related calculations

4. Custom time-related calculations

The **Standard time-related calculations** pattern is implemented using regular DAX time intelligence functions. It works based on the assumption that your calendar is a regular Gregorian calendar and that your fiscal calendar starts at the beginning of a Gregorian quarter. For example, DAX time intelligence functions work fine if your fiscal calendar starts on July 1 (start of the third quarter of a Gregorian calendar). Yet, they might provide unexpected results if your fiscal calendar starts on March 1 – both because March does not start a Gregorian quarter, and because of a historical bug in handling leap years with fiscal calendars. Despite these limitations, the pattern is easy to use and implement because it relies on standard DAX functions and works with a regular date table, with few requirements.

The next three patterns do not use DAX time intelligence calculations. Rather, they are written using basic DAX functions – which leaves much more flexibility in the definition of what a calendar is in terms of quarters, months, and weeks. These patterns require you to build a *Date* table whose columns are required for the DAX measures to identify the fractions of the year. For example, you need one column containing the year, one for the quarter, one for the month, plus additional columns to simplify the calculations.

Moreover, many details need to be considered when detecting and filtering periods. Many calculations that look easy to humans prove to be very complicated for a computer. When you compare one quarter against the previous one, you need to select a different number of days for the two quarters: the January-March quarter is shorter than the April-June quarter. The same goes for the months: January is longer than February, but if you want to make a comparison month-over-month, you need two date selections of different lengths.

If standard time intelligence functions do not meet your needs, then you need to implement one of the other three patterns. All of them require the creation of your own *Date* table.

The **Month-related calculations** pattern is the easiest one. It implements all the calculations assuming that you are not interested in the daily details. For example, if you need calculations and reports that compare one month against another, then the pattern is a good fit. The pattern does not support sub-month selections. If you want to compare three days in a quarter against the same three days in the previous quarter, then you exceed the potential of the pattern: it just does not work. Despite strong limitations in its analytical power (limited to monthly granularity) the month-related pattern is extremely fast and simple to implement. Moreover, it can handle scenarios where you have more than 12 months seamlessly. It comes with the flexibility of a custom-made pattern, and it is simpler than the standard time-related pattern. If you are ok with its limitation about the month granularity, this should be the pattern of choice.

In the **Week-related calculations** pattern, the week is the foundation of the calendar. The ISO 8601 is one of the standards that provide a definition of a week date system – even though many countries adopt different national standards to identify years, quarters, and weeks. One year has 52 or 53 weeks, one quarter has 13 weeks, and each quarter is subdivided into 5+4+4 weeks, 4+5+4 weeks, or 4+4+5 weeks. When there are 53 weeks in a year, there are 14 weeks in one of the quarters. Because a week is not necessarily entirely included in a month, the group of weeks within a quarter should be called a "period" even though it is often referred to as a month. For this reason, we refer to the month names as "periods" in the following description.

Because weeks are the main entity, there is no correspondence between a year in a Gregorian calendar and a year in a week-based calendar. A week-based calendar always starts on the same weekday, like Monday or Sunday. Therefore, only occasionally does this day happen to fall on January 1. For a weekly year, it is totally fine to start on December 29 of the previous year, or on January 3 of the current year. Despite being somewhat unusual, weekly calendars come with some great characteristics: every "month" in a quarter includes the same number of weekdays. Comparing one quarter against another means comparing the same number of days and the same distribution of weekdays.

Week-based calendars require a dedicated *Date* table with several columns to drive the DAX calculations. Moreover, there are no pre-existing DAX functions available to compute calculations over such calendars. Therefore, week-based calculations are implemented with custom DAX code. The complexity is higher than the month-related pattern because the week-related pattern lets you filter any time period, down to the day level. If you have a calendar based on weeks, the week-based calculations pattern is what you have to implement.

The **Custom time-related calculations** pattern is the most flexible (and complex) one. This last pattern provides the same calculations as the standard time-related pattern. The relevant difference is that the entire pattern is written using basic DAX functions: we do not use any DAX time intelligence functions. Consequently, the pattern is extremely flexible because you can freely change the behavior of the calculations. With greater flexibility comes greater complexity.

The DAX code of the last pattern is not trivial. It requires much attention to small details. Use it only if none of the other patterns satisfies your business requirements, and you really need the complete flexibility it provides.

Finally, which pattern should you choose?

- If your requirements are satisfied by a regular Gregorian calendar, the **Standard time-related calculations** pattern is the obvious choice.

- If the month granularity is enough for your reporting needs – which is often the case, more often than expected – then the **Month-related calculations** pattern is the optimal choice: fast and simple.

- If you work with a calendar based on weeks, then you need the **Week-related calculations** pattern.

- If none of the above is enough and you really need total flexibility, be prepared for a long and fascinating trip into the intricacies of filter contexts and dive straight into the **Custom time-related calculations** pattern.

Remember: with a Business Intelligence project, simpler is better. Choose the most straightforward pattern that satisfies your needs. Needless to say, if you are curious about the differences between the various implementations, it might be useful to have a quick read through all four chapters before making your choice.

## CHAPTER 2

Standard time-related calculations

Download sample files: **https://sql.bi/dax-201**

In this pattern, we show you how to compute time-related calculations, like year-to-date, same period last year, and percentage growth using a standard calendar. The great advantage of working with a standard calendar is that you can rely on several built-in time intelligence functions. The built-in functions are designed in such a way that they provide the correct result for the most common requirements.

In case your requirement cannot be fulfilled by the built-in functions, or if you have a non-standard calendar, then you should use regular (non-time-related) DAX functions to reach the same goal. This way, you customize the result of your code at will. That said, if you need custom calculations, then you also need to enrich your date table with a set of columns that are needed by the DAX formulas to move the filter. These custom calculations are covered in the **Custom time-related calculations** pattern.

If you are using a regular Gregorian calendar, then the formulas in this pattern are the easiest and most effective way of producing time intelligence calculations. Keep in mind that standard DAX time intelligence functions only support a regular Gregorian calendar – that is a calendar with 12 months, each month with its Gregorian number of days, quarters made up of three months, and all the regular aspects of a calendar that we are used to.

Introduction to time intelligence calculations

In order to use any time intelligence calculation, you need a well-formed date table. The *Date* table must satisfy the following requirements:

- All dates need to be present for the years required. The *Date* table must always start on January 1 and end on December 31, including all the days in this range. If the report only references fiscal years, then the date table must include all the dates from the first to the last day of a fiscal year. For example, if the fiscal year 2008 starts on July 1, 2007, then the *Date* table must include all the days from July 1, 2007 to June 30, 2008.

- There needs to be a column with a *DateTime* or *Date* data type containing unique values. This column is usually called *Date*. Even though the *Date* column is often used to define relationships with other tables, this is not required. Still, the *Date* column must contain unique values and should be referenced by the Mark as Date Table feature. In case the column also contains a time part, no time should be used – for example, the time should always be 12:00 am.

- The *Date* table must be marked as a date table in the model, in case the relationship between the *Date* table and any other table (like *Sales* in our example) is not based on the *Date* column.

There are several ways to build a *Date* table. The way you build the *Date* table does not affect how you use the standard time intelligence calculations, as long as the date table satisfies the requirements. If you already have a *Date* table that works well for your report, just import it and mark it as a date table after having checked that it satisfies the minimum requirements. If you do not have a *Date* table, you can create one using a DAX calculated table as described later.

It is a best practice to apply the Mark as a Date Table setting to the *Date* table used for time intelligence calculations. The Mark as a Date Table setting adds a REMOVEFILTERS modifier over the *Date* table every time a filter is applied to the *Date* column. This action (applying a filter on the *Date* column) is performed by all the time intelligence functions used in CALCULATE. DAX implements the same behavior if you define the relationship between *Sales* and *Date* using the *Date* column. Nevertheless, applying the Mark as a Date Table setting to a date table is a best practice. If you have multiple date tables, you can mark all of them as date tables.

If you do not use the Mark as a Date Table setting and you do not use the date column for the relationship, then you must add a REMOVEFILTERS over the *Date* table whenever you use a time intelligence function in CALCULATE. This behavior is described in more detail in the article Time Intelligence in Power BI Desktop (https://sql.bi/28211).

What are standard DAX time intelligence functions

The standard time intelligence functions are table functions returning a list of dates used as a filter in CALCULATE. The result of a time intelligence function can be obtained by writing a more complex filter expression. For example, the DATESYTD function returns all the dates in the same year between the first day of the year and the last day visible in the filter context. The following expression:

```
DATESYTD ( 'Date'[Date] )
```

corresponds to the following FILTER expression:

```
VAR LastDateAvailable = MAX ( 'Date'[Date] )
VAR FirstJanuaryOfLastDate = DATE ( YEAR ( LastDateAvailable ), 1, 1 )
RETURN
    FILTER (
        ALL ( 'Date'[Date] ),
        AND (
            'Date'[Date] >= FirstJanuaryOfLastDate,
            'Date'[Date] <= LastDateAvailable
        )
    )
```

There are many time intelligence functions, most of which we present in this pattern. Be mindful: time intelligence functions should be used as filter arguments of CALCULATE, and sometimes you will resort to variables to achieve that. It is dangerous to use time intelligence functions in iterators, because of the implicit context transition that is triggered to retrieve the dates active from the filter context. More details about this behavior are available in the DAX Guide documentation, like https://dax.guide/datesytd/ .

The following is a quick guide to the best practices when using time intelligence functions:

- Use time intelligence functions like DATESYTD only in filter arguments of CALCULATE / CALCULATETABLE, or to assign filters to variables.
- Use scalar functions like EDATE and EOMONTH in DAX formulas returning a value – also known as scalar expressions. These functions are not time intelligence functions and can be used in expressions evaluated in a row context.
- Use CONVERT to convert a date into a number and vice versa.
- A complete updated list of time intelligence functions is available at https://dax.guide/.

DAX beginners often confuse time intelligence functions with regular – scalar – time functions. This confusion leads to common mistakes that can be avoided by following these suggestions:

- **DO NOT** use DATEADD to return the previous or the following day. You can use simple mathematical operators to do that.
- **DO NOT** use PREVIOUSDAY to compute the previous day in a scalar expression. You can just subtract one from a date to obtain the previous day in a scalar expression.
- **DO NOT** use EOMONTH as a filter – use ENDOFMONTH instead. EOMONTH is a scalar expression. ENDOFMONTH is a time intelligence function. Always pay attention to the return type of a function: only table functions are time intelligence functions, and they should not be used in scalar expressions.

Disabling the Auto Date/Time

Power BI can automatically add a *Date* table to a data model. **Yet, we strongly suggest disabling the automatic *Date* table created by Power BI** and importing or creating an explicit *Date* table instead. More details are included in the article Automatic time intelligence in Power BI (https://sql.bi/137706).

The presence of an automatic *Date* table also enables a specific syntax called column variation. Column variations are expressed with a dot after the date column, followed by a column of the date table that is created automatically:

```
Sales[Order Date].[Date]
```

Power BI quick measures make extensive use of column variations when used over an automatic *Date* table. We do not rely on the date tables created automatically in Power BI because we want to maintain maximum flexibility and maximum control over our model. The syntax of column variations is not used for Date tables that are part of the model and thus are not created automatically.

Limitations of standard time intelligence functions

The standard time intelligence functions work on a regular Gregorian calendar. They have several limitations, listed in this section. When your requirements are not compatible with these limitations, you need another pattern (see **Custom time-related calculations** and **Week-related calculations**).

- The year starts on the first of January. There is limited support for fiscal calendars starting at a different date. However, the first day of the fiscal year must always be the same for every year and cannot be the first of March, because of historical bugs related to leap years.

- The quarters always start on the first of January, April, July, and October. The range of a quarter cannot be modified.

- A month is always a calendar month.

- Filters of additional columns such as *Day of Week* or *Working Day* might not be supported correctly by standard time intelligence functions. More details about possible workarounds are available in the section, "Filtering other date attributes".

Consequently, many advanced calculations like calculations over weeks are not supported by the standard time intelligence calculations. These advanced calculations require a custom calendar.

Building a *Date* table

DAX time intelligence functions work on any standard Gregorian calendar table. If you already have a *Date* table, you can import the table and use it without any issue. If a *Date* table is not available, you can create one using a DAX calculated table. As an example, the following DAX expression defines the simple *Date* table used in this chapter:

Calculated table

```
Date =
VAR FirstFiscalMonth = 7   -- First month of the fiscal year
VAR FirstDayOfWeek = 0     -- 0 = Sunday, 1 = Monday, ...
VAR FirstYear =            -- Customizes the first year to use
    YEAR ( MIN ( Sales[Order Date] ))
RETURN
GENERATE (
    FILTER (
        CALENDARAUTO (),
        YEAR ( [Date] ) >= FirstYear
    ),
    VAR Yr = YEAR ( [Date] )           -- Year Number
    VAR Mn = MONTH ( [Date] )          -- Month Number (1-12)
    VAR Qr = QUARTER ( [Date] )        -- Quarter Number (1-4)
    VAR MnQ = Mn - 3 * (Qr - 1)        -- Month in Quarter (1-3)
    VAR Wd = WEEKDAY ( [Date], 1 ) - 1 -- Weekday Number (0 = Sunday, 1 = Monday, ...)
    VAR Fyr =                          -- Fiscal Year Number
        Yr + 1 * ( FirstFiscalMonth > 1 && Mn >= FirstFiscalMonth )
    VAR Fqr =                          -- Fiscal Quarter (string)
        FORMAT ( EOMONTH ( [Date], 1 - FirstFiscalMonth ), "\QQ" )
    RETURN ROW (
        "Year", DATE ( Yr, 12, 31 ),
        "Year Quarter", FORMAT ( [Date], "\QQ-YYYY" ),
        "Year Quarter Date", EOMONTH ( [Date], 3 - MnQ ),
        "Quarter", FORMAT ( [Date], "\QQ" ),
        "Year Month", EOMONTH ( [Date], 0 ),
        "Month", DATE ( 1900, MONTH ( [Date] ), 1 ),
        "Day of Week", DATE ( 1900, 1, 7 + Wd + (7 * (Wd < FirstDayOfWeek)) ),
        "Fiscal Year", DATE ( Fyr + (FirstFiscalMonth = 1), FirstFiscalMonth, 1 ) - 1,
        "Fiscal Year Quarter", "F" & Fqr & "-" & Fyr,
        "Fiscal Year Quarter Date", EOMONTH ( [Date], 3 - MnQ ),
        "Fiscal Quarter", "F" & Fqr
    )
)
```

You can customize the first three variables to build a *Date* table that meets specific business requirements. In order to obtain the correct result, the columns must be configured in the data model as follows – when the column is not text, it is a *Date* data type with standard or custom format:

- *Date*: m/dd/yyyy (8/14/2007), used as a column to mark as date table
- *Year*: yyyy (2007)
- *Year Quarter*: Text (Q3-2008)
- *Year Quarter Date*: Hidden (9/30/2008)

- *Quarter*: Text (Q1)
- *Year Month*: mmm yyyy (Aug 2007)
- *Month*: mmm (Aug)
- *Day of Week*: ddd (Tue)
- *Fiscal Year*: \F\Y yyyy (FY 2008)
- *Fiscal Year Quarter*: Text (FQ1-2008)
- *Fiscal Year Quarter Date*: Hidden (9/30/2008)
- *Fiscal Quarter*: Text (FQ1)

The *Date* table in this pattern has two hierarchies:

- Calendar: Year (*Year*), Quarter (*Year Quarter*), Month (*Year Month*)
- Fiscal: Year (*Fiscal Year*), Quarter (*Fiscal Year Quarter*), Month (*Year Month*)

Regardless of the source, the *Date* table must also include a hidden *DateWithSales* calculated column to use the formulas of this pattern:

Calculated column in the Date table

```
DateWithSales =
'Date'[Date] <= MAX ( Sales[Order Date] )
```

The *Date[DateWithSales]* column is *TRUE* if the date is on or before the last date with transactions in the Sales table; it is *FALSE* otherwise. In other words, *DateWithSales* is *TRUE* for "past" dates and *FALSE* for "future" dates, where "past" and "future" are relative to the last date with transactions in *Sales*.

Controlling the visualization in future dates

Most of the time intelligence calculations should not display values for dates after the last date available. For example, a year-to-date calculation can also show values for future dates, but we want to hide those values. The dataset used in these examples ends on August 15, 2009. Therefore, we consider the month of August 2009, the third quarter of 2009 (Q3-2009), and the year 2009 as the last periods with data. Any date later than August 15, 2019 is considered as future, and we want to hide values there.

In order to avoid showing results in future dates, we use the following *ShowValueForDates* measure. *ShowValueForDates* returns TRUE if the time period selected is not after the last period with data:

Measure (hidden) in the Date table

```
ShowValueForDates :=
VAR LastDateWithData =
    CALCULATE (
        MAX ( 'Sales'[Order Date] ),
        REMOVEFILTERS ()
    )
VAR FirstDateVisible =
    MIN ( 'Date'[Date] )
VAR Result =
    FirstDateVisible <= LastDateWithData
RETURN
    Result
```

The *ShowValueForDates* measure is hidden. It is a technical measure created to reuse the same logic in many different time-related calculations, and the user should not use *ShowValueForDates* directly in a report.

Naming convention

This section describes the naming convention we adopted to reference the time intelligence calculations. A simple categorization shows whether a calculation:

- shifts over a period of time, for example the same period in the previous year;

- performs an aggregation, for example year-to-date; or

- compares two time periods, for example this year compared to last year.

Acronym	Description	Shift	Aggregation	Comparison
YTD	Year-to-date		X	
QTD	Quarter-to-date		X	
MTD	Month-to-date		X	
MAT	Moving annual total		X	
PY	Previous year	X		
PQ	Previous quarter	X		
PM	Previous month	X		
PYC	Previous year complete	X		
PQC	Previous quarter complete	X		
PMC	Previous month complete	X		
PP	Previous period (automatically selects year, quarter, or month)	X		
PYMAT	Previous year moving annual total	X	X	

Acronym	Description	Shift	Aggregation	Comparison
YOY	Year-over-year			X
QOQ	Quarter-over-quarter			X
MOM	Month-over-month			X
MATG	Moving annual total growth	X	X	X
POP	Period-over-period (automatically selects year, quarter, or month)			X
PYTD	Previous year-to-date	X	X	
PQTD	Previous quarter-to-date	X	X	
PMTD	Previous month-to-date	X	X	
YOYTD	Year-over-year-to-date	X	X	X
QOQTD	Quarter-over-quarter-to-date	X	X	X
MOMTD	Month-over-month-to-date	X	X	X
YTDOPY	Year-to-date-over-previous-year	X	X	X
QTDOPQ	Quarter-to-date-over-previous-quarter	X	X	X
MTDOPM	Month-to-date-over-previous-month	X	X	X

Computing period-to-date totals

The year-to-date, quarter-to-date, and month-to-date calculations modify the filter context for the *Date* table, applying a range of dates as a filter that overwrites the filter for the period selected.

All these calculations can be implemented using a regular CALCULATE with a time intelligence function, or with one of the TOTAL functions such as TOTALYTD. TOTAL functions are just syntactic sugar for the CALCULATE version. We show them as a reference, even though we prefer the CALCULATE version – indeed, using CALCULATE makes the formula logic more evident, and it provides more flexibility than TOTAL functions do. The formulas using the TOTAL functions are marked as (2) in the following examples. The purpose of showing them is only to show that they return the same values as the CALCULATE version does.

Year-to-date total

The year-to-date aggregates data starting on January 1 of the year, as shown in Figure 2-1.

Year	Sales Amount	Sales YTD (simple)	Sales YTD	Sales YTD (2)
⊞ **2007**	**9,008,591.74**	**9,008,591.74**	**9,008,591.74**	**9,008,591.74**
⊞ **2008**	**9,927,582.99**	**9,927,582.99**	**9,927,582.99**	**9,927,582.99**
⊟ **2009**	**5,725,632.34**	**5,725,632.34**	**5,725,632.34**	**5,725,632.34**
Jan 2009	580,901.05	580,901.05	580,901.05	580,901.05
Feb 2009	622,581.14	1,203,482.19	1,203,482.19	1,203,482.19
Mar 2009	496,137.87	1,699,620.05	1,699,620.05	1,699,620.05
Apr 2009	678,893.22	2,378,513.27	2,378,513.27	2,378,513.27
May 2009	1,067,165.23	3,445,678.50	3,445,678.50	3,445,678.50
Jun 2009	872,586.20	4,318,264.70	4,318,264.70	4,318,264.70
Jul 2009	1,068,396.58	5,386,661.27	5,386,661.27	5,386,661.27
Aug 2009	338,971.06	5,725,632.34	5,725,632.34	5,725,632.34
Sep 2009		5,725,632.34		
Oct 2009		5,725,632.34		
Nov 2009		5,725,632.34		
Dec 2009		5,725,632.34		
Total	**24,661,807.07**			

FIGURE 2-1 *Sales YTD (simple)* shows the value for any time period, whereas *Sales YTD* and *Sales YTD (2)* hide the result after the last period with data.

The year-to-date total of a measure can rely on the DATESYTD function this way:

Measure in the Sales table

```
Sales YTD (simple) :=
CALCULATE (
    [Sales Amount],
    DATESYTD ( 'Date'[Date] )
)
```

DATESYTD returns the set of dates from the first day of the current year, up to the last date visible in the filter context. Therefore, the *Sales YTD (simple)* measure shows data even for future dates in the year. We can avoid this behavior in the *Sales YTD* measure by returning a result only when the *ShowValueForDates* measure returns TRUE:

Measure in the Sales table

```
Sales YTD :=
IF (
    [ShowValueForDates],
    CALCULATE (
        [Sales Amount],
        DATESYTD ( 'Date'[Date] )
    )
)
```

If the report is based on a fiscal year that does not correspond to the calendar year, DATESYTD requires an additional argument to identify the last day of the fiscal year. Take for example, the report in Figure 2-2.

Year	Sales Amount	Sales Fiscal YTD	Sales Fiscal YTD (2)
⊞ **FY 2007**	**3,391,921.03**	**3,391,921.03**	**3,391,921.03**
⊞ **FY 2008**	**10,171,096.65**	**10,171,096.65**	**10,171,096.65**
⊟ **FY 2009**	**9,691,421.74**	**9,691,421.74**	**9,691,421.74**
Jul 2008	890,547.41	890,547.41	890,547.41
Aug 2008	721,560.95	1,612,108.36	1,612,108.36
Sep 2008	963,437.23	2,575,545.59	2,575,545.59
Oct 2008	719,792.99	3,295,338.58	3,295,338.58
Nov 2008	1,156,109.32	4,451,447.90	4,451,447.90
Dec 2008	921,709.14	5,373,157.05	5,373,157.05
Jan 2009	580,901.05	5,954,058.10	5,954,058.10
Feb 2009	622,581.14	6,576,639.23	6,576,639.23
Mar 2009	496,137.87	7,072,777.10	7,072,777.10
Apr 2009	678,893.22	7,751,670.32	7,751,670.32
May 2009	1,067,165.23	8,818,835.55	8,818,835.55
Jun 2009	872,586.20	9,691,421.74	9,691,421.74
⊟ **FY 2010**	**1,407,367.64**	**1,407,367.64**	**1,407,367.64**
Jul 2009	1,068,396.58	1,068,396.58	1,068,396.58
Aug 2009	338,971.06	1,407,367.64	1,407,367.64
Total	**24,661,807.07**		

FIGURE 2-2 *Sales Fiscal YTD* and *Sales Fiscal YTD (2)* show the year-to-date based on fiscal years.

The *Sales Fiscal YTD* measure specifies the last day and month of the fiscal year in the second argument of DATESYTD. The following measure uses June 30 as the last day of the fiscal year. The second argument of DATESYTD must be a constant value (also called a literal) corresponding to the definition of the fiscal year in the *Date* table; it cannot be computed dynamically:

Measure in the Sales table

```
Sales Fiscal YTD :=
IF (
    [ShowValueForDates],
    CALCULATE (
        [Sales Amount],
        DATESYTD ( 'Date'[Date], "6-30" )
    )
)
```

The TOTALYTD function is a possible alternative to DATESYTD:

Measure in the Sales table

```
Sales YTD (2) :=
IF (
    [ShowValueForDates],
    TOTALYTD (
        [Sales Amount],
        'Date'[Date]
    )
)
```

Measure in the Sales table

```
Sales Fiscal YTD (2) :=
IF (
    [ShowValueForDates],
    TOTALYTD (
        [Sales Amount],
        'Date'[Date],
        "6-30"
    )
)
```

Quarter-to-date total

The quarter to date aggregates data from the first day of the quarter, as shown in Figure 2-3.

Year	Sales Amount	Sales QTD	Sales QTD (2)
⊞ **2007**	**9,008,591.74**	**2,731,424.16**	**2,731,424.16**
⊞ **2008**	**9,927,582.99**	**2,797,611.46**	**2,797,611.46**
⊟ **2009**	**5,725,632.34**		
⊞ **Q1-2009**	**1,699,620.05**	**1,699,620.05**	**1,699,620.05**
⊟ **Q2-2009**	**2,618,644.64**	**2,618,644.64**	**2,618,644.64**
Apr 2009	678,893.22	678,893.22	678,893.22
May 2009	1,067,165.23	1,746,058.45	1,746,058.45
Jun 2009	872,586.20	2,618,644.64	2,618,644.64
⊟ **Q3-2009**	**1,407,367.64**	**1,407,367.64**	**1,407,367.64**
Jul 2009	1,068,396.58	1,068,396.58	1,068,396.58
Aug 2009	338,971.06	1,407,367.64	1,407,367.64
Total	**24,661,807.07**		

FIGURE 2-3 *Sales QTD* shows the quarter-to-date amount, which is blank for 2009 because there is no data in Q4-2009.

The quarter-to-date total of a measure is computed with the DATESQTD function as follows:

Measure in the Sales table

```
Sales QTD :=
IF (
    [ShowValueForDates],
    CALCULATE (
        [Sales Amount],
        DATESQTD ( 'Date'[Date] )
    )
)
```

The TOTALQTD is a possible alternative to DATESQTD:

Measure in the Sales table

```
Sales QTD (2) :=
IF (
    [ShowValueForDates],
    TOTALQTD (
        [Sales Amount],
        'Date'[Date]
    )
)
```

Month-to-date total

The month to date aggregates data from the first day of the month, as shown in Figure 2-4.

Year	Sales Amount	Sales MTD	Sales MTD (2)
⊞ 2007	9,008,591.74	991,548.75	991,548.75
⊞ 2008	9,927,582.99	921,709.14	921,709.14
⊟ 2009	5,725,632.34		
⊞ Q1-2009	1,699,620.05	496,137.87	496,137.87
⊞ Q2-2009	2,618,644.64	872,586.20	872,586.20
⊟ Q3-2009	1,407,367.64		
⊞ Jul 2009	1,068,396.58	1,068,396.58	1,068,396.58
⊟ Aug 2009	338,971.06	338,971.06	338,971.06
8/1/2009	37,750.10	37,750.10	37,750.10
8/2/2009	8,203.42	45,953.52	45,953.52
8/3/2009	337.68	46,291.20	46,291.20
8/4/2009	4,482.94	50,774.14	50,774.14
8/5/2009	14,319.18	65,093.32	65,093.32
8/6/2009	26,941.94	92,035.26	92,035.26
8/7/2009	2,518.99	94,554.25	94,554.25
8/8/2009	22,619.84	117,174.10	117,174.10
8/9/2009	21,983.18	139,157.27	139,157.27
8/10/2009	4,211.87	143,369.15	143,369.15
8/11/2009	79,245.09	222,614.24	222,614.24
8/12/2009	1,497.50	224,111.74	224,111.74
8/13/2009	13,784.34	237,896.08	237,896.08
8/14/2009	100,059.00	337,955.08	337,955.08
8/15/2009	1,015.98	338,971.06	338,971.06
Total	24,661,807.07		

FIGURE 2-4 *Sales MTD* shows the month-to-date amount, which is blank for CY 2009 and Q3-2009 because there is no data after August 15, 2009.

The month-to-date total of a measure is computed with the DATESMTD function this way:

Measure in the Sales table

```
Sales MTD :=
IF (
    [ShowValueForDates],
    CALCULATE (
        [Sales Amount],
        DATESMTD ( 'Date'[Date] )
    )
)
```

The TOTALMTD is a possible alternative to DATESMTD :

Measure in the Sales table

```
Sales MTD (2) :=
IF (
    [ShowValueForDates],
    TOTALMTD (
        [Sales Amount],
        'Date'[Date]
    )
)
```

Computing period-over-period growth

A common requirement is to compare a time period with the same time period in the previous year, quarter, or month. The last month/quarter/year could be incomplete; so in order to achieve a fair comparison, the comparison should consider an equivalent period. For these reasons, the calculations shown in this section use the *Date[DateWithSales]* calculated column, as described in the article Hiding future dates for calculations in DAX (https://sql.bi/78171).

Year-over-year growth

Year-over-year compares a period to the equivalent period in the previous year. In this example, data is available until August 15, 2009. For this reason, *Sales PY* shows numbers related to 2008 only considering transactions prior to August 15, 2008. Figure 2-5 shows that *Sales Amount* of August 2008 is 721,560.95, whereas *Sales PY* for August 2009 returns 296,529.51 because the measure only considers sales up to August 15, 2008.

Year	Sales Amount	Sales PY	Sales YOY	Sales YOY %
⊞ 2007	9,008,591.74			
⊟ 2008	9,927,582.99	9,008,591.74	918,991.25	10.20%
⊞ Q1-2008	1,816,385.21	345,319.01	1,471,066.20	426.00%
⊞ Q2-2008	2,738,040.73	3,046,602.02	-308,561.29	-10.13%
⊟ Q3-2008	2,575,545.59	2,885,246.55	-309,700.96	-10.73%
Jul 2008	890,547.41	922,542.98	-31,995.58	-3.47%
Aug 2008	721,560.95	952,834.59	-231,273.63	-24.27%
Sep 2008	963,437.23	1,009,868.98	-46,431.76	-4.60%
⊞ Q4-2008	2,797,611.46	2,731,424.16	66,187.30	2.42%
⊟ 2009	5,725,632.34	5,741,502.86	-15,870.52	-0.28%
⊞ Q1-2009	1,699,620.05	1,816,385.21	-116,765.16	-6.43%
⊞ Q2-2009	2,618,644.64	2,738,040.73	-119,396.09	-4.36%
⊟ Q3-2009	1,407,367.64	1,187,076.92	220,290.72	18.56%
Jul 2009	1,068,396.58	890,547.41	177,849.17	19.97%
Aug 2009	338,971.06	296,529.51	42,441.55	14.31%
Total	24,661,807.07	14,750,094.60	9,911,712.47	67.20%

FIGURE 2-5 For August 2009, *Sales PY* shows the amount for August 1-15, 2008, because there is no data after August 15, 2009.

Sales PY uses DATEADD and filters *Date[DateWithSales]* to guarantee a fair comparison of the last period with data. The year-over-year growth is computed as an amount in *Sales YOY*, and as a percentage in *Sales YOY %*. Both measures use *Sales PY* to only consider dates up to August 15, 2009:

Measure in the Sales table

```
Sales PY :=
IF (
    [ShowValueForDates],
    CALCULATE (
        [Sales Amount],
        CALCULATETABLE (
            DATEADD ( 'Date'[Date], -1, YEAR ),
            'Date'[DateWithSales] = TRUE
        )
    )
)
```

Measure in the Sales table

```
Sales YOY :=
VAR ValueCurrentPeriod = [Sales Amount]
VAR ValuePreviousPeriod = [Sales PY]
VAR Result =
    IF (
        NOT ISBLANK ( ValueCurrentPeriod ) && NOT ISBLANK ( ValuePreviousPeriod ),
        ValueCurrentPeriod - ValuePreviousPeriod
    )
RETURN
    Result
```

Measure in the Sales table

```
Sales YOY % :=
DIVIDE (
    [Sales YOY],
    [Sales PY]
)
```

Sales PY can also be written using SAMEPERIODLASTYEAR. SAMEPERIODLASTYEAR is easier to read, but it does not offer any performance benefit. This is because internally, it is translated into the DATEADD function used in previous formulas:

Measure in the Sales table

```
Sales PY (2) :=
IF (
    [ShowValueForDates],
    CALCULATE (
        [Sales Amount],
        CALCULATETABLE (
            SAMEPERIODLASTYEAR ( 'Date'[Date] ),
            'Date'[DateWithSales] = TRUE
        )
    )
)
```

Quarter-over-quarter growth

Quarter-over-quarter compares a period with the equivalent period in the previous quarter. In this example, data is available until August 15, 2009, which is the first half of the third quarter of 2009. Therefore, *Sales PQ* for August 2009 (the second month of the third quarter) shows sales until May 15, 2009, which is the first half of the second month of the previous quarter. Figure 2-6 shows that *Sales Amount* of May 2009 is 1,067,165.23, whereas *Sales PQ* for August 2009 returns 435,306.10, only taking into account sales made prior to May 15, 2009.

Year	Sales Amount	Sales PQ	Sales QOQ	Sales QOQ %
⊞ 2007	9,008,591.74	6,277,167.58	2,731,424.16	43.51%
⊞ 2008	9,927,582.99	9,861,395.69	66,187.30	0.67%
⊟ 2009	5,725,632.34	5,611,430.83	114,201.51	2.04%
⊞ Q1-2009	1,699,620.05	2,797,611.46	-1,097,991.40	-39.25%
⊟ Q2-2009	2,618,644.64	1,699,620.05	919,024.59	54.07%
Apr 2009	678,893.22	580,901.05	97,992.17	16.87%
May 2009	1,067,165.23	622,581.14	444,584.09	71.41%
Jun 2009	872,586.20	496,137.87	376,448.33	75.88%
⊟ Q3-2009	1,407,367.64	1,114,199.32	293,168.32	26.31%
Jul 2009	1,068,396.58	678,893.22	389,503.36	57.37%
Aug 2009	338,971.06	435,306.10	-96,335.04	-22.13%
Total	24,661,807.07	21,749,994.10	2,911,812.97	13.39%

FIGURE 2-6 For August 2009, *Sales PQ shows* the amount for May 1-15, 2009; indeed, there is no data after August 15, 2009.

Sales PQ uses DATEADD and filters *Date[DateWithSales]* to guarantee a fair comparison with the last period with data. The quarter-over-quarter growth is computed as an amount in *Sales QOQ* and as a percentage in *Sales QOQ %*. Both measures use *Sales PQ* to guarantee the same fair comparison:

Measure in the Sales table

```
Sales PQ :=
IF (
    [ShowValueForDates],
    CALCULATE (
        [Sales Amount],
        CALCULATETABLE (
            DATEADD ( 'Date'[Date], -1, QUARTER ),
            'Date'[DateWithSales] = TRUE
        )
    )
)
```

Measure in the Sales table

```
Sales QOQ :=
VAR ValueCurrentPeriod = [Sales Amount]
VAR ValuePreviousPeriod = [Sales PQ]
VAR Result =
    IF (
        NOT ISBLANK ( ValueCurrentPeriod ) && NOT ISBLANK ( ValuePreviousPeriod ),
        ValueCurrentPeriod - ValuePreviousPeriod
    )
RETURN
    Result
```

Measure in the Sales table

```
Sales QOQ % :=
DIVIDE (
    [Sales QOQ],
    [Sales PQ]
)
```

Month-over-month growth

Month-over-month compares a time period with its equivalent in the previous month. In this example, data is only available until August 15, 2009. For this reason, *Sales PM* only considers sales between July 1-15, 2009 in order to return a value for August 2009. That way, it only returns the corresponding portion of the previous month. Figure 2-7 shows that *Sales Amount* for July 2009 is 1,068,396.58, whereas *Sales PM* of August 2019 returns 584,212.78, since it only takes into account sales prior to July 15, 2009.

Year	Sales Amount	Sales PM	Sales MOM	Sales MOM %
⊞ **2007**	**9,008,591.74**	**8,017,042.99**	**991,548.75**	**12.37%**
⊞ **2008**	**9,927,582.99**	**9,997,422.60**	**-69,839.61**	**-0.70%**
⊟ **2009**	**5,725,632.34**	**5,824,186.61**	**-98,554.28**	**-1.69%**
⊞ **Q1-2009**	**1,699,620.05**	**2,125,191.33**	**-425,571.27**	**-20.03%**
⊟ **Q2-2009**	**2,618,644.64**	**2,242,196.31**	**376,448.33**	**16.79%**
Apr 2009	678,893.22	496,137.87	182,755.35	36.84%
May 2009	1,067,165.23	678,893.22	388,272.01	57.19%
Jun 2009	872,586.20	1,067,165.23	-194,579.03	-18.23%
⊟ **Q3-2009**	**1,407,367.64**	**1,456,798.97**	**-49,431.33**	**-3.39%**
Jul 2009	1,068,396.58	872,586.20	195,810.38	22.44%
Aug 2009	338,971.06	584,212.78	-245,241.71	-41.98%
Total	**24,661,807.07**	**23,838,652.20**	**823,154.87**	**3.45%**

FIGURE 2-7 For August 2009, *Sales PM* shows the amount in the July 1-15, 2009 time period; indeed, there is no data after August 15, 2009.

Sales PM uses DATEADD and filters the *Date[DateWithSales]* column to guarantee a fair comparison of the last period with data. The month-over-month growth is computed as an amount in *Sales MOM* and as a percentage in *Sales MOM %*. Both measures use *Sales PM* to guarantee the same fair comparison:

Measure in the Sales table

```
Sales PM :=
IF (
    [ShowValueForDates],
    CALCULATE (
        [Sales Amount],
        CALCULATETABLE (
            DATEADD ( 'Date'[Date], -1, MONTH ),
            'Date'[DateWithSales] = TRUE
        )
    )
)
```

Measure in the Sales table

```
Sales MOM :=
VAR ValueCurrentPeriod = [Sales Amount]
VAR ValuePreviousPeriod = [Sales PM]
VAR Result =
    IF (
        NOT ISBLANK ( ValueCurrentPeriod )
            && NOT ISBLANK ( ValuePreviousPeriod ),
        ValueCurrentPeriod - ValuePreviousPeriod
    )
RETURN
    Result
```

Measure in the Sales table

```
Sales MOM % :=
DIVIDE (
    [Sales MOM],
    [Sales PM]
)
```

Period-over-period growth

Period-over-period growth automatically selects one of the measures previously described in this section based on the current selection of the visualization. For example, it returns the value of month-over-month growth measures if the visualization displays data at the month level, switching to year-over-year growth measures if the visualization shows the total at the year level. The expected result is visible in Figure 2-8.

Year	Sales Amount	Sales PP	Sales POP	Sales POP %
⊞ 2007	9,008,591.74			
⊟ 2008	9,927,582.99	9,008,591.74	918,991.25	10.20%
⊞ Q1-2008	1,816,385.21	2,731,424.16	-915,038.95	-33.50%
⊞ Q2-2008	2,738,040.73	1,816,385.21	921,655.52	50.74%
⊟ Q3-2008	2,575,545.59	2,738,040.73	-162,495.14	-5.93%
Jul 2008	890,547.41	845,141.60	45,405.81	5.37%
Aug 2008	721,560.95	890,547.41	-168,986.45	-18.98%
Sep 2008	963,437.23	721,560.95	241,876.27	33.52%
⊟ Q4-2008	2,797,611.46	2,575,545.59	222,065.87	8.62%
Oct 2008	719,792.99	963,437.23	-243,644.24	-25.29%
Nov 2008	1,156,109.32	719,792.99	436,316.33	60.62%
Dec 2008	921,709.14	1,156,109.32	-234,400.18	-20.27%
⊟ 2009	5,725,632.34	5,741,502.86	-15,870.52	-0.28%
⊞ Q1-2009	1,699,620.05	2,797,611.46	-1,097,991.40	-39.25%
⊟ Q2-2009	2,618,644.64	1,699,620.05	919,024.59	54.07%
Apr 2009	678,893.22	496,137.87	182,755.35	36.84%
May 2009	1,067,165.23	678,893.22	388,272.01	57.19%
Jun 2009	872,586.20	1,067,165.23	-194,579.03	-18.23%
⊟ Q3-2009	1,407,367.64	1,114,199.32	293,168.32	26.31%
Jul 2009	1,068,396.58	872,586.20	195,810.38	22.44%
Aug 2009	338,971.06	584,212.78	-245,241.71	-41.98%
Total	24,661,807.07			

FIGURE 2-8 *Sales PP* shows the value of the previous month at the month level, of the previous quarter at the quarter level, and of the previous year at the year level.

The three measures *Sales PP*, *Sales POP*, and *Sales POP %* redirect the evaluation to the corresponding year, quarter, and month measures depending on the level selected in the report. The ISINSCOPE function detects the level used in the report. The arguments passed to ISINSCOPE are the attributes used in the rows of the Matrix visual in Figure 2-8. The measures are defined as follows:

Measure in the Sales table

```
Sales POP % :=
SWITCH (
    TRUE,
    ISINSCOPE ( 'Date'[Year Month] ), [Sales MOM %],
    ISINSCOPE ( 'Date'[Year Quarter] ), [Sales QOQ %],
    ISINSCOPE ( 'Date'[Year] ), [Sales YOY %]
)
```

Measure in the Sales table

```
Sales POP :=
SWITCH (
    TRUE,
    ISINSCOPE ( 'Date'[Year Month] ), [Sales MOM],
    ISINSCOPE ( 'Date'[Year Quarter] ), [Sales QOQ],
    ISINSCOPE ( 'Date'[Year] ), [Sales YOY]
)
```

Measure in the Sales table

```
Sales PP :=
SWITCH (
    TRUE,
    ISINSCOPE ( 'Date'[Year Month] ), [Sales PM],
    ISINSCOPE ( 'Date'[Year Quarter] ), [Sales PQ],
    ISINSCOPE ( 'Date'[Year] ), [Sales PY]
)
```

Computing period-to-date growth

The growth of a "to-date" measure is the comparison of the "to-date" measure with the same measure over an equivalent period with a specific offset. For example, you can compare a year-to-date aggregation against the year-to-date in the previous year, that is with an offset of one year.

All the measures in this set of calculations take care of partial periods. Because data is available only until August 15, 2009 in our example, the measures make sure that data in the previous year does not consider dates after August 15, 2019.

Year-over-year-to-date growth

Year-over-year-to-date growth compares the year-to-date at a specific date with the year-to-date at an equivalent date in the previous year. Figure 2-9 shows that *Sales PYTD* in 2009 is only considering transactions until August 15, 2008. For this reason, *Sales YTD* of Q3-2008 is 7,129,971.53, whereas *Sales PYTD* for Q3-2009 is less: 5,741,502.86.

Year	Sales Amount	Sales YTD	Sales PYTD	Sales YOYTD	Sales YOYTD %	Sales PYTD (2)
2007	**9,008,591.74**	**9,008,591.74**				
Q1-2007	345,319.01	345,319.01				
Q2-2007	3,046,602.02	3,391,921.03				
Q3-2007	2,885,246.55	6,277,167.58				
Q4-2007	2,731,424.16	9,008,591.74				
2008	**9,927,582.99**	**9,927,582.99**	**9,008,591.74**	**918,991.25**	**10.20%**	**9,008,591.74**
Q1-2008	1,816,385.21	1,816,385.21	345,319.01	1,471,066.20	426.00%	345,319.01
Q2-2008	2,738,040.73	4,554,425.94	3,391,921.03	1,162,504.91	34.27%	3,391,921.03
Q3-2008	2,575,545.59	7,129,971.53	6,277,167.58	852,803.95	13.59%	6,277,167.58
Q4-2008	2,797,611.46	9,927,582.99	9,008,591.74	918,991.25	10.20%	9,008,591.74
2009	**5,725,632.34**	**5,725,632.34**	**5,741,502.86**	**-15,870.52**	**-0.28%**	**5,741,502.86**
Q1-2009	1,699,620.05	1,699,620.05	1,816,385.21	-116,765.16	-6.43%	1,816,385.21
Q2-2009	2,618,644.64	4,318,264.70	4,554,425.94	-236,161.25	-5.19%	4,554,425.94
Q3-2009	1,407,367.64	5,725,632.34	5,741,502.86	-15,870.52	-0.28%	5,741,502.86
Total	**24,661,807.07**		**5,741,502.86**			**5,741,502.86**

FIGURE 2-9 For Q3-2009, *Sales PYTD* shows the amount of January 1-August 15, 2008 because there is no data after August 15, 2009.

Sales PYTD uses DATEADD and filters the *Date[DateWithSales]* column to guarantee a fair comparison of the last period with data. *Sales YOYTD* and *Sales YOYTD %* rely on *Sales PYTD* to guarantee the same fair comparison:

Measure in the Sales table

```
Sales PYTD :=
IF (
    [ShowValueForDates],
    CALCULATE (
        [Sales YTD],
        CALCULATETABLE (
            DATEADD ( 'Date'[Date], -1, YEAR ),
            'Date'[DateWithSales] = TRUE
        )
    )
)
```

Measure in the Sales table

```
Sales YOYTD :=
VAR ValueCurrentPeriod = [Sales YTD]
VAR ValuePreviousPeriod = [Sales PYTD]
VAR Result =
    IF (
        NOT ISBLANK ( ValueCurrentPeriod )
            && NOT ISBLANK ( ValuePreviousPeriod ),
        ValueCurrentPeriod - ValuePreviousPeriod
    )
RETURN
    Result
```

Measure in the Sales table

```
Sales YOYTD % :=
DIVIDE (
    [Sales YOYTD],
    [Sales PYTD]
)
```

Sales PYTD shifts the date filter back one year by using DATEADD. Using DATEADD makes it easy to apply shifts of two or more years. However, to shift dates back by one year *Sales PYTD* can also be written using SAMEPERIODLASTYEAR as in the following example, which internally uses DATEADD as in the previous example:

Measure in the Sales table

```
Sales PYTD (2) :=
IF (
    [ShowValueForDates],
    CALCULATE (
        [Sales YTD],
        CALCULATETABLE (
            SAMEPERIODLASTYEAR ( 'Date'[Date] ),
            'Date'[DateWithSales] = TRUE
        )
    )
)
```

Quarter-over-quarter-to-date growth

Quarter-over-quarter-to-date growth compares the quarter-to-date at a specific date with the quarter-to-date at an equivalent date in the previous quarter. Figure 2-10 shows that *Sales PQ* in August 2009 is only considering transactions until May 15, 2008, to only get the first half of the previous quarter. For this reason *Sales QTD* of May 2009 is 1,746,058.45, whereas *Sales PQTD* for August 2009 is lower: 1,114,199.32.

Year	Sales Amount	Sales QTD	Sales PQTD	Sales QOQTD	Sales QOQTD %
⊞ 2007	9,008,591.74	2,731,424.16	2,885,246.55	-153,822.39	-5.33%
⊞ 2008	9,927,582.99	2,797,611.46	2,575,545.59	222,065.87	8.62%
⊟ 2009	5,725,632.34		1,114,199.32		
⊞ Q1-2009	1,699,620.05	1,699,620.05	2,797,611.46	-1,097,991.40	-39.25%
⊟ Q2-2009	2,618,644.64	2,618,644.64	1,699,620.05	919,024.59	54.07%
Apr 2009	678,893.22	678,893.22	580,901.05	97,992.17	16.87%
May 2009	1,067,165.23	1,746,058.45	1,203,482.19	542,576.26	45.08%
Jun 2009	872,586.20	2,618,644.64	1,699,620.05	919,024.59	54.07%
⊟ Q3-2009	1,407,367.64	1,407,367.64	1,114,199.32	293,168.32	26.31%
Jul 2009	1,068,396.58	1,068,396.58	678,893.22	389,503.36	57.37%
Aug 2009	338,971.06	1,407,367.64	1,114,199.32	293,168.32	26.31%
Total	24,661,807.07		1,114,199.32		

FIGURE 2-10 *Sales PQTD* shows for Aug 2009 the amount of the period April 1-May 15, 2009, because there is no data after August 15, 2009.

Sales *PQTD* uses DATEADD and filters the *Date[DateWithSales]* column to guarantee a fair comparison of the last period with data. *Sales QOQTD* and *Sales QOQTD %* rely on *Sales PQTD* to guarantee the same fair comparison:

Measure in the Sales table

```
Sales PQTD :=
IF (
    [ShowValueForDates],
    CALCULATE (
        [Sales QTD],
        CALCULATETABLE (
            DATEADD ( 'Date'[Date], -1, QUARTER ),
            'Date'[DateWithSales] = TRUE
        )
    )
)
```

Measure in the Sales table

```
Sales QOQTD :=
VAR ValueCurrentPeriod = [Sales QTD]
VAR ValuePreviousPeriod = [Sales PQTD]
VAR Result =
    IF (
        NOT ISBLANK ( ValueCurrentPeriod )
            && NOT ISBLANK ( ValuePreviousPeriod ),
        ValueCurrentPeriod - ValuePreviousPeriod
    )
RETURN
    Result
```

Measure in the Sales table

```
Sales QOQTD % :=
DIVIDE (
    [Sales QOQTD],
    [Sales PQTD]
)
```

Month-over-month-to-date growth

Month-over-month-to-date growth compares a month-to-date at a specific date with the month-to-date at an equivalent date in the previous month. Figure 2-11 shows that *Sales PMTD* in August 2009 is only considering sales until July 15, 2009, to only get the corresponding portion of the previous month. For this reason *Sales MTD* of July 2009 is 1,068,396.58, whereas *Sales PMTD* for August 2009 is less: 584,212.78.

Year	Sales Amount	Sales MTD	Sales PMTD	Sales MOMTD	Sales MOMTD %
⊞ 2007	9,008,591.74	991,548.75	825,601.87	165,946.88	20.10%
⊞ 2008	9,927,582.99	921,709.14	1,156,109.32	-234,400.18	-20.27%
⊟ 2009	5,725,632.34		584,212.78		
⊞ Q1-2009	1,699,620.05	496,137.87	622,581.14	-126,443.27	-20.31%
⊞ Q2-2009	2,618,644.64	872,586.20	1,067,165.23	-194,579.03	-18.23%
⊟ Q3-2009	1,407,367.64		584,212.78		
⊞ Jul 2009	1,068,396.58	1,068,396.58	872,586.20	195,810.38	22.44%
⊟ Aug 2009	338,971.06	338,971.06	584,212.78	-245,241.71	-41.98%
8/1/2009	37,750.10	37,750.10	64,551.47	-26,801.36	-41.52%
8/2/2009	8,203.42	45,953.52	90,074.93	-44,121.41	-48.98%
8/3/2009	337.68	46,291.20	153,054.51	-106,763.31	-69.76%
8/4/2009	4,482.94	50,774.14	171,310.23	-120,536.08	-70.36%
8/5/2009	14,319.18	65,093.32	248,443.99	-183,350.66	-73.80%
8/6/2009	26,941.94	92,035.26	272,277.89	-180,242.62	-66.20%
8/7/2009	2,518.99	94,554.25	296,502.87	-201,948.61	-68.11%
8/8/2009	22,619.84	117,174.10	315,987.54	-198,813.44	-62.92%
8/9/2009	21,983.18	139,157.27	369,855.95	-230,698.67	-62.38%
8/10/2009	4,211.87	143,369.15	370,871.93	-227,502.78	-61.34%
8/11/2009	79,245.09	222,614.24	422,203.83	-199,589.59	-47.27%
8/12/2009	1,497.50	224,111.74	484,757.36	-260,645.62	-53.77%
8/13/2009	13,784.34	237,896.08	510,540.43	-272,644.35	-53.40%
8/14/2009	100,059.00	337,955.08	533,703.16	-195,748.08	-36.68%
8/15/2009	1,015.98	338,971.06	584,212.78	-245,241.71	-41.98%
Total	24,661,807.07		584,212.78		

FIGURE 2-11 For Aug 2009, *Sales PQTD* shows the amount of the period July 1-July 15, 2009, because there is no data after August 15, 2009.

Sales PMTD uses DATEADD and filters the *Date[DateWithSales]* column to guarantee a fair comparison of the last period with data. *Sales MOMTD* and *Sales MOMTD %* rely on the *Sales PMTD* measure to guarantee the same fair comparison:

Measure in the Sales table

```
Sales PMTD :=
IF (
    [ShowValueForDates],
    CALCULATE (
        [Sales MTD],
        CALCULATETABLE (
            DATEADD ( 'Date'[Date], -1, MONTH ),
            'Date'[DateWithSales] = TRUE
        )
    )
)
```

Measure in the Sales table

```
Sales MOMTD :=
VAR ValueCurrentPeriod = [Sales MTD]
VAR ValuePreviousPeriod = [Sales PMTD]
VAR Result =
    IF (
        NOT ISBLANK ( ValueCurrentPeriod )
            && NOT ISBLANK ( ValuePreviousPeriod ),
        ValueCurrentPeriod - ValuePreviousPeriod
    )
RETURN
    Result
```

Measure in the Sales table

```
Sales MOMTD % :=
DIVIDE (
    [Sales MOMTD],
    [Sales PMTD]
)
```

Comparing period-to-date with previous full period

Comparing a to-date aggregation with the previous full period is useful when you consider the previous period as a benchmark. Once the current year-to-date reaches 100% of the full previous year, this means we have reached the same performance as the previous full period, hopefully in fewer days.

Year-to-date over the full previous year

The year-to-date over the full previous year compares the year-to-date against the entire previous year. Figure 2-12 shows that in November 2008 *Sales YTD* almost reaches *Sales Amount* for the entire year 2007. *Sales YTDOPY%* provides an immediate comparison of the year-to-date with the total of the previous year; it shows growth over the previous year when the percentage is positive, as is the case starting December 1, 2008.

Year	Sales Amount	Sales YTD	Sales PYC	Sales YTDOPY	Sales YTDOPY %
⊞ **2007**	**9,008,591.74**	**9,008,591.74**			
⊟ **2008**	**9,927,582.99**	**9,927,582.99**	**9,008,591.74**	**918,991.25**	**10.20%**
⊞ **Q1-2008**	**1,816,385.21**	**1,816,385.21**	**9,008,591.74**	**-7,192,206.53**	**-79.84%**
⊞ **Q2-2008**	**2,738,040.73**	**4,554,425.94**	**9,008,591.74**	**-4,454,165.80**	**-49.44%**
⊞ **Q3-2008**	**2,575,545.59**	**7,129,971.53**	**9,008,591.74**	**-1,878,620.21**	**-20.85%**
⊟ **Q4-2008**	**2,797,611.46**	**9,927,582.99**	**9,008,591.74**	**918,991.25**	**10.20%**
⊞ **Oct 2008**	**719,792.99**	**7,849,764.52**	**9,008,591.74**	**-1,158,827.22**	**-12.86%**
⊞ **Nov 2008**	**1,156,109.32**	**9,005,873.85**	**9,008,591.74**	**-2,717.90**	**-0.03%**
⊟ **Dec 2008**	**921,709.14**	**9,927,582.99**	**9,008,591.74**	**918,991.25**	**10.20%**
12/1/2008	4,605.06	9,010,478.90	9,008,591.74	1,887.16	0.02%
12/2/2008	447.22	9,010,926.12	9,008,591.74	2,334.38	0.03%
12/3/2008	40,643.69	9,051,569.82	9,008,591.74	42,978.07	0.48%
Total	**24,661,807.07**				

FIGURE 2-12 *Sales YTDOPY %* shows a positive percentage from December 1, 2008, when the *Sales YTD* starts to be greater than *Sales Amount* for 2007.

The year-to-date-over-previous-year growth is computed by the *Sales YTDOPY* and *Sales YTDOPY %* measures; these rely on the *Sales YTD* measure to compute the year-to-date value, and on the *Sales PYC* measure to get the sales amount of the entire previous year:

Measure in the Sales table

```
Sales PYC :=
IF (
    [ShowValueForDates],
    CALCULATE (
        [Sales Amount],
        PARALLELPERIOD ( 'Date'[Date], -1, YEAR )
    )
)
```

Measure in the Sales table

```
Sales YTDOPY :=
VAR ValueCurrentPeriod = [Sales YTD]
VAR ValuePreviousPeriod = [Sales PYC]
VAR Result =
    IF (
        NOT ISBLANK ( ValueCurrentPeriod )
            && NOT ISBLANK ( ValuePreviousPeriod ),
        ValueCurrentPeriod - ValuePreviousPeriod
    )
RETURN
    Result
```

Measure in the Sales table

```
Sales YTDOPY % :=
DIVIDE (
    [Sales YTDOPY],
    [Sales PYC]
)
```

The *Sales PYC* measure can also be written using PREVIOUSYEAR, whose behavior is similar to PARALLELPERIOD (the difference is not relevant for this example):

Measure in the Sales table

```
Sales PYC (2) :=
IF (
    [ShowValueForDates],
    CALCULATE (
        [Sales Amount],
        PREVIOUSYEAR ( 'Date'[Date] )
    )
)
```

PREVIOUSYEAR is mandatory if the comparison uses the fiscal year because PREVIOUSYEAR accepts a second argument to specify the last day of the fiscal year. Look at the following report in Figure 2-13, which is slicing the measures by fiscal periods.

Year	Sales Amount	Sales Fiscal YTD	Sales Fiscal PYC	Sales Fiscal YTDOPY	Sales Fiscal YTDOPY %
⊞ **FY 2007**	**3,391,921.03**	**3,391,921.03**			
⊟ **FY 2008**	**10,171,096.65**	**10,171,096.65**	**3,391,921.03**	**6,779,175.62**	**199.86%**
⊞ FQ1-2008	2,885,246.55	2,885,246.55	3,391,921.03	-506,674.48	-14.94%
⊞ FQ2-2008	2,731,424.16	5,616,670.71	3,391,921.03	2,224,749.68	65.59%
⊞ FQ3-2008	1,816,385.21	7,433,055.92	3,391,921.03	4,041,134.89	119.14%
⊞ FQ4-2008	2,738,040.73	10,171,096.65	3,391,921.03	6,779,175.62	199.86%
⊟ **FY 2009**	**9,691,421.74**	**9,691,421.74**	**10,171,096.65**	**-479,674.91**	**-4.72%**
⊞ FQ1-2009	2,575,545.59	2,575,545.59	10,171,096.65	-7,595,551.06	-74.68%
⊞ FQ2-2009	2,797,611.46	5,373,157.05	10,171,096.65	-4,797,939.61	-47.17%
⊞ FQ3-2009	1,699,620.05	7,072,777.10	10,171,096.65	-3,098,319.55	-30.46%
⊞ FQ4-2009	2,618,644.64	9,691,421.74	10,171,096.65	-479,674.91	-4.72%
⊟ **FY 2010**	**1,407,367.64**	**1,407,367.64**	**9,691,421.74**	**-8,284,054.10**	**-85.48%**
⊞ FQ1-2010	1,407,367.64	1,407,367.64	9,691,421.74	-8,284,054.10	-85.48%
Total	**24,661,807.07**				

FIGURE 2-13 *Sales Fiscal YTDOPY %* compares *Sales YTD* with the *Sales Amount* of the previous fiscal year.

The measures used in the report are defined as follows. Please pay attention to the second argument of PREVIOUSYEAR in *Sales Fiscal PYC*:

Measure in the Sales table

```
Sales Fiscal PYC :=
IF (
    [ShowValueForDates],
    CALCULATE (
        [Sales Amount],
        PREVIOUSYEAR ( 'Date'[Date], "06-30" )
    )
)
```

Measure in the Sales table

```
Sales Fiscal YTDOPY :=
VAR ValueCurrentPeriod = [Sales Fiscal YTD]
VAR ValuePreviousPeriod = [Sales Fiscal PYC]
VAR Result =
    IF (
        NOT ISBLANK ( ValueCurrentPeriod )
            && NOT ISBLANK ( ValuePreviousPeriod ),
        ValueCurrentPeriod - ValuePreviousPeriod
    )
RETURN
    Result
```

Measure in the Sales table

```
Sales Fiscal YTDOPY % :=
DIVIDE (
    [Sales Fiscal YTDOPY],
    [Sales Fiscal PYC]
)
```

Quarter-to-date over full previous quarter

The quarter-to-date over full previous quarter compares the quarter-to-date against the entire previous quarter. Figure 2-14 shows that *Sales QTD* in May 2008 surpasses the total *Sales Amount* for Q1-2008. *Sales QTDOPQ%* provides an immediate comparison of the quarter-to-date with the total of the previous quarter; it shows growth over the previous quarter when the percentage is positive, as is the case starting in May 2008.

Year	Sales Amount	Sales QTD	Sales PQC	Sales QTDOPQ	Sales QTDOPQ %
⊞ 2007	9,008,591.74	2,731,424.16			
⊟ 2008	9,927,582.99	2,797,611.46			
⊞ Q1-2008	1,816,385.21	1,816,385.21	2,731,424.16	-915,038.95	-33.50%
⊟ Q2-2008	2,738,040.73	2,738,040.73	1,816,385.21	921,655.52	50.74%
⊞ Apr 2008	999,667.17	999,667.17	1,816,385.21	-816,718.04	-44.96%
⊞ May 2008	893,231.96	1,892,899.13	1,816,385.21	76,513.92	4.21%
⊞ Jun 2008	845,141.60	2,738,040.73	1,816,385.21	921,655.52	50.74%
⊞ Q3-2008	2,575,545.59	2,575,545.59	2,738,040.73	-162,495.14	-5.93%
⊞ Q4-2008	2,797,611.46	2,797,611.46	2,575,545.59	222,065.87	8.62%
⊞ 2009	5,725,632.34				
Total	24,661,807.07				

FIGURE 2-14 *Sales QTDOPQ %* shows a positive percentage from May 2008, when *Sales QTD* starts to be greater than the *Sales Amount* for Q1-2008.

The quarter-to-date-over-previous-quarter growth is computed with the *Sales QTDOPQ* and *Sales QTDOPQ %* measures; these rely on the *Sales QTD* measure to compute the quarter-to-date value and on the *Sales PQC* measure to get the sales amount of the entire previous quarter:

Measure in the Sales table

```
Sales PQC :=
IF (
    [ShowValueForDates] && HASONEVALUE ( 'Date'[Year Quarter] ),
    CALCULATE (
        [Sales Amount],
        PARALLELPERIOD ( 'Date'[Date], -1, QUARTER )
    )
)
```

Measure in the Sales table

```
Sales QTDOPQ :=
VAR ValueCurrentPeriod = [Sales QTD]
VAR ValuePreviousPeriod = [Sales PQC]
VAR Result =
    IF (
        NOT ISBLANK ( ValueCurrentPeriod )
            && NOT ISBLANK ( ValuePreviousPeriod ),
        ValueCurrentPeriod - ValuePreviousPeriod
    )
RETURN
    Result
```

Measure in the Sales table

```
Sales QTDOPQ % :=
DIVIDE (
    [Sales QTDOPQ],
    [Sales PQC]
)
```

The *Sales PQC* measure can also be written using PREVIOUSQUARTER, as long as it is not used at the year level for more than one quarter:

Measure in the Sales table

```
Sales PQC (2) :=
IF (
    [ShowValueForDates] && HASONEVALUE ( 'Date'[Year Quarter] ),
    CALCULATE (
        [Sales Amount],
        PREVIOUSQUARTER ( 'Date'[Date] )
    )
)
```

Month-to-date over full previous month

The month-to-date over full previous month compares the month-to-date against the entire previous month. Figure 2-15 shows that *Sales MTD* during April 2008 surpasses the total *Sales Amount* for March 2008. The *Sales MTDOPM%* provides an immediate comparison of the month-to-date with the total of the previous month; it shows growth over the previous month when the percentage is positive as is the case starting April 19, 2008.

Year	Sales Amount	Sales MTD	Sales PMC	Sales MTDOPM	Sales MTDOPM %
⊞ 2007	9,008,591.74	991,548.75			
⊟ 2008	9,927,582.99	921,709.14			
⊟ Q1-2008	1,816,385.21	559,538.52			
⊞ Jan 2008	656,766.69	656,766.69	991,548.75	-334,782.06	-33.76%
⊞ Feb 2008	600,080.00	600,080.00	656,766.69	-56,686.70	-8.63%
⊞ Mar 2008	559,538.52	559,538.52	600,080.00	-40,541.48	-6.76%
⊟ Q2-2008	2,738,040.73	845,141.60			
⊟ Apr 2008	999,667.17	999,667.17	559,538.52	440,128.65	78.66%
4/1/2008	13,557.28	13,557.28	559,538.52	-545,981.24	-97.58%
4/2/2008	9,065.70	22,622.98	559,538.52	-536,915.54	-95.96%
4/3/2008	31,133.36	53,756.34	559,538.52	-505,782.18	-90.39%
4/4/2008	24,122.38	77,878.72	559,538.52	-481,659.80	-86.08%
4/5/2008	43,296.27	121,174.99	559,538.52	-438,363.53	-78.34%
4/6/2008	47,212.95	168,387.94	559,538.52	-391,150.58	-69.91%
4/7/2008	29,037.93	197,425.87	559,538.52	-362,112.65	-64.72%
4/8/2008	16,857.91	214,283.78	559,538.52	-345,254.74	-61.70%
4/9/2008	1,561.36	215,845.13	559,538.52	-343,693.39	-61.42%
4/10/2008	378.55	216,223.68	559,538.52	-343,314.84	-61.36%
4/11/2008	42,286.96	258,510.64	559,538.52	-301,027.88	-53.80%
4/12/2008	38,560.80	297,071.44	559,538.52	-262,467.08	-46.91%
4/13/2008	6,511.76	303,583.20	559,538.52	-255,955.32	-45.74%
4/14/2008	57,402.73	360,985.93	559,538.52	-198,552.59	-35.49%
4/15/2008	56,015.09	417,001.02	559,538.52	-142,537.50	-25.47%
4/16/2008	35,205.64	452,206.66	559,538.52	-107,331.86	-19.18%
4/17/2008	59,922.32	512,128.98	559,538.52	-47,409.54	-8.47%
4/18/2008	22,947.10	535,076.08	559,538.52	-24,462.44	-4.37%
4/19/2008	61,693.67	596,769.75	559,538.52	37,231.23	6.65%
Total	**24,661,807.07**				

FIGURE 2-15 *Sales MTDOPM %* shows a positive percentage from April 19, 2008, when *Sales MTD* starts to be greater than the *Sales Amount* for March 2008.

The month-to-date-over-previous-month growth is computed with the *Sales MTDOPM %* and *Sales MTDOPM* measures; these rely on the *Sales MTD* measure to compute the month-to-date value and on the *Sales PMC* measure to get the sales amount of the entire previous month:

Measure in the Sales table

```
Sales PMC :=
IF (
    [ShowValueForDates] && HASONEVALUE ( 'Date'[Year Month] ),
    CALCULATE (
        [Sales Amount],
        PARALLELPERIOD ( 'Date'[Date], -1, MONTH )
    )
)
```

Measure in the Sales table

```
Sales MTDOPM :=
VAR ValueCurrentPeriod = [Sales MTD]
VAR ValuePreviousPeriod = [Sales PMC]
VAR Result =
    IF (
        NOT ISBLANK ( ValueCurrentPeriod )
            && NOT ISBLANK ( ValuePreviousPeriod ),
        ValueCurrentPeriod - ValuePreviousPeriod
    )
RETURN
    Result
```

Measure in the Sales table

```
Sales MTDOPM % :=
DIVIDE (
    [Sales MTDOPM],
    [Sales PMC]
)
```

The *Sales PMC* measure can also be written using PREVIOUSMONTH, as long as it is not used at the quarter or year level for more than one month:

Measure in the Sales table

```
Sales PMC (2) :=
IF (
    [ShowValueForDates] && HASONEVALUE ( 'Date'[Year Month] ),
    CALCULATE (
        [Sales Amount],
        PREVIOUSMONTH ( 'Date'[Date] )
    )
)
```

Using moving annual total calculations

A common way to aggregate data over several months is by using the moving annual total instead of the year-to-date. The moving annual total includes the last 12 months of data. For example, the moving annual total for March 2008 includes data from April 2007 to March 2008.

Moving annual total

The *Sales MAT* measure computes the moving annual total, as shown in Figure 2-16.

Year	Sales Amount	Sales MAT	Sales PYMAT	Sales MATG	Sales MATG %
⊟ 2007	9,008,591.74	9,008,591.74			
Mar 2007	345,319.01	345,319.01			
Apr 2007	1,128,104.82	1,473,423.82			
May 2007	936,192.74	2,409,616.57			
Jun 2007	982,304.46	3,391,921.03			
Jul 2007	922,542.98	4,314,464.01			
Aug 2007	952,834.59	5,267,298.60			
Sep 2007	1,009,868.98	6,277,167.58			
Oct 2007	914,273.54	7,191,441.12			
Nov 2007	825,601.87	8,017,042.99			
Dec 2007	991,548.75	9,008,591.74			
⊟ 2008	9,927,582.99	9,927,582.99	9,008,591.74	918,991.25	10.20%
Jan 2008	656,766.69	9,665,358.44			
Feb 2008	600,080.00	10,265,438.43			
Mar 2008	559,538.52	10,479,657.94	345,319.01	10,134,338.94	2934.78%
Apr 2008	999,667.17	10,351,220.30	1,473,423.82	8,877,796.47	602.53%
May 2008	893,231.96	10,308,259.51	2,409,616.57	7,898,642.95	327.80%
Jun 2008	845,141.60	10,171,096.65	3,391,921.03	6,779,175.62	199.86%
Jul 2008	890,547.41	10,139,101.08	4,314,464.01	5,824,637.07	135.00%
Aug 2008	721,560.95	9,907,827.45	5,267,298.60	4,640,528.85	88.10%
Sep 2008	963,437.23	9,861,395.69	6,277,167.58	3,584,228.11	57.10%
Oct 2008	719,792.99	9,666,915.14	7,191,441.12	2,475,474.02	34.42%
Nov 2008	1,156,109.32	9,997,422.60	8,017,042.99	1,980,379.60	24.70%
Dec 2008	921,709.14	9,927,582.99	9,008,591.74	918,991.25	10.20%
⊟ 2009	5,725,632.34	5,725,632.34	9,927,582.99	-4,201,950.65	-42.33%
Jan 2009	580,901.05	9,851,717.35	9,665,358.44	186,358.91	1.93%
Total	24,661,807.07		5,725,632.34		

FIGURE 2-16 *Sales MAT* in March 2008 aggregates *Sales Amount* from April 2007 to March 2008.

The moving annual total uses DATESINPERIOD to select the previous year:

Measure in the Sales table

```
Sales MAT :=
IF (
    [ShowValueForDates],
    CALCULATE (
        [Sales Amount],
        DATESINPERIOD (
            'Date'[Date],
            MAX ( 'Date'[Date] ),
            -1,
            YEAR
        )
    )
)
```

DATESINPERIOD returns the set of dates starting from the date passed in the second argument and applying an offset specified in the third and fourth arguments. For example, the *Sales MAT* measure returns the dates included in the full year before the last date available in the filter context. The same result could have been obtained by specifying -12 and MONTH in the third and fourth arguments, respectively.

Moving annual total growth

The moving annual total growth is computed with the *Sales PYMAT*, *Sales MATG*, and *Sales MATG %* measures, which rely on the *Sales MAT* measure. The *Sales MAT* measure provides a correct value one year after the first sale ever (when it collects one full year of data), and it is not protected in case the current time period is shorter than a full year. For example, the amount for the full year 2009 of *Sales PYMAT* is 9,927,582.99, which corresponds to the *Sales Amount* of 2008 as shown in Figure 2-17. When compared with sales in 2009, this produces a comparison of less than 8 months – data being only available until August 15, 2009 – with a full year 2008. Similarly, you can see that *Sales MATG %* starts in 2008 with very high values and stabilizes after a year. The first values are due to the effect of having no sales in the previous year. This behavior is by design: the moving annual total is usually computed at the month or day granularity to show trends in a chart.

Year	Sales Amount	Sales MAT	Sales PYMAT	Sales MATG	Sales MATG %
⊞ **2007**	**9,008,591.74**	**9,008,591.74**			
⊟ **2008**	**9,927,582.99**	**9,927,582.99**	**9,008,591.74**	**918,991.25**	**10.20%**
Jan 2008	656,766.69	9,665,358.44			
Feb 2008	600,080.00	10,265,438.43			
Mar 2008	559,538.52	10,479,657.94	345,319.01	10,134,338.94	2934.78%
Apr 2008	999,667.17	10,351,220.30	1,473,423.82	8,877,796.47	602.53%
May 2008	893,231.96	10,308,259.51	2,409,616.57	7,898,642.95	327.80%
Jun 2008	845,141.60	10,171,096.65	3,391,921.03	6,779,175.62	199.86%
Jul 2008	890,547.41	10,139,101.08	4,314,464.01	5,824,637.07	135.00%
Aug 2008	721,560.95	9,907,827.45	5,267,298.60	4,640,528.85	88.10%
Sep 2008	963,437.23	9,861,395.69	6,277,167.58	3,584,228.11	57.10%
Oct 2008	719,792.99	9,666,915.14	7,191,441.12	2,475,474.02	34.42%
Nov 2008	1,156,109.32	9,997,422.60	8,017,042.99	1,980,379.60	24.70%
Dec 2008	921,709.14	9,927,582.99	9,008,591.74	918,991.25	10.20%
⊟ **2009**	**5,725,632.34**	**5,725,632.34**	**9,927,582.99**	**-4,201,950.65**	**-42.33%**
Jan 2009	580,901.05	9,851,717.35	9,665,358.44	186,358.91	1.93%
Feb 2009	622,581.14	9,874,218.49	10,265,438.43	-391,219.95	-3.81%
Mar 2009	496,137.87	9,810,817.83	10,479,657.94	-668,840.11	-6.38%
Apr 2009	678,893.22	9,490,043.88	10,351,220.30	-861,176.42	-8.32%
May 2009	1,067,165.23	9,663,977.15	10,308,259.51	-644,282.36	-6.25%
Jun 2009	872,586.20	9,691,421.74	10,171,096.65	-479,674.91	-4.72%
Jul 2009	1,068,396.58	9,869,270.91	10,139,101.08	-269,830.17	-2.66%
Aug 2009	338,971.06	9,486,681.02	9,907,827.45	-421,146.43	-4.25%
Total	**24,661,807.07**		**5,725,632.34**		

FIGURE 2-17 *Sales MATG %* shows the growth between *Sales MAT* and *Sales PYMAT* as a percentage.

The measures are defined as follows:

Measure in the Sales table

```
Sales PYMAT :=
IF (
    [ShowValueForDates],
    CALCULATE (
        [Sales MAT],
        DATEADD ( 'Date'[Date], -1, YEAR )
    )
)
```

Measure in the Sales table

```
Sales MATG :=
VAR ValueCurrentPeriod = [Sales MAT]
VAR ValuePreviousPeriod = [Sales PYMAT]
VAR Result =
    IF (
        NOT ISBLANK ( ValueCurrentPeriod )
            && NOT ISBLANK ( ValuePreviousPeriod ),
        ValueCurrentPeriod - ValuePreviousPeriod
    )
RETURN
    Result
```

Measure in the Sales table

```
Sales MATG % :=
DIVIDE (
    [Sales MATG],
    [Sales PYMAT]
)
```

The *Sales PYMAT* measure can also be written using SAMEPERIODLASTYEAR as in the following example, which internally uses DATEADD as in the previous example:

Measure in the Sales table

```
Sales PYMAT (2) :=
IF (
    [ShowValueForDates],
    CALCULATE (
        [Sales MAT],
        SAMEPERIODLASTYEAR ( 'Date'[Date] )
    )
)
```

Moving averages

The moving average is typically used to display trends in line charts. Figure 2-18 includes the moving average of *Sales Amount* over 30 days (*Sales AVG 30D*), three months (*Sales AVG 3M*), and a year (*Sales AVG 1Y*).

Sales AVG 30D, Sales AVG 3M and Sales AVG 1Y by Date

FIGURE 2-18 *Sales AVG 30D*, *Sales AVG 3M*, and *Sales AVG 1Y* show the moving average over 30 days, three months, and one year, respectively.

Moving average 30 days

The *Sales AVG 30D* measure computes the moving average over 30 days by iterating a list of the last 30 dates obtained by DATESINPERIOD:

Measure in the Sales table

```
Sales AVG 30D :=
VAR Period30D =
    CALCULATETABLE (
        DATESINPERIOD (
            'Date'[Date],
            MAX ( 'Date'[Date] ),
            -30,
            DAY
        ),
        'Date'[DateWithSales] = TRUE
    )
VAR FirstDayWithData =
    CALCULATE (
        MIN ( Sales[Order Date] ),
        REMOVEFILTERS ()
    )
VAR FirstDayInPeriod =
    MINX ( Period 30D, 'Date'[Date] )
VAR Result =
    IF (
        FirstDayWithData <= FirstDayInPeriod,
        AVERAGEX (
            Period 30D,
            [Sales Amount]
        )
    )
RETURN
    Result
```

This pattern is very flexible. But for a regular additive calculation, *Result* can be implemented using a different and faster formula:

```
VAR Result =
    IF (
        FirstDayWithData <= FirstDayInPeriod,
        CALCULATE (
            DIVIDE (
                [Sales Amount],
                DISTINCTCOUNT ( Sales[Order Date] )
            ),
            Period30D
        )
    )
```

Moving average 3 months

The *Sales AVG 3M* measure computes the moving average over three months by iterating a list of the dates in the last three months obtained by DATESINPERIOD:

Measure in the Sales table

```
Sales AVG 3M :=
VAR Period3M =
    CALCULATETABLE (
        DATESINPERIOD (
            'Date'[Date],
            MAX ( 'Date'[Date] ),
            -3,
            MONTH
        ),
        'Date'[DateWithSales] = TRUE
    )
VAR FirstDayWithData =
    CALCULATE (
        MIN ( Sales[Order Date] ),
        REMOVEFILTERS ()
    )
VAR FirstDayInPeriod =
    MINX ( Period3M, 'Date'[Date] )
VAR Result =
    IF (
        FirstDayWithData <= FirstDayInPeriod,
        AVERAGEX (
            Period3M,
            [Sales Amount]
        )
    )
RETURN
    Result
```

For simple additive measures, the pattern based on DIVIDE which is shown for the moving average over 30 days can also be used for the average over three months.

Moving average 1 year

The *Sales AVG 1Y* measure computes the moving average over one year by iterating a list of the dates in the last year obtained by DATESINPERIOD:

Measure in the Sales table

```
Sales AVG 1Y :=
VAR Period1Y =
    CALCULATETABLE (
        DATESINPERIOD (
            'Date'[Date],
            MAX ( 'Date'[Date] ),
            -1,
            YEAR
        ),
        'Date'[DateWithSales] = TRUE
    )
VAR FirstDayWithData =
    CALCULATE (
        MIN ( Sales[Order Date] ),
        REMOVEFILTERS ()
    )
VAR FirstDayInPeriod =
    MINX ( Period1Y, 'Date'[Date] )
VAR Result =
    IF (
        FirstDayWithData <= FirstDayInPeriod,
        AVERAGEX (
            Period1Y,
            [Sales Amount]
        )
    )
RETURN
    Result
```

For simple additive measures, the same pattern based on DIVIDE, shown for the moving average over 30 days can also be used for the average over one year.

Filtering other date attributes

Once you mark the Date table as a date table, DAX automatically removes any filter from the *Date* table every time CALCULATE filters the date column of the *Date* table. This behavior is by design. Its goal is to simplify the writing of time intelligence calculations. Indeed, if DAX did not remove the filters, it would be necessary to manually add a REMOVEFILTERS over the *Date* table every time a DAX time intelligence function is used, resulting in a negative development experience.

The automatic removal of the filters from the *Date* table might introduce issues for some particular reports. For example, if a report computes the year-to-date of sales by slicing the amount by day of the week, the result obtained by only using the time intelligence function DATESYTD is wrong. Figure 2-19 shows that the result of *Sales YTD* for each day of the week is slightly smaller or equal to the row total, which is showing the value for all the days of the week.

Year	Sun	Mon	Tue	Wed	Thu	Fri	Sat	Total
⊟ **2007**	**2,028,110.40**	**2,033,290.41**	**1,986,595.75**	**1,986,595.75**	**2,001,546.40**	**2,023,061.60**	**2,023,061.60**	**2,033,290.41**
⊞ Q1-2007	33,191.68	33,191.68	37,278.73	67,516.57	67,516.57	67,687.57	70,663.35	**70,663.35**
⊞ Q2-2007	715,161.10	726,556.88	726,556.88	726,556.88	726,556.88	752,340.65	752,340.65	**752,340.65**
⊞ Q3-2007	1,299,615.31	1,275,404.66	1,275,584.60	1,275,584.60	1,279,868.45	1,280,683.45	1,283,923.34	**1,299,615.31**
⊞ Q4-2007	2,028,110.40	2,033,290.41	1,986,595.75	1,986,595.75	2,001,546.40	2,023,061.60	2,023,061.60	**2,033,290.41**
⊟ **2008**	**3,863,166.63**	**3,945,581.66**	**3,961,357.00**	**3,962,572.24**	**3,834,546.99**	**3,838,405.66**	**3,847,341.31**	**3,962,572.24**
⊞ Q1-2008	652,523.41	653,510.79	603,654.94	621,113.72	646,903.21	646,903.21	652,523.41	**653,510.79**
⊞ Q2-2008	1,897,398.57	1,905,436.47	1,897,236.73	1,897,236.73	1,897,236.73	1,897,236.73	1,897,236.73	**1,905,436.47**
⊞ Q3-2008	2,938,716.78	2,961,218.27	2,971,689.41	2,933,658.94	2,938,230.94	2,938,716.78	2,938,716.78	**2,971,689.41**
⊞ Q4-2008	3,863,166.63	3,945,581.66	3,961,357.00	3,962,572.24	3,834,546.99	3,838,405.66	3,847,341.31	**3,962,572.24**
⊟ **2009**	**2,106,851.27**	**2,106,851.27**	**2,106,851.27**	**2,106,851.27**	**2,106,851.27**	**2,106,851.27**	**2,106,851.27**	**2,106,851.27**
⊞ Q1-2009	607,441.51	607,441.51	607,441.51	602,032.63	607,441.51	607,441.51	607,441.51	**607,441.51**
⊞ Q2-2009	1,606,849.46	1,637,729.02	1,655,456.71	1,585,978.86	1,585,978.86	1,587,634.79	1,603,263.58	**1,655,456.71**
⊞ Q3-2009	2,106,851.27	2,106,851.27	2,106,851.27	2,106,851.27	2,106,851.27	2,106,851.27	2,106,851.27	**2,106,851.27**
Total								

FIGURE 2-19 Slicing the measure *Sales YTD* by day of the week produces an inaccurate result.

The reason for the inaccurate value is that DATESYTD applies a filter on the *Date[Date]* column. Because *Date* is marked as a date table, DAX automatically applies a *REMOVEFILTERS('Date')* modifier to the same CALCULATE where DATESYTD is used in a filter argument – thus removing the filter on the day of the week. Therefore, the number shown is the year-to-date regardless of any filter on the weekday. The day-of-week filter only affects the last day of the period specified on the rows of the report – year or quarter. The correct result, shown in Figure 2-20, requires a different approach.

Year	Sun	Mon	Tue	Wed	Thu	Fri	Sat	Total
⊟ 2007	387,892.31	256,494.86	351,518.69	167,564.95	325,372.54	234,028.12	310,418.94	2,033,290.41
⊞ Q1-2007	7,494.33	269.59	4,087.06	37,797.73	8,092.55	171.00	12,751.10	70,663.35
⊞ Q2-2007	157,152.33	104,206.69	94,556.88	53,180.25	65,739.02	98,845.73	178,659.77	752,340.65
⊞ Q3-2007	294,136.91	146,961.86	197,450.85	114,226.73	191,722.65	140,318.84	214,797.46	1,299,615.31
⊞ Q4-2007	387,892.31	256,494.86	351,518.69	167,564.95	325,372.54	234,028.12	310,418.94	2,033,290.41
⊟ 2008	481,984.57	748,049.69	672,542.60	612,707.54	456,627.54	536,158.70	454,501.59	3,962,572.24
⊞ Q1-2008	99,539.00	114,336.96	127,790.20	73,790.35	166,717.34	36,881.39	34,455.55	653,510.79
⊞ Q2-2008	235,012.67	372,938.93	375,364.30	254,736.08	275,116.22	145,657.29	246,610.98	1,905,436.47
⊞ Q3-2008	336,763.20	502,666.56	540,890.53	451,235.48	368,948.90	422,201.81	348,982.93	2,971,689.41
⊞ Q4-2008	481,984.57	748,049.69	672,542.60	612,707.54	456,627.54	536,158.70	454,501.59	3,962,572.24
⊟ 2009	319,764.21	317,954.65	229,012.06	242,739.71	269,741.35	436,190.22	291,449.07	2,106,851.27
⊞ Q1-2009	92,797.03	150,013.12	51,059.31	46,155.11	65,152.15	112,963.49	89,301.31	607,441.51
⊞ Q2-2009	272,649.29	268,634.97	165,391.40	196,429.31	183,913.29	358,525.74	209,912.72	1,655,456.71
⊞ Q3-2009	319,764.21	317,954.65	229,012.06	242,739.71	269,741.35	436,190.22	291,449.07	2,106,851.27
Total								

FIGURE 2-20 Slicing *Sales YTD (day of week)* by day of the week produces the correct result.

There are two options to obtain the correct value: either reiterate the filter over the day of the week in the CALCULATE statement, or update the data model.

Restoring the filter over the day of the week requires adding *VALUES (Date[Day of Week])* only if the columns are filtered, like in the following code:

Measure in the Sales table

```
Sales YTD (day of week) :=
IF (
    [ShowValueForDates],
    IF (
        ISFILTERED ( 'Date'[Day of Week] ),
        CALCULATE (
            [Sales Amount],
            DATESYTD ( 'Date'[Date] ),
            VALUES ( 'Date'[Day of Week] )
        ),
        CALCULATE (
            [Sales Amount],
            DATESYTD ( 'Date'[Date] )
        )
    )
)
```

This first solution works well, but it comes with a significant shortcoming: there are two different versions of the calculation depending on whether the *Date[Day of Week]* column is filtered or not. On large models, this might have a noticeable impact on performance.

There is another solution to this scenario that requires updating the data model. Instead of using the *Date* table to select the day of the week, we can store the day of the week in a separate table that filters

Sales without being related to *Date*. This way, the automatic filter removal over *Date* does not affect the existing filter over the day of the week. For example, the *Day of Week* table can be created as a calculated table:

Calculated table

```
Day of Week =
SELECTCOLUMNS (
    'Date',
    "Date", 'Date'[Date],
    "Day of Week", 'Date'[Day of Week]
)
```

The *Day of week* table must have a relationship between *Sales[Order Date]* and *'Day of week'[Date]*, meaning the model must look like the one in Figure 2-21.

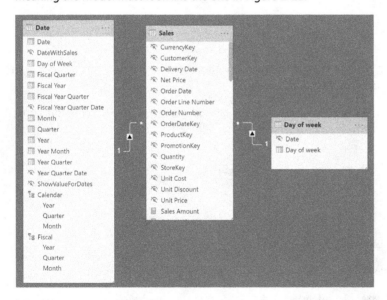

FIGURE 2-21 The new *Day of Week* table is related to the same *Order Date* column used by *Date*.

Please note that we created the new *Day of Week* table using all the dates in *Date* to create the relationship with the existing *Sales[Order Date]* column. It is possible to obtain the same behavior by creating a table with only seven values (Sunday through Saturday), but that choice requires an additional column in the *Sales* table – thus consuming more memory for the data model.

Slicing by *Day of Week* in the newly created table is compatible with any time intelligence calculation and respects any filter on the *Day of Week* table; this is because the two filters (*Date* and *Day of the week*) belong to two different tables.

The additional table could consolidate any set of attributes required by specific business rules. We built an example with the day of the week, but you can use any other set of attributes (like working days, holidays, seasons), provided that such attributes depend on *Order Date*.

Month-related calculations

This pattern describes how to compute month-related calculations such as year-to-date, same period last year, and percentage growth using a month granularity. This pattern does not rely on DAX built-in time intelligence functions.

You can use the Month-related calculations pattern if the analysis over sales is executed at the month level (or above) only. In other words, the formulas stop working if you drill down to the date level. Because the pattern does not use real dates to link to sales, you can also implement fiscal calendars with 13 months and any non-standard time-related calculation – provided that the maximum level of detail of the reports is the month and not weeks or days. The report cannot filter or group by week, day of week, or working days; despite the fact that the granularity of the *Date* table can be at the date level, these columns must not be part of the *Date* table because they are not compatible with the formulas in this pattern.

The Month-related calculations pattern is useful to create simple formulas and optimal performance in all those cases where the day granularity is not required. Moreover, this is the only pattern that allows the creation of additional months, like a 13th virtual month for a fiscal year that contains year-end adjustments in accounting systems. If you manage time-related calculations over time periods based on months and you need the day granularity, consider using the **Custom time-related calculations** pattern. If you manage time-related calculations over time periods based on weeks, consider using the **Week-related calculations** pattern.

Introduction to month-related time intelligence calculations

The time intelligence calculations in this pattern modify the filter context over the *Date* table to obtain the result. The formulas are designed to apply filters at the month granularity to improve query performance, regardless of the cardinality of the *Date* table. For example, many calculations modify the filter context at the month level instead of the individual dates. This technique reduces the cost of computing the new filter and applying it to the filter context. This optimization is especially useful when using DirectQuery, even though it also improves performance on models imported in memory.

The pattern does not rely on the standard time intelligence functions; therefore, the *Date* table does not have the requirements needed for standard DAX time intelligence functions. The formulas are identical whether you have one row for each month or one row for each day.

If the *Date* table has a *Date* column, the Mark as Date Table setting is allowed but not required. The formulas in this pattern do not rely on the automatic REMOVEFILTERS applied over the *Date* table when the *Date* column is filtered. Instead, all the formulas use a specific REMOVEFILTERS over the *Date* table to get rid of the existing filters, in turn replacing them with the minimal number of filters that guarantee the desired result.

Building a *Date* table

The *Date* table used for month-related calculations can be built in many ways. The requirement for the pattern is to expose columns related to the months and any aggregation over months, such as quarters and years. The months could be different from those defined in the standard Gregorian calendar, as is the case when a 13th month is required. The sample files available for this pattern include four different scenarios for the *Date* table:

1. One row for each date based on the Gregorian calendar, using *Date* as the primary key. In this case, the behavior is close to the standard time intelligence calculations, with the noticeable difference that the formulas are faster.

2. One row for each month based on the Gregorian calendar, using *Year Month Number* as the primary key. This pattern is even better than the previous one, because the date table is significantly smaller.

3. One row for each month in an accounting calendar with 13 fiscal months, where the 13th fiscal month is projected as an additional month in the Gregorian calendar between the last month of a fiscal year and the first month of the following fiscal year. Performance is close to that of the second pattern.

4. One row for each month in an accounting calendar with 13 fiscal months, where the 13th fiscal month is projected in the last fiscal month on the Gregorian calendar. Performance and behavior are very close to what is observed in the third example.

In case there is one row for each month in the *Date* table, you should not use a date to link the *Sales* and *Date* tables – unless you use specific dates to identify each month. For example, December 1 for December and December 31 for the 13th month of the year.

The *Date* table in this pattern must have all the months included in the range between the first and the last date referenced in the *Sales* table. Therefore, if the last sale was processed in August 2009, the last month in the Date table must be August 2009. This requirement is different from the requirement of the standard time-intelligence functions in DAX, where all the months of a year must be present in the *Date* table to guarantee the correct behavior.

If you already have a *Date* table, you can import the table and use it by showing only the columns required for this pattern while hiding columns with a day or week granularity. If a *Date* table is not available, you can create one using a DAX calculated table. As an example, the following DAX expression defines the *Date* table used in the first three scenarios described earlier:

Calculated table

```
Date =
VAR FirstFiscalMonth = 3    -- First month of the fiscal year
VAR MonthsInYear = 12       -- Must be 12 for GranularityByDate
                            -- can be different for GranularityByMonth
VAR CalendarFirstDate = MIN ( Sales[Order Date]  )
VAR CalendarLastDate = MAX ( Sales[Order Date]  )
VAR CalendarFirstYear = YEAR ( CalendarFirstDate )
VAR CalendarFirstMonth = MONTH ( CalendarFirstDate )
VAR CalendarLastYear = YEAR ( CalendarLastDate )
VAR CalendarLastMonth = MONTH ( CalendarLastDate )


------------------------
-- Internal calculations
------------------------
VAR GranularityByDate =
    ADDCOLUMNS (
        CALENDAR (
            DATE ( CalendarFirstYear, CalendarFirstMonth, 1 ),
            EOMONTH (
                DATE ( CalendarLastYear, CalendarLastMonth, 1 ),
                0
            )
        ),
        "Year Month Number", YEAR ( [Date] ) * MonthsInYear
            + MONTH ( [Date] ) - 1
    )
VAR GranularityByMonth =
    SELECTCOLUMNS (
        GENERATESERIES (
            CalendarFirstYear * MonthsInYear + CalendarFirstMonth - 1
                - (MonthsInYear - 12) * (CalendarFirstMonth < FirstFiscalMonth),
            CalendarLastYear * MonthsInYear + CalendarLastMonth - 1
                - (MonthsInYear - 12) * (CalendarLastMonth < FirstFiscalMonth),
            1
        ),
        "Year Month Number", [Value]
    )
RETURN GENERATE (
    GranularityByDate,       -- Use GranularityByMonth to get one row for each month
    VAR YearMonthNumber = [Year Month Number]
    VAR FiscalMonthNumber =
        MOD (
            YearMonthNumber + 1
                * (FirstFiscalMonth > 1)
                * (MonthsInYear + 1 - FirstFiscalMonth),
            MonthsInYear
        ) + 1
    VAR FiscalYearNumber =
        QUOTIENT (
            YearMonthNumber + 1
                * (FirstFiscalMonth > 1)
                * (MonthsInYear + 1 - FirstFiscalMonth),
            MonthsInYear
        )
    VAR OffsetFiscalMonthNumber = MonthsInYear + 1 - (MonthsInYear - 12)
```

```
    VAR MonthNumber =
        IF (
            FiscalMonthNumber <= 12 && FirstFiscalMonth > 1,
            FiscalMonthNumber + FirstFiscalMonth
                - IF (
                    FiscalMonthNumber > (OffsetFiscalMonthNumber - FirstFiscalMonth),
                    OffsetFiscalMonthNumber,
                    1
                ),
            FiscalMonthNumber
        )
    VAR YearNumber = FiscalYearNumber - 1 * (MonthNumber > FiscalMonthNumber)
    VAR YearMonthKey = YearNumber * 100 + MonthNumber

    VAR MonthDate = DATE ( YearNumber, MonthNumber, 1 )
    VAR FiscalQuarterNumber = MIN ( ROUNDUP ( FiscalMonthNumber / 3, 0 ), 4 )
    VAR FiscalYearQuarterNumber = FiscalYearNumber * 4 + FiscalQuarterNumber - 1
    VAR FiscalMonthInQuarterNumber =
        MOD ( FiscalMonthNumber - 1, 3 ) + 1 + 3 * (MonthNumber > 12)
    VAR MonthInQuarterNumber = MOD ( MonthNumber - 1, 3 ) + 1 + 3 * (MonthNumber > 12)
    VAR QuarterNumber = MIN ( ROUNDUP ( MonthNumber / 3, 0 ), 4 )
    VAR YearQuarterNumber = YearNumber * 4 + QuarterNumber - 1
    RETURN ROW (
        "Year Month Key", YearMonthKey,
        "Year", YearNumber,
        "Year Quarter", FORMAT ( QuarterNumber, "\Q0" )
            & "-" & FORMAT ( YearNumber, "0000" ),
        "Year Quarter Number", YearQuarterNumber,
        "Quarter", FORMAT ( QuarterNumber, "\Q0" ),
        "Year Month", IF (
            MonthNumber > 12,
            FORMAT ( MonthNumber, "\M00" ) & FORMAT ( YearNumber, " 0000" ),
            FORMAT ( MonthDate, "mmm yyyy" )
        ),
        "Month", IF (
            MonthNumber > 12,
            FORMAT ( MonthNumber, "\M00" ),
            FORMAT ( MonthDate, "mmm" )
        ),
        "Month Number", MonthNumber,
        "Month In Quarter Number", MonthInQuarterNumber,
        "Fiscal Year", FORMAT ( FiscalYearNumber, "\F\Y 0000" ),
        "Fiscal Year Number", FiscalYearNumber,
        "Fiscal Year Quarter", FORMAT ( FiscalQuarterNumber, "\F\Q0" ) & "-"
            & FORMAT ( FiscalYearNumber, "0000" ),
        "Fiscal Year Quarter Number", FiscalYearQuarterNumber,
        "Fiscal Quarter", FORMAT ( FiscalQuarterNumber, "\F\Q0" ),
        "Fiscal Month", IF (
            MonthNumber > 12,
            FORMAT ( MonthNumber, "\M00" ),
            FORMAT ( MonthDate, "mmm" )
        ),
        "Fiscal Month Number", FiscalMonthNumber,
        "Fiscal Month In Quarter Number", FiscalMonthInQuarterNumber
    )
)
```

You can customize the first two variables to build a *Date* table that meets specific business requirements. The *FirstFiscalMonth* variable defines the first fiscal month in the year, and the *MonthsInYear* variable defines the number of months for each fiscal year. The other customization is the first argument of GENERATE, which can be:

- *GranularityByMonth* to generate one row for each month;
- *GranularityByDate* to generate one row for each date.

The *GranularityByDate* argument is used in the first scenario (one row for every date), whereas *GranularityByMonth* is used in the other three scenarios (one row for every month). The *Year Month* column has one value for each month; the month description is the same for both the fiscal and Gregorian calendar hierarchies. The fourth scenario includes a few additional columns to get a different value between *Month* and *Fiscal Month*. This is required to manage the 13th month differently, depending on the hierarchy.

In order to obtain the correct visualization, the **calendar columns** must be configured in the data model as follows. For each column we show the data type followed by a sample value assuming a fiscal month starting in March where there are 12 months in the fiscal year:

- *Date*: Date, Hidden (8/14/2007), used only for the first scenario
- *Year Month Key*: Whole Number, Hidden (200708), used to define relationships
- *Year Month*: Text (Aug 2007)
- *Year Quarter*: Text (Q3-2007)
- *Year Quarter Number*: Whole Number, Hidden (8030)
- *Quarter*: Text (Q3)
- *Year Month Number*: Whole Number, Hidden (24091)
- *Month*: Text (Aug)
- *Month Number*: Whole Number, Hidden (8)
- *Month In Quarter Number*: Whole Number, Hidden (2)
- *Fiscal Month*: Text (Aug)
- *Fiscal Month Number*: Whole Number, Hidden (6)
- *Fiscal Month in Quarter Number*: Whole Number, Hidden (3)
- *Fiscal Year*: Text (FY 2008)
- *Fiscal Year Number*: Whole Number, Hidden (2008)
- *Fiscal Year Quarter*: Text (FQ2-2008)
- *Fiscal Year Quarter* Number: Whole Number, Hidden (8033)
- *Fiscal Quarter*: Text (FQ2)

The *Date* table in this pattern has four hierarchies:

- Fiscal Year-Quarter: Year (*Fiscal Year*), Quarter (*Fiscal Year Quarter*), Month (*Year Month*)
- Fiscal Year-Month: Year (*Fiscal Year*), Month (*Year Month*)
- Year-Quarter: Year (*Year*), Quarter (*Year Quarter*), Month (*Year Month*)
- Year-Month: Year (*Year*), Month (*Year Month*)

Several columns serve the only purpose of simplifying the formulas used in custom time-related calculations. The *Year Month Key* column is only used to define a relationship with the *Sales* table using an integer in the format *YYYYMM*. This numeric format to identify a month is common in many data sources that manage data at the month granularity.

The *Date* table has only the range of months required by the data available. For example, in the example the *Date* table includes only the months from March 2007 to August 2009. This pattern does not come with the constraint of including all the months in one year. For this reason, there is no need for additional calculated columns like the *DateWithSales* used in the **Standard time-related calculations** pattern.

Naming convention

This section describes the naming convention we adopted to reference the time intelligence calculations. A simple categorization shows whether a calculation:

- shifts over a period of time, for example the same period in the previous year;

- performs an aggregation, for example year-to-date; or

- compares two time periods, for example this year compared to last year.

Acronym	Description	Shift	Aggregation	Comparison
YTD	Year-to-date		X	
QTD	Quarter-to-date		X	
MAT	Moving annual total		X	
PY	Previous year	X		
PQ	Previous quarter	X		
PM	Previous month	X		
PYC	Previous year complete	X		
PQC	Previous quarter complete	X		
PMC	Previous month complete	X		
PP	Previous period; automatically selects year, quarter, or month	X		
PYMAT	Previous year moving annual total	X	X	
YOY	Year-over-year			X
QOQ	Quarter-over-quarter			X
MOM	Month-over-month			X
MATG	Moving annual total growth	X	X	X
POP	Period-over-period; automatically selects year, quarter, or month			X
PYTD	Previous year-to-date	X	X	
PQTD	Previous quarter-to-date	X	X	
YOYTD	Year-over-year-to-date	X	X	X
QOQTD	Quarter-over-quarter-to-date	X	X	X
YTDOPY	Year-to-date-over-previous-year	X	X	X
QTDOPQ	Quarter-to-date-over-previous-quarter	X	X	X

Computing period-to-date totals

The year-to-date, quarter-to-date, and month-to-date calculations modify the filter context for the *Date* table, so to include the dates from the beginning of the period to the currently selected month.

Year-to-date total

The year-to-date aggregates data starting from the first day of the year, as shown in Figure 3-1.

Year	Sales Amount	Sales YTD	^	Year	Sales Amount	Sales Fiscal YTD	^
⊟ **2007**	**9,008,591.74**	**9,008,591.74**		⊟ **FY 2008**	**10,265,438.43**	**10,265,438.43**	
Mar 2007	345,319.01	345,319.01		Mar 2007	345,319.01	345,319.01	
Apr 2007	1,128,104.82	1,473,423.82		Apr 2007	1,128,104.82	1,473,423.82	
May 2007	936,192.74	2,409,616.57		May 2007	936,192.74	2,409,616.57	
Jun 2007	982,304.46	3,391,921.03		Jun 2007	982,304.46	3,391,921.03	
Jul 2007	922,542.98	4,314,464.01		Jul 2007	922,542.98	4,314,464.01	
Aug 2007	952,834.59	5,267,298.60		Aug 2007	952,834.59	5,267,298.60	
Sep 2007	1,009,868.98	6,277,167.58		Sep 2007	1,009,868.98	6,277,167.58	
Oct 2007	914,273.54	7,191,441.12		Oct 2007	914,273.54	7,191,441.12	
Nov 2007	825,601.87	8,017,042.99		Nov 2007	825,601.87	8,017,042.99	
Dec 2007	991,548.75	9,008,591.74		Dec 2007	991,548.75	9,008,591.74	
⊟ **2008**	**9,927,582.99**	**9,927,582.99**		Jan 2008	656,766.69	9,665,358.44	
Jan 2008	656,766.69	656,766.69		Feb 2008	600,080.00	10,265,438.43	
Feb 2008	600,080.00	1,256,846.69		⊟ **FY 2009**	**9,874,218.49**	**9,874,218.49**	
Mar 2008	559,538.52	1,816,385.21		Mar 2008	559,538.52	559,538.52	
Apr 2008	999,667.17	2,816,052.38		Apr 2008	999,667.17	1,559,205.69	
May 2008	893,231.96	3,709,284.34		May 2008	893,231.96	2,452,437.65	

FIGURE 3-1 *Sales YTD* shows the aggregated value from the beginning of the year, whereas *Sales Fiscal YTD* aggregates the value starting from the beginning of the fiscal year.

The year-to-date total of a measure filters all the months that are in the year of the last date available in the filter context, and whose month is less than or equal to the month of that date:

Measure in the Sales table

```
Sales YTD :=
VAR LastMonthAvailable = MAX ( 'Date'[Year Month Number] )
VAR LastYearAvailable = MAX ( 'Date'[Year] )
VAR Result =
    CALCULATE (
        [Sales Amount],
        REMOVEFILTERS ( 'Date' ),
        'Date'[Year Month Number] <= LastMonthAvailable,
        'Date'[Year] = LastYearAvailable
    )
RETURN
    Result
```

If the report uses a hierarchy based on the fiscal year, then the measure must filter the corresponding columns with the word "Fiscal" before the acronym identifying the time intelligence calculation. For example, the *Sales Fiscal YTD* measure uses *Fiscal Year Number* instead of *Year*; however, it does not change the filter over *Year Month Number* because that column is identical for both fiscal and calendar hierarchies:

Measure in the Sales table

```
Sales Fiscal YTD :=
VAR LastMonthAvailable = MAX ( 'Date'[Year Month Number] )
VAR LastFiscalYearAvailable = MAX ( 'Date'[Fiscal Year Number] )
VAR Result =
    CALCULATE (
        [Sales Amount],
        REMOVEFILTERS ( 'Date' ),
        'Date'[Year Month Number] <= LastMonthAvailable,
        'Date'[Fiscal Year Number] = LastFiscalYearAvailable
    )
RETURN
    Result
```

Quarter-to-date total

The quarter to date aggregates data from the first month of the fiscal quarter, as shown in Figure 3-2.

Year	Sales Amount	Sales QTD
⊞ **2007**	**9,008,591.74**	**2,731,424.16**
⊞ **2008**	**9,927,582.99**	**2,797,611.46**
⊟ **2009**	**5,725,632.34**	**1,407,367.64**
⊟ **Q1-2009**	**1,699,620.05**	**1,699,620.05**
Jan 2009	580,901.05	580,901.05
Feb 2009	622,581.14	1,203,482.19
Mar 2009	496,137.87	1,699,620.05
⊟ **Q2-2009**	**2,618,644.64**	**2,618,644.64**
Apr 2009	678,893.22	678,893.22
May 2009	1,067,165.23	1,746,058.45
Jun 2009	872,586.20	2,618,644.64
⊟ **Q3-2009**	**1,407,367.64**	**1,407,367.64**
Jul 2009	1,068,396.58	1,068,396.58
Aug 2009	338,971.06	1,407,367.64
Total	**24,661,807.07**	**1,407,367.64**

FIGURE 3-2 *Sales QTD* shows the quarter-to-date amount, which is the value of the last quarter available at the year level.

The quarter-to-date total of a measure is computed with the technique used for the year-to-date total. The only difference is that the filter is now on *Year Quarter Number* instead of *Year*:

Measure in the Sales table

```
Sales QTD :=
VAR LastMonthAvailable = MAX ( 'Date'[Year Month Number] )
VAR LastYearQuarterAvailable = MAX ( 'Date'[Year Quarter Number] )
VAR Result =
    CALCULATE (
        [Sales Amount],
        REMOVEFILTERS ( 'Date' ),
        'Date'[Year Month Number] <= LastMonthAvailable,
        'Date'[Year Quarter Number] = LastYearQuarterAvailable
    )
RETURN
    Result
```

Computing period-over-period growth

A common requirement is to compare a time period with the same time period in the previous year, quarter, or month. In order to achieve a fair comparison, the measure takes into account the same relative months in the previous year, or the same relative months in the previous quarter.

Year-over-year growth

Year-over-year compares a time period to its equivalent in the previous year. In this example, data is available until August 2009. For this reason, *Sales PY* shows numbers related to the year 2009 considering transactions only from before August 2008. Figure 3-3 shows that the *Sales Amount* of 2008 is 9,927,582.99, whereas *Sales PY* for 2009 returns 6,166,534.30 because the measure involves sales only up to August 2008.

Year	Sales Amount	Sales PY	Sales YOY	Sales YOY %
⊞ 2007	9,008,591.74			
⊟ 2008	9,927,582.99	9,008,591.74	918,991.25	10.20%
⊞ Q1-2008	1,816,385.21	345,319.01	1,471,066.20	426.00%
⊞ Q2-2008	2,738,040.73	3,046,602.02	-308,561.29	-10.13%
⊟ Q3-2008	2,575,545.59	2,885,246.55	-309,700.96	-10.73%
Jul 2008	890,547.41	922,542.98	-31,995.58	-3.47%
Aug 2008	721,560.95	952,834.59	-231,273.63	-24.27%
Sep 2008	963,437.23	1,009,868.98	-46,431.76	-4.60%
⊞ Q4-2008	2,797,611.46	2,731,424.16	66,187.30	2.42%
⊟ 2009	5,725,632.34	6,166,534.30	-440,901.97	-7.15%
⊞ Q1-2009	1,699,620.05	1,816,385.21	-116,765.16	-6.43%
⊞ Q2-2009	2,618,644.64	2,738,040.73	-119,396.09	-4.36%
⊟ Q3-2009	1,407,367.64	1,612,108.36	-204,740.72	-12.70%
Jul 2009	1,068,396.58	890,547.41	177,849.17	19.97%
Aug 2009	338,971.06	721,560.95	-382,589.89	-53.02%
Total	24,661,807.07			

FIGURE 3-3 For the year 2009, *Sales PY* shows the amount from January to August 2008, because there is no data after August 2009.

Sales PY removes all the filters from the *Date* table; it filters the *Year* column by using the previous year, and by using *VALUES* it retrieves the months visible in the current filter context to then filter the *Month Number* column. The *Date* table must hold only the months with sales, instead of holding all the months of the year as required by the standard time intelligence functions in DAX. This way, any direct or indirect selection of months is applied to the previous year:

Measure in the Sales table

```
Sales PY :=
VAR CurrentYearNumber = SELECTEDVALUE ( 'Date'[Year] )
VAR PreviousYearNumber = CurrentYearNumber - 1
VAR Result =
    CALCULATE (
        [Sales Amount],
        REMOVEFILTERS ( 'Date' ),
        'Date'[Year] = PreviousYearNumber,
        VALUES ( 'Date'[Month Number] )
    )
RETURN
    Result
```

Year-over-year growth is computed as an amount in *Sales YOY,* and as a percentage in *Sales YOY %.* Both measures use *Sales PY* to take into account dates only up to August 2009:

Measure in the Sales table

```
Sales YOY :=
VAR ValueCurrentPeriod = [Sales Amount]
VAR ValuePreviousPeriod = [Sales PY]
VAR Result =
    IF (
        NOT ISBLANK ( ValueCurrentPeriod ) && NOT ISBLANK ( ValuePreviousPeriod ),
        ValueCurrentPeriod - ValuePreviousPeriod
    )
RETURN
    Result
```

Measure in the Sales table

```
Sales YOY % :=
DIVIDE (
    [Sales YOY],
    [Sales PY]
)
```

Quarter-over-quarter growth

Quarter-over-quarter compares a time period to its equivalent in the previous quarter. In this example, data is available until August 2009. For this reason, *Sales PQ* shows numbers related to Q3-2009 considering only transactions before the second month of Q2-2009. Figure 3-4 shows that the *Sales Amount* of Q2-2009 is 2,618,644.64, whereas *Sales PY* for Q3-2009 returns 1,746,058.45. This is because the measure takes into account the sales of only the first two months of Q2-2009.

Year	Sales Amount	Sales PQ	Sales QOQ	Sales QOQ %
⊞ 2007	9,008,591.74			
⊞ 2008	9,927,582.99			
⊟ 2009	5,725,632.34			
⊞ Q1-2009	1,699,620.05	2,797,611.46	-1,097,991.40	-39.25%
⊟ Q2-2009	2,618,644.64	1,699,620.05	919,024.59	54.07%
Apr 2009	678,893.22	580,901.05	97,992.17	16.87%
May 2009	1,067,165.23	622,581.14	444,584.09	71.41%
Jun 2009	872,586.20	496,137.87	376,448.33	75.88%
⊟ Q3-2009	1,407,367.64	1,746,058.45	-338,690.80	-19.40%
Jul 2009	1,068,396.58	678,893.22	389,503.36	57.37%
Aug 2009	338,971.06	1,067,165.23	-728,194.17	-68.24%
Total	24,661,807.07			

FIGURE 3-4 For Q3-2009, *Sales PQ shows* the sum of Apr 2009 and May 2009, because there are only two months in Q3-2009 to be compared to Q2-2009.

Sales PQ removes all the filters from the *Date* table; it filters the *Year Quarter Number* column using the previous quarter, and with VALUES which retrieves the months visible in the filter context it filters the *Month In Quarter Number* column. This way, any direct or indirect selection of months is applied to the previous quarter:

Measure in the Sales table

```
Sales PQ :=
VAR CurrentYearQuarterNumber = SELECTEDVALUE ( 'Date'[Year Quarter Number] )
VAR PreviousYearQuarterNumber = CurrentYearQuarterNumber - 1
VAR Result =
    CALCULATE (
        [Sales Amount],
        REMOVEFILTERS ( 'Date' ),
        'Date'[Year Quarter Number] = PreviousYearQuarterNumber,
        VALUES ( 'Date'[Month In Quarter Number] )
    )
RETURN
    Result
```

Quarter-over-quarter growth is computed as an amount in *Sales QOQ* and as a percentage in *Sales QOQ %*. Both measures use *Sales PQ* to guarantee a fair comparison:

Measure in the Sales table

```
Sales QOQ :=
VAR ValueCurrentPeriod = [Sales Amount]
VAR ValuePreviousPeriod = [Sales PQ]
VAR Result =
    IF (
        NOT ISBLANK ( ValueCurrentPeriod )
            && NOT ISBLANK ( ValuePreviousPeriod ),
        ValueCurrentPeriod - ValuePreviousPeriod
    )
RETURN
    Result
```

Measure in the Sales table

```
Sales QOQ % :=
DIVIDE (
    [Sales QOQ],
    [Sales PQ]
)
```

Month-over-month growth

Month-over-month compares a time period to its equivalent in the previous month. Figure 3-5 shows that *Sales PM* always corresponds to the *Sales Amount* of the previous month and does not produce any result at the quarter and at the year levels (only the year level is visible in Figure 3-5).

Year	Sales Amount	Sales PM	Sales MOM	Sales MOM %
⊞ **2007**	**9,008,591.74**			
⊞ **2008**	**9,927,582.99**			
⊟ **2009**	**5,725,632.34**			
Jan 2009	580,901.05	921,709.14	-340,808.09	-36.98%
Feb 2009	622,581.14	580,901.05	41,680.09	7.18%
Mar 2009	496,137.87	622,581.14	-126,443.27	-20.31%
Apr 2009	678,893.22	496,137.87	182,755.35	36.84%
May 2009	1,067,165.23	678,893.22	388,272.01	57.19%
Jun 2009	872,586.20	1,067,165.23	-194,579.03	-18.23%
Jul 2009	1,068,396.58	872,586.20	195,810.38	22.44%
Aug 2009	338,971.06	1,068,396.58	-729,425.52	-68.27%
Total	**24,661,807.07**			

FIGURE 3-5 *Sales PM* always corresponds to the *Sales Amount* of the previous month.

Sales PM removes all the filters from the *Date* table and only filters the *Year Month Number* column using the previous month:

Measure in the Sales table

```
Sales PM :=
VAR CurrentYearMonthNumber = SELECTEDVALUE ( 'Date'[Year Month Number] )
VAR PreviousYearMonthNumber = CurrentYearMonthNumber - 1
VAR Result =
    CALCULATE (
        [Sales Amount],
        REMOVEFILTERS ( 'Date' ),
        'Date'[Year Month Number] = PreviousYearMonthNumber
    )
RETURN
    Result
```

The month-over-month growth is computed as an amount in *Sales MOM* and as a percentage in *Sales MOM %*:

Measure in the Sales table

```
Sales MOM :=
VAR ValueCurrentPeriod = [Sales Amount]
VAR ValuePreviousPeriod = [Sales PM]
VAR Result =
    IF (
        NOT ISBLANK ( ValueCurrentPeriod ) && NOT ISBLANK ( ValuePreviousPeriod ),
        ValueCurrentPeriod - ValuePreviousPeriod
    )
RETURN
    Result
```

Measure in the Sales table

```
Sales MOM % :=
DIVIDE (
    [Sales MOM],
    [Sales PM]
)
```

Period-over-period growth

Period-over-period growth automatically selects one of the measures previously described in this section based on the current selection in the visualization. For example, it returns the value of month-over-month growth measures if the visualization displays data at the month level, but switches to year-over-year growth measures if the visualization shows the total at the year level. The result you would expect is visible in Figure 3-6.

Year	Sales Amount	Sales PP	Sales POP	Sales POP %
⊞ **2007**	**9,008,591.74**			
⊟ **2008**	**9,927,582.99**	**9,008,591.74**	**918,991.25**	**10.20%**
⊞ **Q1-2008**	**1,816,385.21**	**2,731,424.16**	**-915,038.95**	**-33.50%**
⊟ **Q2-2008**	**2,738,040.73**	**1,816,385.21**	**921,655.52**	**50.74%**
Apr 2008	999,667.17	559,538.52	440,128.65	78.66%
May 2008	893,231.96	999,667.17	-106,435.21	-10.65%
Jun 2008	845,141.60	893,231.96	-48,090.36	-5.38%
⊟ **Q3-2008**	**2,575,545.59**	**2,738,040.73**	**-162,495.14**	**-5.93%**
Jul 2008	890,547.41	845,141.60	45,405.81	5.37%
Aug 2008	721,560.95	890,547.41	-168,986.45	-18.98%
Sep 2008	963,437.23	721,560.95	241,876.27	33.52%
⊞ **Q4-2008**	**2,797,611.46**	**2,575,545.59**	**222,065.87**	**8.62%**
⊟ **2009**	**5,725,632.34**	**6,166,534.30**	**-440,901.97**	**-7.15%**
⊞ **Q1-2009**	**1,699,620.05**	**2,797,611.46**	**-1,097,991.40**	**-39.25%**
⊟ **Q2-2009**	**2,618,644.64**	**1,699,620.05**	**919,024.59**	**54.07%**
Apr 2009	678,893.22	496,137.87	182,755.35	36.84%
May 2009	1,067,165.23	678,893.22	388,272.01	57.19%
Jun 2009	872,586.20	1,067,165.23	-194,579.03	-18.23%
⊟ **Q3-2009**	**1,407,367.64**	**1,746,058.45**	**-338,690.80**	**-19.40%**
Jul 2009	1,068,396.58	872,586.20	195,810.38	22.44%
Aug 2009	338,971.06	1,068,396.58	-729,425.52	-68.27%
Total	**24,661,807.07**			

FIGURE 3-6 *Sales PP* shows the value of the previous month at the month level, of the previous quarter at the quarter level, and of the previous year at the year level.

The three measures *Sales PP*, *Sales POP*, and *Sales POP %* redirect the evaluation to the corresponding year, quarter, and month measures depending on the level selected in the report. The ISINSCOPE function detects the level used in the report. The arguments passed to ISINSCOPE are the attributes used in the rows of the Matrix visual from Figure 3-6. The measures are defined as follows:

Measure in the Sales table

```
Sales POP % :=
SWITCH (
    TRUE,
    ISINSCOPE ( 'Date'[Year Month] ), [Sales MOM %],
    ISINSCOPE ( 'Date'[Year Quarter] ), [Sales QOQ %],
    ISINSCOPE ( 'Date'[Year] ), [Sales YOY %]
)
```

Measure in the Sales table

```
Sales POP :=
SWITCH (
    TRUE,
    ISINSCOPE ( 'Date'[Year Month] ), [Sales MOM],
    ISINSCOPE ( 'Date'[Year Quarter] ), [Sales QOQ],
    ISINSCOPE ( 'Date'[Year] ), [Sales YOY]
)
```

Measure in the Sales table

```
Sales PP :=
SWITCH (
    TRUE,
    ISINSCOPE ( 'Date'[Year Month] ), [Sales PM],
    ISINSCOPE ( 'Date'[Year Quarter] ), [Sales PQ],
    ISINSCOPE ( 'Date'[Year] ), [Sales PY]
)
```

Computing period-to-date growth

The growth of a "to-date" measure is the comparison of said "to-date" measure with the same measure over an equivalent time period with a specific offset. For example, you can compare a year-to-date aggregation against the year-to-date in the previous year, that is with an offset of one year.

All the measures in this set of calculations take care of partial periods. Because data is available only until August 2009 in our example, the measures make sure the previous year does not report dates after August 2008.

Year-over-year-to-date growth

Year-over-year-to-date growth compares the year-to-date at a specific date with the year-to-date in an equivalent month in the previous year. Figure 3-7 shows that *Sales PYTD* in 2009 is taking into account transactions only until August 2008. For this reason, *Sales YTD* of Q3-2008 is 7,129,971.53, whereas *Sales PYTD* for Q3-2009 is less: 6,166,534.30.

Year	Sales Amount	Sales YTD	Sales PYTD	Sales YOYTD	Sales YOYTD %
⊞ **2007**	**9,008,591.74**	**9,008,591.74**			
⊟ **2008**	**9,927,582.99**	**9,927,582.99**	**9,008,591.74**	**918,991.25**	**10.20%**
⊞ **Q1-2008**	**1,816,385.21**	**1,816,385.21**	**345,319.01**	**1,471,066.20**	**426.00%**
⊞ **Q2-2008**	**2,738,040.73**	**4,554,425.94**	**3,391,921.03**	**1,162,504.91**	**34.27%**
⊟ **Q3-2008**	**2,575,545.59**	**7,129,971.53**	**6,277,167.58**	**852,803.95**	**13.59%**
Jul 2008	890,547.41	5,444,973.35	4,314,464.01	1,130,509.34	26.20%
Aug 2008	721,560.95	6,166,534.30	5,267,298.60	899,235.71	17.07%
Sep 2008	963,437.23	7,129,971.53	6,277,167.58	852,803.95	13.59%
⊞ **Q4-2008**	**2,797,611.46**	**9,927,582.99**	**9,008,591.74**	**918,991.25**	**10.20%**
⊟ **2009**	**5,725,632.34**	**5,725,632.34**	**6,166,534.30**	**-440,901.97**	**-7.15%**
⊞ **Q1-2009**	**1,699,620.05**	**1,699,620.05**	**1,816,385.21**	**-116,765.16**	**-6.43%**
⊞ **Q2-2009**	**2,618,644.64**	**4,318,264.70**	**4,554,425.94**	**-236,161.25**	**-5.19%**
⊟ **Q3-2009**	**1,407,367.64**	**5,725,632.34**	**6,166,534.30**	**-440,901.97**	**-7.15%**
Jul 2009	1,068,396.58	5,386,661.27	5,444,973.35	-58,312.08	-1.07%
Aug 2009	338,971.06	5,725,632.34	6,166,534.30	-440,901.97	-7.15%
Total	**24,661,807.07**	**5,725,632.34**			

FIGURE 3-7 For Q3-2009, *Sales PYTD* shows the amount of July-August 2008 because there is no data after August 2009.

Sales PYTD filters the previous value in *Year* and all the months in the year less than or equal to the last month visible in the filter context:

Measure in the Sales table

```
Sales PYTD :=
VAR LastMonthInYearAvailable = MAX ( 'Date'[Month Number] )
VAR LastYearAvailable = SELECTEDVALUE ( 'Date'[Year] )
VAR PreviousYearAvailable = LastYearAvailable - 1
VAR Result =
    CALCULATE (
        [Sales Amount],
        REMOVEFILTERS ( 'Date' ),
        'Date'[Month Number] <= LastMonthInYearAvailable,
        'Date'[Year] = PreviousYearAvailable
    )
RETURN
    Result
```

Sales YOYTD and *Sales YOYTD %* rely on *Sales PYTD* to provide their result:

Measure in the Sales table

```
Sales YOYTD :=
VAR ValueCurrentPeriod = [Sales YTD]
VAR ValuePreviousPeriod = [Sales PYTD]
VAR Result =
    IF (
        NOT ISBLANK ( ValueCurrentPeriod ) && NOT ISBLANK ( ValuePreviousPeriod ),
        ValueCurrentPeriod - ValuePreviousPeriod
    )
RETURN
    Result
```

Measure in the Sales table

```
Sales YOYTD % :=
DIVIDE (
    [Sales YOYTD],
    [Sales PYTD]
)
```

Quarter-over-quarter-to-date growth

Quarter-over-quarter-to-date growth compares the quarter-to-date at a specific date with the quarter-to-date at an equivalent month in the previous quarter. Figure 3-8 shows that *Sales PQTD* in 2009 is taking into account transactions only until May 2009, which is the second month in the quarter. For this reason, *Sales QTD* of Q2-2009 is 2,618,644.64, whereas *Sales PQTD* for Q3-2009 is less: 1,746,058.45.

Year	Sales Amount	Sales QTD	Sales PQTD	Sales QOQTD	Sales QOQTD %
⊞ 2007	9,008,591.74	2,731,424.16	2,885,246.55	-153,822.39	-5.33%
⊞ 2008	9,927,582.99	2,797,611.46	2,575,545.59	222,065.87	8.62%
⊟ 2009	5,725,632.34	1,407,367.64	2,618,644.64	-1,211,277.00	-46.26%
⊞ Q1-2009	1,699,620.05	1,699,620.05	2,797,611.46	-1,097,991.40	-39.25%
⊟ Q2-2009	2,618,644.64	2,618,644.64	1,699,620.05	919,024.59	54.07%
Apr 2009	678,893.22	678,893.22	580,901.05	97,992.17	16.87%
May 2009	1,067,165.23	1,746,058.45	1,203,482.19	542,576.26	45.08%
Jun 2009	872,586.20	2,618,644.64	1,699,620.05	919,024.59	54.07%
⊟ Q3-2009	1,407,367.64	1,407,367.64	1,746,058.45	-338,690.80	-19.40%
Jul 2009	1,068,396.58	1,068,396.58	678,893.22	389,503.36	57.37%
Aug 2009	338,971.06	1,407,367.64	1,746,058.45	-338,690.80	-19.40%
Total	24,661,807.07	1,407,367.64	2,618,644.64	-1,211,277.00	-46.26%

FIGURE 3-8 *Sales PQTD* shows for Q3-2009 the amount of the period April-May 2009, because there is no data after August 2009.

Sales PQTD filters the previous value in *Year Quarter Number,* and through *Month In Quarter Number* filters all the months in the quarter less than or equal to the last relative month of the quarter visible in the filter context:

Measure in the Sales table

```
Sales PQTD :=
VAR LastMonthInQuarterAvailable = MAX ( 'Date'[Month In Quarter Number] )
VAR LastYearQuarterAvailable = MAX ( 'Date'[Year Quarter Number] )
VAR PreviousYearQuarterAvailable = LastYearQuarterAvailable - 1
VAR Result =
    CALCULATE (
        [Sales Amount],
        REMOVEFILTERS ( 'Date' ),
        'Date'[Month In Quarter Number] <= LastMonthInQuarterAvailable,
        'Date'[Year Quarter Number] = PreviousYearQuarterAvailable
    )
RETURN
    Result
```

Sales QOQTD and *Sales QOQTD %* rely on *Sales PQTD* to guarantee a fair comparison:

Measure in the Sales table

```
Sales QOQTD :=
VAR ValueCurrentPeriod = [Sales QTD]
VAR ValuePreviousPeriod = [Sales PQTD]
VAR Result =
    IF (
        NOT ISBLANK ( ValueCurrentPeriod ) && NOT ISBLANK ( ValuePreviousPeriod ),
        ValueCurrentPeriod - ValuePreviousPeriod
    )
RETURN
    Result
```

Measure in the Sales table

```
Sales QOQTD % :=
DIVIDE (
    [Sales QOQTD],
    [Sales PQTD]
)
```

Comparing period-to-date with a previous full period

Comparing a to-date aggregation with the previous full period is useful when you consider the previous period as a benchmark. Once the current year-to-date reaches 100% of the full previous year, this means we have reached the performance of the previous full period – hopefully in fewer days.

Year-to-date over the full previous year

As the name indicates, the year-to-date over the full previous year compares the year-to-date against the entire previous year. Figure 3-9 shows that in November 2008 (which is close to the end of the year 2008) *Sales YTD* almost reached the value of *Sales Amount* for the entire year 2007. *Sales YTDOPY %* provides an immediate comparison of the year-to-date with the total of the previous year; it shows growth over the previous year when the percentage is positive, which is the case in December 2008.

Year	Sales Amount	Sales YTD	Sales PYC	Sales YTDOPY	Sales YTDOPY %
⊞ **2007**	**9,008,591.74**	**9,008,591.74**			
⊟ **2008**	**9,927,582.99**	**9,927,582.99**	**9,008,591.74**	**918,991.25**	**10.20%**
⊞ **Q1-2008**	**1,816,385.21**	**1,816,385.21**	**9,008,591.74**	**-7,192,206.53**	**-79.84%**
⊞ **Q2-2008**	**2,738,040.73**	**4,554,425.94**	**9,008,591.74**	**-4,454,165.80**	**-49.44%**
⊞ **Q3-2008**	**2,575,545.59**	**7,129,971.53**	**9,008,591.74**	**-1,878,620.21**	**-20.85%**
⊟ **Q4-2008**	**2,797,611.46**	**9,927,582.99**	**9,008,591.74**	**918,991.25**	**10.20%**
Oct 2008	719,792.99	7,849,764.52	9,008,591.74	-1,158,827.22	-12.86%
Nov 2008	1,156,109.32	9,005,873.85	9,008,591.74	-2,717.90	-0.03%
Dec 2008	921,709.14	9,927,582.99	9,008,591.74	918,991.25	10.20%
⊞ **2009**	**5,725,632.34**	**5,725,632.34**	**9,927,582.99**	**-4,201,950.65**	**-42.33%**
Total	**24,661,807.07**	**5,725,632.34**			

FIGURE 3-9 *Sales YTDOPY %* shows a negative value corresponding to the missing percentage of *Sales YTD* to reach the total *Sales Amount* of the previous year.

The year-to-date-over-previous-year growth is computed by using the *Sales YTDOPY* and *Sales YTDOPY %* measures; these in turn rely on the *Sales YTD* measure to compute the year-to-date value, and on the *Sales PYC* measure to get the sales amount of the entire previous year:

Measure in the Sales table

```
Sales PYC :=
VAR CurrentYearNumber = SELECTEDVALUE ( 'Date'[Year] )
VAR PreviousYearNumber = CurrentYearNumber - 1
VAR Result =
    CALCULATE (
        [Sales Amount],
        REMOVEFILTERS ( 'Date' ),
        'Date'[Year] = PreviousYearNumber
    )
RETURN
    Result
```

Measure in the Sales table

```
Sales YTDOPY :=
VAR ValueCurrentPeriod = [Sales YTD]
VAR ValuePreviousPeriod = [Sales PYC]
VAR Result =
    IF (
        NOT ISBLANK ( ValueCurrentPeriod ) && NOT ISBLANK ( ValuePreviousPeriod ),
        ValueCurrentPeriod - ValuePreviousPeriod
    )
RETURN
    Result
```

Measure in the Sales table

```
Sales YTDOPY % :=
DIVIDE (
    [Sales YTDOPY],
    [Sales PYC]
)
```

Quarter-to-date over full previous quarter

As the name indicates, the quarter-to-date over the full previous quarter compares the quarter-to-date against the entire previous quarter. Figure 3-10 shows that in May 2009, *Sales QTD* exceeded the value of *Sales Amount* for the entire previous quarter (Q1-2009). *Sales QTDOPQ%* provides an immediate comparison of the quarter-to-date with the total of the previous quarter; it shows growth over the previous quarter when the percentage is positive, which is the case in May and June 2009.

Year	Sales Amount	Sales QTD	Sales PQC	Sales QTDOPQ	Sales QTDOPQ %
⊞ 2007	9,008,591.74	2,731,424.16			
⊞ 2008	9,927,582.99	2,797,611.46			
⊟ 2009	5,725,632.34	1,407,367.64			
⊟ Q1-2009	1,699,620.05	1,699,620.05	2,797,611.46	-1,097,991.40	-39.25%
Jan 2009	580,901.05	580,901.05	2,797,611.46	-2,216,710.41	-79.24%
Feb 2009	622,581.14	1,203,482.19	2,797,611.46	-1,594,129.27	-56.98%
Mar 2009	496,137.87	1,699,620.05	2,797,611.46	-1,097,991.40	-39.25%
⊟ Q2-2009	2,618,644.64	2,618,644.64	1,699,620.05	919,024.59	54.07%
Apr 2009	678,893.22	678,893.22	1,699,620.05	-1,020,726.84	-60.06%
May 2009	1,067,165.23	1,746,058.45	1,699,620.05	46,438.39	2.73%
Jun 2009	872,586.20	2,618,644.64	1,699,620.05	919,024.59	54.07%
⊞ Q3-2009	1,407,367.64	1,407,367.64	2,618,644.64	-1,211,277.00	-46.26%
Total	24,661,807.07	1,407,367.64			

FIGURE 3-10 *Sales QTDOPQ %* shows a positive percentage in May 2009 and June 2009, when *Sales QTD* starts to be greater than the *Sales Amount* for Q1-2009.

The quarter-to-date-over-previous-quarter growth is computed by using the *Sales QTDOPQ* and *Sales QTDOPQ %* measures; these in turn rely on the *Sales QTD* measure to compute the quarter-to-date value and on the *Sales PQC* measure to get the sales amount of the entire previous quarter:

Measure in the Sales table

```
Sales PQC :=
VAR CurrentYearQuarterNumber = SELECTEDVALUE ( 'Date'[Year Quarter Number] )
VAR PreviousYearQuarterNumber = CurrentYearQuarterNumber - 1
VAR Result =
    CALCULATE (
        [Sales Amount],
        REMOVEFILTERS ( 'Date' ),
        'Date'[Year Quarter Number] = PreviousYearQuarterNumber
    )
RETURN
    Result
```

Measure in the Sales table

```
Sales QTDOPQ :=
VAR ValueCurrentPeriod = [Sales QTD]
VAR ValuePreviousPeriod = [Sales PQC]
VAR Result =
    IF (
        NOT ISBLANK ( ValueCurrentPeriod )
            && NOT ISBLANK ( ValuePreviousPeriod ),
        ValueCurrentPeriod - ValuePreviousPeriod
    )
RETURN
    Result
```

Measure in the Sales table

```
Sales QTDOPQ % :=
DIVIDE (
    [Sales QTDOPQ],
    [Sales PQC]
)
```

Using moving annual total calculations

A common way to aggregate data over several months is by using the moving annual total instead of the year-to-date. The moving annual total includes the last 12 months of data. For example, the moving annual total for March 2009 includes data from April 2008 to March 2009.

Moving annual total

Sales MAT computes the moving annual total, as shown in Figure 3-11.

Year	Sales Amount	Sales MAT	Sales PYMAT	Sales MATG	Sales MATG %
⊞ **2007**	**9,008,591.74**	**9,008,591.74**			
⊟ **2008**	**9,927,582.99**	**9,927,582.99**	**9,008,591.74**	**918,991.25**	**10.20%**
Jan 2008	656,766.69	9,665,358.44			
Feb 2008	600,080.00	10,265,438.43			
Mar 2008	559,538.52	10,479,657.94	345,319.01	10,134,338.94	2934.78%
Apr 2008	999,667.17	10,351,220.30	1,473,423.82	8,877,796.47	602.53%
May 2008	893,231.96	10,308,259.51	2,409,616.57	7,898,642.95	327.80%
Jun 2008	845,141.60	10,171,096.65	3,391,921.03	6,779,175.62	199.86%
Jul 2008	890,547.41	10,139,101.08	4,314,464.01	5,824,637.07	135.00%
Aug 2008	721,560.95	9,907,827.45	5,267,298.60	4,640,528.85	88.10%
Sep 2008	963,437.23	9,861,395.69	6,277,167.58	3,584,228.11	57.10%
Oct 2008	719,792.99	9,666,915.14	7,191,441.12	2,475,474.02	34.42%
Nov 2008	1,156,109.32	9,997,422.60	8,017,042.99	1,980,379.60	24.70%
Dec 2008	921,709.14	9,927,582.99	9,008,591.74	918,991.25	10.20%
⊟ **2009**	**5,725,632.34**	**9,486,681.02**	**9,907,827.45**	**-421,146.43**	**-4.25%**
Jan 2009	580,901.05	9,851,717.35	9,665,358.44	186,358.91	1.93%
Feb 2009	622,581.14	9,874,218.49	10,265,438.43	-391,219.95	-3.81%
Mar 2009	496,137.87	9,810,817.83	10,479,657.94	-668,840.11	-6.38%
Apr 2009	678,893.22	9,490,043.88	10,351,220.30	-861,176.42	-8.32%
May 2009	1,067,165.23	9,663,977.15	10,308,259.51	-644,282.36	-6.25%
Jun 2009	872,586.20	9,691,421.74	10,171,096.65	-479,674.91	-4.72%
Jul 2009	1,068,396.58	9,869,270.91	10,139,101.08	-269,830.17	-2.66%
Aug 2009	338,971.06	9,486,681.02	9,907,827.45	-421,146.43	-4.25%
Total	**24,661,807.07**	**9,486,681.02**	**9,907,827.45**	**-421,146.43**	**-4.25%**

FIGURE 3-11 *Sales MAT* in March 2009 aggregates *Sales Amount* from April 2008 to March 2009.

The *Sales MAT* measure defines a range over the *Year Month Number* column that includes the months of one complete year from the last month in the filter context:

Measure in the Sales table

```
Sales MAT :=
VAR MonthsInRange = 12
VAR LastMonthRange = MAX ( 'Date'[Year Month Number] )
VAR FirstMonthRange = LastMonthRange - MonthsInRange + 1
VAR Result =
    CALCULATE (
        [Sales Amount],
        REMOVEFILTERS ( 'Date' ),
        'Date'[Year Month Number] >= FirstMonthRange
            && 'Date'[Year Month Number] <= LastMonthRange
    )
RETURN
    Result
```

Moving annual total growth

The moving annual total growth is computed by using the *Sales PYMAT*, *Sales MATG*, and *Sales MATG %* measures, which in turn rely on the *Sales MAT* measure. The *Sales MAT* measure starts to provide accurate values one year after the first sale ever – once it has been able to collect one full year of data – and it is not protected in case the current time period is shorter than a full year.

For example, the amount for the year 2009 of *Sales PYMAT* is 9,927,582.99, which corresponds to the *Sales Amount* of the entire year 2008 as shown in Figure 3-11 (see previous section). When compared with sales in 2009, this produces a comparison of 8 months – data being only available until August 2009 – with the whole year 2008. Similarly, you can see that *Sales MATG %* starts in March 2008 with very high values and stabilizes after a year. This behavior is by design: the moving annual total is usually computed at the month granularity to show trends in a chart.

The measures are defined as follows:

Measure in the Sales table

```
Sales PYMAT :=
VAR MonthsInRange = 12
VAR LastMonthRange =
    MAX ( 'Date'[Year Month Number] ) - MonthsInRange
VAR FirstMonthRange =
    LastMonthRange - MonthsInRange + 1
VAR Result =
    CALCULATE (
        [Sales Amount],
        REMOVEFILTERS ( 'Date' ),
        'Date'[Year Month Number] >= FirstMonthRange
            && 'Date'[Year Month Number] <= LastMonthRange
    )
RETURN
    Result
```

Measure in the Sales table

```
Sales MATG :=
VAR ValueCurrentPeriod = [Sales MAT]
VAR ValuePreviousPeriod = [Sales PYMAT]
VAR Result =
    IF (
        NOT ISBLANK ( ValueCurrentPeriod )
            && NOT ISBLANK ( ValuePreviousPeriod ),
        ValueCurrentPeriod - ValuePreviousPeriod
    )
RETURN
    Result
```

Measure in the Sales table

```
Sales MATG % :=
DIVIDE (
    [Sales MATG],
    [Sales PYMAT]
)
```

Moving averages

The moving average is typically used to display trends in line charts. Figure 3-12 includes the moving average of three months (*Sales AVG 3M*) and a year (*Sales AVG 1Y*).

FIGURE 3-12 *Sales AVG 3M* and *Sales AVG 1Y* show the moving average over three months and one year, respectively.

Moving average 3 months

The *Sales AVG 3M* measure computes the moving average over three months by iterating the last three months obtained in the *Period3M* variable:

Measure in the Sales table

```
Sales AVG 3M :=
VAR MonthsInRange = 3
VAR LastMonthRange =
    MAX ( 'Date'[Year Month Number] )
VAR FirstMonthRange =
    LastMonthRange - MonthsInRange + 1
VAR Period3M =
    FILTER (
        ALL ( 'Date'[Year Month Number] ),
        'Date'[Year Month Number] >= FirstMonthRange
            && 'Date'[Year Month Number] <= LastMonthRange
    )
VAR Result =
    IF (
        COUNTROWS ( Period3M ) >= MonthsInRange,
        CALCULATE (
            AVERAGEX ( Period3M, [Sales Amount] ),
            REMOVEFILTERS ( 'Date' )
        )
    )
RETURN
    Result
```

Moving average 1 year

The *Sales AVG 1Y* measure computes the moving average over one year by iterating the last 12 months stored in the *Period1Y* variable:

Measure in the Sales table

```
Sales AVG 1Y :=
VAR MonthsInRange = 12
VAR LastMonthRange =
    MAX ( 'Date'[Year Month Number] )
VAR FirstMonthRange =
    LastMonthRange - MonthsInRange + 1
VAR Period1Y =
    FILTER (
        ALL ( 'Date'[Year Month Number] ),
        'Date'[Year Month Number] >= FirstMonthRange
            && 'Date'[Year Month Number] <= LastMonthRange
    )
VAR Result =
    IF (
        COUNTROWS ( Period1Y ) >= MonthsInRange,
        CALCULATE (
            AVERAGEX ( Period1Y, [Sales Amount] ),
            REMOVEFILTERS ( 'Date' )
        )
    )
RETURN
    Result
```

Managing years with more than 12 months

As we stated in the introduction, this pattern works even in scenarios where one year contains more than 12 months. For example, accounting oftentimes requires a 13th month containing the year-end adjustments. In these scenarios, it is important to set the values in the *Date* table correctly. Specifically, the *Year Month Number* column must store a sequential number for each month of the year; therefore, the same month in the previous year can be obtained by just subtracting 13 from the value of the current month if the year contains 13 months.

Moreover, you need to pay attention to the content of the *Month* and *Year Month* columns. Indeed, these columns must contain a proper name for the 13th month, and that choice depends on how you plan to show the month in both the fiscal and Gregorian calendars.

If the report shows only the fiscal year, you can choose any name and you will always show 13 months. If you need to show both fiscal and Gregorian calendar hierarchies, then you should decide between the following options: you can show the 13th month as a separate month in the Gregorian calendar; or you can decide to merge it under the corresponding Gregorian month, which means you are still showing 12 months when displaying the Gregorian calendar.

For example, Figure 3-13 shows the 13th month named "M13". Its position is right after June, because the fiscal calendar ends in June. The month is visible both in the fiscal and in the Gregorian calendars.

Year	Sales Amount	Sales YTD		Year	Sales Amount	Sales Fiscal YTD
⊟ **2007**	**9,008,591.74**	**9,008,591.74**		⊟ **FY 2007**	**3,477,295.86**	**3,477,295.86**
Mar 2007	293,034.81	293,034.81		Mar 2007	293,034.81	293,034.81
Apr 2007	1,128,104.82	1,421,139.63		Apr 2007	1,128,104.82	1,421,139.63
May 2007	929,599.70	2,350,739.33		May 2007	929,599.70	2,350,739.33
Jun 2007	982,304.46	3,333,043.79		Jun 2007	982,304.46	3,333,043.79
M13 2007	144,252.07	3,477,295.86		M13 2007	144,252.07	3,477,295.86
Jul 2007	891,679.09	4,368,974.95		⊟ **FY 2008**	**10,147,195.35**	**10,147,195.35**
Aug 2007	934,606.97	5,303,581.92		Jul 2007	891,679.09	891,679.09
Sep 2007	1,009,868.98	6,313,450.90		Aug 2007	934,606.97	1,826,286.06
Oct 2007	884,842.16	7,198,293.07		Sep 2007	1,009,868.98	2,836,155.05
Nov 2007	825,601.87	8,023,894.94		Oct 2007	884,842.16	3,720,997.21
Dec 2007	984,696.81	9,008,591.74		Nov 2007	825,601.87	4,546,599.08
⊟ **2008**	**9,927,582.99**	**9,927,582.99**		Dec 2007	984,696.81	5,531,295.88
Jan 2008	656,380.18	656,380.18		Jan 2008	656,380.18	6,187,676.07
Feb 2008	600,080.00	1,256,460.18		Feb 2008	600,080.00	6,787,756.06
Mar 2008	540,948.01	1,797,408.19		Mar 2008	540,948.01	7,328,704.07

FIGURE 3-13 13 fiscal months and 13 calendar months.

Figure 3-14 shows the result of a different choice, where the 13th month is visible only in the fiscal calendar. When the report is being browsed by the Gregorian calendar, the value of the 13th month is merged with that of June. Therefore, the Gregorian calendar is still showing 12 months.

Year	Sales Amount	Sales YTD		Year	Sales Amount	Sales Fiscal YTD
⊟ **2007**	**9,008,591.74**	**9,008,591.74**		⊟ **FY 2007**	**3,477,295.86**	**3,477,295.86**
Mar 2007	293,034.81	293,034.81		Mar 2007	293,034.81	293,034.81
Apr 2007	1,128,104.82	1,421,139.63		Apr 2007	1,128,104.82	1,421,139.63
May 2007	929,599.70	2,350,739.33		May 2007	929,599.70	2,350,739.33
Jun 2007	1,126,556.53	3,477,295.86		Jun 2007	982,304.46	3,333,043.79
Jul 2007	891,679.09	4,368,974.95		M13 2007	144,252.07	3,477,295.86
Aug 2007	934,606.97	5,303,581.92		⊟ **FY 2008**	**10,147,195.35**	**10,147,195.35**
Sep 2007	1,009,868.98	6,313,450.90		Jul 2007	891,679.09	891,679.09
Oct 2007	884,842.16	7,198,293.07		Aug 2007	934,606.97	1,826,286.06
Nov 2007	825,601.87	8,023,894.94		Sep 2007	1,009,868.98	2,836,155.05
Dec 2007	984,696.81	9,008,591.74		Oct 2007	884,842.16	3,720,997.21
⊟ **2008**	**9,927,582.99**	**9,927,582.99**		Nov 2007	825,601.87	4,546,599.08
Jan 2008	656,380.18	656,380.18		Dec 2007	984,696.81	5,531,295.88
Feb 2008	600,080.00	1,256,460.18		Jan 2008	656,380.18	6,187,676.07
Mar 2008	540,948.01	1,797,408.19		Feb 2008	600,080.00	6,787,756.06
Apr 2008	999,667.17	2,797,075.36		Mar 2008	540,948.01	7,328,704.07

FIGURE 3-14 13 fiscal months and 12 calendar months.

If you want to merge June with the 13th month as shown on the left side of Figure 3-14, then you must assign the proper values to the columns in the *Date* table; it is then no longer possible to share the same columns for both fiscal and Gregorian calendars. The columns for the fiscal calendar must differentiate between the 12th and 13th months, whereas the columns for the Gregorian calendar will share the values for the month name and number. Therefore, the *Date* table still contains 13 months, but two of them share the same values in the Gregorian set of columns. By doing so, the report merges rows with the same value in the months columns and the user obtains the desired result.

You can find the set of values for the figures shown in this section in the demo files *"Month-related calculations - 13 Fiscal and 13 Calendar Months.pbix"* and *"Month-related calculations - 13 Fiscal and 12 Calendar Months.pbix"*, respectively, where the *Year Month*, *Year Month Number*, *Month*, and *Month Number* columns for the Gregorian calendar have corresponding *Fiscal Year Month*, *Fiscal Year Month Number*, *Fiscal Month*, and *Fiscal Month* Number columns for the fiscal calendar.

## CHAPTER 4

Week-related calculations

Download sample files: **https://sql.bi/dax-203**

This pattern describes how to compute week-related calculations, such as year-to-date, same period last year, and percentage growth using a week granularity. This pattern does not rely on DAX built-in time intelligence functions. All the measures refer to the fiscal calendar because the nature of a calendar based on weeks is not compatible with the definition of months in a regular Gregorian calendar. You can use the **Standard time-related calculations** pattern for time-related calculations based on a Gregorian calendar.

Every time a fiscal calendar is based on weeks, this pattern should be used instead of other patterns based on calendar months. There are many different standards adopted worldwide to define a week-based calendar. The assumptions in this pattern are:

- Every year is a set of complete weeks;
- Every period within the year (quarter, month) is a set of complete weeks;
- The fiscal year always starts on the same day of the week, so it does not always start on January 1.
- The fiscal month and the fiscal quarter always start on the same day of the week, so they do not always start on the first day of a month.

Introduction to week-related time intelligence calculations

The time intelligence calculations in this pattern modify the filter context over the *Date* table to obtain the result. The formulas are designed to apply filters at a granularity corresponding to the calculation requirements, without removing filters applied to attributes like working day and day of week; this is so that the report granularity is not limited by the implementation of the pattern.

The pattern does not rely on the standard time intelligence functions. Therefore, the *Date* table does not have the requirements needed for standard DAX time intelligence functions. The formulas are identical whether you have one row for each week or one row for each day. The examples contain one row for each day, in order to create a relationship with the *Sales* table through the *Sales[Order Date]* column.

If there is a *Date* column in the *Date* table, the Mark as a Date Table setting is allowed but not required. The formulas in this pattern do not rely on the automatic REMOVEFILTERS being applied over the *Date* table when the *Date* column is filtered. Instead, all the formulas use a specific REMOVEFILTERS over the *Date* table to get rid of the existing filters, replacing them with the minimum number of filters that guarantee the result.

Building a *Date* table

The *Date* table used for week-related calculations must include the right definition of all the fiscal periods required – quarter, month, week. The requirement for the pattern is to expose columns related to the week and any aggregation over weeks, such as quarters and years. The months could be different from those defined in the standard Gregorian calendar, as it happens when you have a 4-4-5 calendar like the one used in the example.

If you already have a *Date* table, you can import the table – but make sure you have the columns required for this pattern, adding them to the *Date* table if necessary. If a *Date* table is not available, you can create one using a DAX calculated table. The *Date* table included in the example dynamically creates a 4-4-5 calendar based on the ISO 8601 definition of weeks in a Gregorian calendar.

The first rows of the formula for the *Date* calculated table included in the example define the type of week-based table to create in specific variables. For example, these are the parameters used for a 4-4-5 calendar starting in January of each year, although the first day of the fiscal year could be in December of the previous calendar year:

Calculated table

```
Date =
VAR FirstFiscalMonth = 1        -- First month of the fiscal year
VAR FirstDayOfWeek = 0          -- 0 = Sunday, 1 = Monday, ...
VAR FirstSalesDate = MIN ( Sales[Order Date] )
VAR LastSalesDate = MAX ( Sales[Order Date] )
VAR TypeStartFiscalYear = 1     -- Fiscal year as Calendar Year of :
                                -- 0 - First day of fiscal year
                                -- 1 - Last day of fiscal year
VAR QuarterWeekType = "445" -- Supports only "445", "454", and "544"
VAR WeeklyType = "Last" -- Use: "Nearest" or "Last"
-- The remaining code of the calculated table is included in the sample file
```

We suggest you read the comments included in the *Date* calculated table in the example to find whether it works with your specific requirements. However, if you already have a *Date* table in your data model, you should just make sure to include the columns described in the following paragraphs.

In order to obtain the correct visualization, the **calendar columns** must be configured in the data model as follows. For each column you can see the data type followed by a sample value:

- *Date*: Date, m/dd/yyyy (8/14/2007), used as a column to mark as date table, which is optional
- *Sequential Day Number*: Whole Number, Hidden (40040) , same value of Date as integer
- *Fiscal Year*: Text (FY 2007)
- *Fiscal Year Number*: Whole Number, Hidden (2007)
- *Fiscal Quarter*: Text (FQ3)
- *Fiscal Quarter Number*: Whole Number, Hidden (3)
- *Fiscal Year Quarter*: Text (FQ3-2007)
- *Fiscal Year Quarter Number*: Whole Number, Hidden (8030)
- *Fiscal Week*: Text (FW33)

- *Fiscal Week Number*: Whole Number, Hidden (33)
- *Fiscal Year Week*: Text (FW33-2007)
- *Fiscal Year Week Number*: Whole Number, Hidden (5564)
- *Fiscal Month*: Text (FM Aug)
- *Fiscal Month Number*: Whole Number, Hidden (8)
- *Fiscal Year Month*: Text (FM Aug 2007)
- *Fiscal Year Month Number*: Whole Number, Hidden (24091)
- *Day of Fiscal Month Number*: Whole Number, Hidden (17)
- *Day of Fiscal Quarter Number*: Whole Number, Hidden (45)
- *Day of Fiscal Year Number*: Whole Number, Hidden (227)

We want to introduce the concept of **filter-safe columns**. In a table, there are columns whose filters need to be preserved. The filters over filter-safe columns are not altered by the time intelligence calculations. They will be affecting the calculations presented in this pattern. The filter-safe columns in our sample table are the following:

- *Day of Week*: ddd (Tue)
- *Day of Week Number*: Whole Number, Hidden (6)
- *Working Day*: Text (Working Day)

We provide a more in-depth description of the behavior of filter-safe columns in the next section.

The *Date* table in this pattern contains several hierarchies:

- Year-Month-Week: Year (*Fiscal Year*), Month (*Fiscal Year Month*), Week (*Fiscal Year Week*)
- Year-Quarter-Month-Week: Year (*Fiscal Year*), Quarter (*Fiscal Year Quarter*), Month (*Fiscal Year Month*), Week (*Fiscal Year Week*)
- Year-Quarter-Week: Year (*Fiscal Year*), Quarter (*Fiscal Year Quarter*), Week (*Fiscal Year Week*)
- Year- Week: Year (*Fiscal Year*), Week (*Fiscal Year Week*)

The columns are designed to simplify the formulas. For example, the *Day of Fiscal Year Number* column contains the number of days since the beginning of the fiscal year; this number makes it easier to find a corresponding range of dates in the previous year.

The *Date* table must also include a hidden *DateWithSales* calculated column, used by some of the formulas of this pattern:

Calculated column in the Date table

```
DateWithSales =
'Date'[Date] <= MAX ( Sales[Order Date] )
```

The *Date[DateWithSales]* column is *TRUE* if the date is on or before the last date with sales; it is *FALSE* otherwise. In other words, *DateWithSales* is *TRUE* for "past" dates and *FALSE* for "future" dates, where "past" and "future" are relative to the last date with sales.

In case you import a *Date* table, you want to create columns that are similar to the ones we describe in this pattern, in that they should behave the same way.

Understanding filter-safe columns

The *Date* table contains two types of columns: regular columns and filter-safe columns. The regular columns are worked on by the measures shown in this pattern. The filters over filter-safe columns are always preserved and never altered by the measures of this pattern. An example clarifies this distinction.

The *Year Quarter Number* column is a regular column: the formulas in this pattern have the option of changing its value during their computation. To compute the previous quarter, the formulas change the filter context by subtracting one to the value of *Year Quarter Number* in the filter context. Conversely, the *Day of Week* column is a filter-safe column. If a user filters Monday to Friday, the formulas do not alter that filter on the day of the week. Therefore, a previous-quarter measure keeps the filter on the day of the week, and replaces only the filter on calendar columns such as year, month, and date.

To implement this pattern, you must identify which columns need to be treated as filter-safe columns, because filter-safe columns require special handling. The following is the classification of the columns used in the *Date* table of this pattern:

- **Calendar columns**: *Date, Fiscal Year, Fiscal Year Number, Fiscal Quarter, Fiscal Quarter Number, Fiscal Year Quarter, Fiscal Year Quarter Number, Fiscal Week, Fiscal Week Number, Fiscal Year Week, Fiscal Year Week Number, Fiscal Month, Fiscal Month Number, Fiscal Year Month, Fiscal Year Month Number, Day of Fiscal Month Number, Day of Fiscal Quarter Number, Day of Fiscal Year Number.*
- **Filter-safe columns**: *Day of Week, Day of Week Number, Working Day.*

The special handling of filter-safe columns revolves around the filter context. Every measure in this pattern manipulates the filter context by replacing filters over all the calendar columns, without altering any filter applied to the filter-safe columns. In other words, every measure follows two rules:

- Remove filters on calendar columns;
- Do not alter filters on filter-safe columns.

The ALLEXCEPT function can implement these requirements if the user specifies the *Date* table in the first argument, and the filter-safe columns in the following arguments:

```
CALCULATE (
    [Sales Amount],
    ALLEXCEPT ( 'Date', 'Date'[Working Day], 'Date'[Day of Week] ),
    ... // Filters over one or more calendar columns
)
```

If the *Date* table did not have any filter-safe column, the filters could be removed by using REMOVEFILTERS over the *Date* table instead of ALLEXCEPT:

```
CALCULATE (
    [Sales Amount],
    REMOVEFILTERS ( 'Date' ),
    ... // Filters over one or more calendar columns
)
```

If your *Date* table does not contain any filter-safe column, then you can use REMOVEFILTERS instead of ALLEXCEPT in all the measures of this pattern. We provide a complete scenario that includes filter-safe columns. Whenever possible, you can simplify it.

While the ALLEXCEPT should include all the filter-safe columns, we skip strictly those hidden filter-safe columns used only to sort other columns. For example, we do not include *Day of Week Number*, which is a hidden column used to sort the *Day of Week* column. The assumption is that the user never applies filters on hidden columns; if this assumption is not true, then the hidden filter-safe columns must also be included in the arguments of ALLEXCEPT. You can find an example of the impact of using REMOVEFILTERS vs. ALLEXCEPT in the **Year-to-date total** section of this pattern.

Controlling the visualization in future dates

Most of the time intelligence calculations should not display values for dates after the last available date. For example, a year-to-date calculation can also show values for future dates, but we want to hide those values. The dataset used in these examples ends on August 15, 2009. Therefore, we consider the fiscal month FM August 2009, the third fiscal quarter of 2009 FQ3-2009, and the fiscal year FY 2009 to be the last periods with data. Any date after August 15, 2019 is considered as future, and we want to hide values there.

In order to avoid showing results in future dates, we use the following *ShowValueForDates* measure. *ShowValueForDates* returns TRUE if the period selected is earlier than the last period with data:

Measure (hidden) in the Date table

```
ShowValueForDates :=
VAR LastDateWithData =
    CALCULATE (
        MAX ( 'Sales'[Order Date] ),
        REMOVEFILTERS ()
    )
VAR FirstDateVisible =
    MIN ( 'Date'[Date] )
VAR Result =
    FirstDateVisible <= LastDateWithData
RETURN
    Result
```

The *ShowValueForDates* measure is hidden. It is a technical measure created to reuse the same logic in many different time-related calculations, and the user should not use *ShowValueForDates* directly in a report. The REMOVEFILTERS function removes the filter from any table in the model, because the purpose is to retrieve the last date used in the *Sales* table regardless of any filter.

Naming convention

This section describes the naming convention we adopted to reference the time intelligence calculations. A simple categorization shows whether a calculation:

- shifts over a period of time, for example the same period in the previous year;

- performs an aggregation, for example year-to-date; or

- compares two time periods, for example this year compared to last year.

Acronym	Description	Shift	Aggregation	Comparison
YTD	Year-to-date		X	
QTD	Quarter-to-date		X	
MTD	Month-to-date		X	
WTD	Week-to-date		X	
MAT	Moving annual total		X	
PY	Previous year	X		
PQ	Previous quarter	X		
PW	Previous week	X		
PYC	Previous year complete	X		
PQC	Previous quarter complete	X		
PWC	Previous week complete	X		
PP	Previous period (automatically selects year, quarter, or week)	X		
PYMAT	Previous year moving annual total	X	X	
YOY	Year-over-year			X
QOQ	Quarter-over-quarter			X
WOW	Week-over-week			X
MATG	Moving annual total growth	X	X	X
POP	Period-over-period (automatically selects year, quarter, or week)			X
PYTD	Previous year-to-date	X	X	
PQTD	Previous quarter-to-date	X	X	
PWTD	Previous week-to-date	X	X	
YOYTD	Year-over-year-to-date	X	X	X
QOQTD	Quarter-over-quarter-to-date	X	X	X
WOWTD	Week-over-week-to-date	X	X	X
YTDOPY	Year-to-date-over-previous-year	X	X	X
QTDOPQ	Quarter-to-date-over-previous-quarter	X	X	X
WTDOPW	Week-to-date-over-previous-week	X	X	X

Computing period-to-date totals

The year-to-date, quarter-to-date, month-to-date, and week-to-date calculations modify the filter context for the *Date* table, showing the values from the beginning of the period up to the last date available in the filter context.

Year-to-date total

The year-to-date aggregates data starting from the first day of the fiscal year, as shown in Figure 4-1.

Year	Sales Amount	Sales YTD (simple)	Sales YTD
⊞ **FY 2007**	**8,942,403.96**	**8,942,403.96**	**8,942,403.96**
⊞ **FY 2008**	**9,788,101.45**	**9,788,101.45**	**9,788,101.45**
⊟ **FY 2009**	**5,931,301.67**	**5,931,301.67**	**5,931,301.67**
⊞ **FQ1-2009**	**1,903,944.38**	**1,903,944.38**	**1,903,944.38**
⊞ **FQ2-2009**	**2,531,034.28**	**4,434,978.66**	**4,434,978.66**
⊟ **FQ3-2009**	**1,496,323.01**	**5,931,301.67**	**5,931,301.67**
FW27-2009	260,265.60	4,695,244.25	4,695,244.25
FW28-2009	250,893.60	4,946,137.85	4,946,137.85
FW29-2009	306,535.20	5,252,673.05	5,252,673.05
FW30-2009	193,712.22	5,446,385.28	5,446,385.28
FW31-2009	183,695.43	5,630,080.71	5,630,080.71
FW32-2009	79,423.99	5,709,504.70	5,709,504.70
FW33-2009	221,796.97	5,931,301.67	5,931,301.67
FW34-2009		5,931,301.67	
FW35-2009		5,931,301.67	
FW36-2009		5,931,301.67	
FW37-2009		5,931,301.67	
FW38-2009		5,931,301.67	
FW39-2009		5,931,301.67	
⊞ **FQ4-2009**		**5,931,301.67**	
Total	**24,661,807.07**	**5,931,301.67**	**5,931,301.67**

FIGURE 4-1 *Sales YTD (simple)* shows the value for any time period, whereas *Sales YTD* hides the result after the last period with data.

The measure filters all the days less than or equal to the last day visible in the last fiscal year. It also filters the last visible *Fiscal Year Number*.

Measure in the Sales table

```
Sales YTD (simple) :=
VAR LastDayAvailable = MAX ( 'Date'[Day of Fiscal Year Number] )
VAR LastFiscalYearAvailable = MAX ( 'Date'[Fiscal Year Number] )
VAR Result =
    CALCULATE (
        [Sales Amount],
        ALLEXCEPT ( 'Date', 'Date'[Working Day], 'Date'[Day of Week] ),
        'Date'[Day of Fiscal Year Number] <= LastDayAvailable,
        'Date'[Fiscal Year Number] = LastFiscalYearAvailable
    )
RETURN
    Result
```

Because *LastDayAvailable* contains the last date visible in the filter context, *Sales YTD (simple)* shows data even for future dates in the year. We can avoid this behavior in the *Sales YTD* measure by returning a result only when *ShowValueForDates* returns TRUE:

Measure in the Sales table

```
Sales YTD :=
IF (
    [ShowValueForDates],
    VAR LastDayAvailable = MAX ( 'Date'[Day of Fiscal Year Number] )
    VAR LastFiscalYearAvailable = MAX ( 'Date'[Fiscal Year Number] )
    VAR Result =
        CALCULATE (
            [Sales Amount],
            ALLEXCEPT ( 'Date', 'Date'[Working Day], 'Date'[Day of Week] ),
            'Date'[Day of Fiscal Year Number] <= LastDayAvailable,
            'Date'[Fiscal Year Number] = LastFiscalYearAvailable
        )
    RETURN
        Result
)
```

ALLEXCEPT is required to preserve the filter-safe columns *Working Day* or *Day of Week* in case they are used in the report. To demonstrate this, we purposely created an incorrect measure: *Sales YTD (wrong)*, which removes the filters from the *Date* table by using REMOVEFILTERS instead of ALLEXCEPT. By doing this, the formula loses the filter on *Working Day* used in the columns of the matrix, thus producing an incorrect result:

Measure in the Sales table

```
Sales YTD (wrong) :=
IF (
    [ShowValueForDates],
    VAR LastDayAvailable = MAX ( 'Date'[Day of Fiscal Year Number] )
    VAR LastFiscalYearAvailable = MAX ( 'Date'[Fiscal Year Number] )
    RETURN
        CALCULATE (
            [Sales Amount],
            REMOVEFILTERS ( 'Date' ),
            'Date'[Day of Fiscal Year Number] <= LastDayAvailable,
            'Date'[Fiscal Year Number] = LastFiscalYearAvailable
        )
)
```

Figure 4-2 shows the comparison of the correct and incorrect measures.

Working Day Year	Non-Working day Sales Amount	Sales YTD	Sales YTD (wrong)	Working Day Sales Amount	Sales YTD	Sales YTD (wrong)
⊞ **FY 2007**	**2,649,347.96**	**2,649,347.96**	**8,942,403.96**	**6,293,056.00**	**6,293,056.00**	**8,942,403.96**
⊞ **FY 2008**	**2,514,575.86**	**2,514,575.86**	**9,788,101.45**	**7,273,525.59**	**7,273,525.59**	**9,776,539.08**
⊟ **FY 2009**	**1,654,106.45**	**1,654,106.45**	**5,931,301.67**	**4,277,195.22**	**4,277,195.22**	**5,931,301.67**
⊟ **FQ1-2009**	**437,943.10**	**437,943.10**	**1,903,944.38**	**1,466,001.28**	**1,466,001.28**	**1,903,519.67**
FW01-2009	48,656.79	48,656.79	270,201.87	221,545.07	221,545.07	244,457.06
FW02-2009	36,818.09	85,474.88	400,260.58	93,240.63	314,785.70	393,593.69
FW03-2009	7,979.08	93,453.96	491,169.04	82,929.38	397,715.08	490,891.65
FW04-2009	62,386.36	155,840.32	704,188.45	150,633.05	548,348.13	675,339.52
FW05-2009	14,542.94	170,383.26	786,570.38	67,838.99	616,187.12	773,382.53
FW06-2009	18,187.30	188,570.57	917,416.48	112,658.80	728,845.91	902,732.22
FW07-2009	33,966.68	222,537.25	1,047,579.85	96,196.69	825,042.60	1,029,216.79
FW08-2009	41,628.88	264,166.13	1,226,407.50	137,198.77	962,241.37	1,199,679.91
FW09-2009	48,340.72	312,506.85	1,409,151.52	134,403.30	1,096,644.67	1,378,964.16
FW10-2009	30,639.72	343,146.57	1,510,053.01	70,261.78	1,166,906.44	1,492,718.35
FW11-2009	42,916.73	386,063.30	1,631,521.08	78,551.34	1,245,457.78	1,629,973.67
FW12-2009	39,550.06	425,613.35	1,788,118.06	117,046.93	1,362,504.71	1,757,457.82
FW13-2009	12,329.75	437,943.10	1,903,944.38	103,496.57	1,466,001.28	1,903,519.67
⊞ **FQ2-2009**	**747,912.55**	**1,185,855.65**	**4,434,978.66**	**1,783,121.73**	**3,249,123.01**	**4,384,604.18**
⊞ **FQ3-2009**	**468,250.80**	**1,654,106.45**	**5,931,301.67**	**1,028,072.21**	**4,277,195.22**	**5,931,301.67**
Total	**6,818,030.26**	**1,654,106.45**	**5,931,301.67**	**17,843,776.81**	**4,277,195.22**	**5,931,301.67**

FIGURE 4-2 *Sales YTD (wrong)* shows *Sales YTD* calculated by ignoring the filter over *Working Day*.

The *Sales YTD (wrong)* measure would work well if the *Date* table did not contain any filter-safe columns. The presence of filter-safe columns requires using ALLEXCEPT instead of REMOVEFILTERS. We used *Sales YTD* as an example, but the same concept is valid for all the other measures in this pattern.

Quarter-to-date total

Quarter-to-date aggregates data from the first day of the fiscal quarter, as shown in Figure 4-3.

Year	Sales Amount	Sales QTD
⊞ **FY 2007**	**8,942,403.96**	**2,717,807.00**
⊞ **FY 2008**	**9,788,101.45**	**2,663,730.18**
⊟ **FY 2009**	**5,931,301.67**	
⊞ **FQ1-2009**	**1,903,944.38**	**1,903,944.38**
⊞ **FQ2-2009**	**2,531,034.28**	**2,531,034.28**
⊟ **FQ3-2009**	**1,496,323.01**	**1,496,323.01**
FW27-2009	260,265.60	260,265.60
FW28-2009	250,893.60	511,159.20
FW29-2009	306,535.20	817,694.40
FW30-2009	193,712.22	1,011,406.62
FW31-2009	183,695.43	1,195,102.05
FW32-2009	79,423.99	1,274,526.04
FW33-2009	221,796.97	1,496,323.01
Total	**24,661,807.07**	

FIGURE 4-3 *Sales QTD* shows the quarter-to-date amount, which is blank for FY 2009 because there is no data in FQ4-2009.

Quarter-to-date is computed with the same technique as the one we used for the year-to-date total. The only differences are the filters on *Fiscal Year Quarter Number* instead of *Fiscal Year Number*, and *Day of Fiscal Quarter Number* instead of *Day of Fiscal Year Number*.

Measure in the Sales table

```
Sales QTD :=
IF (
    [ShowValueForDates],
    VAR LastDayAvailable =  MAX ( 'Date'[Day of Fiscal Quarter Number] )
    VAR LastFiscalYearQuarterAvailable = MAX ( 'Date'[Fiscal Year Quarter Number] )
    VAR Result =
        CALCULATE (
            [Sales Amount],
            ALLEXCEPT ( 'Date', 'Date'[Working Day], 'Date'[Day of Week] ),
            'Date'[Day of Fiscal Quarter Number] <= LastDayAvailable,
            'Date'[Fiscal Year Quarter Number] = LastFiscalYearQuarterAvailable
        )
    RETURN
        Result
)
```

Month-to-date total

Month-to-date aggregates data starting from the first day of the fiscal month, as shown in Figure 4-4.

Year	Sales Amount	Sales MTD
⊞ **FY 2007**	**8,942,403.96**	**1,046,500.07**
⊞ **FY 2008**	**9,788,101.45**	**984,333.18**
⊟ **FY 2009**	**5,931,301.67**	
⊞ **FQ1-2009**	**1,903,944.38**	**677,536.88**
⊞ **FQ2-2009**	**2,531,034.28**	**1,119,492.29**
⊟ **FQ3-2009**	**1,496,323.01**	
⊟ **FM Jul 2009**	**1,011,406.62**	**1,011,406.62**
FW27-2009	260,265.60	260,265.60
FW28-2009	250,893.60	511,159.20
FW29-2009	306,535.20	817,694.40
FW30-2009	193,712.22	1,011,406.62
⊟ **FM Aug 2009**	**484,916.39**	**484,916.39**
FW31-2009	183,695.43	183,695.43
FW32-2009	79,423.99	263,119.42
FW33-2009	221,796.97	484,916.39
Total	**24,661,807.07**	

FIGURE 4-4 *Sales MTD* shows the month-to-date amount, which is blank for FY 2009 and FQ3-2009 because there is no data after August 15, 2009.

The month-to-date total is computed with a technique similar to those used in year-to-date total and quarter-to-date total, which filter all the days that are less than or equal to the last day visible in the last fiscal month. The filters are applied to the *Day of Month Number* and *Year Month Number* columns:

Measure in the Sales table

```
Sales MTD :=
IF (
    [ShowValueForDates],
    VAR LastDayAvailable =  MAX ( 'Date'[Day of Fiscal Month Number] )
    VAR LastFiscalYearMonthAvailable = MAX ( 'Date'[Fiscal Year Month Number] )
    VAR Result =
        CALCULATE (
            [Sales Amount],
            ALLEXCEPT ( 'Date', 'Date'[Working Day], 'Date'[Day of Week] ),
            'Date'[Day of Fiscal Month Number] <= LastDayAvailable,
            'Date'[Fiscal Year Month Number] = LastFiscalYearMonthAvailable
        )
    RETURN
        Result
)
```

The measure filters *Day of Fiscal Month Number* instead of *Day of Fiscal Year Number*. The reason is to filter a column with a lower number of unique values, which is a best practice from a query performance standpoint.

Week-to-date total

Week-to-date aggregates data from the first day of the week, as shown in Figure 4-5.

Year	Sales Amount	Sales WTD
⊞ **FY 2007**	**8,942,403.96**	**201,146.30**
⊞ **FY 2008**	**9,788,101.45**	**165,554.93**
⊟ **FY 2009**	**5,931,301.67**	
⊞ **FQ1-2009**	**1,903,944.38**	**115,826.31**
⊞ **FQ2-2009**	**2,531,034.28**	**201,675.45**
⊟ **FQ3-2009**	**1,496,323.01**	
⊞ **FM Jul 2009**	**1,011,406.62**	**193,712.22**
⊟ **FM Aug 2009**	**484,916.39**	
⊞ **FW31-2009**	**183,695.43**	**183,695.43**
⊞ **FW32-2009**	**79,423.99**	**79,423.99**
⊟ **FW33-2009**	**221,796.97**	**221,796.97**
8/9/2009	21,983.18	21,983.18
8/10/2009	4,211.87	26,195.05
8/11/2009	79,245.09	105,440.14
8/12/2009	1,497.50	106,937.64
8/13/2009	13,784.34	120,721.98
8/14/2009	100,059.00	220,780.98
8/15/2009	1,015.98	221,796.97
Total	**24,661,807.07**	

FIGURE 4-5 *Sales WTD* shows the week-to-date amount, which is blank for FY 2009, FQ3-2009, and FM Aug 2009 because there is no data after August 15, 2009.

The week-to-date total is computed with a technique similar to those used in year-to-date total and quarter-to-date total, which filters all the days that are less than or equal to the last weekday day number visible in the last fiscal week. The filters are applied to the *Day of Week Number* and *Fiscal Year Week Number* columns:

Measure in the Sales table

```
Sales WTD :=
IF (
    [ShowValueForDates],
    VAR LastDayOfWeekAvailable =  MAX ( 'Date'[Day of Week Number] )
    VAR LastFiscalYearWeekAvailable = MAX ( 'Date'[Fiscal Year Week Number] )
    VAR Result =
        CALCULATE (
            [Sales Amount],
            ALLEXCEPT ( 'Date', 'Date'[Working Day], 'Date'[Day of Week] ),
            'Date'[Day of Week Number] <= LastDayOfWeekAvailable,
            'Date'[Fiscal Year Week Number] = LastFiscalYearWeekAvailable
        )
    RETURN
        Result
)
```

The measure filters *Day of Week Number* instead of *Day of Fiscal Year Number*. This is to filter a column with a lower number of unique values, which is a best practice from a query performance standpoint.

Computing period-over-period growth

A common requirement is to compare a time period with the same time period in the previous year, quarter, or week. We do not look at the comparison over the previous month because in a 4-4-5 calendar there may be a different number of weeks within the months. In order to achieve a fair comparison, the measure should work with an equivalent period, also taking into account that the last week/quarter/year could be incomplete. For these reasons, the calculations shown in this section use the *Date[DateWithSales]* calculated column, as described in the article, Hiding future dates for calculations in DAX (https://sql. bi/78171).

Year-over-year growth

Year-over-year compares a time period to the equivalent time period in the previous year. In this example, data is available until August 15, 2009. For this reason, *Sales PY* shows numbers related to FY 2009 and takes into account only transactions before August 15, 2008. Figure 4-6 shows that *Sales Amount* of FQ3-2008 is 2,573,182.08, whereas *Sales PY* for FQ3-2009 returns 1,270,748.28 because the measure considers only sales up to August 15, 2008.

Year	Sales Amount	Sales PY	Sales YOY	Sales YOY %
⊞ **FY 2007**	**8,942,403.96**			
⊟ **FY 2008**	**9,788,101.45**	**8,942,403.96**	**845,697.49**	**9.46%**
⊞ FQ1-2008	1,856,813.65	345,319.01	1,511,494.64	437.71%
⊞ FQ2-2008	2,694,375.54	3,046,602.02	-352,226.48	-11.56%
⊞ FQ3-2008	2,573,182.08	2,832,675.92	-259,493.84	-9.16%
⊞ FQ4-2008	2,663,730.18	2,717,807.00	-54,076.82	-1.99%
⊟ **FY 2009**	**5,931,301.67**	**5,821,937.47**	**109,364.20**	**1.88%**
⊞ FQ1-2009	1,903,944.38	1,856,813.65	47,130.73	2.54%
⊞ FQ2-2009	2,531,034.28	2,694,375.54	-163,341.26	-6.06%
⊞ FQ3-2009	1,496,323.01	1,270,748.28	225,574.73	17.75%
Total	**24,661,807.07**	**14,764,341.42**	**9,897,465.65**	**67.04%**

FIGURE 4-6 For FQ3-2009, *Sales PY* shows the amount of FQ3-2008 until August 15, 2008, because there is no data after August 15, 2009.

Sales PY uses a standard technique that shifts the selection by the number of months defined in the *MonthsOffset* variable. In *Sales PY* the variable is set to 12, to move back in time by 12 months. The next measures, *Sales PQ* and *Sales PM*, use the same code. The only difference is the value assigned to *MonthsOffset*.

Sales PY iterates every year active in the filter context. For each year, it retrieves the days selected in the year while ignoring the filter-safe columns (*Working Day*, *Day of Week* and *Day of Week Number* in our example). The days are evaluated using the relative day number within the year. These days are applied as a filter on the previous year. The filters over filter-safe columns are kept in the filter context by using ALLEXCEPT:

Measure in the Sales table

```
Sales PY :=
IF (
    [ShowValueForDates],
    SUMX (
        VALUES ( 'Date'[Fiscal Year Number] ),
        VAR CurrentFiscalYearNumber = 'Date'[Fiscal Year Number]
        VAR DaysSelected =
            CALCULATETABLE (
                VALUES ( 'Date'[Day of Fiscal Year Number] ),
                REMOVEFILTERS (
                    'Date'[Working Day],
                    'Date'[Day of Week],
                    'Date'[Day of Week Number]
                ),
                'Date'[DateWithSales] = TRUE
            )
        RETURN
            CALCULATE (
                [Sales Amount],
                'Date'[Fiscal Year Number] = CurrentFiscalYearNumber - 1,
                DaysSelected,
                ALLEXCEPT ( 'Date', 'Date'[Working Day], 'Date'[Day of Week] )
            )
    )
)
```

The year-over-year growth is computed as an amount in *Sales YOY* and as a percentage in *Sales YOY %*. Both measures use *Sales PY* to take into account only dates up to August 15, 2009:

Measure in the Sales table

```
Sales YOY :=
VAR ValueCurrentPeriod = [Sales Amount]
VAR ValuePreviousPeriod = [Sales PY]
VAR Result =
    IF (
        NOT ISBLANK ( ValueCurrentPeriod )
            && NOT ISBLANK ( ValuePreviousPeriod ),
        ValueCurrentPeriod - ValuePreviousPeriod
    )
RETURN
    Result
```

Measure in the Sales table

```
Sales YOY % :=
DIVIDE (
    [Sales YOY],
    [Sales PY]
)
```

Quarter-over-quarter growth

Quarter-over-quarter compares a time period with the equivalent time period in the previous quarter. In this example, data is available until August 15, 2009, which is more than half of the third quarter of FY 2009 – it is day 49 in that quarter. Therefore, *Sales PQ* for August 2009 – the second month of the third quarter – shows sales until May 16, 2009, which is day 49 in the previous quarter, FQ2-2009. Figure 4-7 shows that *Sales Amount* of FQ2-2009 is 2,531,034.28, whereas *Sales PQ* for FQ3-2009 returns 1,140,186.77, restricted to sales performed up to May 16, 2009.

Year	Sales Amount	Sales PQ	Sales QOQ	Sales QOQ %
⊞ **FY 2007**	**8,942,403.96**	**6,224,596.95**	**2,717,807.00**	**43.66%**
⊞ **FY 2008**	**9,788,101.45**	**9,842,178.27**	**-54,076.82**	**-0.55%**
⊟ **FY 2009**	**5,931,301.67**	**5,707,861.33**	**223,440.34**	**3.91%**
⊞ **FQ1-2009**	**1,903,944.38**	**2,663,730.18**	**-759,785.80**	**-28.52%**
⊟ **FQ2-2009**	**2,531,034.28**	**1,903,944.38**	**627,089.91**	**32.94%**
FW14-2009	156,901.21	270,201.87	-113,300.65	-41.93%
FW15-2009	89,762.79	130,058.72	-40,295.93	-30.98%
FW16-2009	190,397.26	90,908.45	99,488.81	109.44%
FW17-2009	157,692.58	213,019.41	-55,326.83	-25.97%
FW18-2009	178,247.24	82,381.93	95,865.31	116.37%
FW19-2009	250,067.09	130,846.10	119,220.99	91.12%
FW20-2009	117,118.60	130,163.37	-13,044.77	-10.02%
FW21-2009	271,355.21	178,827.65	92,527.56	51.74%
FW22-2009	302,268.61	182,744.02	119,524.59	65.41%
FW23-2009	194,482.52	100,901.50	93,581.02	92.74%
FW24-2009	229,129.53	121,468.07	107,661.46	88.63%
FW25-2009	191,936.18	156,596.98	35,339.20	22.57%
FW26-2009	201,675.45	115,826.31	85,849.14	74.12%
⊟ **FQ3-2009**	**1,496,323.01**	**1,140,186.77**	**356,136.24**	**31.23%**
FW27-2009	260,265.60	156,901.21	103,364.38	65.88%
FW28-2009	250,893.60	89,762.79	161,130.81	179.51%
FW29-2009	306,535.20	190,397.26	116,137.94	61.00%
FW30-2009	193,712.22	157,692.58	36,019.64	22.84%
FW31-2009	183,695.43	178,247.24	5,448.19	3.06%
FW32-2009	79,423.99	250,067.09	-170,643.10	-68.24%
FW33-2009	221,796.97	117,118.60	104,678.37	89.38%
Total	**24,661,807.07**	**21,774,636.55**	**2,887,170.52**	**13.26%**

FIGURE 4-7 For FQ3-2009, *Sales PQ* shows the values of FQ2-2009 until May 16, 2009; indeed, there is no data after August 15, 2009, which sits at the same relative position in the quarter (day 49).

Sales PQ uses the technique described for *Sales PY*. The only difference is that instead of iterating *Fiscal Year Number*, it iterates *Fiscal Year Quarter Number* and applies the filter over *Day of Fiscal Quarter Number* instead of over *Day of Fiscal Year Number*.

Measure in the Sales table

```
Sales PQ :=
IF (
    [ShowValueForDates],
    SUMX (
        VALUES ( 'Date'[Fiscal Year Quarter Number] ),
        VAR CurrentFiscalYearQuarterNumber = 'Date'[Fiscal Year Quarter Number]
        VAR DaysSelected =
            CALCULATETABLE (
                VALUES ( 'Date'[Day of Fiscal Quarter Number] ),
                REMOVEFILTERS (
                    'Date'[Working Day],
                    'Date'[Day of Week],
                    'Date'[Day of Week Number]
                ),
                'Date'[DateWithSales] = TRUE
            )
        RETURN
            CALCULATE (
                [Sales Amount],
                'Date'[Fiscal Year Quarter Number] = CurrentFiscalYearQuarterNumber - 1,
                DaysSelected,
                ALLEXCEPT ( 'Date', 'Date'[Working Day], 'Date'[Day of Week] )
            )
    )
)
```

The quarter-over-quarter growth is computed as an amount in *Sales QOQ* and as a percentage in *Sales QOQ %*. Both measures use *Sales PQ* to guarantee a fair comparison:

Measure in the Sales table

```
Sales QOQ :=
VAR ValueCurrentPeriod = [Sales Amount]
VAR ValuePreviousPeriod = [Sales PQ]
VAR Result =
    IF (
        NOT ISBLANK ( ValueCurrentPeriod ) && NOT ISBLANK ( ValuePreviousPeriod ),
        ValueCurrentPeriod - ValuePreviousPeriod
    )
RETURN
    Result
```

Measure in the Sales table

```
Sales QOQ % :=
DIVIDE (
    [Sales QOQ],
    [Sales PQ]
)
```

Week-over-week growth

Week-over-week compares a time period with its equivalent in the previous week. The calculation is similar to year-over-year and quarter-over-quarter growth, even though the data available does not show a specific example of a partial week corresponding to the last day available (August 15, 2019). The *Sales PW* measure sums all the weeks of the period shifted back by one week if the report aggregates more weeks, like at the year and quarter level. Figure 4-8 shows an example of the result.

Year	Sales Amount	Sales PW	Sales WOW	Sales WOW %
⊞ **FY 2007**	**8,942,403.96**	**8,741,257.66**	**201,146.30**	**2.30%**
⊞ **FY 2008**	**9,788,101.45**	**9,823,692.82**	**-35,591.37**	**-0.36%**
⊟ **FY 2009**	**5,931,301.67**	**5,875,059.63**	**56,242.04**	**0.96%**
⊞ **FQ1-2009**	**1,903,944.38**	**1,953,672.99**	**-49,728.62**	**-2.55%**
⊞ **FQ2-2009**	**2,531,034.28**	**2,445,185.14**	**85,849.14**	**3.51%**
⊟ **FQ3-2009**	**1,496,323.01**	**1,476,201.50**	**20,121.51**	**1.36%**
FW27-2009	260,265.60	201,675.45	58,590.14	29.05%
FW28-2009	250,893.60	260,265.60	-9,371.99	-3.60%
FW29-2009	306,535.20	250,893.60	55,641.60	22.18%
FW30-2009	193,712.22	306,535.20	-112,822.98	-36.81%
FW31-2009	183,695.43	193,712.22	-10,016.79	-5.17%
FW32-2009	79,423.99	183,695.43	-104,271.44	-56.76%
FW33-2009	221,796.97	79,423.99	142,372.97	179.26%
Total	**24,661,807.07**	**24,440,010.10**	**221,796.97**	**0.91%**

FIGURE 4-8 The *Sales PW* measure shows the *Sales Amount* of the previous week.

Sales PW uses the technique described for *Sales PY*. The only difference is that instead of iterating *Fiscal Year Number*, it iterates *Fiscal Year Week Number* and applies the filter over *Day of Week Number* instead of over *Day of Fiscal Year Number*:

Measure in the Sales table

```
Sales PW :=
IF (
    [ShowValueForDates],
    SUMX (
        VALUES ( 'Date'[Fiscal Year Week Number] ),
        VAR CurrentFiscalYearWeekNumber = 'Date'[Fiscal Year Week Number]
        VAR DaysSelected =
            CALCULATETABLE (
                VALUES ( 'Date'[Day of Week Number] ),
                REMOVEFILTERS (
                    'Date'[Working Day],
                    'Date'[Day of Week],
                    'Date'[Day of Week Number]
                ),
                'Date'[DateWithSales] = TRUE
            )
        RETURN
            CALCULATE (
                [Sales Amount],
                'Date'[Fiscal Year Week Number] = CurrentFiscalYearWeekNumber - 1,
                KEEPFILTERS ( DaysSelected ),
                ALLEXCEPT ( 'Date', 'Date'[Working Day], 'Date'[Day of Week] )
            )
    )
)
```

The week-over-week growth is computed as an amount in *Sales WOW* and as a percentage in *Sales WOW %*. Both measures use *Sales PW* to guarantee a fair comparison:

Measure in the Sales table

```
Sales WOW :=
VAR ValueCurrentPeriod = [Sales Amount]
VAR ValuePreviousPeriod = [Sales PW]
VAR Result =
    IF (
        NOT ISBLANK ( ValueCurrentPeriod ) && NOT ISBLANK ( ValuePreviousPeriod ),
        ValueCurrentPeriod - ValuePreviousPeriod
    )
RETURN
    Result
```

Measure in the Sales table

```
Sales WOW % :=
DIVIDE (
    [Sales WOW],
    [Sales PW]
)
```

Period-over-period growth

Period-over-period growth automatically selects one of the measures described earlier in this section based on the current selection of the visualization. For example, it returns the value of week-over-week growth measures if the visualization displays data at the week level, and switches to quarter-over-quarter or year-over-year growth measures if the visualization shows the total at the quarter or year level, respectively. The month level is not supported on a 4-4-5 calendar. The expected result is visible in Figure 4-9.

Year	Sales Amount	Sales PP	Sales POP	Sales POP %
⊞ **FY 2007**	**8,942,403.96**			
⊟ **FY 2008**	**9,788,101.45**	**8,942,403.96**	**845,697.49**	**9.46%**
⊞ **FQ1-2008**	**1,856,813.65**	**2,717,807.00**	**-860,993.36**	**-31.68%**
⊞ **FQ2-2008**	**2,694,375.54**	**1,856,813.65**	**837,561.90**	**45.11%**
⊞ **FQ3-2008**	**2,573,182.08**	**2,694,375.54**	**-121,193.46**	**-4.50%**
⊞ **FQ4-2008**	**2,663,730.18**	**2,573,182.08**	**90,548.10**	**3.52%**
⊟ **FY 2009**	**5,931,301.67**	**5,821,937.47**	**109,364.20**	**1.88%**
⊞ **FQ1-2009**	**1,903,944.38**	**2,663,730.18**	**-759,785.80**	**-28.52%**
⊞ **FQ2-2009**	**2,531,034.28**	**1,903,944.38**	**627,089.91**	**32.94%**
⊟ **FQ3-2009**	**1,496,323.01**	**1,140,186.77**	**356,136.24**	**31.23%**
FW27-2009	260,265.60	201,675.45	58,590.14	29.05%
FW28-2009	250,893.60	260,265.60	-9,371.99	-3.60%
FW29-2009	306,535.20	250,893.60	55,641.60	22.18%
FW30-2009	193,712.22	306,535.20	-112,822.98	-36.81%
FW31-2009	183,695.43	193,712.22	-10,016.79	-5.17%
FW32-2009	79,423.99	183,695.43	-104,271.44	-56.76%
FW33-2009	221,796.97	79,423.99	142,372.97	179.26%
Total	**24,661,807.07**			

FIGURE 4-9 *Sales PP* shows the value of the previous week at the week level, of the previous quarter at the quarter level, and of the previous year at the year level.

The three measures *Sales PP*, *Sales POP*, and *Sales POP %* redirect the evaluation to the corresponding year, quarter, and week measures depending on the level selected in the report. ISINSCOPE detects the level used in the report. The arguments passed to ISINSCOPE are the attributes used in the rows of the Matrix visual in Figure 4-9. The measures are defined as follows:

Measure in the Sales table

```
Sales POP % :=
SWITCH (
    TRUE,
    ISINSCOPE ( 'Date'[Fiscal Year Week] ), [Sales WOW %],
    -- The month level should not be managed in a 445 calendar
    ISINSCOPE ( 'Date'[Fiscal Year Quarter] ), [Sales QOQ %],
    ISINSCOPE ( 'Date'[Fiscal Year] ), [Sales YOY %]
)
```

Measure in the Sales table

```
Sales POP :=
SWITCH (
    TRUE,
    ISINSCOPE ( 'Date'[Fiscal Year Week] ), [Sales WOW],
    -- The month level should not be managed in a 445 calendar
    ISINSCOPE ( 'Date'[Fiscal Year Quarter] ), [Sales QOQ],
    ISINSCOPE ( 'Date'[Fiscal Year] ), [Sales YOY]
)
```

Measure in the Sales table

```
Sales PP :=
SWITCH (
    TRUE,
    ISINSCOPE ( 'Date'[Fiscal Year Week] ), [Sales PW],
    -- The month level should not be managed in a 445 calendar
    ISINSCOPE ( 'Date'[Fiscal Year Quarter] ), [Sales PQ],
    ISINSCOPE ( 'Date'[Fiscal Year] ), [Sales PY]
)
```

Computing period-to-date growth

The growth of a "to-date" measure is the comparison of the "to-date" measure with the same measure over an equivalent time period with a specific offset. For example, you can compare a year-to-date aggregation against the year-to-date in the previous fiscal year, that is with an offset of one fiscal year.

All the measures in this set of calculations take care of partial periods. Because data is available only until August 15, 2009 in our example, the measures make sure the previous year does not report dates after August 15, 2008.

Year-over-year-to-date growth

Year-over-year-to-date growth compares the year-to-date on a specific date with the year-to-date on an equivalent date in the previous year. Figure 4-10 shows that *Sales PYTD* in FY 2009 is considering only sales until August 16, 2008, because it is the same relative day within FY 2008 as is August 15, 2009 for FY 2009. For this reason, *Sales YTD* of FQ3-2008 is 7,124,371.27, whereas *Sales PYTD* for FQ3-2009 is less: 5,821,937.47.

Year	Sales Amount	Sales YTD	Sales PYTD	Sales YOYTD	Sales YOYTD %
⊞ **FY 2007**	**8,942,403.96**	**8,942,403.96**			
⊟ **FY 2008**	**9,788,101.45**	**9,788,101.45**	**8,942,403.96**	**845,697.49**	**9.46%**
⊞ **FQ1-2008**	**1,856,813.65**	**1,856,813.65**	**345,319.01**	**1,511,494.64**	**437.71%**
⊞ **FQ2-2008**	**2,694,375.54**	**4,551,189.19**	**3,391,921.03**	**1,159,268.16**	**34.18%**
⊟ **FQ3-2008**	**2,573,182.08**	**7,124,371.27**	**6,224,596.95**	**899,774.32**	**14.46%**
⊞ FM Jul 2008	855,061.83	5,406,251.02	4,201,119.08	1,205,131.94	28.69%
⊞ FM Aug 2008	608,473.34	6,014,724.36	5,065,511.79	949,212.57	18.74%
⊞ FM Sep 2008	1,109,646.91	7,124,371.27	6,224,596.95	899,774.32	14.46%
⊞ **FQ4-2008**	**2,663,730.18**	**9,788,101.45**	**8,942,403.96**	**845,697.49**	**9.46%**
⊟ **FY 2009**	**5,931,301.67**	**5,931,301.67**	**5,821,937.47**	**109,364.20**	**1.88%**
⊞ **FQ1-2009**	**1,903,944.38**	**1,903,944.38**	**1,856,813.65**	**47,130.73**	**2.54%**
⊞ **FQ2-2009**	**2,531,034.28**	**4,434,978.66**	**4,551,189.19**	**-116,210.53**	**-2.55%**
⊟ **FQ3-2009**	**1,496,323.01**	**5,931,301.67**	**5,821,937.47**	**109,364.20**	**1.88%**
⊞ FM Jul 2009	1,011,406.62	5,446,385.28	5,406,251.02	40,134.26	0.74%
⊞ FM Aug 2009	484,916.39	5,931,301.67	5,821,937.47	109,364.20	1.88%
Total	**24,661,807.07**	**5,931,301.67**	**9,788,101.45**	**-3,856,799.78**	**-39.40%**

FIGURE 4-10 For FQ3-2009, *Sales PYTD* shows the amount of the days in FQ3-2008 until August 16, 2008 because there is no data after August 15, 2009.

Sales PYTD is like *Sales YTD*: it filters the previous value in *Fiscal Year Number* instead of the last year visible in the filter context. The main difference is the evaluation of *LastDayOfFiscalYearAvailable*, which must consider only dates with sales while ignoring the filter on filter-safe columns, which are considered in the evaluation of *Sales Amount*:

Measure in the Sales table

```
Sales PYTD :=
IF (
    [ShowValueForDates],
    VAR PreviousFiscalYear = MAX ( 'Date'[Fiscal Year Number] ) - 1
    VAR LastDayOfFiscalYearAvailable =
        CALCULATE (
            MAX ( 'Date'[Day of Fiscal Year Number] ),
            REMOVEFILTERS (                   -- Remove filters from
                'Date'[Working Day],          -- filter-safe columns
                'Date'[Day of Week],          -- to get the last day with data
                'Date'[Day of Week Number]    -- selected in the report
            ),
            'Date'[DateWithSales] = TRUE
        )
    VAR Result =
        CALCULATE (
            [Sales Amount],
            ALLEXCEPT ( 'Date', 'Date'[Working Day], 'Date'[Day of Week] ),
            'Date'[Fiscal Year Number] = PreviousFiscalYear,
            'Date'[Day of Fiscal Year Number] <= LastDayOfFiscalYearAvailable,
            'Date'[DateWithSales] = TRUE
        )
    RETURN
        Result
)
```

Sales YOYTD and *Sales YOYTD %* rely on *Sales PYTD* to guarantee a fair comparison:

Measure in the Sales table

```
Sales YOYTD :=
VAR ValueCurrentPeriod = [Sales YTD]
VAR ValuePreviousPeriod = [Sales PYTD]
VAR Result =
    IF (
        NOT ISBLANK ( ValueCurrentPeriod ) && NOT ISBLANK ( ValuePreviousPeriod ),
        ValueCurrentPeriod - ValuePreviousPeriod
    )
RETURN
    Result
```

Measure in the Sales table

```
Sales YOYTD % :=
DIVIDE (
    [Sales YOYTD],
    [Sales PYTD]
)
```

Quarter-over-quarter-to-date growth

Quarter-over-quarter-to-date growth compares the quarter-to-date on a specific date with the quarter-to-date on an equivalent date in the previous quarter. Figure 4-11 shows that *Sales PQTD* in FW August 2009 is considering only transactions that occurred prior to May 16, 2009, to get the corresponding part of the previous quarter. For this reason *Sales QTD* of FW May 2009 is 1,411,541.99, whereas *Sales PQTD* for FW August 2009 is lower: 1,140,186.77.

Year	Sales Amount	Sales QTD	Sales PQTD	Sales QOQTD	Sales QOQTD %
⊞ **FY 2007**	**8,942,403.96**	**2,717,807.00**	**2,832,675.92**	**-114,868.92**	**-4.06%**
⊞ **FY 2008**	**9,788,101.45**	**2,663,730.18**	**2,573,182.08**	**90,548.10**	**3.52%**
⊟ **FY 2009**	**5,931,301.67**		**1,496,323.01**		
⊞ **FQ1-2009**	**1,903,944.38**	**1,903,944.38**	**2,663,730.18**	**-759,785.80**	**-28.52%**
⊟ **FQ2-2009**	**2,531,034.28**	**2,531,034.28**	**1,903,944.38**	**627,089.91**	**32.94%**
⊞ FM Apr 2009	594,753.85	594,753.85	704,188.45	-109,434.60	-15.54%
⊞ FM May 2009	816,788.14	1,411,541.99	1,226,407.50	185,134.49	15.10%
⊞ FM Jun 2009	1,119,492.29	2,531,034.28	1,903,944.38	627,089.91	32.94%
⊟ **FQ3-2009**	**1,496,323.01**	**1,496,323.01**	**1,140,186.77**	**356,136.24**	**31.23%**
⊞ FM Jul 2009	1,011,406.62	1,011,406.62	594,753.85	416,652.77	70.05%
⊞ FM Aug 2009	484,916.39	1,496,323.01	1,140,186.77	356,136.24	31.23%
Total	**24,661,807.07**		**1,496,323.01**		

FIGURE 4-11 For Aug 2009, *Sales PQTD* shows the amount for March 29-May 16, 2009, because there is no data after August 15, 2009. The comparison only uses the first 49 days of the quarter.

Sales PQTD is like *Sales QTD*; it filters the previous value in *Fiscal Year Quarter Number* instead of the last quarter visible in the filter context. The main difference is the evaluation of *LastDayOfFiscalYearQuarterAvailable*, which must consider only dates with sales while ignoring the filter on filter-safe columns, which are considered in the evaluation of *Sales Amount*:

Measure in the Sales table

```
Sales PQTD :=
IF (
    [ShowValueForDates],
    VAR PreviousFiscalYearQuarter = MAX ( 'Date'[Fiscal Year Quarter Number] ) - 1
    VAR LastDayOfFiscalYearQuarterAvailable =
        CALCULATE (
            MAX ( 'Date'[Day of Fiscal Quarter Number] ),
            REMOVEFILTERS (                      -- Remove filters from
                'Date'[Working Day],             -- filter-safe columns
                'Date'[Day of Week],             -- to get the last day with data
                'Date'[Day of Week Number] -- selected in the report
            ),
            'Date'[DateWithSales] = TRUE
        )
    VAR Result =
        CALCULATE (
            [Sales Amount],
            ALLEXCEPT ( 'Date', 'Date'[Working Day], 'Date'[Day of Week] ),
            'Date'[Fiscal Year Quarter Number] = PreviousFiscalYearQuarter,
            'Date'[Day of Fiscal Quarter Number] <= LastDayOfFiscalYearQuarterAvailable,
            'Date'[DateWithSales] = TRUE
        )
    RETURN
        Result
)
```

Sales QOQTD and *Sales QOQTD %* rely on *Sales PQTD* to guarantee a fair comparison:

Measure in the Sales table

```
Sales QOQTD :=
VAR ValueCurrentPeriod = [Sales QTD]
VAR ValuePreviousPeriod = [Sales PQTD]
VAR Result =
    IF (
        NOT ISBLANK ( ValueCurrentPeriod ) && NOT ISBLANK ( ValuePreviousPeriod ),
        ValueCurrentPeriod - ValuePreviousPeriod
    )
RETURN
    Result
```

Measure in the Sales table

```
Sales QOQTD % :=
DIVIDE (
    [Sales QOQTD],
    [Sales PQTD]
)
```

Week-over-week-to-date growth

Week-over-week-to-date growth compares a week-to-date on a specific date with the week-to-date on an equivalent date in the previous week. The calculation is similar to year-over-year and quarter-over-quarter growth, even though the data available does not show a specific example of a partial week corresponding to the last day available (August 15, 2019). Figure 4-12 shows an example of the result.

Year	Sales Amount	Sales WTD	Sales PWTD	Sales WOWTD	Sales WOWTD %
⊞ FY 2007	8,942,403.96	201,146.30	200,343.92	802.38	0.40%
⊞ FY 2008	9,788,101.45	165,554.93	152,052.00	13,502.93	8.88%
⊟ FY 2009	5,931,301.67				
⊞ FQ1-2009	1,903,944.38	115,826.31	156,596.98	-40,770.67	-26.04%
⊞ FQ2-2009	2,531,034.28	201,675.45	191,936.18	9,739.27	5.07%
⊟ FQ3-2009	1,496,323.01				
⊞ FW27-2009	260,265.60	260,265.60	201,675.45	58,590.14	29.05%
⊞ FW28-2009	250,893.60	250,893.60	260,265.60	-9,371.99	-3.60%
⊞ FW29-2009	306,535.20	306,535.20	250,893.60	55,641.60	22.18%
⊞ FW30-2009	193,712.22	193,712.22	306,535.20	-112,822.98	-36.81%
⊞ FW31-2009	183,695.43	183,695.43	193,712.22	-10,016.79	-5.17%
⊟ FW32-2009	79,423.99	79,423.99	183,695.43	-104,271.44	-56.76%
8/2/2009	8,203.42	8,203.42	17,995.31	-9,791.89	-54.41%
8/3/2009	337.68	8,541.10	19,090.63	-10,549.53	-55.26%
8/4/2009	4,482.94	13,024.04	32,875.76	-19,851.72	-60.38%
8/5/2009	14,319.18	27,343.22	35,135.57	-7,792.35	-22.18%
8/6/2009	26,941.94	54,285.16	98,335.49	-44,050.34	-44.80%
8/7/2009	2,518.99	56,804.15	145,945.33	-89,141.18	-61.08%
8/8/2009	22,619.84	79,423.99	183,695.43	-104,271.44	-56.76%
⊟ FW33-2009	221,796.97	221,796.97	79,423.99	142,372.97	179.26%
8/9/2009	21,983.18	21,983.18	8,203.42	13,779.76	167.98%
8/10/2009	4,211.87	26,195.05	8,541.10	17,653.95	206.69%
8/11/2009	79,245.09	105,440.14	13,024.04	92,416.10	709.58%
8/12/2009	1,497.50	106,937.64	27,343.22	79,594.42	291.09%
8/13/2009	13,784.34	120,721.98	54,285.16	66,436.83	122.38%
8/14/2009	100,059.00	220,780.98	56,804.15	163,976.83	288.67%
8/15/2009	1,015.98	221,796.97	79,423.99	142,372.97	179.26%
Total	24,661,807.07				

FIGURE 4-12 The *Sales PWTD* measure shows the *Sales WTD* of the previous week.

Sales PWTD is like *Sales WTD*; it filters the previous value in *Fiscal Year Week Number* instead of the last week visible in the filter context. The main difference is the evaluation of *LastDayOfFiscalYearWeekAvailable*, which must consider only dates with sales while ignoring the filter on filter-safe columns, which are considered in the evaluation of *Sales Amount*:

Measure in the Sales table

```
Sales PWTD :=
IF (
    [ShowValueForDates],
    VAR PreviousFiscalYearWeek = MAX ( 'Date'[Fiscal Year Week Number] ) - 1
    VAR LastDayOfWeekAvailable =
        CALCULATE (
            MAX ( 'Date'[Day of Week Number] ),
            REMOVEFILTERS (                      -- Remove filters from
                'Date'[Working Day],             -- filter-safe columns
                'Date'[Day of Week],             -- to get the last day with data
                'Date'[Day of Week Number]       -- selected in the report
            ),
            'Date'[DateWithSales] = TRUE
        )
    VAR Result =
        CALCULATE (
            [Sales Amount],
            ALLEXCEPT ( 'Date', 'Date'[Working Day], 'Date'[Day of Week] ),
            'Date'[Fiscal Year Week Number] = PreviousFiscalYearWeek,
            'Date'[Day of Week Number] <= LastDayOfWeekAvailable,
            'Date'[DateWithSales] = TRUE
        )
    RETURN
        Result
)
```

Sales WOWTD and *Sales WOWTD %* rely on the *Sales PWTD* measure to guarantee a fair comparison:

Measure in the Sales table

```
Sales WOWTD :=
VAR ValueCurrentPeriod = [Sales WTD]
VAR ValuePreviousPeriod = [Sales PWTD]
VAR Result =
    IF (
        NOT ISBLANK ( ValueCurrentPeriod )
            && NOT ISBLANK ( ValuePreviousPeriod ),
        ValueCurrentPeriod - ValuePreviousPeriod
    )
RETURN
    Result
```

Measure in the Sales table

```
Sales WOWTD % :=
DIVIDE (
    [Sales WOWTD],
    [Sales PWTD]
)
```

Comparing period-to-date with previous full period

Comparing a to-date aggregation with the previous full period is useful when you consider the previous period as a benchmark. Once the current year-to-date reaches 100% of the full previous year, this means we have reached the same performance as the previous full period, hopefully in fewer days.

Year-to-date over the full previous year

Year-to-date over the full previous year compares the year-to-date against the entire previous year. Figure 4-13 shows that in FW48-2008 *Sales YTD* surpassed the value of *Sales Amount* for the entire fiscal year 2007. *Sales YTDOPY %* provides an immediate comparison of the year-to-date with the total of the previous fiscal year; it shows growth over the previous fiscal year when the percentage is positive.

Year	Sales Amount	Sales YTD	Sales PYC	Sales YTDOPY	Sales YTDOPY %
⊞ FY 2007	8,942,403.96	8,942,403.96			
⊟ FY 2008	9,788,101.45	9,788,101.45	8,942,403.96	845,697.49	9.46%
⊞ FQ1-2008	1,856,813.65	1,856,813.65	8,942,403.96	-7,085,590.31	-79.24%
⊞ FQ2-2008	2,694,375.54	4,551,189.19	8,942,403.96	-4,391,214.77	-49.11%
⊞ FQ3-2008	2,573,182.08	7,124,371.27	8,942,403.96	-1,818,032.69	-20.33%
⊟ FQ4-2008	2,663,730.18	9,788,101.45	8,942,403.96	845,697.49	9.46%
⊞ FM Oct 2008	659,306.74	7,783,678.01	8,942,403.96	-1,158,725.94	-12.96%
⊞ FM Nov 2008	1,020,090.26	8,803,768.27	8,942,403.96	-138,635.69	-1.55%
⊟ FM Dec 2008	984,333.18	9,788,101.45	8,942,403.96	845,697.49	9.46%
FW48-2008	245,714.96	9,049,483.23	8,942,403.96	107,079.27	1.20%
FW49-2008	145,259.35	9,194,742.58	8,942,403.96	252,338.62	2.82%
FW50-2008	275,751.94	9,470,494.52	8,942,403.96	528,090.57	5.91%
FW51-2008	152,052.00	9,622,546.52	8,942,403.96	680,142.56	7.61%
FW52-2008	165,554.93	9,788,101.45	8,942,403.96	845,697.49	9.46%
⊞ FY 2009	5,931,301.67	5,931,301.67	9,788,101.45	-3,856,799.78	-39.40%
Total	24,661,807.07	5,931,301.67			

FIGURE 4-13 *Sales YTDOPY %* shows a positive value when *Sales YTD* is greater than the total *Sales Amount* of the previous fiscal year.

The year-to-date-over-previous-year growth is computed by the *Sales YTDOPY* and *Sales YTDOPY %* measures; these rely on the *Sales YTD* measure to compute the year-to-date value, and on the *Sales PYC* measure to get the sales amount of the entire previous fiscal year:

Measure in the Sales table

```
Sales PYC :=
IF (
    [ShowValueForDates] && HASONEVALUE ( 'Date'[Fiscal Year Number] ),
    VAR PreviousFiscalYear = MAX ( 'Date'[Fiscal Year Number] ) - 1
    VAR Result =
        CALCULATE (
            [Sales Amount],
            ALLEXCEPT ( 'Date', 'Date'[Working Day], 'Date'[Day of Week] ),
            'Date'[Fiscal Year Number] = PreviousFiscalYear
        )
    RETURN
        Result
)
```

Measure in the Sales table

```
Sales YTDOPY :=
VAR ValueCurrentPeriod = [Sales YTD]
VAR ValuePreviousPeriod = [Sales PYC]
VAR Result =
    IF (
        NOT ISBLANK ( ValueCurrentPeriod ) && NOT ISBLANK ( ValuePreviousPeriod ),
        ValueCurrentPeriod - ValuePreviousPeriod
    )
RETURN
    Result
```

Measure in the Sales table

```
Sales YTDOPY % :=
DIVIDE (
    [Sales YTDOPY],
    [Sales PYC]
)
```

Quarter-to-date over the full previous quarter

Quarter-to-date over the full previous quarter compares the quarter-to-date against the entire previous fiscal quarter. Figure 4-14 shows that *Sales QTD* surpassed the total *Sales Amount* for FQ1-2009 in FW23-2009. *Sales QTDOPQ %* provides an immediate comparison of the quarter-to-date with the total of the previous quarter; it shows growth over the previous quarter when the percentage is positive.

Year	Sales Amount	Sales QTD	Sales PQC	Sales QTDOPQ	Sales QTDOPQ %
⊞ **FY 2007**	**8,942,403.96**	**2,717,807.00**			
⊞ **FY 2008**	**9,788,101.45**	**2,663,730.18**			
⊟ **FY 2009**	**5,931,301.67**				
⊞ **FQ1-2009**	**1,903,944.38**	**1,903,944.38**	**2,663,730.18**	**-759,785.80**	**-28.52%**
⊟ **FQ2-2009**	**2,531,034.28**	**2,531,034.28**	**1,903,944.38**	**627,089.91**	**32.94%**
⊞ **FM Apr 2009**	**594,753.85**	**594,753.85**	**1,903,944.38**	**-1,309,190.53**	**-68.76%**
⊞ **FM May 2009**	**816,788.14**	**1,411,541.99**	**1,903,944.38**	**-492,402.39**	**-25.86%**
⊟ **FM Jun 2009**	**1,119,492.29**	**2,531,034.28**	**1,903,944.38**	**627,089.91**	**32.94%**
FW22-2009	302,268.61	1,713,810.60	1,903,944.38	-190,133.78	-9.99%
FW23-2009	194,482.52	1,908,293.11	1,903,944.38	4,348.74	0.23%
FW24-2009	229,129.53	2,137,422.65	1,903,944.38	233,478.27	12.26%
FW25-2009	191,936.18	2,329,358.83	1,903,944.38	425,414.45	22.34%
FW26-2009	201,675.45	2,531,034.28	1,903,944.38	627,089.91	32.94%
⊞ **FQ3-2009**	**1,496,323.01**	**1,496,323.01**	**2,531,034.28**	**-1,034,711.27**	**-40.88%**
Total	**24,661,807.07**				

FIGURE 4-14 *Sales QTDOPQ %* shows a positive percentage from FW23-2009, when *Sales QTD* starts to be greater than the *Sales Amount* for FQ1-2009.

The quarter-to-date-over-previous-quarter growth is computed with the *Sales QTDOPQ* and *Sales QTDOPQ %* measures. These rely on the *Sales QTD* measure to compute the quarter-to-date value, and on the *Sales PQC* measure to get the sales amount of the entire previous quarter:

Measure in the Sales table

```
Sales PQC :=
IF (
    [ShowValueForDates] && HASONEVALUE ( 'Date'[Fiscal Year Quarter Number] ),
    VAR PreviousFiscalYearQuarter = MAX ( 'Date'[Fiscal Year Quarter Number] ) - 1
    VAR Result =
        CALCULATE (
            [Sales Amount],
            ALLEXCEPT ( 'Date', 'Date'[Working Day], 'Date'[Day of Week] ),
            'Date'[Fiscal Year Quarter Number] = PreviousFiscalYearQuarter
        )
    RETURN
        Result
)
```

Measure in the Sales table

```
Sales QTDOPQ :=
VAR ValueCurrentPeriod = [Sales QTD]
VAR ValuePreviousPeriod = [Sales PQC]
VAR Result =
    IF (
        NOT ISBLANK ( ValueCurrentPeriod ) && NOT ISBLANK ( ValuePreviousPeriod ),
        ValueCurrentPeriod - ValuePreviousPeriod
    )
RETURN
    Result
```

Measure in the Sales table

```
Sales QTDOPQ % :=
DIVIDE (
    [Sales QTDOPQ],
    [Sales PQC]
)
```

Week-to-date over the full previous week

The week-to-date over the full previous week compares the week-to-date against the entire previous week. Figure 4-15 shows that *Sales WTD* during FW33-2009 surpasses the total *Sales Amount* for FW32-2009. *Sales WTDOPW%* provides an immediate comparison of the week-to-date with the total of the previous week; it shows growth over the previous week when the percentage is positive, as is the case starting from August 11, 2009.

Year	Sales Amount	Sales WTD	Sales PWC	Sales WTDOPW	Sales WTDOPW %
⊞ FY 2007	8,942,403.96	201,146.30			
⊞ FY 2008	9,788,101.45	165,554.93			
⊟ FY 2009	5,931,301.67				
⊞ FQ1-2009	1,903,944.38	115,826.31			
⊞ FQ2-2009	2,531,034.28	201,675.45			
⊟ FQ3-2009	1,496,323.01				
⊞ FW27-2009	260,265.60	260,265.60	201,675.45	58,590.14	29.05%
⊞ FW28-2009	250,893.60	250,893.60	260,265.60	-9,371.99	-3.60%
⊞ FW29-2009	306,535.20	306,535.20	250,893.60	55,641.60	22.18%
⊞ FW30-2009	193,712.22	193,712.22	306,535.20	-112,822.98	-36.81%
⊞ FW31-2009	183,695.43	183,695.43	193,712.22	-10,016.79	-5.17%
⊞ FW32-2009	79,423.99	79,423.99	183,695.43	-104,271.44	-56.76%
⊟ FW33-2009	221,796.97	221,796.97	79,423.99	142,372.97	179.26%
8/9/2009	21,983.18	21,983.18	79,423.99	-57,440.82	-72.32%
8/10/2009	4,211.87	26,195.05	79,423.99	-53,228.94	-67.02%
8/11/2009	79,245.09	105,440.14	79,423.99	26,016.15	32.76%
8/12/2009	1,497.50	106,937.64	79,423.99	27,513.65	34.64%
8/13/2009	13,784.34	120,721.98	79,423.99	41,297.99	52.00%
8/14/2009	100,059.00	220,780.98	79,423.99	141,356.99	177.98%
8/15/2009	1,015.98	221,796.97	79,423.99	142,372.97	179.26%
Total	24,661,807.07				

FIGURE 4-15 *Sales WTDOPW %* shows a positive percentage starting from August 11, 2009, when *Sales WTD* starts to be greater than the *Sales Amount* for FW32-2009.

The week-to-date-over-previous-week growth is computed with the *Sales WTDOPW %* and *Sales WTDOPW* measures. These rely on the *Sales WTD* measure to compute the week-to-date value, and on the *Sales PWC* measure to get the sales amount of the entire previous week:

Measure in the Sales table

```
Sales PWC :=
IF (
    [ShowValueForDates] && HASONEVALUE ( 'Date'[Fiscal Year Week Number] ),
    VAR PreviousFiscalYearWeek = MAX ( 'Date'[Fiscal Year Week Number] ) - 1
    VAR Result =
        CALCULATE (
            [Sales Amount],
            ALLEXCEPT ( 'Date', 'Date'[Working Day], 'Date'[Day of Week] ),
            'Date'[Fiscal Year Week Number] = PreviousFiscalYearWeek
        )
    RETURN
        Result
)
```

Measure in the Sales table

```
Sales WTDOPW :=
VAR ValueCurrentPeriod = [Sales WTD]
VAR ValuePreviousPeriod = [Sales PWC]
VAR Result =
    IF (
        NOT ISBLANK ( ValueCurrentPeriod ) && NOT ISBLANK ( ValuePreviousPeriod ),
        ValueCurrentPeriod - ValuePreviousPeriod
    )
RETURN
    Result
```

Measure in the Sales table

```
Sales WTDOPW % :=
DIVIDE (
    [Sales WTDOPW],
    [Sales PWC]
)
```

Using moving annual total calculations

A common way to aggregate data over several months is by using the moving annual total instead of the year-to-date. In the week-based calendar, the moving annual total includes the last 52 weeks (364 days) of data.

Moving annual total

Sales MAT (364) computes the moving annual total, as shown in Figure 4-16.

Year	Sales Amount	Sales MAT (364)	Sales PYMAT (364)	Sales MATG	Sales MATG %
⊞ FY 2007	8,942,403.96	8,942,403.96			
⊟ FY 2008	9,788,101.45	9,788,101.45	8,942,403.96	845,697.49	9.46%
⊞ FQ1-2008	1,856,813.65	10,453,898.59	345,319.01	10,108,579.58	2927.32%
⊞ FQ2-2008	2,694,375.54	10,101,672.11	3,391,921.03	6,709,751.08	197.82%
⊞ FQ3-2008	2,573,182.08	9,842,178.27	6,224,596.95	3,617,581.32	58.12%
⊞ FQ4-2008	2,663,730.18	9,788,101.45	8,942,403.96	845,697.49	9.46%
⊟ FY 2009	5,931,301.67	5,931,301.67	9,788,101.45	-3,856,799.78	-39.40%
⊞ FQ1-2009	1,903,944.38	9,835,232.18	10,453,898.59	-618,666.42	-5.92%
⊞ FQ2-2009	2,531,034.28	9,671,890.91	10,101,672.11	-429,781.20	-4.25%
⊟ FQ3-2009	1,496,323.01	8,595,031.84	9,842,178.27	-1,247,146.43	-12.67%
FW27-2009	260,265.60	9,721,895.85	10,146,028.07	-424,132.23	-4.18%
FW28-2009	250,893.60	9,808,892.25	9,913,448.59	-104,556.34	-1.05%
FW29-2009	306,535.20	9,918,120.11	9,920,475.38	-2,355.27	-0.02%
FW30-2009	193,712.22	9,828,235.71	10,147,535.89	-319,300.18	-3.15%
FW31-2009	183,695.43	9,877,768.06	10,097,325.83	-219,557.77	-2.17%
FW32-2009	79,423.99	9,837,876.30	10,003,938.08	-166,061.78	-1.66%
FW33-2009	221,796.97	9,897,465.65	9,938,077.40	-40,611.75	-0.41%
Total	**24,661,807.07**	**5,931,301.67**	**9,788,101.45**	**-3,856,799.78**	**-39.40%**

FIGURE 4-16 *Sales MAT (364)* in FQ3-2009 aggregates *Sales Amount* from FQ4-2008 to FQ3-2009.

The *Sales MAT (364)* measure defines a range over the *Date[Date]* column that includes the days of one complete year from the last day in the filter context:

Measure in the Sales table

```
Sales MAT (364) :=
IF (
    [ShowValueForDates],
    VAR LastDayMAT = MAX ( 'Date'[Sequential Day Number] )
    VAR FirstDayMAT = LastDayMAT - 363
    VAR Result =
        CALCULATE (
            [Sales Amount],
            ALLEXCEPT ( 'Date', 'Date'[Working Day], 'Date'[Day of Week] ),
            'Date'[Sequential Day Number] >= FirstDayMAT
                && 'Date'[Sequential Day Number] <= LastDayMAT
        )
    RETURN
        Result
)
```

The *Sales MAT (364)* does not correspond to a year total in case the year has more than 52 weeks, as is the case every 5-6 years in the 4-4-5 calendar. Yet, it is a better measure to evaluate trends over time because it always includes the same number of days and weeks.

Moving annual total growth

The moving annual total growth is computed with the *Sales PYMAT (364)*, *Sales MATG*, and *Sales MATG %* measures, which rely on the *Sales MAT (364)* measure. *Sales MAT (364)* provides a correct value one year after the first sale ever, once it has collected one full year of data; it is not protected in case the current time period is shorter than a full year. For example, the amount for the fiscal year FY 2009 of *Sales PYMAT (364)* is 9,788,101.45, which corresponds to the *Sales Amount* of FY 2008 as shown in Figure 4-17. When compared with sales in FY 2009, this produces a comparison of less than 6 months – data being only available until August 15, 2009 – with a full fiscal year 2009. Similarly, you can see that *Sales MATG %* starts in FY 2008 with very high values and stabilizes after a year. This behavior is by design: the moving annual total is usually computed at the month or day granularity to show trends in a chart.

Year	Sales Amount	Sales MAT (364)	Sales PYMAT (364)	Sales MATG	Sales MATG %
⊞ **FY 2007**	**8,942,403.96**	**8,942,403.96**			
⊟ **FY 2008**	**9,788,101.45**	**9,788,101.45**	**8,942,403.96**	**845,697.49**	**9.46%**
⊞ FQ1-2008	1,856,813.65	10,453,898.59	345,319.01	10,108,579.58	2927.32%
⊞ FQ2-2008	2,694,375.54	10,101,672.11	3,391,921.03	6,709,751.08	197.82%
⊞ FQ3-2008	2,573,182.08	9,842,178.27	6,224,596.95	3,617,581.32	58.12%
⊞ FQ4-2008	2,663,730.18	9,788,101.45	8,942,403.96	845,697.49	9.46%
⊟ **FY 2009**	**5,931,301.67**	**5,931,301.67**	**9,788,101.45**	**-3,856,799.78**	**-39.40%**
⊞ FQ1-2009	1,903,944.38	9,835,232.18	10,453,898.59	-618,666.42	-5.92%
⊞ FQ2-2009	2,531,034.28	9,671,890.91	10,101,672.11	-429,781.20	-4.25%
⊞ FQ3-2009	1,496,323.01	8,595,031.84	9,842,178.27	-1,247,146.43	-12.67%
Total	**24,661,807.07**	**5,931,301.67**	**9,788,101.45**	**-3,856,799.78**	**-39.40%**

FIGURE 4-17 *Sales MATG %* shows the growth between *Sales MAT (364)* and *Sales PYMAT (364)* as a percentage.

The measures are defined as follows:

Measure in the Sales table

```
Sales PYMAT (364) :=
IF (
    [ShowValueForDates],
    VAR LastDayAvailable = MAX ( 'Date'[Sequential Day Number] )
    VAR LastDayMAT = LastDayAvailable - 364 -- go back 52 weeks
    VAR FirstDayMAT = LastDayMAT - 363
    VAR Result =
        CALCULATE (
            [Sales Amount],
            ALLEXCEPT ( 'Date', 'Date'[Working Day], 'Date'[Day of Week] ),
            'Date'[Sequential Day Number] >= FirstDayMAT
                && 'Date'[Sequential Day Number] <= LastDayMAT
        )
    RETURN
        Result
)
```

Measure in the Sales table

```
Sales MATG :=
VAR ValueCurrentPeriod = [Sales MAT (364)]
VAR ValuePreviousPeriod = [Sales PYMAT (364)]
VAR Result =
    IF (
        NOT ISBLANK ( ValueCurrentPeriod ) && NOT ISBLANK ( ValuePreviousPeriod ),
        ValueCurrentPeriod - ValuePreviousPeriod
    )
RETURN
    Result
```

Measure in the Sales table

```
Sales MATG % :=
DIVIDE (
    [Sales MATG],
    [Sales PYMAT (364)]
)
```

Moving averages

The moving average is typically used to display trends in line charts. Figure 4-18 includes the moving average of *Sales Amount* over four weeks (*Sales AVG 4W*), one quarter (*Sales AVG 1Q*), and a fiscal year (*Sales AVG 1Y*).

Sales AVG 4W, Sales AVG 1Q and Sales AVG 1Y by Date

FIGURE 4-18 *Sales AVG 4W*, *Sales AVG 1Q*, and *Sales AVG 1Y* show the moving average over four weeks, one quarter, and one year, respectively.

Moving average 4 weeks

The *Sales AVG 4W* measure computes the moving average over four weeks by iterating a list of the last 28 dates obtained in the *Period4W* variable. The *Period4W* variable retrieves the dates visible in the last 28 days with two exceptions; it ignores dates without sales, and it applies the filters existing on filter-safe columns in the *Date* table:

Measure in the Sales table

```
Sales AVG 4W :=
IF (
    [ShowValueForDates],
    VAR LastDayMAT =
        MAX ( 'Date'[Sequential Day Number] )
    VAR FirstDayMAT = LastDayMAT - 27
    VAR Period4W =
        CALCULATETABLE (
            VALUES ( 'Date'[Sequential Day Number] ),
            ALLEXCEPT (
                'Date',
                'Date'[Working Day],
                'Date'[Day of Week]
            ),
            'Date'[Sequential Day Number] >= FirstDayMAT
                && 'Date'[Sequential Day Number] <= LastDayMAT,
            'Date'[DateWithSales] = TRUE
        )
    VAR FirstDayWithData =
        CALCULATE (
            MIN ( Sales[Order Date] ),
            REMOVEFILTERS ()
        )
    VAR FirstDayInPeriod =
        MINX (
            Period4W,
            'Date'[Sequential Day Number]
        )
    VAR Result =
        IF (
            FirstDayWithData <= FirstDayInPeriod,
            CALCULATE (
                AVERAGEX ( Period4W, [Sales Amount] ),
                REMOVEFILTERS ( 'Date' )
            )
        )
    RETURN
        Result
)
```

This pattern is very flexible because it also works for non-additive measures. With that said, for a regular additive calculation *Result* can be implemented using a different and faster formula:

```
VAR Result =
    IF (
        FirstDayWithData <= FirstDayInPeriod,
        CALCULATE (
            DIVIDE (
                [Sales Amount],
                DISTINCTCOUNT ( Sales[Order Date] )
            ),
            REMOVEFILTERS ( 'Date' ),
            Period4W
        )
    )
```

Moving average 1 quarter

The *Sales AVG 1Q* measure computes the moving average over 13 weeks by iterating a list of the dates in the last quarter obtained in the *Period1Q* variable. The *Period1Q* variable retrieves the dates visible included in the last 13 weeks (91 days) with two exceptions; it ignores dates without sales, and it applies the filters existing on filter-safe columns in the *Date* table:

Measure in the Sales table

```
Sales AVG 1Q :=
IF (
    [ShowValueForDates],
    VAR LastDayMAT =
        MAX ( 'Date'[Sequential Day Number] )
    VAR FirstDayMAT = LastDayMAT - 13 * 7 + 1
    VAR Period1Q =
        CALCULATETABLE (
            VALUES ( 'Date'[Sequential Day Number] ),
            ALLEXCEPT ( 'Date', 'Date'[Working Day], 'Date'[Day of Week] ),
            'Date'[Sequential Day Number] >= FirstDayMAT
                && 'Date'[Sequential Day Number] <= LastDayMAT,
            'Date'[DateWithSales] = TRUE
        )
    VAR FirstDayWithData =
        CALCULATE (
            MIN ( Sales[Order Date] ),
            REMOVEFILTERS ()
        )
    VAR FirstDayInPeriod =
        MINX (
            Period1Q,
            'Date'[Sequential Day Number]
        )
    VAR Result =
        IF (
            FirstDayWithData <= FirstDayInPeriod,
            CALCULATE (
                AVERAGEX ( Period1Q, [Sales Amount] ),
                REMOVEFILTERS ( 'Date' )
            )
        )
    RETURN
        Result
)
```

For simple additive measures, the pattern based on DIVIDE which is shown for the moving average over four weeks (28 days) can also be used for the average over 91 days.

Moving average 1 year

The *Sales AVG 1Y* measure computes the moving average over one year by iterating a list of the dates in the last 364 days in the *Period1Y* variable. The *Period1Y* variable retrieves the dates visible included in the last fiscal year (only including 52 weeks) with two exceptions; it ignores dates without sales, and it applies the filters existing on filter-safe columns in the *Date* table:

Measure in the Sales table

```
Sales AVG 1Y :=
IF (
    [ShowValueForDates],
    VAR LastDayMAT =
        MAX ( 'Date'[Sequential Day Number] )
    VAR FirstDayMAT = LastDayMAT - 363
    VAR Period1Y =
        CALCULATETABLE (
            VALUES ( 'Date'[Sequential Day Number] ),
            ALLEXCEPT (
                'Date',
                'Date'[Working Day],
                'Date'[Day of Week]
            ),
            'Date'[Sequential Day Number] >= FirstDayMAT
                && 'Date'[Sequential Day Number] <= LastDayMAT,
            'Date'[DateWithSales] = TRUE
        )
    VAR FirstDayWithData =
        CALCULATE (
            MIN ( Sales[Order Date] ),
            REMOVEFILTERS ()
        )
    VAR FirstDayInPeriod =
        MINX (
            Period1Y,
            'Date'[Sequential Day Number]
        )
    VAR Result =
        IF (
            FirstDayWithData <= FirstDayInPeriod,
            CALCULATE (
                AVERAGEX ( Period1Y, [Sales Amount] ),
                REMOVEFILTERS ( 'Date' )
            )
        )
    RETURN
        Result
)
```

For simple additive measures, the pattern based on DIVIDE shown for the moving average over four weeks (28 days) can also be used for the average over 364 days.

Custom time-related calculations

This pattern shows how to compute time-related calculations like year-to-date, same period last year, and percentage growth using a custom calendar. This pattern does not rely on DAX built-in time intelligence functions. All the measures refer to the fiscal calendar because the same measures, with a regular Gregorian calendar, can be obtained using the **Standard time-related calculations** pattern.

There are several scenarios where the DAX built-in functions for time intelligence cannot provide the right answers. For example, if your fiscal year starts on a month other than January, April, July, or October, then you cannot use the DAX time intelligence functions for quarterly-related calculations. In these scenarios, you need to rewrite the time intelligence logic of the built-in functions by using plain DAX functions like FILTER and CALCULATE. Moreover, you must create a *Date* table that contains additional columns to compute time periods like the previous quarter or a whole year. Indeed, the standard time intelligence functions derive this information from the *Date* column in the *Date* table. The custom time-related calculations pattern does not extract the information from the *Date* column and requires additional columns.

The measures in this pattern work on a regular Gregorian calendar with the following assumptions:

- Years and quarters always start on the first day of a month.

- A month is always a calendar month.

In simpler words, this pattern works fine if the fiscal year starts on the first day of a month, and a quarter is made of three regular months. For example, if the fiscal year starts on March 3, or all the fiscal quarters must have 90 days, then the formulas do not work.

An example of a calendar that does not satisfy the requirements of this pattern is a week-based calendar. If you need calculations over periods based on weeks, you should use the **Week-related calculations** pattern.

Introduction to custom time intelligence calculations

The custom time intelligence calculations in this pattern modify the filter context over the *Date* table to obtain the required result. The formulas are designed to apply filters to the lowest granularity required to improve query performances. For example, a calculation over months works by modifying the filter context at the month level, instead of the individual dates. This technique reduces the cost of computing the new filter and applying it to the filter context. This optimization is especially useful when using DirectQuery, even though it also improves performance on models imported in memory.

Because the pattern does not rely on the standard time intelligence functions, the *Date* table does not have the requirements needed for standard DAX time intelligence functions.

For example, the Mark as Date Table setting is suggested, but not required. The formulas in this pattern do not rely on the automatic REMOVEFILTERS applied over the *Date* table when the *Date* column is filtered. Instead, the *Date* table must contain specific columns required by the measures. Therefore, although you might already have a *Date* table in your model, you must read the next section (Building a *Date* table) to verify that all the required columns are present in the *Date* table.

Building a *Date* table

The *Date* table used for custom time-related calculations is based on the months of the standard Gregorian calendar table. If you already have a *Date* table, you can import the table and – if necessary – extend it to include a set of columns containing the information required by the DAX formulas. We describe these columns later in this section.

If a *Date* table is not available, you can create one using a DAX calculated table. As an example, the following DAX expression defines the *Date* table used in this pattern, which has a fiscal year starting on March 1:

Calculated table

```
Date =
VAR FirstFiscalMonth = 3   -- First month of the fiscal year
VAR FirstDayOfWeek = 0     -- 0 = Sunday, 1 = Monday, ...
VAR FirstSalesDate = MIN ( Sales[Order Date] )
VAR LastSalesDate = MAX ( Sales[Order Date] )
VAR FirstFiscalYear =      -- Customizes the first fiscal year to use
    YEAR ( FirstSalesDate )
    + 1 * ( MONTH ( FirstSalesDate ) >= FirstFiscalMonth && FirstFiscalMonth > 1)
VAR LastFiscalYear =       -- Customizes the last fiscal year to use
    YEAR ( LastSalesDate )
    + 1 * ( MONTH ( LastSalesDate ) >= FirstFiscalMonth && FirstFiscalMonth > 1)
RETURN
GENERATE (
    VAR FirstDay =
        DATE (
            FirstFiscalYear - 1 * (FirstFiscalMonth > 1),
            FirstFiscalMonth,
            1
        )
```

```
            VAR LastDay =
                DATE (
                    LastFiscalYear + 1 * (FirstFiscalMonth = 1),
                    FirstFiscalMonth, 1
                ) - 1
            RETURN
                CALENDAR ( FirstDay, LastDay ),

            VAR CurrentDate = [Date]
            VAR Yr = YEAR ( CurrentDate )           -- Year Number
            VAR Mn = MONTH ( CurrentDate )          -- Month Number (1-12)
            VAR Mdn = DAY ( CurrentDate )           -- Day of Month
            VAR DateKey = Yr*10000+Mn*100+Mdn
            VAR Wd =                                -- Weekday Number (0 = Sunday, 1 = Monday, ...)
                WEEKDAY ( CurrentDate + 7 - FirstDayOfWeek, 1 )
            VAR WorkingDay =                        -- Working Day (1 = working, 0 = non-working)
                ( WEEKDAY ( CurrentDate, 1 ) IN { 2, 3, 4, 5, 6 } )
            VAR Fyr =                               -- Fiscal Year Number
                Yr + 1 * ( FirstFiscalMonth > 1 && Mn >= FirstFiscalMonth )
            VAR Fmn =                               -- Fiscal Month Number (1-12)
                Mn - FirstFiscalMonth + 1 + 12 * (Mn < FirstFiscalMonth)
            VAR Fqrn =                              -- Fiscal Quarter (string)
                ROUNDUP ( Fmn / 3, 0 )
            VAR Fmqn =
                MOD ( FMn - 1, 3 ) + 1
            VAR Fqr =                               -- Fiscal Quarter (string)
                FORMAT ( Fqrn, "\Q0" )
            VAR FirstDayOfYear =
                DATE ( Fyr - 1 * (FirstFiscalMonth > 1), FirstFiscalMonth, 1 )
            VAR Fydn =
                SUMX (
                    CALENDAR ( FirstDayOfYear, CurrentDate ),
                    1 * ( MONTH ( [Date] ) <> 2 || DAY ( [Date] ) <> 29 )
                )
            RETURN ROW (
                "DateKey", INT ( DateKey ),
                "Sequential Day Number", INT ( [Date] ),
                "Year Month", FORMAT ( CurrentDate, "mmm yyyy" ),
                "Year Month Number", Yr * 12 + Mn - 1,
                "Fiscal Year", "FY " & Fyr,
                "Fiscal Year Number", Fyr,
                "Fiscal Year Quarter", "F" & Fqr & "-" & Fyr,
                "Fiscal Year Quarter Number", CONVERT ( Fyr * 4 + FQrn - 1, INTEGER ),
                "Fiscal Quarter", "F" & Fqr,
                "Month", FORMAT ( CurrentDate, "mmm" ),
                "Fiscal Month Number", Fmn,
                "Fiscal Month in Quarter Number",  Fmqn,
                "Day of Week", FORMAT ( CurrentDate, "ddd" ),
                "Day of Week Number", Wd,
                "Day of Month Number", Mdn,
                "Day of Fiscal Year Number", Fydn,
                "Working Day", IF ( WorkingDay, "Working Day", "Non-Working Day" )
            )
        )
```

The first two variables are useful to customize the beginning of both the fiscal year and the week. The next variables detect the range of fiscal years required, based on the transactions in *Sales*. You can customize *FirstSalesDate* and *LastSalesDate* to retrieve the first and last transaction date in your model, or you can assign the first and last fiscal year in the *FirstFiscalYear* and *LastFiscalYear* variables.

The quarters are computed starting from the first month of the fiscal year. The *Date* table contains hidden columns to support the correct sorting of years, quarters, and months. These hidden columns are populated with sequential numbers that make it easy to apply filters to retrieve previous or following years, quarters, and months, without relying on complex calculations at query time.

Among the many columns, one is worth expanding on. The **Year Month Number** column contains the year number multiplied by 12, plus the month. The resulting number is hard to read, but it allows math over months. Given the *Year Month Number* value, you can just subtract 12 to go back one year; this gives you the value of *Year Month Number* corresponding to the same month in the previous year. Many formulas use this characteristic to perform time-shifts.

In order to obtain the right visualization, the **calendar columns** must be configured in the data model as follows – for each column you can see the data type and the format string, followed by a sample value:

- *Date*: Date, m/dd/yyyy (8/14/2007), used as a column to mark as date table (not required)
- *DateKey*: Whole Number, (20070814), used as an alternate key for relationships
- *Sequential Day Number*: Whole Number, Hidden (40040), same value of Date as integer
- *Year Month*: Text (Aug 2007)
- *Year Month Number*: Whole Number, Hidden (24091)
- *Month*: Text (Aug)
- *Fiscal Month Number*: Whole Number, Hidden (6)
- *Fiscal Month in Quarter Number*: Whole Number, Hidden (3)
- *Fiscal Year*: Text (FY 2008)
- *Fiscal Year Number*: Whole Number, Hidden (2008)
- *Fiscal Year Quarter*: Text (FQ2-2008)
- *Fiscal Year Quarter* Number: Whole Number, Hidden (8033)
- *Fiscal Quarter*: Text (FQ2)
- *Day of Fiscal Year Number*: Whole Number, Hidden (167)
- *Day of Month Number*: Whole Number, Hidden (14)

We want to introduce the concept of **filter-safe columns**. In a table, there are columns whose filters need to be preserved. The filters over filter-safe columns are not altered by the time intelligence calculations. They will be affecting the calculations presented in this pattern. The filter-safe columns in our sample table are the following:

- *Day of Week*: ddd (Tue)
- *Day of Week Number*: Whole Number, Hidden (6)
- *Working Day*: Text (Working Day)

We further describe the behavior of filter-safe columns in the next section.

The *Date* table in this pattern has one hierarchy:

- Fiscal: Year (*Fiscal Year*), Quarter (*Fiscal Year Quarter*), Month (*Year Month*)

The columns are designed to simplify the formulas. For example, the *Day of Fiscal Year Number* column contains the number of days since the beginning of the fiscal year, ignoring February 29 in leap years; this number makes it easier to find a corresponding range of dates in the previous year.

The *Date* table must also include a hidden *DateWithSales* calculated column, used by some of the formulas of this pattern:

Calculated column in the Date table

```
DateWithSales =
'Date'[Date] <= MAX ( Sales[Order Date] )
```

The *Date[DateWithSales]* column is *TRUE* if the date is on or before the last date with sales; it is *FALSE* otherwise. In other words, *DateWithSales* is *TRUE* for "past" dates and *FALSE* for "future" dates, where "past" and "future" are relative to the last date with sales.

In case you import a *Date* table, you want to create columns that are similar to the ones we describe in this pattern, in that they should behave the same way.

Understanding filter-safe columns

The *Date* table contains two types of columns: regular columns and filter-safe columns. The regular columns are manipulated by the measures shown in this pattern. The filters over filter-safe columns are always preserved and never altered by the measures of this pattern. An example clarifies this distinction. The *Year Month Number* column is a regular column: the formulas in this pattern have the option of changing its value during their computation.

For example, in order to compute the previous month the formulas change the filter context by subtracting one to the value of *Year Month Number* in the filter context. Conversely, the *Day of Week* column is a filter-safe column. If a user filters Monday to Friday, the formulas do not alter that filter on the day of the week. Therefore, a previous-year measure keeps the filter on the day of the week; it replaces only the filter on calendar columns such as year, month, and date.

To implement this pattern, you must identify which columns need to be treated as filter-safe columns, because filter-safe columns require special handling. The following is the classification of the columns used in the *Date* table of this pattern:

- **Calendar columns**: *Date, DateKey, Sequential Day Number, Year Month, Year Month Number, Month, Fiscal Month Number, Fiscal Month in Quarter Number, Fiscal Year, Fiscal Year Number, Fiscal Year Quarter, Fiscal Year Quarter Number, Fiscal Quarter, Day of Fiscal Year Number, Day of Month Number* .
- **Filter-safe columns**: *Day of Week, Day of Week Number, Working Day*.

The special handling of filter-safe columns pertains to the filter context. Every measure in this pattern manipulates the filter context by replacing filters over all the calendar columns, without altering any filter applied to the filter-safe columns. In other words, every measure follows two rules:

- Remove filters on calendar columns;
- Keep filters on filter-safe columns.

The ALLEXCEPT function can implement these requirements; specify the *Date* table in the first argument, and the filter-safe columns in the following arguments:

```
CALCULATE (
    [Sales Amount],
    ALLEXCEPT ( 'Date', 'Date'[Working Day], 'Date'[Day of Week] ),
    ... // Filters over one or more calendar columns
)
```

If the *Date* table did not have any filter-safe column, the filters could be removed by using REMOVEFILTERS over the *Date* table instead of ALLEXCEPT:

```
CALCULATE (
    [Sales Amount],
    REMOVEFILTERS ( 'Date' ),
    ... // Filters over one or more calendar columns
)
```

If your *Date* table does not contain any filter-safe column, then you can use REMOVEFILTERS instead of ALLEXCEPT in all the measures of this pattern. We provide a complete scenario that includes filter-safe columns. Whenever possible, you can simplify it.

While the ALLEXCEPT should include all the filter-safe columns, we skip specifically the hidden filter-safe columns used only to sort other columns. For example, we do not include *Day of Week Number*, which is a hidden column used to sort the *Day of Week* column. The assumption is that the user never applies filters on hidden columns; if this assumption is not true, then the hidden filter-safe columns must also be included in the ALLEXCEPT arguments. You can find an example of the different results of using REMOVEFILTERS and ALLEXCEPT in the **Year-to-date total** section of this pattern.

Controlling the visualization on future dates

Most of the time intelligence calculations should not display values for dates after the last date available. For example, a year-to-date calculation can also show values for future dates, but we want to hide those values. The dataset used in these examples ends on August 15, 2009. Therefore, we consider the month of August 2009, the third quarter of 2009 (Q3-2009), and the year 2009 as the last time periods with data. Any date later than August 15, 2019 is considered future, and we want to hide its values.

In order to avoid showing results in future dates, we use the following *ShowValueForDates* measure. *ShowValueForDates* returns TRUE if the period selected is earlier than the last period with data:

Measure (hidden) in the Date table

```
ShowValueForDates :=
VAR LastDateWithData =
    CALCULATE (
        MAX ( 'Sales'[Order Date] ),
        REMOVEFILTERS ()
    )
VAR FirstDateVisible =
    MIN ( 'Date'[Date] )
VAR Result =
    FirstDateVisible <= LastDateWithData
RETURN
    Result
```

The *ShowValueForDates* measure is hidden. It is a technical measure created to reuse the same logic in many different time-related calculations, and the user should not use *ShowValueForDates* directly in a report. The REMOVEFILTERS function removes filters from all tables in the model, because the purpose is to retrieve the last date used in the *Sales* table regardless of filters.

Naming convention

This section describes the naming convention we adopted to reference the time intelligence calculations. A simple categorization shows whether a calculation:

- Shifts over a period of time, for example the same period in the previous year;

- Performs an aggregation, for example year-to-date; or,

- Compares two time periods, for example this year compared to last year.

Acronym	Description	Shift	Aggregation	Comparison
YTD	Year-to-date		X	
QTD	Quarter-to-date		X	
MTD	Month-to-date		X	
MAT	Moving annual total		X	
PY	Previous year	X		
PQ	Previous quarter	X		
PM	Previous month	X		
PYC	Previous year complete	X		
PQC	Previous quarter complete	X		
PMC	Previous month complete	X		
PP	Previous period (automatically selects year, quarter, or month)	X		
PYMAT	Previous year moving annual total	X	X	
YOY	Year-over-year			X
QOQ	Quarter-over-quarter			X
MOM	Month-over-month			X
MATG	Moving annual total growth	X	X	X
POP	Period-over-period (automatically selects year, quarter, or month)			X
PYTD	Previous year-to-date	X	X	
PQTD	Previous quarter-to-date	X	X	
PMTD	Previous month-to-date	X	X	
YOYTD	Year-over-year-to-date	X	X	X
QOQTD	Quarter-over-quarter-to-date	X	X	X
MOMTD	Month-over-month-to-date	X	X	X
YTDOPY	Year-to-date-over-previous-year	X	X	X
QTDOPQ	Quarter-to-date-over-previous-quarter	X	X	X
MTDOPM	Month-to-date-over-previous-month	X	X	X

Computing period-to-date totals

The year-to-date, quarter-to-date, and month-to-date calculations modify the filter context for the *Date* table, showing the values from the beginning of the period up to the last date available in the filter context.

Year-to-date total

The year-to-date aggregates data starting from the first day of the fiscal year, as shown in Figure 5-1.

Year	Sales Amount	Sales YTD (simple)	Sales YTD
⊞ **FY 2008**	**10,265,438.43**	**10,265,438.43**	**10,265,438.43**
⊞ **FY 2009**	**9,874,218.49**	**9,874,218.49**	**9,874,218.49**
⊟ **FY 2010**	**4,522,150.15**	**4,522,150.15**	**4,522,150.15**
Mar 2009	496,137.87	496,137.87	496,137.87
Apr 2009	678,893.22	1,175,031.08	1,175,031.08
May 2009	1,067,165.23	2,242,196.31	2,242,196.31
Jun 2009	872,586.20	3,114,782.51	3,114,782.51
Jul 2009	1,068,396.58	4,183,179.09	4,183,179.09
Aug 2009	338,971.06	4,522,150.15	4,522,150.15
Sep 2009		4,522,150.15	
Oct 2009		4,522,150.15	
Nov 2009		4,522,150.15	
Dec 2009		4,522,150.15	
Jan 2010		4,522,150.15	
Feb 2010		4,522,150.15	
Total	**24,661,807.07**	**4,522,150.15**	**4,522,150.15**

FIGURE 5-1 *Sales YTD (simple)* shows the value for any time period, whereas *Sales YTD* hides the result after the last period with data.

The measure filters all the days less than or equal to the last day visible in the last fiscal year. It also filters the last visible *Fiscal Year Number*.

Measure in the Sales table

```
Sales YTD (simple) :=
VAR LastDayAvailable = MAX ( 'Date'[Day of Fiscal Year Number] )
VAR LastFiscalYearAvailable = MAX ( 'Date'[Fiscal Year Number] )
VAR Result =
    CALCULATE (
        [Sales Amount],
        ALLEXCEPT ( 'Date', 'Date'[Working Day], 'Date'[Day of Week] ),
        'Date'[Day of Fiscal Year Number] <= LastDayAvailable,
        'Date'[Fiscal Year Number] = LastFiscalYearAvailable
    )
RETURN
    Result
```

Because *LastDayAvailable* contains the last date visible in the filter context, *Sales YTD (simple)* shows data even for future dates in the year. We can prevent this behavior in the *Sales YTD* measure by returning a result only when *ShowValueForDates* returns TRUE:

Measure in the Sales table

```
Sales YTD :=
IF (
    [ShowValueForDates],
    VAR LastDayAvailable =  MAX ( 'Date'[Day of Fiscal Year Number] )
    VAR LastFiscalYearAvailable = MAX ( 'Date'[Fiscal Year Number] )
    VAR Result =
        CALCULATE (
            [Sales Amount],
            ALLEXCEPT ( 'Date', 'Date'[Working Day], 'Date'[Day of Week] ),
            'Date'[Day of Fiscal Year Number] <= LastDayAvailable,
            'Date'[Fiscal Year Number] = LastFiscalYearAvailable
        )
    RETURN
        Result
)
```

ALLEXCEPT is required to preserve the filter-safe columns *Working Day* or *Day of Week* in case they are used in the report. To demonstrate this, we created an incorrect measure: *Sales YTD (wrong)*, which removes the filters from the *Date* table by using REMOVEFILTERS instead of ALLEXCEPT. By doing this, the formula loses the filter on *Working Day* used in the columns of the matrix, thus returning an inaccurate result:

Measure in the Sales table

```
Sales YTD (wrong) :=
IF (
    [ShowValueForDates],
    VAR LastDayAvailable =  MAX ( 'Date'[Day of Fiscal Year Number] )
    VAR LastFiscalYearAvailable = MAX ( 'Date'[Fiscal Year Number] )
    VAR Result =
        CALCULATE (
            [Sales Amount],
            REMOVEFILTERS ( 'Date' ),
            'Date'[Day of Fiscal Year Number] <= LastDayAvailable,
            'Date'[Fiscal Year Number] = LastFiscalYearAvailable
        )
    RETURN
        Result
)
```

Figure 5-2 shows the comparison of the correct and incorrect measures.

| Working Day | Non-Working Day | | | Working Day | | |
Year	Sales Amount	Sales YTD	Sales YTD (wrong)	Sales Amount	Sales YTD	Sales YTD (wrong)
⊞ **FY 2008**	**3,007,658.58**	**3,007,658.58**	**10,183,163.40**	**7,257,779.85**	**7,257,779.85**	**10,265,438.43**
⊞ **FY 2009**	**2,468,772.08**	**2,468,772.08**	**9,874,218.49**	**7,405,446.41**	**7,405,446.41**	**9,844,031.13**
⊟ **FY 2010**	**1,341,599.60**	**1,341,599.60**	**4,522,150.15**	**3,180,550.55**	**3,180,550.55**	**4,522,150.15**
Mar 2009	126,171.07	126,171.07	495,527.68	369,966.79	369,966.79	496,137.87
Apr 2009	170,253.83	296,424.91	1,106,238.81	508,639.39	878,606.18	1,175,031.08
May 2009	383,512.28	679,937.19	2,242,196.31	683,652.95	1,562,259.13	2,145,367.97
Jun 2009	218,911.51	898,848.70	3,051,327.04	653,674.69	2,215,933.81	3,114,782.51
Jul 2009	351,178.38	1,250,027.07	4,055,229.07	717,218.20	2,933,152.01	4,183,179.09
Aug 2009	91,572.52	1,341,599.60	4,522,150.15	247,398.54	3,180,550.55	4,522,150.15
Total	**6,818,030.26**	**1,341,599.60**	**4,522,150.15**	**17,843,776.81**	**3,180,550.55**	**4,522,150.15**

FIGURE 5-2 *Sales YTD (wrong)* shows Sales YTD calculated by ignoring the filter over *Working Day*.

The *Sales YTD (wrong)* measure would work well if the *Date* table did not contain any filter-safe columns. The presence of filter-safe columns requires the use of ALLEXCEPT instead of REMOVEFILTERS. We used *Sales YTD* as an example, but the same concept is valid for all the other measures in this pattern.

Quarter-to-date total

Quarter-to-date aggregates data starting from the first day of the fiscal quarter, as shown in Figure 5-3.

Year	Sales Amount	Sales QTD
⊞ **FY 2008**	**10,265,438.43**	**2,248,395.44**
⊞ **FY 2009**	**9,874,218.49**	**2,125,191.33**
⊟ **FY 2010**	**4,522,150.15**	
⊟ **FQ1-2010**	**2,242,196.31**	**2,242,196.31**
Mar 2009	496,137.87	496,137.87
Apr 2009	678,893.22	1,175,031.08
May 2009	1,067,165.23	2,242,196.31
⊟ **FQ2-2010**	**2,279,953.84**	**2,279,953.84**
Jun 2009	872,586.20	872,586.20
Jul 2009	1,068,396.58	1,940,982.78
Aug 2009	338,971.06	2,279,953.84
Total	**24,661,807.07**	

FIGURE 5-3 *Sales QTD* shows the quarter-to-date amount, which is blank for FY 2010 because there is no data in FQ4-2010.

The quarter-to-date value is computed using the same technique as the one used for the year-to-date total. The only difference is the filter on *Fiscal Year Quarter Number* instead of on *Fiscal Year Number*.

Measure in the Sales table

```
Sales QTD :=
IF (
    [ShowValueForDates],
    VAR LastDayAvailable = MAX ( 'Date'[Day of Fiscal Year Number] )
    VAR LastFiscalYearQuarterAvailable = MAX ( 'Date'[Fiscal Year Quarter Number] )
    VAR Result =
        CALCULATE (
            [Sales Amount],
            ALLEXCEPT ( 'Date', 'Date'[Working Day], 'Date'[Day of Week] ),
            'Date'[Day of Fiscal Year Number] <= LastDayAvailable,
            'Date'[Fiscal Year Quarter Number] = LastFiscalYearQuarterAvailable
        )
    RETURN
        Result
)
```

Month-to-date total

The month-to-date aggregates data from the first day of the month, as shown in Figure 5-4.

Year	Sales Amount	Sales MTD
⊞ **FY 2008**	**10,265,438.43**	**600,080.00**
⊞ **FY 2009**	**9,874,218.49**	**622,581.14**
⊟ **FY 2010**	**4,522,150.15**	
⊞ **FQ1-2010**	**2,242,196.31**	**1,067,165.23**
⊟ **FQ2-2010**	**2,279,953.84**	**338,971.06**
⊞ **Jun 2009**	**872,586.20**	**872,586.20**
⊞ **Jul 2009**	**1,068,396.58**	**1,068,396.58**
⊟ **Aug 2009**	**338,971.06**	**338,971.06**
8/1/2009	37,750.10	37,750.10
8/2/2009	8,203.42	45,953.52
8/3/2009	337.68	46,291.20
8/4/2009	4,482.94	50,774.14
8/5/2009	14,319.18	65,093.32
8/6/2009	26,941.94	92,035.26
8/7/2009	2,518.99	94,554.25
8/8/2009	22,619.84	117,174.10
8/9/2009	21,983.18	139,157.27
8/10/2009	4,211.87	143,369.15
8/11/2009	79,245.09	222,614.24
8/12/2009	1,497.50	224,111.74
8/13/2009	13,784.34	237,896.08
8/14/2009	100,059.00	337,955.08
8/15/2009	1,015.98	338,971.06
Total	**24,661,807.07**	

FIGURE 5-4 *Sales MTD* shows the month-to-date amount, which is blank for FY 2010 because there is no data after August 15, 2009.

The month-to-date total is computed with a technique similar to the technique used in year-to-date total and quarter-to-date total. It filters all the days that are less than or equal to the last day visible in the last month. The filters are applied to the *Day of Month Number* and *Year Month Number* columns:

Measure in the Sales table

```
Sales MTD :=
IF (
    [ShowValueForDates],
    VAR LastDayAvailable =  MAX ( 'Date'[Day of Month Number] )
    VAR LastFiscalYearMonthAvailable = MAX ( 'Date'[Year Month Number] )
    VAR Result =
        CALCULATE (
            [Sales Amount],
            ALLEXCEPT ( 'Date', 'Date'[Working Day], 'Date'[Day of Week] ),
            'Date'[Day of Month Number] <= LastDayAvailable,
            'Date'[Year Month Number] = LastFiscalYearMonthAvailable
        )
    RETURN
        Result
)
```

The measure filters *Day of Month Number* instead of *Day of Fiscal Year Number*. The goal is to filter a column with a lower number of unique values, which is a best practice from a query performance standpoint (the quarter-to-date total does not apply this optimization because the performance advantage would be minimal).

Computing period-over-period growth

A common requirement is to compare a time period with the same period in the previous year, quarter, or month. The last month/quarter/year could be incomplete. In order to achieve a fair comparison, the measure should work on an equivalent time period. For these reasons, the calculations shown in this section use the *Date[DateWithSales]* calculated column as described in the article, Hiding future dates for calculations in DAX (https://sql.bi/78171).

Year-over-year growth

Year-over-year compares a time period to its equivalent in the previous year. In this example, data is available until August 15, 2009. For this reason, *Sales PY* shows numbers related to FY 2010, and just considers transactions made before August 15, 2008. Figure 5-5 shows that *Sales Amount* in August 2009 is 721,560.95, whereas *Sales PY* in August 2009 returns 296,529.51 because the measure considers only the sales made up to August 15, 2008.

Year	Sales Amount	Sales PY	Sales YOY	Sales YOY %
⊞ **FY 2008**	**10,265,438.43**			
⊟ **FY 2009**	**9,874,218.49**	**10,265,438.43**	**-391,219.95**	**-3.81%**
⊞ **FQ1-2009**	**2,452,437.65**	**2,409,616.57**	**42,821.08**	**1.78%**
⊟ **FQ2-2009**	**2,457,249.97**	**2,857,682.03**	**-400,432.07**	**-14.01%**
Jun 2008	845,141.60	982,304.46	-137,162.86	-13.96%
Jul 2008	890,547.41	922,542.98	-31,995.58	-3.47%
Aug 2008	721,560.95	952,834.59	-231,273.63	-24.27%
⊞ **FQ3-2009**	**2,839,339.54**	**2,749,744.39**	**89,595.15**	**3.26%**
⊞ **FQ4-2009**	**2,125,191.33**	**2,248,395.44**	**-123,204.11**	**-5.48%**
⊟ **FY 2010**	**4,522,150.15**	**4,484,656.17**	**37,493.98**	**0.84%**
⊞ **FQ1-2010**	**2,242,196.31**	**2,452,437.65**	**-210,241.34**	**-8.57%**
⊟ **FQ2-2010**	**2,279,953.84**	**2,032,218.52**	**247,735.32**	**12.19%**
Jun 2009	872,586.20	845,141.60	27,444.59	3.25%
Jul 2009	1,068,396.58	890,547.41	177,849.17	19.97%
Aug 2009	338,971.06	296,529.51	42,441.55	14.31%
Total	**24,661,807.07**	**14,750,094.60**	**9,911,712.47**	**67.20%**

FIGURE 5-5 For August 2009, *Sales PY* shows the amount for August 1-15, 2008 because there is no data after August 15, 2009.

Sales PY uses a standard technique that shifts the selection by the number of months defined in the *MonthsOffset* variable. In *Sales PY* the variable is set to 12, to move time back by 12 months. The next measures *Sales PQ* and *Sales PM* use the same code, the only difference being the value assigned to *MonthsOffset*.

Sales PY iterates every month active in the filter context. For each month, it checks whether the days selected in the month correspond to all the days of the month, taking into account the filter-safe columns – *Working Day* and *Day of Week* in our example. If all the days are selected, it means that the current filter context includes a full month. Therefore, the filter is shifted back to the previous full month. If not all the days are selected, it means that the user has placed one or more filters on calendar columns that show a partial month. In that case, the selected days are shifted back in the corresponding month of the previous year. The filter over *Date[DateWithSales]* guarantees a fair comparison with the last period with data:

Measure in the Sales table

```
Sales PY :=
VAR MonthsOffset = 12
RETURN IF (
    [ShowValueForDates],
    SUMX (
        SUMMARIZE ( 'Date', 'Date'[Year Month Number] ),
        VAR CurrentYearMonthNumber = 'Date'[Year Month Number]
        VAR PreviousYearMonthNumber = CurrentYearMonthNumber - MonthsOffset
        VAR DaysOnMonth =
            CALCULATE (
                COUNTROWS ( 'Date' ),
                ALLEXCEPT (
                    'Date',
                    'Date'[Year Month Number],    -- Year Month granularity
                    'Date'[Working Day],          -- Filter-safe Date column
                    'Date'[Day of week]           -- Filter-safe Date column
                )
            )
        VAR DaysSelected =
            CALCULATE (
                COUNTROWS ( 'Date' ),
                'Date'[DateWithSales] = TRUE
            )
        RETURN IF (
            DaysOnMonth = DaysSelected,

            -- Selection of all days in the month
            CALCULATE (
                [Sales Amount],
                ALLEXCEPT ( 'Date', 'Date'[Working Day], 'Date'[Day of Week] ),
                'Date'[Year Month Number] = PreviousYearMonthNumber
            ),

            -- Partial selection of days in a month
            CALCULATE (
                [Sales Amount],
                ALLEXCEPT ( 'Date', 'Date'[Working Day], 'Date'[Day of Week] ),
                'Date'[Year Month Number] = PreviousYearMonthNumber,
                CALCULATETABLE (
                    VALUES ( 'Date'[Day of Month Number] ),
                    ALLEXCEPT (                       -- Removes filters from all the
                        'Date',                       -- columns that do not have a day
                        'Date'[Day of Month Number],  -- granularity, keeping only
                        'Date'[Date]                  -- Date and Day of Month Number
                    ),
                    'Date'[Year Month Number] = CurrentYearMonthNumber,
                    'Date'[DateWithSales] = TRUE
                )
            )
        )
    )
)
```

The year-over-year growth is computed as an amount in *Sales YOY,* and as a percentage in *Sales YOY %.* Both measures use *Sales PY* to consider only dates up to August 15, 2009:

Measure in the Sales table

```
Sales YOY :=
VAR ValueCurrentPeriod = [Sales Amount]
VAR ValuePreviousPeriod = [Sales PY]
VAR Result =
    IF (
        NOT ISBLANK ( ValueCurrentPeriod )
            && NOT ISBLANK ( ValuePreviousPeriod ),
        ValueCurrentPeriod - ValuePreviousPeriod
    )
RETURN
    Result
```

Measure in the Sales table

```
Sales YOY % :=
DIVIDE (
    [Sales YOY],
    [Sales PY]
)
```

Quarter-over-quarter growth

Quarter-over-quarter compares a time period with its equivalent in the previous quarter. In this example, data is available until August 15, 2009, which is the first 15 days of the third month in the second quarter of FY 2010. Therefore, *Sales PQ* for August 2009 (the third month of the second quarter) shows sales until May 15, 2009, which is the first 15 days of the third month of the previous quarter. Figure 5-6 shows that *Sales Amount* in May 2009 is 1,067,165.23, whereas *Sales PQ* in August 2009 returns 435,306.10 thus only taking into account sales made up to May 15, 2009.

Year	Sales Amount	Sales PQ	Sales QOQ	Sales QOQ %
⊞ **FY 2008**	**10,265,438.43**	**8,017,042.99**	**2,248,395.44**	**28.05%**
⊞ **FY 2009**	**9,874,218.49**	**9,997,422.60**	**-123,204.11**	**-1.23%**
⊟ **FY 2010**	**4,522,150.15**	**3,735,528.51**	**786,621.64**	**21.06%**
⊟ **FQ1-2010**	**2,242,196.31**	**2,125,191.33**	**117,004.98**	**5.51%**
Mar 2009	496,137.87	921,709.14	-425,571.27	-46.17%
Apr 2009	678,893.22	580,901.05	97,992.17	16.87%
May 2009	1,067,165.23	622,581.14	444,584.09	71.41%
⊟ **FQ2-2010**	**2,279,953.84**	**1,610,337.18**	**669,616.65**	**41.58%**
Jun 2009	872,586.20	496,137.87	376,448.33	75.88%
Jul 2009	1,068,396.58	678,893.22	389,503.36	57.37%
Aug 2009	338,971.06	435,306.10	-96,335.04	-22.13%
Total	**24,661,807.07**	**21,749,994.10**	**2,911,812.97**	**13.39%**

FIGURE 5-6 For August 2009, *Sales PQ shows* the amount for May 1-15, 2009; indeed, there is no data after August 15, 2009.

Sales PQ also uses the technique described for *Sales PY*. The only difference is that *MonthsOffset* is set to 3 months instead of 12:

Measure in the Sales table

```
Sales PQ :=
VAR MonthsOffset = 3
... // Same definition as Sales PY
```

The quarter-over-quarter growth is computed as an amount in *Sales QOQ* and as a percentage in *Sales QOQ %*. Both measures use *Sales PQ* to guarantee a fair comparison:

Measure in the Sales table

```
Sales QOQ :=
VAR ValueCurrentPeriod = [Sales Amount]
VAR ValuePreviousPeriod = [Sales PQ]
VAR Result =
    IF (
        NOT ISBLANK ( ValueCurrentPeriod )
            && NOT ISBLANK ( ValuePreviousPeriod ),
        ValueCurrentPeriod - ValuePreviousPeriod
    )
RETURN
    Result
```

Measure in the Sales table

```
Sales QOQ % :=
DIVIDE (
    [Sales QOQ],
    [Sales PQ]
)
```

Month-over-month growth

Month-over-month compares a time period with its equivalent in the previous month. In this example, data is only available until August 15, 2009. For this reason, *Sales PM* only takes sales between July 1-15, 2009 into account in order to return a value for August 2009. That way, it only returns the corresponding portion of the previous month. Figure 5-7 shows that *Sales Amount* for July 2009 is 1,068,396.58, whereas *Sales PM* of August 2019 returns 584,212.78 – since it only takes into account sales up to July 15, 2009.

Year	Sales Amount	Sales PM	Sales MOM	Sales MOM %
⊞ **FY 2008**	**10,265,438.43**	**9,665,358.44**	**600,080.00**	**6.21%**
⊞ **FY 2009**	**9,874,218.49**	**9,851,717.35**	**22,501.14**	**0.23%**
⊟ **FY 2010**	**4,522,150.15**	**4,321,576.42**	**200,573.73**	**4.64%**
⊟ **FQ1-2010**	**2,242,196.31**	**1,797,612.22**	**444,584.09**	**24.73%**
Mar 2009	496,137.87	622,581.14	-126,443.27	-20.31%
Apr 2009	678,893.22	496,137.87	182,755.35	36.84%
May 2009	1,067,165.23	678,893.22	388,272.01	57.19%
⊟ **FQ2-2010**	**2,279,953.84**	**2,523,964.20**	**-244,010.36**	**-9.67%**
Jun 2009	872,586.20	1,067,165.23	-194,579.03	-18.23%
Jul 2009	1,068,396.58	872,586.20	195,810.38	22.44%
Aug 2009	338,971.06	584,212.78	-245,241.71	-41.98%
Total	**24,661,807.07**	**23,838,652.20**	**823,154.87**	**3.45%**

FIGURE 5-7 For August 2009, *Sales PM* shows the amount in the July 1-15, 2009 time period; indeed, there is no data after August 15, 2009.

Sales PM uses the technique described for *Sales PY*. The only difference is that *MonthsOffset* is set to 1 month instead of 12:

Measure in the Sales table

```
Sales PM :=
VAR MonthsOffset = 1
... // Same definition as Sales PY
```

The month-over-month growth is computed as an amount in *Sales MOM* and as a percentage in *Sales MOM %*. Both measures use *Sales PM* to guarantee a fair comparison:

Measure in the Sales table

```
Sales MOM :=
VAR ValueCurrentPeriod = [Sales Amount]
VAR ValuePreviousPeriod = [Sales PM]
VAR Result =
    IF (
        NOT ISBLANK ( ValueCurrentPeriod )
            && NOT ISBLANK ( ValuePreviousPeriod ),
        ValueCurrentPeriod - ValuePreviousPeriod
    )
RETURN
    Result
```

Measure in the Sales table

```
Sales MOM % :=
DIVIDE (
    [Sales MOM],
    [Sales PM]
)
```

Period-over-period growth

Period-over-period growth automatically selects one of the measures previously described in this section based on the current selection of the visualization. For example, it returns the value of month-over-month growth measures if the visualization displays data at the month level; but it switches to year-over-year growth measures if the visualization shows the total at the year level. The result is visible in Figure 5-8.

Year	Sales Amount	Sales PP	Sales POP	Sales POP %
⊞ **FY 2008**	**10,265,438.43**			
⊟ **FY 2009**	**9,874,218.49**	**10,265,438.43**	**-391,219.95**	**-3.81%**
⊟ **FQ1-2009**	**2,452,437.65**	**2,248,395.44**	**204,042.21**	**9.08%**
Mar 2008	559,538.52	600,080.00	-40,541.48	-6.76%
Apr 2008	999,667.17	559,538.52	440,128.65	78.66%
May 2008	893,231.96	999,667.17	-106,435.21	-10.65%
⊟ **FQ2-2009**	**2,457,249.97**	**2,452,437.65**	**4,812.32**	**0.20%**
Jun 2008	845,141.60	893,231.96	-48,090.36	-5.38%
Jul 2008	890,547.41	845,141.60	45,405.81	5.37%
Aug 2008	721,560.95	890,547.41	-168,986.45	-18.98%
⊞ **FQ3-2009**	**2,839,339.54**	**2,457,249.97**	**382,089.58**	**15.55%**
⊞ **FQ4-2009**	**2,125,191.33**	**2,839,339.54**	**-714,148.21**	**-25.15%**
⊟ **FY 2010**	**4,522,150.15**	**9,874,218.49**	**-5,352,068.33**	**-54.20%**
⊟ **FQ1-2010**	**2,242,196.31**	**2,125,191.33**	**117,004.98**	**5.51%**
Mar 2009	496,137.87	622,581.14	-126,443.27	-20.31%
Apr 2009	678,893.22	496,137.87	182,755.35	36.84%
May 2009	1,067,165.23	678,893.22	388,272.01	57.19%
⊟ **FQ2-2010**	**2,279,953.84**	**2,242,196.31**	**37,757.53**	**1.68%**
Jun 2009	872,586.20	1,067,165.23	-194,579.03	-18.23%
Jul 2009	1,068,396.58	872,586.20	195,810.38	22.44%
Aug 2009	338,971.06	1,068,396.58	-729,425.52	-68.27%
Total	**24,661,807.07**			

FIGURE 5-8 *Sales PP* shows the value of the previous month at the month level, of the previous quarter at the quarter level, and of the previous year at the year level.

The three measures *Sales PP*, *Sales POP*, and *Sales POP %* redirect the evaluation to the corresponding year, quarter, and month measures depending on the level selected in the report. ISINSCOPE detects the level used in the report. The arguments passed to ISINSCOPE are the attributes used in the rows of the Matrix visual in Figure 5-8. The measures are defined as follows:

Measure in the Sales table

```
Sales POP % :=
SWITCH (
    TRUE,
    ISINSCOPE ( 'Date'[Year Month] ), [Sales MOM %],
    ISINSCOPE ( 'Date'[Fiscal Year Quarter] ), [Sales QOQ %],
    ISINSCOPE ( 'Date'[Fiscal Year] ), [Sales YOY %]
)
```

Measure in the Sales table

```
Sales POP :=
SWITCH (
    TRUE,
    ISINSCOPE ( 'Date'[Year Month] ), [Sales MOM],
    ISINSCOPE ( 'Date'[Fiscal Year Quarter] ), [Sales QOQ],
    ISINSCOPE ( 'Date'[Fiscal Year] ), [Sales YOY]
)
```

Measure in the Sales table

```
Sales PP :=
SWITCH (
    TRUE,
    ISINSCOPE ( 'Date'[Year Month] ), [Sales PM],
    ISINSCOPE ( 'Date'[Fiscal Year Quarter] ), [Sales PQ],
    ISINSCOPE ( 'Date'[Fiscal Year] ), [Sales PY]
)
```

Computing period-to-date growth

The growth of a "to-date" measure is the comparison of the "to-date" measure with the same measure over an equivalent period with a specific offset. For example, you can compare a year-to-date aggregation against the year-to-date in the previous year, that is with an offset of one year.

All the measures in this set of calculations take care of partial time periods. Because data is available only until August 15, 2009 in our example, the measures make sure the previous year does not report dates after August 15, 2008.

Year-over-year-to-date growth

Year-over-year-to-date growth compares the year-to-date at a specific date with the year-to-date at an equivalent date in the previous year. Figure 5-9 shows that *Sales PYTD* in FY 2010 is considering only sales until August 15, 2008. For this reason, *Sales YTD* of FQ2-2009 is 4,909,687.61, whereas *Sales PYTD* for FQ2-2010 is less at 4,484,656.17.

Year	Sales Amount	Sales YTD	Sales PYTD	Sales YOYTD	Sales YOYTD %
⊟ **FY 2008**	**10,265,438.43**	**10,265,438.43**			
⊞ **FQ1-2008**	**2,409,616.57**	**2,409,616.57**			
⊞ **FQ2-2008**	**2,857,682.03**	**5,267,298.60**			
⊞ **FQ3-2008**	**2,749,744.39**	**8,017,042.99**			
⊞ **FQ4-2008**	**2,248,395.44**	**10,265,438.43**			
⊟ **FY 2009**	**9,874,218.49**	**9,874,218.49**	**10,265,438.43**	**-391,219.95**	**-3.81%**
⊞ **FQ1-2009**	**2,452,437.65**	**2,452,437.65**	**2,409,616.57**	**42,821.08**	**1.78%**
⊟ **FQ2-2009**	**2,457,249.97**	**4,909,687.61**	**5,267,298.60**	**-357,610.98**	**-6.79%**
Jun 2008	845,141.60	3,297,579.25	3,391,921.03	-94,341.78	-2.78%
Jul 2008	890,547.41	4,188,126.66	4,314,464.01	-126,337.35	-2.93%
Aug 2008	721,560.95	4,909,687.61	5,267,298.60	-357,610.98	-6.79%
⊞ **FQ3-2009**	**2,839,339.54**	**7,749,027.16**	**8,017,042.99**	**-268,015.84**	**-3.34%**
⊞ **FQ4-2009**	**2,125,191.33**	**9,874,218.49**	**10,265,438.43**	**-391,219.95**	**-3.81%**
⊟ **FY 2010**	**4,522,150.15**	**4,522,150.15**	**4,484,656.17**	**37,493.98**	**0.84%**
⊞ **FQ1-2010**	**2,242,196.31**	**2,242,196.31**	**2,452,437.65**	**-210,241.34**	**-8.57%**
⊟ **FQ2-2010**	**2,279,953.84**	**4,522,150.15**	**4,484,656.17**	**37,493.98**	**0.84%**
Jun 2009	872,586.20	3,114,782.51	3,297,579.25	-182,796.74	-5.54%
Jul 2009	1,068,396.58	4,183,179.09	4,188,126.66	-4,947.57	-0.12%
Aug 2009	338,971.06	4,522,150.15	4,484,656.17	37,493.98	0.84%
Total	**24,661,807.07**	**4,522,150.15**	**9,874,218.49**	**-5,352,068.33**	**-54.20%**

FIGURE 5-9 For FQ2-2010, *Sales PYTD* shows the amount of March 1-August 15, 2008 because there is no data after August 15, 2009.

Sales PYTD is like *Sales YTD*, in that it filters the previous value in *Fiscal Year Number* instead of the last year visible in the filter context. The main difference is the evaluation of *LastDayOfFiscalYearAvailable*; it must take into account only dates with sales, and ignore the filter on filter-safe columns which matter in the evaluation of *Sales Amount*:

Measure in the Sales table

```
Sales PYTD :=
IF (
    [ShowValueForDates],
    VAR PreviousFiscalYear = MAX ( 'Date'[Fiscal Year Number] ) - 1
    VAR LastDayOfFiscalYearAvailable =
        CALCULATE (
            MAX ( 'Date'[Day of Fiscal Year Number] ),
            REMOVEFILTERS (                   -- Removes filters from
                'Date'[Working Day],          -- filter-safe columns
                'Date'[Day of Week],          -- to get the last day with data
                'Date'[Day of Week Number]    -- selected in the report
            ),
            'Date'[DateWithSales] = TRUE
        )
    VAR Result =
        CALCULATE (
            [Sales Amount],
            ALLEXCEPT ( 'Date', 'Date'[Working Day], 'Date'[Day of Week] ),
            'Date'[Fiscal Year Number] = PreviousFiscalYear,
            'Date'[Day of Fiscal Year Number] <= LastDayOfFiscalYearAvailable,
            'Date'[DateWithSales] = TRUE
        )
    RETURN
        Result
)
```

Sales YOYTD and *Sales YOYTD %* rely on *Sales PYTD* to guarantee a fair comparison:

Measure in the Sales table

```
Sales YOYTD :=
VAR ValueCurrentPeriod = [Sales YTD]
VAR ValuePreviousPeriod = [Sales PYTD]
VAR Result =
    IF (
        NOT ISBLANK ( ValueCurrentPeriod ) && NOT ISBLANK ( ValuePreviousPeriod ),
        ValueCurrentPeriod - ValuePreviousPeriod
    )
RETURN
    Result
```

Measure in the Sales table

```
Sales YOYTD % :=
DIVIDE (
    [Sales YOYTD],
    [Sales PYTD]
)
```

Quarter-over-quarter-to-date growth

Quarter-over-quarter-to-date growth compares the quarter-to-date at a specific date with the quarter-to-date at an equivalent date in the previous quarter. Figure 5-10 shows that *Sales PQ* in August 2009 is just taking into account transactions performed up to May 15, 2008, to get the corresponding part of the previous quarter. For this reason *Sales QTD* of May 2009 is 2,242,196.31, whereas *Sales PQTD* for August 2009 is lower at 1,610,337.18.

Year	Sales Amount	Sales QTD	Sales PQTD	Sales QOQTD	Sales QOQTD %
⊞ **FY 2008**	**10,265,438.43**	**2,248,395.44**	**2,749,744.39**	**-501,348.95**	**-18.23%**
⊞ **FY 2009**	**9,874,218.49**	**2,125,191.33**	**2,839,339.54**	**-714,148.21**	**-25.15%**
⊟ **FY 2010**	**4,522,150.15**				
⊟ **FQ1-2010**	**2,242,196.31**	**2,242,196.31**	**2,125,191.33**	**117,004.98**	**5.51%**
Mar 2009	496,137.87	496,137.87	921,709.14	-425,571.27	-46.17%
Apr 2009	678,893.22	1,175,031.08	1,502,610.19	-327,579.11	-21.80%
May 2009	1,067,165.23	2,242,196.31	2,125,191.33	117,004.98	5.51%
⊟ **FQ2-2010**	**2,279,953.84**	**2,279,953.84**	**2,242,196.31**	**37,757.53**	**1.68%**
Jun 2009	872,586.20	872,586.20	496,137.87	376,448.33	75.88%
Jul 2009	1,068,396.58	1,940,982.78	1,175,031.08	765,951.69	65.19%
Aug 2009	338,971.06	2,279,953.84	1,610,337.18	669,616.65	41.58%
Total	**24,661,807.07**				

FIGURE 5-10 *Sales PQTD* shows for Aug 2009 the amount of the March 1-May 15, 2009 period, because there is no data after August 15, 2009.

Sales PQTD performs several steps, some of which are somewhat complex. The first two variables are quite easy: *LastMonthSelected* contains the last month visible in the filter context, while *DaysOnLastMonth* contains the number of days in *LastMonthSelected*.

It is important to note that if *DaysOnLastMonth* is equal to *DaysLastMonthSelected*, it means that the current filter context includes the end of a month; therefore the corresponding selection in the previous quarter must include the entire relative month. If *DaysOnLastMonth* is not equal to *DaysLastMonthSelected*, then the filter context is restricting the number of visible days. Consequently, we compute the last day of the month with data and we restrict the result to go only up to the same day number in the relative month within the previous quarter. This calculation takes place in *LastDayOfMonthWithSales*, which contains the last day of the month with sales regardless of the filter-safe columns.

If the selection in the last month includes the whole month, then *LastDayOfMonthWithSales* contains the fixed value 31, which is a number greater than or equal to all the other days of a month. A similar calculation occurs with *LastMonthInQuarterWithSales*, this time with the month number. These two variables are used to compute *FilterQTD* in the last step. *FilterQTD* contains all the pairs of (*FiscalMonthInQuarter*, *FiscalDayInMonth*) that are less than or equal to the pair (*LastMonthInQuarterWithSales*, *LastDayOfMonthWithSales*). By using ISONORAFTER (..., DESC) we obtain the effect we would get by using NOT ISONORAFTER with the default ASC sort order:

Measure in the Sales table

```
Sales PQTD :=
IF (
    [ShowValueForDates],
    VAR LastMonthSelected =
        MAX ( 'Date'[Year Month Number] )
    VAR DaysOnLastMonth =
        CALCULATE (
            COUNTROWS ( 'Date' ),
            ALLEXCEPT ( 'Date', 'Date'[Working Day], 'Date'[Day of week] ),
            'Date'[Year Month Number] = LastMonthSelected
        )
    VAR DaysLastMonthSelected =
        CALCULATE (
            COUNTROWS ( 'Date' ),
            'Date'[DateWithSales] = TRUE,
            'Date'[Year Month Number] = LastMonthSelected
        )
    VAR LastDayOfMonthWithSales =
        MAX (
            -- End of month of any month
            31 * (DaysOnLastMonth = DaysLastMonthSelected),
            -- or last day selected with data
            CALCULATE (
                MAX ( 'Date'[Day of Month Number] ),
                REMOVEFILTERS (                       -- Removes filters from all of the
                    'Date'[Working Day],              -- filter-safe columns
                    'Date'[Day of Week],              -- to get the last day with data
                    'Date'[Day of Week Number] -- selected in the report
                ),
                'Date'[DateWithSales] = TRUE
            )
        )
    VAR LastMonthInQuarterWithSales =
        CALCULATE (
            MAX ( 'Date'[Fiscal Month In Quarter Number] ),
            REMOVEFILTERS (                       -- Removes filters from all of the
                'Date'[Working Day],              -- filter-safe columns
                'Date'[Day of Week],              -- to get the last day with data
                'Date'[Day of Week Number] -- selected in the report
            ),
            'Date'[DateWithSales] = TRUE
        )
    VAR PreviousFiscalYearQuarter =
        MAX ( 'Date'[Fiscal Year Quarter Number] ) - 1
    VAR FilterQTD =
        FILTER (
            ALL ( 'Date'[Fiscal Month In Quarter Number], 'Date'[Day of Month Number] ),
            ISONORAFTER (
                'Date'[Fiscal Month In Quarter Number], LastMonthInQuarterWithSales, DESC,
                'Date'[Day of Month Number], LastDayOfMonthWithSales, DESC
            )
        )
```

```
    VAR Result =
        CALCULATE (
            [Sales Amount],
            ALLEXCEPT ( 'Date', 'Date'[Working Day], 'Date'[Day of Week] ),
            'Date'[Fiscal Year Quarter Number] = PreviousFiscalYearQuarter,
            FilterQTD
        )
    RETURN
        Result
)
```

Sales QOQTD and *Sales QOQTD %* rely on *Sales PQTD* to guarantee a fair comparison:

Measure in the Sales table

```
Sales QOQTD :=
VAR ValueCurrentPeriod = [Sales QTD]
VAR ValuePreviousPeriod = [Sales PQTD]
VAR Result =
    IF (
        NOT ISBLANK ( ValueCurrentPeriod ) && NOT ISBLANK ( ValuePreviousPeriod ),
        ValueCurrentPeriod - ValuePreviousPeriod
    )
RETURN
    Result
```

Measure in the Sales table

```
Sales QOQTD % :=
DIVIDE (
    [Sales QOQTD],
    [Sales PQTD]
)
```

Month-over-month-to-date growth

Month-over-month-to-date growth compares a month-to-date at a specific date with the month-to-date at an equivalent date in the previous month. Figure 5-11 shows that *Sales PMTD* in August 2009 is only taking sales made up to July 15, 2009 into account, to get the corresponding portion of the previous month. For this reason *Sales MTD* of July 2009 is 1,068,396.58, whereas *Sales PMTD* for August 2009 is lower: 584,212.78.

Year	Sales Amount	Sales MTD	Sales PMTD	Sales MOMTD	Sales MOMTD %
⊞ FY 2008	10,265,438.43	600,080.00	656,766.69	-56,686.70	-8.63%
⊞ FY 2009	9,874,218.49	622,581.14	580,901.05	41,680.09	7.18%
⊟ FY 2010	4,522,150.15				
⊟ FQ1-2010	2,242,196.31	1,067,165.23	678,893.22	388,272.01	57.19%
⊞ Mar 2009	496,137.87	496,137.87	622,581.14	-126,443.27	-20.31%
⊞ Apr 2009	678,893.22	678,893.22	496,137.87	182,755.35	36.84%
⊞ May 2009	1,067,165.23	1,067,165.23	678,893.22	388,272.01	57.19%
⊟ FQ2-2010	2,279,953.84	338,971.06	1,068,396.58	-729,425.52	-68.27%
⊞ Jun 2009	872,586.20	872,586.20	1,067,165.23	-194,579.03	-18.23%
⊞ Jul 2009	1,068,396.58	1,068,396.58	872,586.20	195,810.38	22.44%
⊟ Aug 2009	338,971.06	338,971.06	584,212.78	-245,241.71	-41.98%
8/1/2009	37,750.10	37,750.10	64,551.47	-26,801.36	-41.52%
8/2/2009	8,203.42	45,953.52	90,074.93	-44,121.41	-48.98%
8/3/2009	337.68	46,291.20	153,054.51	-106,763.31	-69.76%
8/4/2009	4,482.94	50,774.14	171,310.23	-120,536.08	-70.36%
8/5/2009	14,319.18	65,093.32	248,443.99	-183,350.66	-73.80%
8/6/2009	26,941.94	92,035.26	272,277.89	-180,242.62	-66.20%
8/7/2009	2,518.99	94,554.25	296,502.87	-201,948.61	-68.11%
8/8/2009	22,619.84	117,174.10	315,987.54	-198,813.44	-62.92%
8/9/2009	21,983.18	139,157.27	369,855.95	-230,698.67	-62.38%
8/10/2009	4,211.87	143,369.15	370,871.93	-227,502.78	-61.34%
8/11/2009	79,245.09	222,614.24	422,203.83	-199,589.59	-47.27%
8/12/2009	1,497.50	224,111.74	484,757.36	-260,645.62	-53.77%
8/13/2009	13,784.34	237,896.08	510,540.43	-272,644.35	-53.40%
8/14/2009	100,059.00	337,955.08	533,703.16	-195,748.08	-36.68%
8/15/2009	1,015.98	338,971.06	584,212.78	-245,241.71	-41.98%
Total	24,661,807.07				

FIGURE 5-11 For Aug 2009, *Sales PQTD* shows the amount of the July 1-15, 2009 period, because there is no sales data after August 15, 2009.

Sales PMTD performs several steps, some of which are somewhat complex. The first two variables are quite easy: *LastMonthSelected* contains the last month visible in the filter context, while *DaysOnLastMonth* contains the number of days in *LastMonthSelected*.

It is important to note that if *DaysOnLastMonth* is equal to *DaysLastMonthSelected*, it means that the current filter context includes the end of a month; therefore the corresponding selection in the previous month must include the complete month. If *DaysOnLastMonth* is not equal to *DaysLastMonthSelected*, then the filter context is restricting the number of visible days. Consequently, we compute the last day of the month with data, and we restrict the result to only go up to the same day number in the previous month. This calculation takes place in *LastDayOfMonthWithSales*, which contains the last day of the month with sales data regardless of the filter-safe columns.

If the selection in the last month includes the whole month, then *LastDayOfMonthWithSales* contains the fixed value 31, which is a number greater than or equal to all the other days of a month. The

LastDayOfMonthWithSales is then used to filter the days in the previous month, which is obtained by subtracting one to the value of *LastMonthSelected*:

Measure in the Sales table

```
Sales PMTD :=
IF (
    [ShowValueForDates],
    VAR LastMonthSelected =
        MAX ( 'Date'[Year Month Number] )
    VAR DaysOnLastMonth =
        CALCULATE (
            COUNTROWS ( 'Date' ),
            ALLEXCEPT ( 'Date', 'Date'[Working Day], 'Date'[Day of week] ),
            'Date'[Year Month Number] = LastMonthSelected
        )
    VAR DaysLastMonthSelected =
        CALCULATE (
            COUNTROWS ( 'Date' ),
            'Date'[DateWithSales] = TRUE,
            'Date'[Year Month Number] = LastMonthSelected
        )
    VAR LastDayOfMonthWithSales =
        MAX (
            -- End of month of any month
            31 * (DaysOnLastMonth = DaysLastMonthSelected),
            -- or last day selected with data
            CALCULATE (
                MAX ( 'Date'[Day of Month Number] ),
                REMOVEFILTERS (                    -- Removes filters from all of the
                    'Date'[Working Day],           -- filter-safe columns
                    'Date'[Day of Week],           -- to get the last day with data
                    'Date'[Day of Week Number]     -- selected in the report
                ),
                'Date'[DateWithSales] = TRUE
            )
        )
    VAR PreviousYearMonth =
        LastMonthSelected - 1
    VAR Result =
        CALCULATE (
            [Sales Amount],
            ALLEXCEPT ( 'Date', 'Date'[Working Day], 'Date'[Day of Week] ),
            'Date'[Year Month Number] = PreviousYearMonth,
            'Date'[Day of Month Number] <= LastDayOfMonthWithSales
        )
    RETURN
        Result
)
```

Sales MOMTD and *Sales MOMTD %* rely on the *Sales PMTD* measure to guarantee a fair comparison:

Measure in the Sales table

```
Sales MOMTD :=
VAR ValueCurrentPeriod = [Sales MTD]
VAR ValuePreviousPeriod = [Sales PMTD]
VAR Result =
    IF (
        NOT ISBLANK ( ValueCurrentPeriod )
            && NOT ISBLANK ( ValuePreviousPeriod ),
        ValueCurrentPeriod - ValuePreviousPeriod
    )
RETURN
    Result
```

Measure in the Sales table

```
Sales MOMTD % :=
DIVIDE (
    [Sales MOMTD],
    [Sales PMTD]
)
```

Comparing period-to-date with a previous full period

Comparing a to-date aggregation with the previous full time period is useful when you look at the previous period as a benchmark. Once the current year-to-date reaches 100% of the full previous year, this means you have reached the same performance as the previous full period, hopefully in fewer days.

Year-to-date over the full previous year

The year-to-date over the full previous year compares the year-to-date against the entire previous year. Figure 5-12 shows that in January 2009 (which is close to the end of FY 2009) *Sales YTD* is 10% lower than *Sales Amount* for the entire fiscal year 2008. *Sales YTDOPY %* provides an immediate comparison of the year-to-date with the total of the previous year; it shows growth over the previous year when the percentage is positive, which never happens in this example.

Year	Sales Amount	Sales YTD	Sales PYC	Sales YTDOPY	Sales YTDOPY %
⊞ **FY 2008**	**10,265,438.43**	**10,265,438.43**			
⊟ **FY 2009**	**9,874,218.49**	**9,874,218.49**	**10,265,438.43**	**-391,219.95**	**-3.81%**
⊞ **FQ1-2009**	**2,452,437.65**	**2,452,437.65**	**10,265,438.43**	**-7,813,000.78**	**-76.11%**
⊞ **FQ2-2009**	**2,457,249.97**	**4,909,687.61**	**10,265,438.43**	**-5,355,750.82**	**-52.17%**
⊞ **FQ3-2009**	**2,839,339.54**	**7,749,027.16**	**10,265,438.43**	**-2,516,411.28**	**-24.51%**
⊟ **FQ4-2009**	**2,125,191.33**	**9,874,218.49**	**10,265,438.43**	**-391,219.95**	**-3.81%**
⊞ **Dec 2008**	**921,709.14**	**8,670,736.30**	**10,265,438.43**	**-1,594,702.13**	**-15.53%**
⊞ **Jan 2009**	**580,901.05**	**9,251,637.35**	**10,265,438.43**	**-1,013,801.08**	**-9.88%**
⊟ **Feb 2009**	**622,581.14**	**9,874,218.49**	**10,265,438.43**	**-391,219.95**	**-3.81%**
2/1/2009	3,503.04	9,255,140.39	10,265,438.43	-1,010,298.04	-9.84%
2/2/2009	55,182.37	9,310,322.76	10,265,438.43	-955,115.68	-9.30%
2/3/2009	19,696.81	9,330,019.57	10,265,438.43	-935,418.86	-9.11%
Total	**24,661,807.07**	**4,522,150.15**			

FIGURE 5-12 *Sales YTDOPY %* shows a negative value corresponding to the missing percentage of *Sales YTD* to reach the total *Sales Amount* of the previous year.

The year-to-date-over-previous-year growth is computed by the *Sales YTDOPY* and *Sales YTDOPY %* measures; these rely on the *Sales YTD* measure to compute the year-to-date value, and on the *Sales PYC* measure to get the sales amount of the entire previous year:

Measure in the Sales table

```
Sales PYC :=
IF (
    [ShowValueForDates] && HASONEVALUE ( 'Date'[Fiscal Year Number] ),
    VAR PreviousFiscalYear = MAX ( 'Date'[Fiscal Year Number] ) - 1
    VAR Result =
        CALCULATE (
            [Sales Amount],
            ALLEXCEPT ( 'Date', 'Date'[Working Day], 'Date'[Day of Week] ),
            'Date'[Fiscal Year Number] = PreviousFiscalYear
        )
    RETURN
        Result
)
```

Measure in the Sales table

```
Sales YTDOPY :=
VAR ValueCurrentPeriod = [Sales YTD]
VAR ValuePreviousPeriod = [Sales PYC]
VAR Result =
    IF (
        NOT ISBLANK ( ValueCurrentPeriod )
            && NOT ISBLANK ( ValuePreviousPeriod ),
        ValueCurrentPeriod - ValuePreviousPeriod
    )
RETURN
    Result
```

Measure in the Sales table

```
Sales YTDOPY % :=
DIVIDE (
    [Sales YTDOPY],
    [Sales PYC]
)
```

Quarter-to-date over the full previous quarter

The quarter-to-date over the full previous quarter compares the quarter-to-date against the entire previous quarter. Figure 5-13 shows that *Sales QTD* surpassed the total *Sales Amount* for FQ1-2008 only in August 2008. *Sales QTDOPQ %* provides an immediate comparison of the quarter-to-date with the total of the previous quarter; it shows growth over the previous quarter when the percentage is positive.

Year	Sales Amount	Sales QTD	Sales PQC	Sales QTDOPQ	Sales QTDOPQ %
⊞ FY 2008	10,265,438.43	2,248,395.44			
⊟ FY 2009	9,874,218.49	2,125,191.33			
⊞ FQ1-2009	2,452,437.65	2,452,437.65	2,248,395.44	204,042.21	9.08%
⊟ FQ2-2009	2,457,249.97	2,457,249.97	2,452,437.65	4,812.32	0.20%
⊞ Jun 2008	845,141.60	845,141.60	2,452,437.65	-1,607,296.05	-65.54%
⊞ Jul 2008	890,547.41	1,735,689.01	2,452,437.65	-716,748.64	-29.23%
⊞ Aug 2008	721,560.95	2,457,249.97	2,452,437.65	4,812.32	0.20%
⊞ FQ3-2009	2,839,339.54	2,839,339.54	2,457,249.97	382,089.58	15.55%
⊞ FQ4-2009	2,125,191.33	2,125,191.33	2,839,339.54	-714,148.21	-25.15%
⊞ FY 2010	4,522,150.15				
Total	24,661,807.07				

FIGURE 5-13 *Sales QTDOPQ %* shows a positive percentage in August 2008, when *Sales QTD* is greater than the *Sales Amount* for FQ1-2008.

The quarter-to-date-over-previous-quarter growth is computed with the *Sales QTDOPQ* and *Sales QTDOPQ %* measures; these rely on the *Sales QTD* measure to compute the quarter-to-date value and on the *Sales PQC* measure to get the sales amount of the entire previous quarter:

Measure in the Sales table

```
Sales PQC :=
IF (
    [ShowValueForDates] && HASONEVALUE ( 'Date'[Fiscal Year Quarter Number] ),
    VAR PreviousFiscalYearQuarter = MAX ( 'Date'[Fiscal Year Quarter Number] ) - 1
    VAR Result =
        CALCULATE (
            [Sales Amount],
            ALLEXCEPT ( 'Date', 'Date'[Working Day], 'Date'[Day of Week] ),
            'Date'[Fiscal Year Quarter Number] = PreviousFiscalYearQuarter
        )
    RETURN
        Result
)
```

Measure in the Sales table

```
Sales QTDOPQ :=
VAR ValueCurrentPeriod = [Sales QTD]
VAR ValuePreviousPeriod = [Sales PQC]
VAR Result =
    IF (
        NOT ISBLANK ( ValueCurrentPeriod )
            && NOT ISBLANK ( ValuePreviousPeriod ),
        ValueCurrentPeriod - ValuePreviousPeriod
    )
RETURN
    Result
```

Measure in the Sales table

```
Sales QTDOPQ % :=
DIVIDE (
    [Sales QTDOPQ],
    [Sales PQC]
)
```

Month-to-date over the full previous month

The month-to-date over the full previous month compares the month-to-date against the entire previous month. Figure 5-14 shows that *Sales MTD* during April 2008 surpasses the total *Sales Amount* for March 2008. *Sales MTDOPM %* provides an immediate comparison of the month-to-date with the total of the previous month; it shows growth over the previous month when the percentage is positive as is the case starting April 19, 2008.

Year	Sales Amount	Sales MTD	Sales PMC	Sales MTDOPM	Sales MTDOPM %
⊞ **FY 2008**	**10,265,438.43**	**600,080.00**			
⊟ **FY 2009**	**9,874,218.49**	**622,581.14**			
⊟ **FQ1-2009**	**2,452,437.65**	**893,231.96**			
⊞ **Mar 2008**	**559,538.52**	**559,538.52**	**600,080.00**	**-40,541.48**	**-6.76%**
⊟ **Apr 2008**	**999,667.17**	**999,667.17**	**559,538.52**	**440,128.65**	**78.66%**
4/1/2008	13,557.28	13,557.28	559,538.52	-545,981.24	-97.58%
4/2/2008	9,065.70	22,622.98	559,538.52	-536,915.54	-95.96%
4/3/2008	31,133.36	53,756.34	559,538.52	-505,782.18	-90.39%
4/4/2008	24,122.38	77,878.72	559,538.52	-481,659.80	-86.08%
4/5/2008	43,296.27	121,174.99	559,538.52	-438,363.53	-78.34%
4/6/2008	47,212.95	168,387.94	559,538.52	-391,150.58	-69.91%
4/7/2008	29,037.93	197,425.87	559,538.52	-362,112.65	-64.72%
4/8/2008	16,857.91	214,283.78	559,538.52	-345,254.74	-61.70%
4/9/2008	1,561.36	215,845.13	559,538.52	-343,693.39	-61.42%
4/10/2008	378.55	216,223.68	559,538.52	-343,314.84	-61.36%
4/11/2008	42,286.96	258,510.64	559,538.52	-301,027.88	-53.80%
4/12/2008	38,560.80	297,071.44	559,538.52	-262,467.08	-46.91%
4/13/2008	6,511.76	303,583.20	559,538.52	-255,955.32	-45.74%
4/14/2008	57,402.73	360,985.93	559,538.52	-198,552.59	-35.49%
4/15/2008	56,015.09	417,001.02	559,538.52	-142,537.50	-25.47%
4/16/2008	35,205.64	452,206.66	559,538.52	-107,331.86	-19.18%
4/17/2008	59,922.32	512,128.98	559,538.52	-47,409.54	-8.47%
4/18/2008	22,947.10	535,076.08	559,538.52	-24,462.44	-4.37%
4/19/2008	61,693.67	596,769.75	559,538.52	37,231.23	6.65%
4/20/2008	75 526.00	672 295.74	559 538.52	112 757.22	20.15%

FIGURE 5-14 *Sales MTDOPM %* shows a positive percentage starting from April 19, 2008, when *Sales MTD* starts to be greater than the *Sales Amount* for March 2008.

The month-to-date-over-previous-month growth is computed with the *Sales MTDOPM %* and *Sales*

MTDOPM measures; these rely on the *Sales MTD* measure to compute the month-to-date value and on the *Sales PMC* measure to get the sales amount of the entire previous month:

Measure in the Sales table

```
Sales PMC :=
IF (
    [ShowValueForDates] && HASONEVALUE ( 'Date'[Year Month Number] ),
    VAR PreviousFiscalYearMonth = MAX ( 'Date'[Year Month Number] ) - 1
    VAR Result =
        CALCULATE (
            [Sales Amount],
            ALLEXCEPT ( 'Date', 'Date'[Working Day], 'Date'[Day of Week] ),
            'Date'[Year Month Number] = PreviousFiscalYearMonth
        )
    RETURN
        Result
)
```

Measure in the Sales table

```
Sales MTDOPM :=
VAR ValueCurrentPeriod = [Sales MTD]
VAR ValuePreviousPeriod = [Sales PMC]
VAR Result =
    IF (
        NOT ISBLANK ( ValueCurrentPeriod )
            && NOT ISBLANK ( ValuePreviousPeriod ),
        ValueCurrentPeriod - ValuePreviousPeriod
    )
RETURN
    Result
```

Measure in the Sales table

```
Sales MTDOPM % :=
DIVIDE (
    [Sales MTDOPM],
    [Sales PMC]
)
```

Using moving annual total calculations

A common way of aggregating data over several months is by using the moving annual total instead of the year-to-date. The moving annual total includes the last 12 months of data. For example, the moving annual total for March 2008 includes data from April 2007 to March 2008.

Moving annual total

Sales MAT computes the moving annual total, as shown in Figure 5-15. The same report also shows *Sales MAT (364):* it is a similar measure with the difference that it uses the last 364 days (corresponding to the last 52 weeks), instead of a full year.

Year	Sales Amount	Sales MAT	Sales MAT (364)	Sales PYMAT	Sales MATG	Sales MATG %
⊟ **FY 2008**	**10,265,438.43**	**10,265,438.43**	**10,265,438.43**			
Mar 2007	345,319.01	345,319.01	345,319.01			
Apr 2007	1,128,104.82	1,473,423.82	1,473,423.82			
May 2007	936,192.74	2,409,616.57	2,409,616.57			
Jun 2007	982,304.46	3,391,921.03	3,391,921.03			
Jul 2007	922,542.98	4,314,464.01	4,314,464.01			
Aug 2007	952,834.59	5,267,298.60	5,267,298.60			
Sep 2007	1,009,868.98	6,277,167.58	6,277,167.58			
Oct 2007	914,273.54	7,191,441.12	7,191,441.12			
Nov 2007	825,601.87	8,017,042.99	8,017,042.99			
Dec 2007	991,548.75	9,008,591.74	9,008,591.74			
Jan 2008	656,766.69	9,665,358.44	9,665,358.44			
Feb 2008	600,080.00	10,265,438.43	10,265,438.43			
⊟ **FY 2009**	**9,874,218.49**	**9,874,218.49**	**9,870,214.20**	**10,265,175.01**	**-390,956.52**	**-3.81%**
Mar 2008	559,538.52	10,479,657.94	10,380,441.35	345,319.01	10,134,338.94	2934.78%
Apr 2008	999,667.17	10,351,220.30	10,333,107.23	1,473,423.82	8,877,796.47	602.53%
May 2008	893,231.96	10,308,259.51	10,282,508.05	2,409,616.57	7,898,642.95	327.80%
Jun 2008	845,141.60	10,171,096.65	10,156,747.85	3,391,921.03	6,779,175.62	199.86%
Jul 2008	890,547.41	10,139,101.08	10,113,997.26	4,314,464.01	5,824,637.07	135.00%
Aug 2008	721,560.95	9,907,827.45	9,823,064.26	5,267,298.60	4,640,528.85	88.10%
Sep 2008	963,437.23	9,861,395.69	9,841,335.70	6,277,167.58	3,584,228.11	57.10%
Oct 2008	719,792.99	9,666,915.14	9,602,561.78	7,191,441.12	2,475,474.02	34.42%
Nov 2008	1,156,109.32	9,997,422.60	9,805,709.73	8,017,042.99	1,980,379.60	24.70%
Dec 2008	921,709.14	9,927,582.99	9,893,708.52	9,008,591.74	918,991.25	10.20%
Jan 2009	580,901.05	9,851,717.35	9,819,091.08	9,665,358.44	186,358.91	1.93%
Feb 2009	622,581.14	9,874,218.49	9,870,214.20	10,265,175.01	-390,956.52	-3.81%
Total	**24,661,807.07**	**4,522,150.15**	**4,508,845.09**	**9,874,218.49**	**-5,352,068.33**	**-54.20%**

FIGURE 5-15 *Sales MAT* in March 2008 aggregates *Sales Amount* from April 2007 to March 2008.

The *Sales MAT* measure defines a range over the *Date[Date]* column that includes the days of one complete year starting from the last day in the filter context:

Measure in the Sales table

```
Sales MAT :=
IF (
    [ShowValueForDates],
    VAR LastDayMAT =  MAX ( 'Date'[Sequential Day Number] )
    VAR FirstDayMAT = INT ( EDATE ( LastDayMAT + 1, -12 ) )
    VAR Result =
        CALCULATE (
            [Sales Amount],
            ALLEXCEPT ( 'Date', 'Date'[Working Day], 'Date'[Day of Week] ),
            'Date'[Sequential Day Number] >= FirstDayMAT
                && 'Date'[Sequential Day Number] <= LastDayMAT
        )
    RETURN
        Result
)
```

Sales MAT (364) does not correspond to a total over the year. Yet, it is a good measure to evaluate trends over time or in a chart because it always includes the same number of days and an integer number of weeks. Consequently, the days of the week are evenly represented in the result. The measure defines a range over the *Date[Date]* column that includes the last 364 days from the last day in the filter context:

Measure in the Sales table

```
Sales MAT (364) :=
IF (
    [ShowValueForDates],
    VAR LastDayMAT =  MAX ( 'Date'[Sequential Day Number] )
    VAR FirstDayMAT = LastDayMAT - 363
    VAR Result =
        CALCULATE (
            [Sales Amount],
            ALLEXCEPT ( 'Date', 'Date'[Working Day], 'Date'[Day of Week] ),
            'Date'[Sequential Day Number] >= FirstDayMAT
                && 'Date'[Sequential Day Number] <= LastDayMAT
        )
    RETURN
        Result
)
```

Moving annual total growth

The moving annual total growth is computed with the *Sales PYMAT*, *Sales MATG*, and *Sales MATG %* measures, which rely on the *Sales MAT* measure. The *Sales MAT* measure provides a correct value one year after the first sale ever (when it collects one full year of data), and it is not protected in case the current time period is shorter than a full year. For example, the amount for the fiscal year 2010 of *Sales PYMAT* is 9,874,218.49, which corresponds to the *Sales Amount* of FY 2009 as shown in Figure 5-16. When compared with sales in FY 2010, this produces a comparison of less than 6 months – data being only available until August 15, 2009 – with the full fiscal year 2009. Similarly, you can see that *Sales MATG %* starts in FY 2009 with very high values and stabilizes after a year. This behavior is by design: the moving annual total is usually computed at the month or day granularity to show trends in a chart.

Year	Sales Amount	Sales MAT	Sales PYMAT	Sales MATG	Sales MATG %
⊞ **2007**	**9,008,591.74**	**9,008,591.74**			
⊟ **2008**	**9,927,582.99**	**9,927,582.99**	**9,008,591.74**	**918,991.25**	**10.20%**
Jan 2008	656,766.69	9,665,358.44			
Feb 2008	600,080.00	10,265,438.43			
Mar 2008	559,538.52	10,479,657.94	345,319.01	10,134,338.94	2934.78%
Apr 2008	999,667.17	10,351,220.30	1,473,423.82	8,877,796.47	602.53%
May 2008	893,231.96	10,308,259.51	2,409,616.57	7,898,642.95	327.80%
Jun 2008	845,141.60	10,171,096.65	3,391,921.03	6,779,175.62	199.86%
Jul 2008	890,547.41	10,139,101.08	4,314,464.01	5,824,637.07	135.00%
Aug 2008	721,560.95	9,907,827.45	5,267,298.60	4,640,528.85	88.10%
Sep 2008	963,437.23	9,861,395.69	6,277,167.58	3,584,228.11	57.10%
Oct 2008	719,792.99	9,666,915.14	7,191,441.12	2,475,474.02	34.42%
Nov 2008	1,156,109.32	9,997,422.60	8,017,042.99	1,980,379.60	24.70%
Dec 2008	921,709.14	9,927,582.99	9,008,591.74	918,991.25	10.20%
⊟ **2009**	**5,725,632.34**	**5,725,632.34**	**9,927,582.99**	**-4,201,950.65**	**-42.33%**
Jan 2009	580,901.05	9,851,717.35	9,665,358.44	186,358.91	1.93%
Feb 2009	622,581.14	9,874,218.49	10,265,438.43	-391,219.95	-3.81%
Mar 2009	496,137.87	9,810,817.83	10,479,657.94	-668,840.11	-6.38%
Apr 2009	678,893.22	9,490,043.88	10,351,220.30	-861,176.42	-8.32%
May 2009	1,067,165.23	9,663,977.15	10,308,259.51	-644,282.36	-6.25%
Jun 2009	872,586.20	9,691,421.74	10,171,096.65	-479,674.91	-4.72%
Jul 2009	1,068,396.58	9,869,270.91	10,139,101.08	-269,830.17	-2.66%
Aug 2009	338,971.06	9,486,681.02	9,907,827.45	-421,146.43	-4.25%
Total	**24,661,807.07**		**5,725,632.34**		

FIGURE 5-16 *Sales MATG %* shows the growth between *Sales MAT* and *Sales PYMAT* as a percentage.

The measures are defined as follows:

Measure in the Sales table

```
Sales PYMAT :=
IF (
    [ShowValueForDates],
    VAR LastDayAvailable = MAX ( 'Date'[Sequential Day Number] )
    VAR LastDayMAT =  INT ( EDATE ( LastDayAvailable, -12 ) )
    VAR FirstDayMAT = INT ( EDATE ( LastDayAvailable + 1, -24 ) )
    VAR Result =
        CALCULATE (
            [Sales Amount],
            ALLEXCEPT ( 'Date', 'Date'[Working Day], 'Date'[Day of Week] ),
            'Date'[Sequential Day Number] >= FirstDayMAT
                && 'Date'[Sequential Day Number] <= LastDayMAT
        )
    RETURN
        Result
)
```

Measure in the Sales table

```
Sales MATG :=
VAR ValueCurrentPeriod = [Sales MAT]
VAR ValuePreviousPeriod = [Sales PYMAT]
VAR Result =
    IF (
        NOT ISBLANK ( ValueCurrentPeriod )
            && NOT ISBLANK ( ValuePreviousPeriod ),
        ValueCurrentPeriod - ValuePreviousPeriod
    )
RETURN
    Result
```

Measure in the Sales table

```
Sales MATG % :=
DIVIDE (
    [Sales MATG],
    [Sales PYMAT]
)
```

The *Sales PYMAT* measure can also be written using the last 364 days, similar to *Sales MAT (364)* – the difference between *Sales PYMAT* and *Sales PYMAT (364)* is the evaluation of the *FirstDayMAT* and the *LastDayMAT* variables:

Measure in the Sales table

```
Sales PYMAT (364) :=
IF (
    [ShowValueForDates],
    VAR LastDayAvailable = MAX ( 'Date'[Sequential Day Number] )
    VAR LastDayMAT = LastDayAvailable - 364
    VAR FirstDayMAT = LastDayMAT - 363
    VAR Result =
        CALCULATE (
            [Sales Amount],
            ALLEXCEPT ( 'Date', 'Date'[Working Day], 'Date'[Day of Week] ),
            'Date'[Sequential Day Number] >= FirstDayMAT
                && 'Date'[Sequential Day Number] <= LastDayMAT
        )
    RETURN
        Result
)
```

Moving averages

The moving average is typically used to display trends in line charts. Figure 5-17 includes the moving average of *Sales Amount* over 30 days (*Sales AVG 30D*), three months (*Sales AVG 3M*), and a year (*Sales AVG 1Y*).

Sales AVG 30D, Sales AVG 3M and Sales AVG 1Y by Date

FIGURE 5-17 *Sales AVG 30D*, *Sales AVG 3M*, and *Sales AVG 1Y* show the moving average over 30 days, three months, and one year, respectively.

Moving average 30 days

The *Sales AVG 30D* measure computes the moving average over 30 days by iterating a list of the last 30 dates obtained in the *Period30D* variable. It does so by fetching the dates visible included in the last 30 days, while ignoring dates without sales and taking into account filters applied by filter-safe columns in the *Date* table:

Measure in the Sales table

```
Sales AVG 30D :=
IF (
    [ShowValueForDates],
    VAR LastDayMAT =
        MAX ( 'Date'[Sequential Day Number] )
    VAR FirstDayMAT = LastDayMAT - 29
    VAR Period30D =
        CALCULATETABLE (
            VALUES ( 'Date'[Sequential Day Number] ),
            ALLEXCEPT (
                'Date',
                'Date'[Working Day],
                'Date'[Day of Week]
            ),
            'Date'[Sequential Day Number] >= FirstDayMAT
                && 'Date'[Sequential Day Number] <= LastDayMAT,
            'Date'[DateWithSales] = TRUE
        )
    VAR FirstDayWithData =
        CALCULATE (
            INT ( MIN ( Sales[Order Date] ) ),
            REMOVEFILTERS ()
        )
    VAR FirstDayInPeriod =
        MINX (
            Period30D,
            'Date'[Sequential Day Number]
        )
    VAR Result =
        IF (
            FirstDayWithData <= FirstDayInPeriod,
            CALCULATE (
                AVERAGEX ( Period30D, [Sales Amount] ),
                REMOVEFILTERS ( 'Date' )
            )
        )
    RETURN
        Result
)
```

This pattern is very flexible because it also works for non-additive measures. With that said, for a regular additive calculation *Result* can be implemented using a different and faster formula:

```
VAR Result =
    IF (
        FirstDayWithData <= FirstDayInPeriod,
        CALCULATE (
            DIVIDE (
                [Sales Amount],
                DISTINCTCOUNT ( Sales[Order Date] )
            ),
            Period30D,
            REMOVEFILTERS ( 'Date' )
        )
    )
```

Moving average 3 months

The *Sales AVG 3M* measure computes the moving average over three months. It iterates a list of the dates in the last three months obtained in the *Period3M* variable by getting the dates visible included in the last 3 months, by ignoring dates without sales and by taking into account the filters applied by filter-safe columns in the *Date* table:

Measure in the Sales table

```
Sales AVG 3M :=
IF (
    [ShowValueForDates],
    VAR LastDayMAT =
        MAX ( 'Date'[Sequential Day Number] )
    VAR FirstDayMAT =
        INT ( EDATE ( LastDayMAT + 1, -3 ) )
    VAR Period3M =
        CALCULATETABLE (
            VALUES ( 'Date'[Sequential Day Number] ),
            ALLEXCEPT (
                'Date',
                'Date'[Working Day],
                'Date'[Day of Week]
            ),
            'Date'[Sequential Day Number] >= FirstDayMAT
                && 'Date'[Sequential Day Number] <= LastDayMAT,
            'Date'[DateWithSales] = TRUE
        )
    VAR FirstDayWithData =
        CALCULATE (
            INT ( MIN ( Sales[Order Date] ) ),
            REMOVEFILTERS ()
        )
    VAR FirstDayInPeriod =
        MINX (
            Period3M,
            'Date'[Sequential Day Number]
        )
    VAR Result =
        IF (
            FirstDayWithData <= FirstDayInPeriod,
            CALCULATE (
                AVERAGEX ( Period3M, [Sales Amount] ),
                REMOVEFILTERS ( 'Date' )
            )
        )
    RETURN
        Result
)
```

For simple additive measures, the pattern based on DIVIDE which is shown for the moving average over 30 days can also be used for the average over three months.

Moving average 1 year

The *Sales AVG 1Y* measure computes the moving average over one year by iterating a list of the dates in the last year in the *Period1Y* variable. It does so by getting the dates visible included in the last year, by ignoring dates without sales and by taking into account filters applied by filter-safe columns in the *Date* table:

Measure in the Sales table

```
Sales AVG 1Y :=
IF (
    [ShowValueForDates],
    VAR LastDayMAT =
        MAX ( 'Date'[Sequential Day Number] )
    VAR FirstDayMAT =
        INT ( EDATE ( LastDayMAT + 1, 12 ) )
    VAR Period1Y =
        CALCULATETABLE (
            VALUES ( 'Date'[Sequential Day Number] ),
            ALLEXCEPT (
                'Date',
                'Date'[Working Day],
                'Date'[Day of Week]
            ),
            'Date'[Sequential Day Number] >= FirstDayMAT
                && 'Date'[Sequential Day Number] <= LastDayMAT,
            'Date'[DateWithSales] = TRUE
        )
    VAR FirstDayWithData =
        CALCULATE (
            INT ( MIN ( Sales[Order Date] ) ),
            REMOVEFILTERS ()
        )
    VAR FirstDayInPeriod =
        MINX (
            Period1Y,
            'Date'[Sequential Day Number]
        )
    VAR Result =
        IF (
            FirstDayWithData <= FirstDayInPeriod,
            CALCULATE (
                AVERAGEX ( Period1Y, [Sales Amount] ),
                REMOVEFILTERS ( 'Date' )
            )
        )
    RETURN
        Result
)
```

For simple additive measures, the pattern based on DIVIDE shown for the moving average over 30 days can also be used for the average over one year.

## CHAPTER 6

Comparing different time periods

Download sample files: **https://sql.bi/dax-205**

This pattern is a useful technique to compare the value of a measure in different time periods. For example, we can compare the sales of the last month against a user-defined period. The two time periods might have a different number of days, like comparing one month against a full year. When the durations of both time periods are different, we should adjust the values to make a fair comparison.

Pattern description

The user selects two different time periods (current, comparison) through slicers. The report in Figure 6-1 shows the sales in the current period and in a comparison period. The sales of the comparison period must be adjusted using the number of days in each period as the allocation factor.

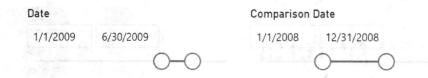

Date		Comparison Date	
1/1/2009	6/30/2009	1/1/2008	12/31/2008

Brand	Sales Amount	Comparison Sales Amount	Adjusted Comp. Sales Amount
A. Datum	208,121.82	463,721.61	229,326.80
Adventure Works	323,361.68	892,674.52	441,459.26
Contoso	1,139,254.63	2,369,167.68	1,171,637.57
Fabrikam	801,063.81	1,993,123.48	985,670.35
Litware	619,337.99	1,487,846.74	735,793.06
Northwind Traders	80,485.83	469,827.70	232,346.49
Proseware	368,315.93	763,586.23	377,620.51
Southridge Video	170,545.60	294,635.04	145,707.49
Tailspin Toys	73,753.75	97,193.87	48,065.82
The Phone Company	248,293.85	355,629.36	175,871.35
Wide World Importers	285,729.80	740,176.76	366,043.70
Total	**4,318,264.70**	**9,927,582.99**	**4,909,542.41**

FIGURE 6-1 The report shows sales in different periods, alongside the adjusted comparison value.

In order to enable the choice of two different time periods, the model must contain two date tables: one to select the current period, one to select the comparison period. As shown in Figure 6-2, the additional *Comparison Date* table is linked to the original *Date* table with an inactive relationship: This simplifies the handling of relationships with other fact tables.

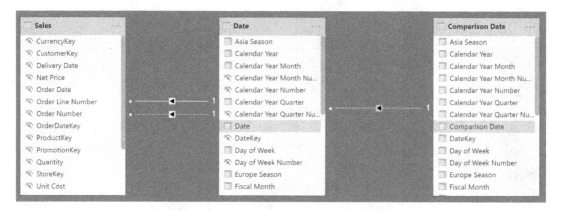

FIGURE 6-2 The *Comparison Date* table is linked to the *Date* table through an inactive relationship.

When a measure evaluates an expression filtered by the *Comparison Date* table, the measure expression activates the relationship between *Comparison Date* and *Date*; it also performs a REMOVEFILTERS on the *Date* table in order to use - in *Sales* - the filter from *Comparison Date*. Using this model, any existing measure can compute the value in the current or comparison period with a simple change in the active relationship.

The following is the definition of the *Comparison Sales Amount* measure:

Measure in the Sales table

```
Comparison Sales Amount :=
VAR ComparisonPeriod =
    CALCULATETABLE (
        VALUES ( 'Date'[Date] ),
        REMOVEFILTERS ( 'Date' ),
        USERELATIONSHIP ( 'Date'[Date], 'Comparison Date'[Comparison Date] )
    )
VAR Result =
    CALCULATE (
        [Sales Amount],
        ComparisonPeriod
    )
RETURN
    Result
```

In order to adjust the value of *Comparison Sales Amount*, we need an allocation method. In the example we use the number of days in the two periods as the allocation factor; the business logic may dictate that only working days should be used for the adjustment. In other words, a different adjustment logic is possible and depends on the business requirements.

In this example of adjustment logic, if the comparison period has more days than the current time period, we reduce the *Comparison Sales Amount* result according to the ratio between the number of days in the two periods:

Measure in the Sales table

```
Adjusted Comp. Sales Amount :=
VAR CurrentPeriod =
    VALUES ( 'Date'[Date] )
VAR ComparisonPeriod =
    CALCULATETABLE (
        VALUES ( 'Date'[Date] ),
        REMOVEFILTERS ( 'Date' ),
        USERELATIONSHIP ( 'Date'[Date], 'Comparison Date'[Comparison Date] )
    )
VAR ComparisonSales =
    CALCULATE ( [Sales Amount], ComparisonPeriod )
VAR DaysInCurrentPeriod =
    COUNTROWS ( CurrentPeriod )
VAR DaysInComparisonPeriod =
    COUNTROWS ( ComparisonPeriod )
VAR DailyComparisonSales =
    DIVIDE (
        ComparisonSales,
        DaysInComparisonPeriod
    )
VAR Result =
    DaysInCurrentPeriod * DailyComparisonSales
RETURN
    Result
```

## CHAPTER 7

Semi-additive calculations

Download sample files: **https://sql.bi/dax-206**

Calculations reporting values at the start or the end of a time period are quite the challenge for any BI developer, and DAX is no exception. These measures are not hard to compute; the complicated part is understanding the desired behavior precisely. These calculations do not work by aggregating values throughout the entire period, as you would typically do for sales amounts. Instead, the calculations should return the value at the beginning or the end of a selected time period. These calculations are also known as semi-additive calculations. They are semi-additive because they do sum up specific attributes, like customers, but not over other attributes, like dates, all the while reporting the value at the beginning or end of the period.

As an example, we use a model that contains the current balance of bank accounts. Over the customers, the measure must be additive: the total balance for all customers is the sum of the balance for each customer. Nevertheless, when aggregating over time you cannot use the SUM function. The balance of a quarter is not the sum of individual monthly balances. Instead, the measure should report the last balance of the quarter.

There are many details that need to be addressed when defining the meaning of *start or end of the period*. This is the reason why this pattern contains many examples. We suggest you read all of them, so to better understand the subtle differences between the different examples before choosing the correct one for your specific scenario.

Introduction

You have a model containing the balance of a few customers' accounts. For each date, the number reported is the balance at that date. There are different reporting dates for different customers, as shown in Figure 7-1.

Date	Katie Jordan	Luis Bonifaz	Maurizio Macagno
12/27/2019	2,130.00		
12/31/2019		1,823.00	1,750.00
01/31/2020	1,687.00	1,470.00	1,500.00
02/29/2020	2,812.00	2,450.00	2,500.00
03/31/2020	3,737.00	3,430.00	3,500.00
04/30/2020	2,250.00	1,960.00	2,000.00
05/31/2020	2,025.00	1,764.00	1,800.00
06/30/2020	2,700.00	2,352.00	2,400.00
07/31/2020	3,600.00	3,136.00	3,200.00
08/31/2020	5,062.00	4,410.00	4,500.00
09/30/2020	2,812.00	2,450.00	2,500.00
10/31/2020		1,960.00	2,000.00
11/15/2020		1,813.00	
11/18/2020			1,850.00

FIGURE 7-1 The source table contains customer account balances at different dates.

Because of the nature of the data, you cannot aggregate using SUM over time. Instead, you need to aggregate values at the month, quarter, and year level using the first or the last value of the period. Before looking at the code, you need to focus on some important details by answering the following questions:

1. What is the end balance of Katie Jordan's account for 2020? Her last available balance is on September 30, so should we consider this to be the final value for 2020? Similarly, is the balance of Luis Bonifaz's account zero or is it 1,813.00 at the end of 2020?

2. What is the total end balance over all three customers for 2020? Is it only the amount on Maurizio Macagno's account – because his balance is the last one – or is it the sum of the last balance for each customer, at their respective dates?

3. What is the starting balance of 2020 for Luis Bonifaz? Is it the balance on January 1, 2020 or December 27/31, 2019?

As you see, there are multiple valid answers to each question, and none of them is more correct than the others. Depending on your requirements, you choose the pattern that best fits your needs. Indeed, all these patterns compute the balance at the start or the end of a period. The only and very relevant difference, is in the definition of what *end of period* means.

First and last date

The first and last date pattern is the simplest one. However, it can only be adopted in the few scenarios where the dataset always contains data at the beginning and at the end of each time period. The formula returns the balance using the first and last date of the *Date* table in the current filter context, regardless of whether data is present on the given date. If there is no balance on that date, its result is blank:

Measure in the Balances table

```
Balance LastDate :=
CALCULATE (
    SUM ( Balances[Balance] ),
    LASTDATE ( 'Date'[Date] )    -- Use FIRSTDATE for Balance FirstDate
)
```

This formula produces the result in Figure 7-2.

Year	Quarter	Month	Katie Jordan	Luis Bonifaz	Maurizio Macagno
⊞ **CY 2019**				**1,823.00**	**1,750.00**
⊟ CY 2020	⊟ Q1	January	1,687.00	1,470.00	1,500.00
		February	2,812.00	2,450.00	2,500.00
		March	3,737.00	3,430.00	3,500.00
		Total	**3,737.00**	**3,430.00**	**3,500.00**
	⊟ Q2	April	2,250.00	1,960.00	2,000.00
		May	2,025.00	1,764.00	1,800.00
		June	2,700.00	2,352.00	2,400.00
		Total	**2,700.00**	**2,352.00**	**2,400.00**
	⊟ Q3	July	3,600.00	3,136.00	3,200.00
		August	5,062.00	4,410.00	4,500.00
		September	2,812.00	2,450.00	2,500.00
		Total	**2,812.00**	**2,450.00**	**2,500.00**
	⊟ Q4	October		1,960.00	2,000.00
		Total			
	Total				
Total					

FIGURE 7-2 The report shows the balance on the last date from the Date table.

On months where data is not available on the last day of the month, the measure reports a blank. This pattern is the fastest among our many examples, but it only returns accurate results when data is stored on each and every day, or at least at the end of each and every time period. Therefore, it is the preferred pattern for example in financial applications where data is reported once every month.

First and last date with data

In this pattern, the formula searches the last date for which there is data in the current filter context. Therefore, instead of finding the last date in the *Date* table, it searches for the last date in the *Balances* table. The result is visible in Figure 7-3.

Year	Quarter	Month	Katie Jordan	Luis Bonifaz	Maurizio Macagno	Total
⊞ **CY 2019**				**1,823.00**	**1,750.00**	**3,573.00**
⊟ CY 2020	⊟ Q1	January	1,687.00	1,470.00	1,500.00	**4,657.00**
		February	2,812.00	2,450.00	2,500.00	**7,762.00**
		March	3,737.00	3,430.00	3,500.00	**10,667.00**
		Total	**3,737.00**	**3,430.00**	**3,500.00**	**10,667.00**
	⊟ Q2	April	2,250.00	1,960.00	2,000.00	**6,210.00**
		May	2,025.00	1,764.00	1,800.00	**5,589.00**
		June	2,700.00	2,352.00	2,400.00	**7,452.00**
		Total	**2,700.00**	**2,352.00**	**2,400.00**	**7,452.00**
	⊟ Q3	July	3,600.00	3,136.00	3,200.00	**9,936.00**
		August	5,062.00	4,410.00	4,500.00	**13,972.00**
		September	2,812.00	2,450.00	2,500.00	**7,762.00**
		Total	**2,812.00**	**2,450.00**	**2,500.00**	**7,762.00**
	⊟ Q4	October		1,960.00	2,000.00	**3,960.00**
		November			1,850.00	**1,850.00**
		Total			**1,850.00**	**1,850.00**
	Total				**1,850.00**	**1,850.00**
Total					**1,850.00**	**1,850.00**

FIGURE 7-3 The report shows the balance on the last date with data.

The formula first finds the last date to use, by finding the last date for which there is any data in the model. It then applies it as a filter:

Measure in the Balances table

```
Balance LastDateWithData :=
VAR MaxBalanceDate =
    CALCULATE (
        MAX ( Balances[Date] ),     -- Use MIN for Balance FirstDateWithData
        ALLEXCEPT (
            Balances,               -- Remove filters from the Balances expanded table
            'Date'                  -- but not from the date
        )
    )
VAR Result =
    CALCULATE (
        SUM ( Balances[Balance] ),
        'Date'[Date] = MaxBalanceDate
    )
RETURN
    Result
```

It is worth noting the presence of ALLEXCEPT in the calculation of *MaxBalanceDate*. ALLEXCEPT is needed in order to avoid obtaining the last date in the current context, which would use a different date for each customer and at the total level. ALLEXCEPT guarantees that the same date is used for all the customers. In your specific scenario you might have to modify that filter to accommodate for further requirements.

In case you do not want to use the same date for all the customers, but instead you want to use a different date for every customer and total those values, then this is not the right pattern. You need to use the *First and last date by customer* pattern.

An alternative implementation of this pattern based on LASTNONBLANK is less efficient. It should only be used when the business logic determining whether a date should be considered or not is more complex than just looking at the presence of a row in the *Balances* table. For example, the following implementation produces the same result as the previous formula with slower execution time and larger memory consumption at query time:

Measure in the Balances table

```
Slower Balance LastDateWithData :=
CALCULATE (
    SUM ( Balances[Balance] ),
    LASTNONBLANK (
        'Date'[Date],
        CALCULATE ( SUM ( Balances[Balance] ) )
    )
)
```

First and last date by customer

If the dataset contains different dates for each customer - or in general for each entity - then the pattern is different. For each customer you must compute its last date, obtaining the subtotals by summing partial results across other non-date attributes. The result is visible in Figure 7-4.

Year	Quarter	Month	Katie Jordan	Luis Bonifaz	Maurizio Macagno	Total
⊞ **CY 2019**			**2,130.00**	**1,823.00**	**1,750.00**	**5,703.00**
⊟ CY 2020	⊟ Q1	January	1,687.00	1,470.00	1,500.00	**4,657.00**
		February	2,812.00	2,450.00	2,500.00	**7,762.00**
		March	3,737.00	3,430.00	3,500.00	**10,667.00**
		Total	**3,737.00**	**3,430.00**	**3,500.00**	**10,667.00**
	⊟ Q2	April	2,250.00	1,960.00	2,000.00	**6,210.00**
		May	2,025.00	1,764.00	1,800.00	**5,589.00**
		June	2,700.00	2,352.00	2,400.00	**7,452.00**
		Total	**2,700.00**	**2,352.00**	**2,400.00**	**7,452.00**
	⊟ Q3	July	3,600.00	3,136.00	3,200.00	**9,936.00**
		August	5,062.00	4,410.00	4,500.00	**13,972.00**
		September	2,812.00	2,450.00	2,500.00	**7,762.00**
		Total	**2,812.00**	**2,450.00**	**2,500.00**	**7,762.00**
	⊟ Q4	October		1,960.00	2,000.00	**3,960.00**
		November		1,813.00	1,850.00	**3,663.00**
		Total		**1,813.00**	**1,850.00**	**3,663.00**
	Total		**2,812.00**	**1,813.00**	**1,850.00**	**6,475.00**
Total			**2,812.00**	**1,813.00**	**1,850.00**	**6,475.00**

FIGURE 7-4 The report shows the balance on the last date by customer, with the Total column computed as sum.

The *Balance LastDateByCustomer* measure provides the desired result:

Measure in the Balances table

```
Balance LastDateByCustomer :=
VAR MaxBalanceDates =
    ADDCOLUMNS (
        SUMMARIZE (              -- Retrieve the customers
            Balances,            -- from the Balances table
            Customers[Name]
        ),
        "@MaxBalanceDate", CALCULATE (      -- Compute for each customer
            MAX ( Balances[Date] )          -- their last date
        )
    )
VAR MaxBalanceDatesWithLineage =
    TREATAS (                    -- Changes the lineage of MaxBalanceDates
        MaxBalanceDates,         -- so to make it filter
        Customers[Name],         -- the customer name
        'Date'[Date]             -- and the date
    )
VAR Result =
    CALCULATE (
        SUM ( Balances[Balance] ),
        MaxBalanceDatesWithLineage
    )
RETURN
    Result
```

In the calculation of the max balance date per customer, you might need to modify the filter further. For example, Katie Jordan reports a blank in Q4 because her last date happens to be outside of the current filter context by quarter. If you need to modify this behavior and report the balance of September forward to the end of the year – and in following years if present – this is achieved by the *Balance LastDateByCustomerEver* measure:

Measure in the Balances table

```
Balance LastDateByCustomerEver :=
VAR MaxDate =
    MAX ( 'Date'[Date] )
VAR MaxBalanceDates =
    CALCULATETABLE (
        ADDCOLUMNS (
            SUMMARIZE ( Balances, Customers[Name] ),
            "@MaxBalanceDate", CALCULATE ( MAX ( Balances[Date] ) )
        ),
        'Date'[Date] <= MaxDate
    )
VAR MaxBalanceDatesWithLineage =
    TREATAS ( MaxBalanceDates, Customers[Name], 'Date'[Date] )
VAR Result =
    CALCULATE ( SUM ( Balances[Balance] ), MaxBalanceDatesWithLineage )
RETURN
    Result
```

You can see the result of the *Balance LastDateByCustomerEver* measure in Figure 7-5.

Year	Quarter	Month	Katie Jordan	Luis Bonifaz	Maurizio Macagno	Total
⊞ **CY 2019**			**2,130.00**	**1,823.00**	**1,750.00**	**5,703.00**
⊟ CY 2020	⊟ Q1	January	1,687.00	1,470.00	1,500.00	**4,657.00**
		February	2,812.00	2,450.00	2,500.00	**7,762.00**
		March	3,737.00	3,430.00	3,500.00	**10,667.00**
		Total	**3,737.00**	**3,430.00**	**3,500.00**	**10,667.00**
	⊟ Q2	April	2,250.00	1,960.00	2,000.00	**6,210.00**
		May	2,025.00	1,764.00	1,800.00	**5,589.00**
		June	2,700.00	2,352.00	2,400.00	**7,452.00**
		Total	**2,700.00**	**2,352.00**	**2,400.00**	**7,452.00**
	⊟ Q3	July	3,600.00	3,136.00	3,200.00	**9,936.00**
		August	5,062.00	4,410.00	4,500.00	**13,972.00**
		September	2,812.00	2,450.00	2,500.00	**7,762.00**
		Total	**2,812.00**	**2,450.00**	**2,500.00**	**7,762.00**
	⊟ Q4	October	2,812.00	1,960.00	2,000.00	**6,772.00**
		November	2,812.00	1,813.00	1,850.00	**6,475.00**
		December	2,812.00	1,813.00	1,850.00	**6,475.00**
		Total	**2,812.00**	**1,813.00**	**1,850.00**	**6,475.00**
	Total		**2,812.00**	**1,813.00**	**1,850.00**	**6,475.00**
Total			**2,812.00**	**1,813.00**	**1,850.00**	**6,475.00**

FIGURE 7-5 The last balance of each customer is moved forward to the end of the year.

Opening and closing balance

The previous calculations to compute a measure for the last date of a period can be used to compute the closing balance; depending on the requirements, you can choose the right technique. However, the same techniques for the first date cannot be used to retrieve the opening balance, which is usually the closing balance of the previous period.

The *Opening* measure filters the day before the first day of the period, whereas the *Closing* measure just gets the last date of the period using LASTDATE:

Measure in the Balances table

```
Opening :=
VAR PreviousClosingDate =
    DATEADD ( FIRSTDATE ( 'Date'[Date] ), -1, DAY )
VAR Result =
    CALCULATE ( SUM ( Balances[Balance] ), PreviousClosingDate )
RETURN
    Result
```

Measure in the Balances table

```
Closing :=
CALCULATE (
    SUM ( Balances[Balance] ),
    LASTDATE ( 'Date'[Date] )
)
```

The result in Figure 7-6 shows that Katie Jordan has an empty opening balance, because the assumption is that the lack of data on December 31, 2019 reflects an empty balance. Indeed, the behavior of the *Opening* and *Closing* measures corresponds to the **First and last date** pattern - which only works if there is a balance for all the customers on the last day of the month.

Year	Quarter	Month	Katie Jordan		Luis Bonifaz		Total	
			Opening	Closing	Opening	Closing	**Opening**	**Closing**
⊞ **CY 2019**							**1,823.00**	**1,823.00**
⊟ CY 2020	⊟ Q1	January		1,687.00	1,823.00	1,470.00	**1,823.00**	**3,157.00**
		February	1,687.00	2,812.00	1,470.00	2,450.00	**3,157.00**	**5,262.00**
		March	2,812.00	3,737.00	2,450.00	3,430.00	**5,262.00**	**7,167.00**
		Total		3,737.00	1,823.00	3,430.00	**1,823.00**	**7,167.00**
	⊟ Q2	April	3,737.00	2,250.00	3,430.00	1,960.00	**7,167.00**	**4,210.00**
		May	2,250.00	2,025.00	1,960.00	1,764.00	**4,210.00**	**3,789.00**
		June	2,025.00	2,700.00	1,764.00	2,352.00	**3,789.00**	**5,052.00**
		Total	3,737.00	2,700.00	3,430.00	2,352.00	**7,167.00**	**5,052.00**
	⊟ Q3	July	2,700.00	3,600.00	2,352.00	3,136.00	**5,052.00**	**6,736.00**
		August	3,600.00	5,062.00	3,136.00	4,410.00	**6,736.00**	**9,472.00**
		September	5,062.00	2,812.00	4,410.00	2,450.00	**9,472.00**	**5,262.00**
		Total	2,700.00	2,812.00	2,352.00	2,450.00	**5,052.00**	**5,262.00**
	⊟ Q4	October	2,812.00		2,450.00	1,960.00	**5,262.00**	**1,960.00**
		November			1,960.00		**1,960.00**	
		Total	2,812.00		2,450.00		**5,262.00**	
	Total				1,823.00		**1,823.00**	
Total								

FIGURE 7-6 Opening and closing balances using standard DAX functions.

DAX also provides time intelligence functions for the same purpose, which are specific for each time period considered - month, quarter, or year. However, these functions are slower and they require a more complex DAX syntax in the measures. They should only be considered for measures that always return the opening or closing balance of a specific granularity regardless of the selection. For example, a measure returns the opening or closing balance of the corresponding year, and though the selection might very well be month or quarter the measure would still return the yearly balance.

In our sample report, the CLOSINGBALANCEMONTH can be used instead of CLOSINGBALANCEQUARTER and CLOSINGBALANCEYEAR because they provide the same result for the last month of a period. Similarly, OPENINGBALANCEMONTH can be used instead of OPENINGBALANCEQUARTER and OPENINGBALANCEYEAR because they provide the same result for the first month of a period.

The definition of the *Opening Dax* and *Closing Dax* measures is the following:

Measure in the Balances table

```
Opening Dax :=
OPENINGBALANCEMONTH (
    SUM ( Balances[Balance] ),
    'Date'[Date]
)
```

Measure in the Balances table

```
Closing Dax :=
CLOSINGBALANCEMONTH (
    SUM ( Balances[Balance] ),
    'Date'[Date]
)
```

If you are looking to achieve a behavior matching the **First and last date by customer** pattern, then you need *Balance LastDateByCustomerEver* for the implementation of the *Closing Ever* measure. With a small variation of the same pattern, we are also able to implement the *Opening Ever* measure:

Measure in the Balances table

```
Opening Ever :=
VAR MinDate =
    MIN ( 'Date'[Date] )
VAR MaxBalanceDates =
    CALCULATETABLE (
        ADDCOLUMNS (
            SUMMARIZE ( Balances, Customers[Name] ),
            "@MaxBalanceDate", CALCULATE ( MAX ( Balances[Date] ) )
        ),
        'Date'[Date] < MinDate
    )
VAR MaxBalanceDatesWithLineage =
    TREATAS ( MaxBalanceDates, Customers[Name], 'Date'[Date] )
VAR Result =
    CALCULATE ( SUM ( Balances[Balance] ), MaxBalanceDatesWithLineage )
RETURN
    Result
```

Measure in the Balances table

```
Closing Ever :=
VAR MaxDate =
    MAX ( 'Date'[Date] )
VAR MaxBalanceDates =
    CALCULATETABLE (
        ADDCOLUMNS (
            SUMMARIZE ( Balances, Customers[Name] ),
            "@MaxBalanceDate", CALCULATE ( MAX ( Balances[Date] ) )
        ),
        'Date'[Date] <= MaxDate
    )
VAR MaxBalanceDatesWithLineage =
    TREATAS ( MaxBalanceDates, Customers[Name], 'Date'[Date] )
VAR Result =
    CALCULATE ( SUM ( Balances[Balance] ), MaxBalanceDatesWithLineage )
RETURN
    Result
```

Figure 7-7 shows that the opening account balance for Katie Jordan for January and Q1 2020 corresponds to the last account balance available in 2019.

Year	Quarter	Month	Katie Jordan Opening Ever	Closing Ever	Luis Bonifaz Opening Ever	Closing Ever	Total Opening Ever	Closing Ever
⊞ **CY 2019**				2,130.00		1,823.00		3,953.00
⊟ CY 2020	⊟ Q1	January	2,130.00	1,687.00	1,823.00	1,470.00	**3,953.00**	**3,157.00**
		February	1,687.00	2,812.00	1,470.00	2,450.00	**3,157.00**	**5,262.00**
		March	2,812.00	3,737.00	2,450.00	3,430.00	**5,262.00**	**7,167.00**
		Total	**2,130.00**	**3,737.00**	**1,823.00**	**3,430.00**	**3,953.00**	**7,167.00**
	⊟ Q2	April	3,737.00	2,250.00	3,430.00	1,960.00	**7,167.00**	**4,210.00**
		May	2,250.00	2,025.00	1,960.00	1,764.00	**4,210.00**	**3,789.00**
		June	2,025.00	2,700.00	1,764.00	2,352.00	**3,789.00**	**5,052.00**
		Total	**3,737.00**	**2,700.00**	**3,430.00**	**2,352.00**	**7,167.00**	**5,052.00**
	⊟ Q3	July	2,700.00	3,600.00	2,352.00	3,136.00	**5,052.00**	**6,736.00**
		August	3,600.00	5,062.00	3,136.00	4,410.00	**6,736.00**	**9,472.00**
		September	5,062.00	2,812.00	4,410.00	2,450.00	**9,472.00**	**5,262.00**
		Total	**2,700.00**	**2,812.00**	**2,352.00**	**2,450.00**	**5,052.00**	**5,262.00**
	⊟ Q4	October	2,812.00	2,812.00	2,450.00	1,960.00	**5,262.00**	**4,772.00**
		November	2,812.00	2,812.00	1,960.00	1,813.00	**4,772.00**	**4,625.00**
		December	2,812.00	2,812.00	1,813.00	1,813.00	**4,625.00**	**4,625.00**
		Total	**2,812.00**	**2,812.00**	**2,450.00**	**1,813.00**	**5,262.00**	**4,625.00**
	Total		**2,130.00**	**2,812.00**	**1,823.00**	**1,813.00**	**3,953.00**	**4,625.00**
Total				2,812.00		1,813.00		4,625.00

FIGURE 7-7 Opening and closing balances using custom calculations.

Growth in period

A useful application of this pattern is to compute the variation of a measure over a selected time period. In our example, we want to compute a new measure that produces the difference between the opening and the closing balance for a selected period. The result is visible in Figure 7-8.

Year	Quarter	Month	Katie Jordan	Luis Bonifaz	Maurizio Macagno	Total
⊟ CY 2020	⊟ Q1	January		-353.00	-250.00	**1,084.00**
		February	1,125.00	980.00	1,000.00	**3,105.00**
		March	925.00	980.00	1,000.00	**2,905.00**
		Total		**1,607.00**	**1,750.00**	**7,094.00**
	⊟ Q2	April	-1,487.00	-1,470.00	-1,500.00	**-4,457.00**
		May	-225.00	-196.00	-200.00	**-621.00**
		June	675.00	588.00	600.00	**1,863.00**
		Total	**-1,037.00**	**-1,078.00**	**-1,100.00**	**-3,215.00**
	⊟ Q3	July	900.00	784.00	800.00	**2,484.00**
		August	1,462.00	1,274.00	1,300.00	**4,036.00**
		September	-2,250.00	-1,960.00	-2,000.00	**-6,210.00**
		Total	**112.00**	**98.00**	**100.00**	**310.00**
	⊟ Q4	October		-490.00	-500.00	**-3,802.00**
		Total				
	Total					
Total						

FIGURE 7-8 The report shows the difference between the opening and closing balance.

The *Growth* measure uses the *Opening* and *Closing* measures based on the ***First and last date*** pattern:

Measure in the Balances table

```
Growth :=
VAR Opening = [Opening] -- Use Opening Ever if required
VAR Closing = [Closing] -- Use Closing Ever if required
VAR Delta =
    IF (
        NOT ISBLANK ( Opening ) && NOT ISBLANK ( Closing ),
        Closing - Opening
    )
VAR Result =
    IF ( Delta <> 0, Delta )
RETURN
    Result
```

As suggested in the comments of the *Growth* measure, it is possible to use a different logic to obtain the opening and closing balance – by changing the assignment to the *Opening* and *Closing* variables.

For example, the *Growth Ever* measure uses the *Opening Ever* and *Closing Ever* measures described in the **Opening and closing balance** pattern:

Measure in the Balances table

```
Growth Ever :=
VAR Opening = [Opening Ever]
VAR Closing = [Closing Ever]
VAR Delta =
    IF (
        NOT ISBLANK ( Opening ) && NOT ISBLANK ( Closing ),
        Closing - Opening
    )
VAR Result =
    IF ( Delta <> 0, Delta )
RETURN
    Result
```

The result of the *Growth Ever* measure is visible in Figure 7-9.

Year	Quarter	Month	Katie Jordan	Luis Bonifaz	Maurizio Macagno	**Total**
⊟ CY 2020	⊟ Q1	January	-443.00	-353.00	-250.00	**-1,046.00**
		February	1,125.00	980.00	1,000.00	**3,105.00**
		March	925.00	980.00	1,000.00	**2,905.00**
		Total	**1,607.00**	**1,607.00**	**1,750.00**	**4,964.00**
	⊟ Q2	April	-1,487.00	-1,470.00	-1,500.00	**-4,457.00**
		May	-225.00	-196.00	-200.00	**-621.00**
		June	675.00	588.00	600.00	**1,863.00**
		Total	**-1,037.00**	**-1,078.00**	**-1,100.00**	**-3,215.00**
	⊟ Q3	July	900.00	784.00	800.00	**2,484.00**
		August	1,462.00	1,274.00	1,300.00	**4,036.00**
		September	-2,250.00	-1,960.00	-2,000.00	**-6,210.00**
		Total	**112.00**	**98.00**	**100.00**	**310.00**
	⊟ Q4	October		-490.00	-500.00	**-990.00**
		November		-147.00	-150.00	**-297.00**
		Total		**-637.00**	**-650.00**	**-1,287.00**
	Total		**682.00**	**-10.00**	**100.00**	**772.00**
Total						

FIGURE 7-9 The report shows the difference between the opening and closing balance (Ever version).

Cumulative total

Download sample files: **https://sql.bi/dax-207**

The cumulative total pattern allows you to perform calculations such as running totals. You can use it to implement warehouse stock and balance sheet calculations using the original transactions instead of using snapshots of data over time.

For example, in order to create an *Inventory* table that shows the stock of each product for every month, you can make that calculation by using the original warehouse movements table, without processing and consolidating data in advance.

The most frequent case of running total is the sum of all the transactions made before a given date. But that same calculation can be used in any scenario where you accumulate values over any sortable column. This is shown in one of the examples of this pattern.

Basic scenario

We want to create a measure that sums all the sales values up to a certain date. The result should look like what we show in Figure 8-1.

Calendar Year	Sales Amount	Sales Amount RT
⊟ **CY 2007**	**2,269,589.88**	**2,269,589.88**
January	215,754.71	215,754.71
February	257,542.99	473,297.70
March	242,605.59	715,903.28
April	265,692.45	981,595.74
May	207,498.55	1,189,094.28
June	159,126.64	1,348,220.92
July	173,146.57	1,521,367.49
August	126,567.16	1,647,934.65
September	184,964.07	1,832,898.72
October	109,991.38	1,942,890.09
November	173,942.39	2,116,832.48
December	152,757.40	2,269,589.88
⊟ **CY 2008**	**919,946.50**	**3,189,536.38**
January	57,707.97	2,327,297.85
February	43,405.70	2,370,703.55
March	72,736.13	2,443,439.68

FIGURE 8-1 The running total accumulates values from the beginning of time up to the current date.

The formula must compute the value of *Sales Amount* for all the dates which are less than or equal to the last one visible in the current filter context. The code also performs an additional check to avoid showing values for future dates – that is, when the minimum visible date is greater than the last date with sales:

Measure in the Sales table

```
Sales Amount RT :=
VAR LastVisibleDate =
    MAX ( 'Date'[Date] )
VAR FirstVisibleDate =
    MIN ( 'Date'[Date] )
VAR LastDateWithSales =
    CALCULATE (
        MAX ( 'Sales'[Order Date] ),
        REMOVEFILTERS ()    -- Use ALL ( Sales ) if REMOVEFILTERS () and ALL ()
                            -- are not available
    )
VAR Result =
    IF (
        FirstVisibleDate <= LastDateWithSales,
        CALCULATE (
            [Sales Amount],
            'Date'[Date] <= LastVisibleDate
        )
    )
RETURN
    Result
```

It is important that the *Date* table is marked as a date table for the formula to work. If not, it is necessary to add REMOVEFILTERS over *Date* as a further CALCULATE modifier, when applying the filter in the computation of the *Result* variable:

```
VAR Result =
    IF (
        FirstVisibleDate <= LastDateWithSales,
        CALCULATE (
            [Sales Amount],
            'Date'[Date] <= LastVisibleDate,
            REMOVEFILTERS ( 'Date' )
        )
    )
```

Either way, the formula of *Sales Amount RT* applies a filter to the *Date* table which removes all the previously existing filters on *Date*. Therefore, if you need to keep existing filters on some columns of the *Date* table, you must apply these filters again. For example, in order to compute the running total while keeping the filter on the day of the week, the code would be the following:

Measure in the Sales table

```
RT Weekdays :=
VAR LastVisibleDate =
    MAX ( 'Date'[Date] )
VAR FirstVisibleDate =
    MIN ( 'Date'[Date] )
VAR LastDateWithSales =
    CALCULATE (
        MAX ( 'Sales'[Order Date] ),
        REMOVEFILTERS ()
    )
VAR Result =
    IF (
        FirstVisibleDate <= LastDateWithSales,
        CALCULATE (
            [Sales Amount],
            'Date'[Date] <= LastVisibleDate,
            VALUES ( 'Date'[Day of Week] )
        )
    )
RETURN
    Result
```

Figure 8-2 shows the two measures *RT Weekdays* and *Sales Amount RT* running totals behaving differently, with and without the additional filter on the days of the week.

Day of Week	Calendar Year	Sales Amount	RT Weekdays	Sales Amount RT
☐ Sunday	⊟ **CY 2007**	**61,702.69**	**61,702.69**	**87,874.44**
☑ Monday	January	9,211.90	9,211.90	9,480.30
☑ Tuesday	February	3,110.90	12,322.80	17,659.46
☑ Wednesday	March	8,766.20	21,089.00	26,527.86
☑ Thursday	April	2,149.97	23,238.97	28,860.95
☑ Friday	May	4,828.72	28,067.68	33,773.00
☐ Saturday	June	3,154.40	31,222.08	36,997.33
	July	194.46	31,416.54	42,425.50

FIGURE 8-2 The *RT Weekdays* measure accurately accumulates values from the beginning of time taking into account just the selected days; *Sales Amount RT* ignores the selection made in the *Day of Week* slicer.

Cumulative total on columns that can be sorted

Most commonly, the cumulative total pattern tends to be based on the date. That said, that pattern can be adapted to any column that can be sorted. The option for a column to be sorted is important because the code includes a "less than or equal to" condition to work properly.

As an example, we classify customers based on sales volumes, according to the table in Figure 8-3.

Customer class number	Customer class	Min Sales	Max Sales
1	Silver	0.00	5,000.00
2	Gold	5,000.00	50,000.00
3	Platinum	50,000.00	150,000.00
4	Titanium	150,000.00	30,591,343.98

FIGURE 8-3 The configuration table controls how to cluster customers based on sales.

We want to produce a report that shows the sales amount of each class along with the running total of sales by customer class, as you can see in Figure 8-4.

Customer Class	Sales Amount	# Customers	Sales Amount RT Class
Silver	6,903,526.35	18,434	6,903,526.35
Gold	5,037,811.96	282	11,941,338.31
Platinum	9,542,895.77	107	21,484,234.08
Titanium	9,107,109.89	46	30,591,343.98
Total	**30,591,343.98**	**18,869**	**30,591,343.98**

FIGURE 8-4 The running total computes the sales amount including "previous" classes of customers.

The code requires us to pay special attention to the Sort by Column. Indeed, because the column shown in the report is *Customer[Customer Class]* and ordering is achieved by *Customer[Customer Class Number]*, the calculation must override the filters on both columns even though the entire calculation is only based on the class number:

Measure in the Sales table

```
Sales Amount RT Class :=
VAR LastVisibleClass =
    MAX ( Customer[Customer Class Number] )
VAR ClassesToSum =
    FILTER (
        ALLSELECTED (
            Customer[Customer Class],
            Customer[Customer Class Number]
        ),
        Customer[Customer Class Number] <= LastVisibleClass
    )
VAR Result =
    CALCULATE (
        [Sales Amount],
        ClassesToSum
    )
RETURN
    Result
```

The ALLSELECTED function used in order to evaluate the *ClassesToSum* variable only takes into account the classes visible in the visual for the running total calculation. In case Sort by Column is not being used, the ALLSELECTED can include the single column to filter.

## CHAPTER 9

Parameter table

Download sample files: **https://sql.bi/dax-210**

The parameter table pattern is used to create parameters in a report, so that users can interact with slicers and dynamically change the behavior of the report itself. For example, a report can show the top N products by category, letting the users decide through a slicer if they want to see 3, 5, 10 or any other number of best products. The values available for a parameter must be stored in one or more disconnected tables, which do not have a relationship with any other tables of the same model. This chapter includes several examples with the parameter table, but this pattern has an even broader range of application.

In this pattern, we create the parameter tables by using DAX code. The Parameter feature of Power BI Desktop uses a similar technique. Indeed, the Parameter feature in Power BI Desktop creates a slicer tied to a calculated table computed with the GENERATESERIES function; it also creates a measure that returns the selected value of the parameter. This is the approach followed in this pattern. The main advantage of writing the calculated table manually in DAX is that it provides greater flexibility in the parameters to use.

Changing the scale of a measure

The user may need to be able to choose whether to show the *Sales Amount* measure as its actual value in dollars, or in thousands, or in millions. This is achieved with a slicer, as in the report visible in Figure 9-1. Though the real value of sales is around 30 million dollars, the measure shows it divided by one thousand as per the slicer selection.

Scale ⌄	Brand	Sales Amount
☐ Units	A. Datum	2,096.18
■ Thousands	Adventure Works	4,011.11
☐ Millions	Contoso	7,352.40
	Fabrikam	5,554.02
	Litware	3,255.70
	Northwind Traders	1,040.55
	Proseware	2,546.14
	Southridge Video	1,384.41
	Tailspin Toys	325.04
	The Phone Company	1,123.82
	Wide World Importers	1,901.96
	Total	**30,591.34**

FIGURE 9-1 The user chooses the scale of the *Sales Amount* measure with the slicer.

The slicer requires a *Scale* table with the list of scales. That table includes two columns: one for the description to use in the slicer (Units, Thousands, Millions) and one to store the actual denominator to use when scaling the measure (1, 1,000, 1,000,000). The *Scale* calculated table can be created using the DATATABLE function:

Calculated table

```
Scale =
DATATABLE (
    "Scale", STRING,
    "Denominator", INTEGER,
    {
        { "Units", 1 },
        { "Thousands", 1000 },
        { "Millions", 1000000 }
    }
)
```

Using the Sort by Column feature to sort *Scale* by the *Denominator* column is a best practice.

The *Sales Amount* measure scales down the result based on the denominator obtained by the current selection in the *Scale[Denominator]* column:

Measure in the Sales table

```
Sales Amount :=
VAR RealValue =
    SUMX ( Sales, Sales[Quantity] * Sales[Net Price] )
VAR Denominator =
    SELECTEDVALUE ( Scale[Denominator], 1 )
VAR Result =
    DIVIDE ( RealValue, Denominator )
RETURN
    Result
```

It is worth noting that despite the slicer being based on the *Scale[Scale]* column, that column also cross-filters the *Scale[Denominator]* column. Therefore, SELECTEDVALUE can query the *Scale[Denominator]* column directly.

If multiple measures must be scaled based on the same slicer, it might be convenient to define a measure returning the denominator value, instead of repeating the same code snippet in every measure that needs to follow the slicer selection:

Measure (hidden) in the Scale table

```
Scale Denominator :=
SELECTEDVALUE ( Scale[Denominator], 1 )
```

Measure in the Sales table

```
Gross Sales :=
DIVIDE (
    SUMX ( Sales, Sales[Quantity] * Sales[Unit Price] ),
    [Scale Denominator]
)
```

Measure in the Sales table

```
Total Cost :=
DIVIDE (
    SUMX ( Sales, Sales[Quantity] * Sales[Unit Cost] ),
    [Scale Denominator]
)
```

Multiple independent parameters

If a calculation depends on multiple parameters, there could be multiple parameter tables in the model - one for each independent parameter.

Imagine the simulation of a discount on orders: when the total number of items in a single order exceeds a given number of articles (*Min Quantity* parameter), the *Discounted Amount* measure applies the *Discount* parameter to the transaction. Users can simulate the effect of their choices on the historical data by using the slicers, as shown in Figure 9-2.

Min Quantity	Discount
☐ 1	☐ 0.00%
☐ 2	☐ 5.00%
☐ 3	☐ 10.00%
☐ 4	■ 15.00%
☐ 5	☐ 20.00%
■ 6	☐ 25.00%
☐ 7	☐ 30.00%
☐ 8	☐ 35.00%
☐ 9	☐ 40.00%
☐ 10	☐ 45.00%
	☐ 50.00%

Brand	Sales Amount	Discounted Amount
A. Datum	2,096,184.64	1,895,755.90
Adventure Works	4,011,112.28	3,643,093.87
Contoso	7,352,399.03	6,610,611.70
Fabrikam	5,554,015.73	4,758,877.76
Litware	3,255,704.03	2,891,437.19
Northwind Traders	1,040,552.13	1,013,975.15
Proseware	2,546,144.16	2,190,424.35
Southridge Video	1,384,413.85	1,259,894.49
Tailspin Toys	325,042.42	314,193.94
The Phone Company	1,123,819.07	964,504.75
Wide World Importers	1,901,956.66	1,636,675.61
Total	**30,591,343.98**	**27,150,725.80**

FIGURE 9-2 *Discounted Amount* applies a 15% discount to the orders with more than 6 products.

The implementation of the *Discounted Amount* measure first prepares a table in the *Orders* variable including the quantity and amount of each order. The result is obtained by iterating over the table in *Orders*, applying the discount to each individual order if the total quantity exceeds the defined boundary:

Measure in the Sales table

```
# Quantity :=
SUM ( Sales[Quantity] )
```

Measure in the Sales table

```
Discounted Amount :=
VAR MinQty =
    SELECTEDVALUE ( 'Min Quantity'[Min Quantity], 1 )
VAR Disc =
    SELECTEDVALUE ( Discount[Discount], 0 )
VAR Orders =
    ADDCOLUMNS (
        SUMMARIZE ( Sales, Sales[Order Number] ),
        "@Qty", [# Quantity],
        "@Amt", [Sales Amount]
    )
VAR Result =
    SUMX (
        Orders,
        IF (
            [@Qty] >= MinQty,
            ( 1 - Disc ) * [@Amt],
            [@Amt]
        )
    )
RETURN
    Result
```

By using multiple parameter tables, the parameters are independent from each other. In other words, a user can choose any combination of the two parameters, and the selection made in one parameter slicer does not affect the values available in other parameter slicers. In order to apply restrictions to the available combinations of parameters in different slicers, it is necessary to implement the multiple dependent parameters pattern.

Multiple dependent parameters

If a calculation depends on multiple parameters with limited available options, then a single table with one column for each parameter can store one row for each valid combination of the parameter values.

Imagine the scenario of the "Multiple independent parameters" pattern with two parameters: *Min Quantity* and *Discount*. The additional requirement is that the discount percentage cannot be greater than 10 times the *Min Quantity*. In other words, if a user selects 3 for *Min Quantity*, the maximum *Discount* available is 30%.

When the user makes a selection in the *Min Quantity* slicer, the *Discount* slicer only shows allowed percentage values according to the *Min Quantity* selected. Figure 9-3 shows an example of this scenario.

Min Quantity	Discount	Brand	Sales Amount	Discounted Amount
☐ 1	☐ 5.00%			
☐ 2	■ 10.00%	A. Datum	2,096,184.64	1,935,508.73
■ 3	☐ 15.00%	Adventure Works	4,011,112.28	3,714,832.14
☐ 4	☐ 20.00%	Contoso	7,352,399.03	6,775,724.69
☐ 5	☐ 25.00%	Fabrikam	5,554,015.73	5,012,971.26
☐ 6	☐ 30.00%	Litware	3,255,704.03	2,984,935.85
☐ 7		Northwind Traders	1,040,552.13	996,140.80
☐ 8		Proseware	2,546,144.16	2,302,708.91
☐ 9		Southridge Video	1,384,413.85	1,281,609.66
☐ 10		Tailspin Toys	325,042.42	309,494.86
		The Phone Company	1,123,819.07	1,015,232.44
		Wide World Importers	1,901,956.66	1,718,789.28
		Total	**30,591,343.98**	**27,962,812.99**

FIGURE 9-3 Because the selection on *Min Quantity* is three, the *Discount* slicer only shows options up to 30%.

The *Discounted Amount* measure is identical to the measure used for the multiple dependent parameters example - it prepares a table in the *Orders* variable that includes the quantity and amount of each order, and then performs the proper calculation by iterating over the table in *Orders*:

Measure in the Sales table

```
# Quantity :=
SUM ( Sales[Quantity] )
```

Measure in the Sales table

```
Discounted Amount :=
VAR MinQty =
    SELECTEDVALUE ( Discount[Min Quantity], 1 )
VAR Disc =
    SELECTEDVALUE ( Discount[Discount], 0 )
VAR Orders =
    ADDCOLUMNS (
        SUMMARIZE ( Sales, Sales[Order Number] ),
        "@Qty", [# Quantity],
        "@Amt", [Sales Amount]
    )
VAR Result =
    SUMX (
        Orders,
        IF (
            [@Qty] >= MinQty,
            ( 1 - Disc ) * [@Amt],
            [@Amt]
        )
    )
RETURN
    Result
```

The Discount table contains both parameters in the Discount[Min Quantity] and Discount[Discount] columns. The Discount table must only include rows corresponding to valid combinations of Min Quantity and Discount. The following definition of the *Discount* calculated table only generates combinations where the *Discount* percentage is less than or equal to 10 times the *Min Quantity*:

Calculated table

```
Discount =
VAR Discounts =
    SELECTCOLUMNS ( GENERATESERIES ( 0, 19, 1 ), "Discount", [Value] / 20 )
VAR Quantities =
    SELECTCOLUMNS ( GENERATESERIES ( 1, 10, 1 ), "Min Quantity", [Value] )
RETURN
    GENERATE (
        Quantities,
        FILTER (
            Discounts,
            [Discount] <= [Min Quantity] / 10
        )
    )
```

The Discount table does not include combinations such as 3 for *Min Quantity* and 50% for *Discount*. Therefore, when the *Min Quantity* slicer selects 3, the *Discount* slicer only shows values less than or equal to 30%. The relationship between two or more parameters is implicitly found in the *Discount* table and directly affects the slicers through cross-filtering.

Selecting top N products dynamically

Imagine needing a report like the one in Figure 9-4, where each column filters a different number of products with the highest *Sales Amount*. Each column shows the *Sales Amount* of only the top N products, where N is determined by the column header. In this case, each visible name of the *TopN* parameter is mapped to a different number, used as the parameter value in the *Top Sales* measure.

Brand	All	Top 1	Top 5	Top 10	Top 20	Top 50
A. Datum	2,096,184.64	725,840.28	918,468.15	1,065,860.16	1,300,034.83	1,688,048.37
Adventure Works	4,011,112.28	1,303,983.46	1,641,157.00	1,946,192.26	2,335,535.74	3,100,295.06
Contoso	7,352,399.03	683,779.95	1,409,240.22	1,900,164.22	2,559,985.29	3,902,806.38
Fabrikam	5,554,015.73	165,594.00	627,603.03	1,015,757.63	1,660,752.83	2,974,789.16
Litware	3,255,704.03	135,039.58	543,539.45	842,969.79	1,261,450.86	2,063,044.45
Northwind Traders	1,040,552.13	151,427.53	502,260.88	744,659.27	996,878.41	1,040,552.13
Proseware	2,546,144.16	160,627.05	609,220.50	850,920.80	1,160,439.55	1,603,259.55
Southridge Video	1,384,413.85	364,714.41	517,333.22	646,492.28	820,429.82	1,149,493.53
Tailspin Toys	325,042.42	10,013.76	46,122.95	77,508.46	125,778.53	217,247.30
The Phone Company	1,123,819.07	32,400.89	136,030.59	229,547.51	389,322.20	734,545.85
Wide World Importers	1,901,956.66	77,615.25	283,817.11	479,833.63	802,336.37	1,384,934.35
Total	**30,591,343.98**	**1,303,983.46**	**3,335,472.85**	**4,146,480.95**	**5,406,168.25**	**7,903,110.28**

FIGURE 9-4 The *TopN Products* parameter assigned to the report columns defines the number of products considered for the Sales Amount calculation.

This visualization is hard to obtain in Power BI, because the Top N visual-level filter can only be applied once in one visual. In this case, every column has a different parameter for the TOPN function used in the *Top Sales* measure.

The parameter table requires two columns: one for the visible name (*TopN Products*) that contains the description of the parameter, and the other column (*TopN*) is a number corresponding to both the result of the parameter selection and the sort order of the *TopN Products* values.

The *TopN Filter* calculated table can be defined with the following code:

Calculated table

```
TopN Filter =
ADDCOLUMNS (
    SELECTCOLUMNS (
        { 0, 1, 5, 10, 20, 50 },
        "TopN", [Value]
    ),
    "TopN Products", IF (
        [TopN] = 0,
        "All",
        "Top " & [TopN]
    )
)
```

The *Top Sales* measure uses the selected value to filter the number of top products by evaluating the *Sales Amount* measure:

Measure in the Sales table

```
Top Sales :=
VAR TopNvalue =
    SELECTEDVALUE ( 'TopN Filter'[TopN], 0 )
VAR TopProducts =
    TOPN (
        TopNvalue,
        'Product',
        [Sales Amount]
    )
VAR AllSales = [Sales Amount]
VAR TopSales =
    CALCULATE (
        [Sales Amount],
        KEEPFILTERS ( TopProducts )
    )
VAR Result =
    IF (
        TopNvalue = 0,
        AllSales,
        TopSales
    )
RETURN
    Result
```

Static segmentation

The static segmentation pattern classifies numerical values into ranges. A typical example is the analysis of sales by price range. You do not want to slice the data by individual price; instead you want to simplify the analysis by grouping prices within ranges of prices. The price ranges are stored in a configuration table and the pattern requires the model to be entirely data-driven. In other words, when the configuration table is updated, the model is updated automatically without requiring any change to the DAX code.

Depending on the size of the data model, there are different options for this pattern. On small models (up to a few million rows) the best option is to use calculated columns and/or calculated relationships. On larger models with hundreds of millions of rows, calculated columns might increase the processing time of the model. Therefore, for large models the best option is to build a calculated table expanding the prices, thereby reducing to a minimum the number of calculated columns in the larger tables.

Basic pattern

You need to analyze sales sliced by price range. To attain this goal, you build a configuration table that stores the price ranges; the price should be greater than or equal to the *Min Price* and less than the *Max Price*, as shown in Figure 10-1.

PriceRangeKey	Price Range	Min Price	Max Price
1	VERY LOW	0.00	100.00
2	LOW	100.00	300.00
3	MEDIUM	300.00	600.00
4	HIGH	600.00	1,500.00
5	VERY HIGH	1,500.00	999,999,999.00

FIGURE 10-1 The configuration table defines the price ranges.

Then, you want to analyze sales by price range, obtaining a report like Figure 10-2.

Price Range	Sales Amount
VERY LOW	1,932,694.35
LOW	7,210,498.15
MEDIUM	9,037,106.68
HIGH	8,000,280.26
VERY HIGH	4,410,764.54
Total	**30,591,343.98**

FIGURE 10-2 The report shows sales sliced by price range.

In the report, the VERY LOW row contains the sales with a net price between 0 and 100.

In order to obtain the desired result, you need a relationship between the configuration table (*Price Ranges*) and the Sales table. In the example, we use *Sales[Net Price]* instead of *Sales[Unit Price]* to determine the sales price, so to consider possible discounts. Indeed, *Sales[Net Price]* might be different than *Sales[Unit price]* because of discounts. The required relationship should use a "between" condition for the join, which is not natively supported by the Tabular engine. Nevertheless, in the *Sales* table we can add a calculated column that stores the key of the price range for each specific row, by using the following code:

Calculated column in the Sales table

```
PriceRangeKey =
VAR CurrentPrice = Sales[Net Price]
VAR FilterSegment =
    FILTER (
        'Price Ranges',
        AND (
            'Price Ranges'[Min Price] < CurrentPrice,
            'Price Ranges'[Max Price] >= CurrentPrice
        )
    )
VAR Result =
    CALCULATE (
        DISTINCT ( 'Price Ranges'[PriceRangeKey] ),
        FilterSegment
    )
RETURN
    Result
```

When building the calculated column, you need to be careful not to use functions that might reference the blank row, such as ALL and VALUES. This is the reason we used DISTINCT instead of VALUES to retrieve the price range key.

Next, you build a relationship between *Sales* and *Price Ranges* based on the new calculated column, like in Figure 10-3.

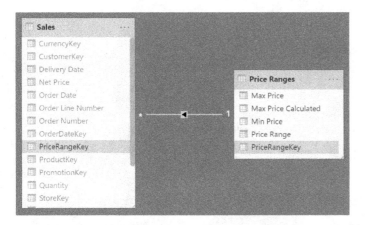

FIGURE 10-3 The relationship is based on a calculated column.

Once the relationship is in place, you can slice sales by *'Price Ranges'[Price Range]*.

You need to make sure that the configuration table is properly designed, so that each price belongs to only one price range. The presence of overlapping segments in the configuration table can generate errors in the evaluation of the *PriceRangeKey* calculated column. If you want to make sure there are no mistakes in the configuration table – such as overlapping ranges – you can generate the *Max Price* column using a calculated column that retrieves the value of *Min Price* for the next segment. This is shown in the following sample code.

Calculated column in the Price Ranges table

```
Max Price Calculated =
VAR CurrentMinPrice = 'Price Ranges'[Min Price]
VAR NextMinPrice =
    CALCULATE (
        MIN ( 'Price Ranges'[Min Price] ),
        REMOVEFILTERS ( 'Price Ranges' ),
        'Price Ranges'[Min Price] > CurrentMinPrice
    )
VAR MaxPrice =
    IF ( ISBLANK ( NextMinPrice ), 999999999, NextMinPrice )
RETURN
    MaxPrice
```

You can also write a safer version of the calculated column that writes a blank or generates an error in the event there are multiple ranges active for one price, as in the following example:

Calculated column in the Sales table

```
PriceRangeKey =
VAR CurrentPrice = Sales[Net Price]
VAR FilterSegment =
    FILTER (
        'Price Ranges',
        AND (
            'Price Ranges'[Min Price] < CurrentPrice,
            'Price Ranges'[Max Price] >= CurrentPrice
        )
    )
VAR FilteredPriceRangeKey =
    CALCULATETABLE (
        DISTINCT ( 'Price Ranges'[PriceRangeKey] ),
        FilterSegment
    )
VAR Result =
    IF (
        COUNTROWS ( FilteredPriceRangeKey ) = 1,
        FilteredPriceRangeKey,
        -- The next line raises a more specific error in the calculated column.
        -- You can replace ERROR with BLANK() in order to just ignore the prices
        -- matching multiple segments, but bear in mind that doing it this way
        -- you would hide possible errors in the report.
        ERROR ( "Overlapping ranges in Price Ranges table" )
    )
RETURN
    Result
```

The code shown in this pattern must satisfy the requirements for calculated columns used in a relationship, in order to avoid circular dependencies (https://sql.bi/59891).

Price ranges by category

A variation of the static segmentation pattern is when the condition to check is not a simple between, but rather a more complex condition. For example, the requirement might be to use different price ranges for different product categories: The LOW price range for games and toys needs to be different from the LOW price range for home appliances.

In this scenario, the configuration table contains an additional column that indicates the category the price range must be applied to. Different categories might have different price ranges, as in Figure 10-4.

PriceRangeKey	Price Range Order	Category	Price Range	Min Price	Max Price
21	1	Cameras and camcorders	VERY LOW	0.00	200.00
22	2	Cameras and camcorders	LOW	200.00	400.00
23	3	Cameras and camcorders	MEDIUM	400.00	800.00
24	4	Cameras and camcorders	HIGH	800.00	1,500.00
25	5	Cameras and camcorders	VERY HIGH	1,500.00	999,999,999.00
31	1	Cell phones	VERY LOW	0.00	100.00
32	2	Cell phones	LOW	100.00	200.00
33	3	Cell phones	MEDIUM	200.00	600.00
34	4	Cell phones	HIGH	600.00	1,000.00
35	5	Cell phones	VERY HIGH	1,000.00	999,999,999.00

FIGURE 10-4 The configuration table also contains the categories.

The pattern here is very similar to the basic pattern, the only noticeable change being in the condition used to find the correct price range key. Indeed, the search must be limited to the row in the *Price Ranges* table with the category of the product being sold and where the net price falls within the desired range:

Calculated column in the Sales table

```
PriceRangeKey =
VAR CurrentPrice = Sales[Net Price]
VAR CurrentCategory = RELATED ( 'Product'[Category] )
VAR FilterSegment =
    FILTER (
        'Price Ranges',
        'Price Ranges'[Category] = CurrentCategory
            && 'Price Ranges'[Min Price] < CurrentPrice
            && 'Price Ranges'[Max Price] >= CurrentPrice
    )
VAR FilteredPriceRangeKey =
    CALCULATETABLE (
        DISTINCT ( 'Price Ranges'[PriceRangeKey] ),
        FilterSegment
    )
VAR Result =
    IF (
        COUNTROWS ( FilteredPriceRangeKey ) = 1,
        FilteredPriceRangeKey,
        ERROR ( "Overlapping ranges in Price Ranges table" )
    )
RETURN
    Result
```

Similarly, you can use any other condition if it is guaranteed that only one row remains visible in the configuration table. In order to make sure that the configuration table does not contain overlapping ranges, you can generate the *Max Price* column using a calculated column similar to the one used in the basic pattern. The important difference is the use of ALLEXCEPT instead of REMOVEFILTERS, so that the filter over *'Price Ranges'[Category]* coming from the context transition is kept in the filter context:

Calculated column in the Price Ranges table

```
Max Price Calculated =
VAR CurrentMinPrice = 'Price Ranges'[Min Price]
VAR NextMinPrice =
    CALCULATE (
        MIN ( 'Price Ranges'[Min Price] ),
        -- ALLEXCEPT is required to filter only the other
        -- segments of the same category
        ALLEXCEPT ( 'Price Ranges', 'Price Ranges'[Category] ),
        'Price Ranges'[Min Price] > CurrentMinPrice
    )
VAR MaxPrice =
    IF ( ISBLANK ( NextMinPrice ), 999999999, NextMinPrice )
RETURN
    MaxPrice
```

Price ranges on large tables

The static segmentation pattern requires the creation of a calculated column in the *Sales* table. The column itself is typically rather small in size, because it contains few distinct values. However, on very large tables the column size might start to grow and you may face another problem: the column needs to be computed for the entire table at every data refresh. On a multi-billion-row table that is likely to be partitioned, the column needs to be recomputed for the entire table whenever one partition is refreshed. This slows down every refresh operation.

In this scenario, it is possible to use a variation of the static segmentation that works without adding any column in the Sales table. Instead of building the relationship with the new calculated column, this pattern uses *Sales[Net Price]* as the key for a relationship with a new calculated table. Indeed, it is not possible to create a relationship between *Sales* and the *Price Ranges* table because the *Price Ranges* table is missing a suitable column. Nevertheless, such column can be created by increasing the number of rows in the configuration table.

The table we want to generate contains one row for each value of *Sales[Net Price]* with the corresponding price range, like in Figure 10-5.

Net Price ▲	Min Price	Max Price	Price Range
98.99	0.00	100.00	VERY LOW
99.00	0.00	100.00	VERY LOW
99.75	0.00	100.00	VERY LOW
99.99	0.00	100.00	VERY LOW
101.37	100.00	300.00	LOW
101.52	100.00	300.00	LOW
101.99	100.00	300.00	LOW

FIGURE 10-5 The expanded configuration contains one row for each value in *Net Price*.

We renamed the original configuration table to *Price Ranges Configuration*. The *Price Ranges* table can be created as a calculated table using the following code:

Calculated table

```
Price Ranges =
GENERATE (
    'Price Ranges Configuration',
    FILTER (
        ALLNOBLANKROW ( Sales[Net Price] ),
        AND (
            Sales[Net Price] > 'Price Ranges Configuration'[Min Price],
            Sales[Net Price] <= 'Price Ranges Configuration'[Max Price]
        )
    )
)
```

This new table contains exactly one row for each distinct value of the *Sales[Net Price]* column. Therefore, it is possible to create a relationship between *Sales* and the new *Price Ranges* calculated table based on the *Net Price* column, as shown in Figure 10-6.

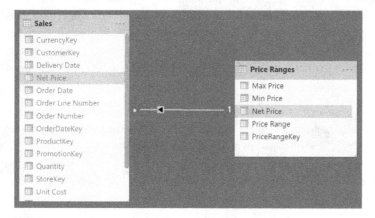

FIGURE 10-6 The relationship is based on the *Net Price* column.

With this optimization, there is no need to create a new column in *Sales*, because the model uses the existing *Sales[Net Price]* column to setup the relationship. Therefore, no calculated column in *Sales* must be recomputed during data refresh. The original *Price Ranges Configuration* table should be hidden in the model in order to avoid any possible confusion for the end users.

On smaller models, creating a calculated column is not an issue. Therefore, the basic solution that does not involve new tables is to be preferred. On larger models, this version reduces the processing time.

Dynamic segmentation

The Dynamic segmentation pattern is useful to perform the classification of entities based on measures. A typical example is to cluster customers based on spending volume. The clustering is dynamic, so that the categorization considers the filters active in the report. Indeed, a customer might belong to different clusters on different dates.

Basic pattern

You need to categorize customers based on spending. Using a configuration table like Figure 11-1, you define the clusters.

Segment	Min Sales	Max Sales
SILVER	0.00	100.00
GOLD	100.00	500.00
PLATINUM	500.00	2,000.00
DIAMOND	2,000.00	999,999,999.00

FIGURE 11-1 The configuration table defines the boundaries of each segment.

Every segment represents a classification for a customer based on their *Sales Amount* computed over one year. Using this configuration, you want to analyze how many customers belong to each segment over time. One same customer might be Silver in one year, and Platinum in a different year.

Segment	CY 2007	CY 2008	CY 2009
SILVER	2,142	1,996	1,929
GOLD	2,126	661	354
PLATINUM	3,031	537	207
DIAMOND	700	300	245
Total	**7,999**	**3,494**	**2,735**

FIGURE 11-2 The report shows the number of customers in each segment for each year.

In the report in Figure 11-2, the first row shows that in 2007 there were 2,142 customers in the SILVER segment. By adding a *Category* slicer to this report, we segment our customers based on their purchases in the chosen category alone, as shown in Figure 11-3.

Category ⌄

☐ Audio
☐ Cameras and camcorders
☐ Cell phones
☐ Computers
☐ Games and Toys
■ Home Appliances
☐ Music, Movies and Audio Books
☐ TV and Video

Segment	CY 2007	CY 2008	CY 2009
SILVER	86		
GOLD	277	26	29
PLATINUM	465	390	90
DIAMOND	210	242	187
Total	**1,038**	**658**	**306**

FIGURE 11-3 The report shows customers in each segment considering sales of the given category alone.

Being dynamic, the pattern is implemented through a measure. The measure finds the customers who belong to the selected cluster. It then uses this table as a filter in CALCULATE to restrict the calculation to the customers found. KEEPFILTERS is needed to intersect the customers list with the customers found:

Measure in the Sales table

```
# Seg. Customers :=
IF (
    HASONEVALUE ( 'Date'[Calendar Year] ),   -- Segmentation only over one year selected
    VAR CustomersInSegment =                  -- Gets the customers in the current segment
        FILTER (
            ALLSELECTED ( Customer ),
            VAR SalesOfCustomer = [Sales Amount] -- Computes Sales Amount for one customer
            VAR SegmentForCustomer =              -- Retrieves the segment
                FILTER (                          -- a customer belongs to
                    'Customer segments',
                    NOT ISBLANK ( SalesOfCustomer )
                        && 'Customer segments'[Min Sales] < SalesOfCustomer
                        && 'Customer segments'[Max Sales] >= SalesOfCustomer
                )
            VAR IsCustomerInSegments = NOT ISEMPTY ( SegmentForCustomer )
            RETURN IsCustomerInSegments
        )
    VAR Result =
        CALCULATE (
            COUNTROWS ( Customer ),                -- Expression to compute
            KEEPFILTERS ( CustomersInSegment )  -- Applies filter for segmented customers
        )
    RETURN Result
)
```

The measure must iterate through all the segments for each customer, to make sure the total is correct with an arbitrary selection of segments, as shown in Figure 11-4.

Segment	CY 2007	CY 2008	CY 2009
SILVER	2,142	1,996	1,929
DIAMOND	700	300	245
Total	**2,842**	**2,296**	**2,174**

Segment filter: ▪ SILVER, ☐ GOLD, ☐ PLATINUM, ▪ DIAMOND

FIGURE 11-4 The report shows an accurate total for each year summing only the selected segments.

By nature, this calculation is non-additive. The previous implementation works at the year level only, which is a good idea to compute the number of customers. This way, the same customer is never summed twice. However, for other measures the segmentation could require an additive behavior. For example, imagine a measure showing the *Sales Amount* of the customer in the segment that should also show a total over multiple years. The following measure implements a calculation that is additive across the years:

Measure in the Sales table

```
Sales Seg. Customers :=
SUMX (
    VALUES ( 'Date'[Calendar Year] ),        -- Repeat segmentation for every year selected
    VAR CustomersInSegment =                 -- Gets the customers in the current segment
        FILTER (
            ALLSELECTED ( Customer ),
            VAR SalesOfCustomer = [Sales Amount] -- Computes Sales Amount for one customer
            VAR SegmentForCustomer =             -- Retrieves the segment
                FILTER (                         -- a customer belongs to
                    'Customer segments',
                    NOT ISBLANK ( SalesOfCustomer )
                        && 'Customer segments'[Min Sales] < SalesOfCustomer
                        && 'Customer segments'[Max Sales] >= SalesOfCustomer
                )
            VAR IsCustomerInSegments = NOT ISEMPTY ( SegmentForCustomer )
            RETURN IsCustomerInSegments
        )
    VAR Result =
        CALCULATE (
            [Sales Amount],                      -- Expression to compute
            KEEPFILTERS ( CustomersInSegment )   -- Applies filter for segmented customers
        )
    RETURN Result
)
```

The result shown in Figure 11-5 provides a total in each row, summing the measure computed for each year.

Segment	CY 2007	CY 2008	CY 2009	**Total**
SILVER	97,088.05	62,909.45	55,474.67	**215,472.18**
DIAMOND	7,652,919.70	9,065,771.51	9,025,545.30	**25,744,236.51**
Total	**7,750,007.76**	**9,128,680.96**	**9,081,019.97**	**25,959,708.69**

Segment filter: ▪ SILVER, ☐ GOLD, ☐ PLATINUM, ▪ DIAMOND

FIGURE 11-5 The Sales Seg. Customers measure is additive over the years.

You need to make sure that the configuration table is designed properly, so that each possible value of *Sales Amount* only belongs to one segment. The presence of overlapping segment boundaries in the configuration table can generate errors in the evaluation of the *CustomersInSegment* variable. If you want to make sure there are no mistakes in the configuration table – such as overlapping ranges – you can generate the *Max Sales* column using a calculated column that retrieves the value of *Min Sales* for the next segment. This is shown in the following sample code:

Calculated column in the Customer Segments table

```
Max Sales Calculated =
VAR CurrentMinSales = 'Customer Segments'[Min Sales]
VAR MaxEverSales = CALCULATE ( [Sales Amount], REMOVEFILTERS ( ) )
VAR NextMinSales =
    CALCULATE (
        MIN ( 'Customer Segments'[Min Sales] ),
        REMOVEFILTERS ( 'Customer Segments' ),
        'Customer Segments'[Min Sales] > CurrentMinSales
    )
VAR MaxSales =
    IF ( ISBLANK ( NextMinSales ), MaxEverSales, NextMinSales )
RETURN
    MaxSales
```

Clustering by product growth

The dynamic segmentation pattern is very flexible, because it allows you to categorize entities based on dynamic calculations. Moreover, one entity might belong to different clusters. A good example of its flexibility is the following: you want to cluster products based on their yearly growth in sales.

In the sample model, if the year-over-year growth of a product falls within the +/-20% range, then it is considered stable; if its growth is lower than -20%, then it is dropping; if it is over 20%, then it is growing. The same product might be dropping in 2008 and stable in 2009, as highlighted in Figure 11-6.

Category	Segment	CY 2008	CY 2009
■ Audio			
	⊟ **DROP**	**2**	**3**
	WWI 1GB Digital Voice Recorder Pen E100 Black		1
	WWI 1GBPulse Smart pen E50 Black	1	
	WWI 2GB Pulse Smart pen M100 Silver	1	
	WWI 2GB Pulse Smart pen M100 White		1
	WWI 4GB Video Recording Pen X200 Pink		1
Subcategory	⊟ **STABLE**	**1**	
☐ Bluetooth Headphones	WWI 2GB Pulse Smart pen M100 Black	1	
☐ MP4&MP3	⊟ **GROW**	**1**	**4**
■ Recording Pen	WWI 1GBPulse Smart pen E50 Black		1
	WWI 2GB Pulse Smart pen M100 Blue		1
	WWI 2GB Pulse Smart pen M100 Silver		1
	WWI 2GB Pulse Smart pen M100 White	1	
	WWI 4GB Video Recording Pen X200 Yellow		1
	Total	**4**	**7**

FIGURE 11-6 The same product belongs to different clusters, in different years.

You start by building the segmentation table. It is shown in Figure 11-7.

Segment	Min Growth	Max Growth
DROP	-100,000.00%	-20.00%
STABLE	-20.00%	20.00%
GROW	20.00%	100,000.00%

FIGURE 11-7 The configuration table defines the boundaries of each segment.

Once the table is in the model, the code to use is a slight variation of the basic model. This time, instead of determining the customers who belong to a segment based on their spending volume, it determines the products that belong to a segment based on product growth. The only difference in the measure is the reference to the *Growth %* measure:

Measure in the Sales table

```
Growth % :=
VAR SalesCY = [Sales Amount]
VAR SalesPY =
    CALCULATE (
        [Sales Amount],
        SAMEPERIODLASTYEAR ( 'Date'[Date] )
    )
VAR Result =
    IF (
        NOT ISBLANK ( SalesCY ) && NOT ISBLANK ( SalesPY ),
        DIVIDE ( SalesCY - SalesPY, SalesPY )
    )
RETURN
    Result
```

Measure in the Sales table

```
# Seg. Products :=
IF (
    HASONEVALUE ( 'Date'[Calendar Year] ),
    VAR ProductsInSegment =               -- Gets the customers in the current segment
        FILTER (
            ALLSELECTED ( 'Product' ),
            VAR GrowthPerc = [Growth %]   -- Computes Growth% for one product
            VAR SegmentForProduct =       -- Retrieves the segment a customer belongs to
                FILTER (
                    'Growth segments',
                    NOT ISBLANK ( GrowthPerc )
                        && 'Growth segments'[Min Growth] < GrowthPerc
                        && 'Growth segments'[Max Growth] >= GrowthPerc
                )
            VAR IsProductInSegments = NOT ISEMPTY ( SegmentForProduct )
            RETURN IsProductInSegments
        )
    VAR Result =
        CALCULATE (
            COUNTROWS ( 'Product' ),             -- Expression to compute
            KEEPFILTERS ( ProductsInSegment )    -- Applies filter for segmented products
        )
    RETURN Result
)
```

Clustering by best status

The dynamic segmentation pattern is also useful to cluster customers based on sales, assigning each customer to exactly one cluster depending on the highest sales for that customer over time.

If the assignment of the cluster to each customer is static, then this is better implemented through the static segmentation pattern. However, if the assignment has to be dynamic but you do not want a customer to belong to different clusters over time, then the dynamic segmentation pattern is the optimal choice.

Starting with the configuration table in Figure 11-8, we assign customers to one cluster depending on the highest yearly sales. Therefore, a customer is PLATINUM if – in a year – they exceeded the amount of 500.00 spent. If it is determined that the customer be platinum, their sales are reported under the PLATINUM segment for all the years.

Segment	Min Sales	Max Sales
SILVER	0.00	100.00
GOLD	100.00	500.00
PLATINUM	500.00	2,000.00
DIAMOND	2,000.00	999,999,999.00

FIGURE 11-8 The configuration table defines the boundaries of each segment.

In the report shown in Figure 11-9, the sales reported under PLATINUM are the sales of all customers that reached the platinum level in one of the selected years. If their sales are reported under PLATINUM, they are not reported in any other cluster.

Segment	CY 2007	CY 2008	CY 2009	Total
SILVER	85,663.91	40,887.42	34,780.18	**161,331.51**
GOLD	537,202.76	123,184.28	64,863.37	**725,250.41**
PLATINUM	2,967,476.36	644,754.32	208,023.71	**3,820,254.40**
DIAMOND	7,719,603.09	9,118,756.97	9,046,147.60	**25,884,507.66**
Total	**11,309,946.12**	**9,927,582.99**	**9,353,814.87**	**30,591,343.98**

FIGURE 11-9 Sales are sliced by best segment reached in a year.

The measure in the report is a variation of the dynamic segmentation pattern. This time it is not necessary to iterate the calculation over the years. The *CustomersInSegment* variable computes the max sales amount for each year in the report using the *Max Yearly Sales* measure, which also ignores any other filter over the *Date* table. The result is applied as a filter to compute the Sales Amount measure:

Measure in the Sales table

```
Max Yearly Sales :=
MAXX (
    ALLSELECTED ( 'Date'[Calendar Year] ),  -- Iterates over selected years
    CALCULATE (
        [Sales Amount],                     -- Computes the Sales Amount of the year
        ALLEXCEPT (                         -- ignoring any other filter
            'Date',                         -- applied to the Date table other than
            'Date'[Calendar Year]           -- the one coming from context transition
        )
    )
)
```

Measure in the Sales table

```
Sales Seg. Customers :=
VAR CustomersInSegment =                           -- Gets the customers in current segment
    FILTER (
        ALLSELECTED ( Customer ),
        VAR SalesOfCustomer = [Max Yearly Sales]   -- Computes Sales Amount for one customer
        VAR SegmentForCustomer =                   -- Retrieves the segment
            FILTER (                               -- a customer belongs to
                'Customer segments',
                NOT ISBLANK ( SalesOfCustomer )
                    && 'Customer segments'[Min Sales] < SalesOfCustomer
                    && 'Customer segments'[Max Sales] >= SalesOfCustomer
            )
        VAR IsCustomerInSegments = NOT ISEMPTY ( SegmentForCustomer )
        RETURN IsCustomerInSegments
    )
VAR Result =
    CALCULATE (
        [Sales Amount],                       -- Expression to compute
        KEEPFILTERS ( CustomersInSegment )    -- Applies filter for segmented customers
    )
RETURN
    Result
```

## CHAPTER 12

ABC classification

Download sample files: **https://sql.bi/dax-213**

The ABC classification pattern classifies entities based on values, grouping entities together that contribute to a certain percentage of the total. A typical example of ABC classification is the segmentation of products (entity) based on sales (value). The best-selling products that contribute to up to 70% of the total sales belong to cluster A. The products making up the next 20% of sales are in cluster B, whereas the products representing the last 10% of sales, belong to class C. Hence, the pattern is named after the three clusters (ABC).

You can use this pattern to determine the core business of a company, typically in terms of best performing products or best customers. You can find more information on ABC classification at *http://en.wikipedia.org/wiki/ABC_analysis*.

ABC classification can be either static or dynamic. Static ABC classification assigns a class to each product statically, so that the class of a product does not change depending on the filters being applied to the report. Dynamic ABC classification computes the class of each product dynamically, based on the report filters. As such, in the dynamic ABC classification the clustering of product needs to be done in measures, resulting in a less efficient – albeit more flexible – algorithm.

There is also a third pattern for this type of clustering, which lies in-between the static and the dynamic versions: the snapshot ABC. For example, if one needs to update the ABC class to a product on a yearly basis, they can accomplish this by creating a snapshot table containing the ABC class of a product for every year.

Static ABC classification

In the example, we cluster products based on sales. Each product is statically assigned to a class that can be used on the rows and columns of a report. The report in Figure 12-1 shows that there are 493 products in class A, making over 21M in sales, whereas 1,455 products in class C only generate 3M in sales.

ABC Class	#Products	Sales Amount
A	493	21,406,089.17
B	569	6,125,052.03
C	1,455	3,060,202.77
Total	**2,517**	**30,591,343.98**

FIGURE 12-1 The ABC class can be used to filter the products into a given class.

The static ABC classification is based on calculated columns. You need four new calculated columns, as shown in Figure 12-2.

Product Name	Product Sales ▼	Cumulated Sales	Cumulated Pct	ABC Class
Adventure Works 26" 720p LCD HDTV M140 Silver	1,303,983.46	1,303,983.46	4.26%	A
A. Datum SLR Camera X137 Grey	725,840.28	2,029,823.74	6.64%	A
Contoso Telephoto Conversion Lens X400 Silver	683,779.95	2,713,603.69	8.87%	A
SV 16xDVD M360 Black	364,714.41	3,078,318.10	10.06%	A
Contoso Projector 1080p X980 White	257,154.75	3,335,472.85	10.90%	A
Contoso Washer & Dryer 21in E210 Pink	182,094.12	3,517,566.97	11.50%	A
Fabrikam Independent filmmaker 1/3" 8.5mm X200 White	165,594.00	3,683,160.97	12.04%	A
Proseware Projector 1080p LCD86 Silver	160,627.05	3,843,788.02	12.56%	A

FIGURE 12-2 The ABC static pattern requires four calculated columns.

The four calculated columns are:

- **Product Sales**: the total sales for the product (current row).

- **Cumulated Sales**: the running total of Product Sales ranked from largest to smallest.

- **Cumulated Pct**: the percentage of Cumulated Sales against the grand total of sales.

- **ABC Class**: the class of the product, which could be A, B, or C.

You define the calculated columns using the following DAX formulas:

Calculated Column in the Product table

```
Product Sales =
[Sales Amount]
```

Calculated Column in the Product table

```
Cumulated Sales =
VAR CurrentProductSales = 'Product'[Product Sales]
VAR BetterProducts =
    FILTER (
        'Product',
        'Product'[Product Sales] >= CurrentProductSales
    )
VAR Result =
    SUMX (
        BetterProducts,
        'Product'[Product Sales]
    )
RETURN
    Result
```

Calculated Column in the Product table

```
Cumulated Pct =
DIVIDE (
    'Product'[Cumulated Sales],
    SUM ( 'Product'[Product Sales] )
)
```

Calculated Column in the Product table

```
ABC Class =
SWITCH (
    TRUE,
    'Product'[Cumulated Pct] <= 0.7, "A",
    'Product'[Cumulated Pct] <= 0.9, "B",
    "C"
)
```

The product class is determined by the value of *Cumulated Pct*. As you can see in Figure 12-3, when the value is below 70% the product class is still A, when it is over 70% the product class becomes B.

Product Name	Product Sales	Cumulated Sales	Cumulated Pct	ABC Class
Adventure Works Coffee Maker Auto 10C M100 Black	16,486.38	21,373,280.97	69.87%	A
A. Datum Point Shoot Digital Camera M500 Black	16,434.00	21,389,714.97	69.92%	A
WWI LCD19 E107 Black	16,374.20	21,406,089.17	69.97%	A
A. Datum Rangefinder Digital Camera X200 Orange	16,370.00	21,422,459.17	70.03%	B
Litware Home Theater System 5.1 Channel M512 Brown	16,356.60	21,438,815.77	70.08%	B
Fabrikam SLR Camera 35" M358 Orange	16,350.80	21,455,166.57	70.13%	B

FIGURE 12-3 Products that fall over the 70% threshold in cumulated values are in class B.

The four columns can be replaced with a single calculated column containing the complete logic, using several variables:

Calculated Column in the Product table

```
ABC Class Optimized =
VAR SalesByProduct = ADDCOLUMNS ( 'Product', "@ProdSales", [Sales Amount] )
VAR CurrentSales = [Sales Amount]
VAR BetterProducts = FILTER ( SalesByProduct, [@ProdSales] >= CurrentSales )
VAR CumulatedSales = SUMX ( BetterProducts, [@ProdSales] )
VAR AllSales = CALCULATE ( [Sales Amount], ALL ( 'Product' ) )
VAR CumulatedPct = DIVIDE ( CumulatedSales, AllSales )
VAR AbcClass =
SWITCH (
    TRUE,
    CumulatedPct <= 0.7, "A",
    CumulatedPct <= 0.9, "B",
    "C"
)
RETURN
    AbcClass
```

Using this version of the code reduces the size of the model, because it creates one column in place of the four needed in the earlier version. Nevertheless, on databases with a large number of products, the column calculation might require an excessive amount of memory.

Snapshot ABC classification

You might need to assign the ABC class to each product on a yearly basis, so that the same product can fall into different ABC classes in different years. In this case, you should build a solution with an additional snapshot table containing the correct ABC class for each product and year. The goal is to produce a report like the one in Figure 12-4 – showing for each year, the number of products that fell in class A, B or C.

| Calendar Year | CY 2007 | | CY 2008 | | CY 2009 | |
ABC Class	# Products	ABC Sales Amount	# Products	ABC Sales Amount	# Products	ABC Sales Amount
A	167	7,904,463.00	342	6,946,534.50	430	6,544,508.84
B	280	2,272,418.98	367	1,988,074.60	394	1,873,490.44
C	811	1,133,064.14	769	992,973.88	689	935,815.59
Total	**1,258**	**11,309,946.12**	**1,478**	**9,927,582.99**	**1,513**	**9,353,814.87**

FIGURE 12-4 The ABC classification evaluates the product class every year.

The model requires an additional table to store the ABC class for each year and product. The *ABC by Year* table does not have relationships with other tables in the model and it contains the product key, the year, and the assigned class, as shown in Figure 12-5.

ProductKey	Calendar Year	ABC Class
7	CY 2008	C
7	CY 2009	C
8	CY 2007	A
8	CY 2009	B
9	CY 2009	C

FIGURE 12-5 The calculated table that computes the ABC class has one row for each year and product.

The code that computes the table is the following:

Calculated table

```
ABC by Year =
VAR ProductsByYear =
    SUMMARIZE (
        Sales,
        'Product'[ProductKey],
        'Date'[Calendar Year]
    )
VAR SaleByYearProduct =
    ADDCOLUMNS (
        ProductsByYear,
        "@ProdSales", [Sales Amount],
        "@YearlySales", CALCULATE (
            [Sales Amount],
            ALL ( 'Product' )
        )
    )
VAR CumulatedSalesByYearProduct =
    ADDCOLUMNS (
        SaleByYearProduct,
        "@CumulatedSales",
        VAR CurrentSales = [@ProdSales]
        VAR CurrentYear = 'Date'[Calendar Year]
        VAR CumulatedSalesWithinYear =
            FILTER (
                SaleByYearProduct,
                AND (
                    'Date'[Calendar Year] = CurrentYear,
                    [@ProdSales] >= CurrentSales
                )
            )
        RETURN
            SUMX (
                CumulatedSalesWithinYear,
                [@ProdSales]
            )
    )
VAR CumulatedPctByYearProduct =
    ADDCOLUMNS (
        CumulatedSalesByYearProduct,
        "@CumulatedPct", DIVIDE (
            [@CumulatedSales],
            [@YearlySales]
        )
    )
VAR ClassByYearProduct =
    ADDCOLUMNS (
        CumulatedPctByYearProduct,
        "@AbcClass", SWITCH (
            TRUE,
            [@CumulatedPct] <= 0.7, "A",
            [@CumulatedPct] <= 0.9, "B",
            "C"
        )
    )
```

```
VAR Result =
    SELECTCOLUMNS (
        ClassByYearProduct,
        "ProductKey", 'Product'[ProductKey],
        "Calendar Year", 'Date'[Calendar Year],
        "ABC Class", [@AbcClass]
    )
RETURN
    Result
```

The result of this code is the final one, shown in Figure 12-5. It helps to visualize the content of the *ClassByYearProduct* variable, which shows the columns added to the intermediate calculation through several steps. You can see this in Figure 12-6.

ProductKey	Calendar Year	@ProdSales	@YearlySales	@CumulatedSales	@CumulatedPct	@AbcClass
153	CY 2007	1,289,602.38	11,309,946.12	1,289,602.38	11.40%	A
1052	CY 2007	716,435.28	11,309,946.12	2,006,037.66	17.74%	A
1293	CY 2007	675,449.95	11,309,946.12	2,681,487.61	23.71%	A
176	CY 2007	362,430.21	11,309,946.12	3,043,917.82	26.91%	A
587	CY 2007	169,256.25	11,309,946.12	3,213,174.07	28.41%	A
1939	CY 2008	135,039.58	9,927,582.99	135,039.58	1.36%	A
1895	CY 2007	124,562.10	11,309,946.12	3,337,736.17	29.51%	A
1897	CY 2009	109,759.66	9,353,814.87	109,759.66	1.17%	A
552	CY 2007	102,459.00	11,309,946.12	3,440,195.17	30.42%	A

FIGURE 12-6 The intermediate calculation evaluated in the *ClassByYearProduct* variable.

Once the table is loaded in the model, the *ABC by Year* table can be used as a filter remapping the data lineage of *ProductKey* and *Calendar Year* to the corresponding columns in the *Product* and *Date* tables. For example, the report shown at the beginning of the section uses these two measures:

Measure in the Sales table

```
# Products :=
VAR RemapFilterAbc =
    TREATAS (
        'ABC by Year',            -- Remap the columns of ABC by Year
        'Product'[ProductKey],    -- so that only the specific
        'Date'[Calendar Year],    -- combinations of product and year
        'ABC by Year'[ABC Class]  -- are included in the filter context
    )
VAR Result =
    CALCULATE (
        DISTINCTCOUNT ( Sales[ProductKey] ),
        KEEPFILTERS ( RemapFilterAbc )
    )
RETURN
    Result
```

Measure in the Sales table

```
ABC Sales Amount :=
VAR RemapFilterAbc =
    TREATAS (
        'ABC by Year',            -- Remap the columns of ABC by Year
        'Product'[ProductKey],    -- so that only the specific
        'Date'[Calendar Year],    -- combinations of product and year
        'ABC by Year'[ABC Class]  -- are included in the filter context
    )
VAR Result =
    CALCULATE (
        [Sales Amount],
        KEEPFILTERS ( RemapFilterAbc )
    )
RETURN
    Result
```

By using TREATAS both measures move the filter from the snapshot to the *Product* and the *Date* tables, obtaining the desired result. It is important to apply *ProductKey* and *Calendar Year* in the same filter, otherwise the measure could include combinations of products and years that are not included in the selected ABC classes.

There is an alternative solution that works better in models with a larger number of products – by using expanded tables. As you can see in Figure 12-7, this requires an intermediate *Years* table linked to *Date* through a relationship with a bidirectional filter (so it is not available in the Excel Power Pivot sample).

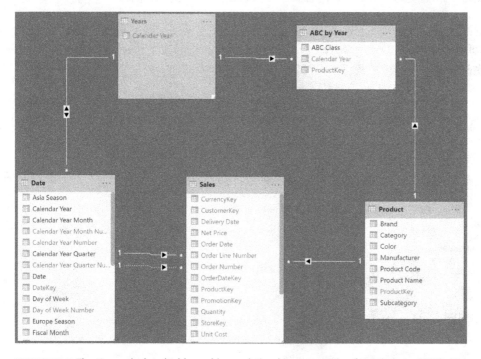

FIGURE 12-7 The *Years* calculated table enables a relationship propagation from *Date* to *ABC by Year*.

The *Years* table is easily computed using a DISTINCT function:

```
Years = DISTINCT ( 'Date'[Calendar Year] )
```

The measures are simpler – though harder to understand – because they rely on table expansion:

Measure in the Sales table

```
# Products Opt :=
CALCULATE (
    DISTINCTCOUNT ( Sales[ProductKey] ),
    'ABC by Year'
)
```

Measure in the Sales table

```
ABC Sales Amount Opt :=
CALCULATE (
    [Sales Amount],
    'ABC by Year'
)
```

The snapshot ABC classification is more dynamic than the static version. The calculated table requires some computational effort. Nevertheless, it is computed at data refresh time and it is very quick at query time. Therefore, the snapshot ABC classification is a very good compromise between speed and flexibility. If flexibility is the main goal, then the slower dynamic ABC classification pattern is a better fit.

Dynamic ABC classification

The dynamic ABC pattern is the most flexible of the three patterns presented, and consequently it is the slowest and most memory-hungry. The goal is to dynamically compute the number of products, the sales amount or any other measure determining the set of products that belong to the given ABC class in the context of the report. For example, in Figure 12-8 the classes are determined considering only the Cell phones category; when the user selects a different category, the whole report is computed with the new filters.

Category	ABC Class	#Products	ABC Sales Amount
☐ Audio			
☐ Cameras and camcorders	A	79	1,117,427.86
■ Cell phones	B	59	325,513.87
☐ Computers	C	147	161,668.53
☐ Games and Toys	**Total**	**285**	**1,604,610.26**
☐ Home Appliances			
☐ Music, Movies and Audio Books			
☐ TV and Video			

FIGURE 12-8 The ABC classification segments the products dynamically, based on the current selection.

Being dynamic, the whole logic is defined in a measure that retrieves the list of products in the desired class, and then uses this list as a filter over the required calculation. Moreover, from the model point of view, there is the need to create an additional *ABC Classes* table that contains the three classes with their boundaries. This is shown in Figure 12-9.

ABC Class	Lower Boundary	Upper Boundary
A	0.00%	70.00%
B	70.00%	90.00%
C	90.00%	100.00%

FIGURE 12-9 The *ABC Classes* table contains the definition of the boundaries for each class.

The measure that computes the *ABC Sales Amount* is the following:

Measure in the Sales table

```
ABC Sales Amount :=
VAR SalesByProduct =
    ADDCOLUMNS (
        ALLSELECTED ( 'Product' ),
        "@ProdSales", [Sales Amount]
    )
VAR AllSales =
    CALCULATE (
        [Sales Amount],
        ALLSELECTED ( 'Product' )
    )
VAR CumulatedPctByProduct =
    ADDCOLUMNS (
        SalesByProduct,
        "@CumulatedPct",
        VAR CurrentSalesAmt = [@ProdSales]
        VAR CumulatedSales =
            FILTER (
                SalesByProduct,
                [@ProdSales] >= CurrentSalesAmt
            )
        VAR CumulatedSalesAmount =
            SUMX (
                CumulatedSales,
                [@ProdSales]
            )
        RETURN
            DIVIDE (
                CumulatedSalesAmount,
                AllSales
            )
    )
VAR ProductsInClass =
    FILTER (
        CROSSJOIN (
            CumulatedPctByProduct,
            'ABC Classes'
        ),
        AND (
            [@CumulatedPct] > 'ABC Classes'[Lower Boundary],
            [@CumulatedPct] <= 'ABC Classes'[Upper Boundary]
        )
    )
VAR Result =
    CALCULATE (               -- The pattern is the same for every measure. Just
        [Sales Amount],       -- change this measure reference for other measures.
        KEEPFILTERS ( ProductsInClass )
    )
RETURN
    Result
```

The complexity of the formula mainly depends on the number of products – the larger the number of products, the slower and more memory-intensive it becomes. Over around ten thousand products, the code will likely start to be too slow to produce an interactive report. This defeats the initial purpose of obtaining a dynamic report.

Finding the ABC class

This pattern describes how to find the ABC class of a product dynamically, producing the result in a measure instead of using a column to classify an existing item. Other ABC segmentation patterns aim to split products into different classes and compute a value, like the sales amount or the number of products. This pattern is useful when you need to show the ABC class of a product dynamically, producing a report like Figure 12-10: The report shows for each product of the Computers category, its ABC class in 2008.

Category	Product Name	Sales Amount	ABC Class
☐ Audio			
☐ Cameras and camcorders	Adventure Works CRT15 E101 Black	1,458.00	C
☐ Cell phones	Adventure Works CRT15 E101 White	1,350.00	C
■ Computers	Adventure Works CRT19 E10 White	607.20	C
☐ Games and Toys	Adventure Works Desktop PC1.60 ED160 Brown	5,641.96	B
☐ Home Appliances	Adventure Works Desktop PC1.60 ED160 Silver	11,229.92	A
☐ Music, Movies and Audio Books	Adventure Works Desktop PC1.80 ED180 Black	6,642.00	B
☐ TV and Video	Adventure Works Desktop PC1.80 ED180 Brown	10,332.00	A
	Adventure Works Desktop PC1.80 ED180 White	17,878.05	A
Calendar Year	Adventure Works Desktop PC1.80 ED182 Black	9,998.00	A
☐ CY 2007	Adventure Works Desktop PC2.30 MD230 Black	34,400.57	A
■ CY 2008	Adventure Works Desktop PC2.30 MD230 Brown	17,817.03	A
☐ CY 2009	Adventure Works Desktop PC2.30 MD230 Silver	17,371.00	A
	Adventure Works Desktop PC2.0 MC200 Black	12,020.20	A
	Total	**2,066,341.75**	

FIGURE 12-10 The ABC classification segments the products dynamically, based on the current selection.

The measure that computes the ABC class is a variation of the dynamic ABC classification. This time, the measure does not need to compute the ABC class of all the products – it is enough to compute the ABC class of the selected product. Therefore, once it computes the list of all products along with their sales, the measure uses the information to compute the correct values only for the current product:

Measure in the Sales table

```
ABC Class :=
IF (
    HASONEVALUE ( 'Product'[ProductKey] ),
    VAR SalesByProduct =
        ADDCOLUMNS (
            ALLSELECTED ( 'Product' ),
            "@ProdSales", [Sales Amount]
        )
    VAR AllSales =
        CALCULATE (
            [Sales Amount],
            ALLSELECTED ( 'Product' )
        )
    VAR CurrentSalesAmt = [Sales Amount]
    VAR CumulatedSales =
        FILTER (
            SalesByProduct,
            [@ProdSales] >= CurrentSalesAmt
        )
    VAR CumulatedSalesAmount =
        SUMX (
            CumulatedSales,
            [@ProdSales]
        )
    VAR CurrentCumulatedPct =
        DIVIDE (
            CumulatedSalesAmount,
            AllSales
        )
    VAR Result =
        SWITCH (
            TRUE,
            ISBLANK ( CurrentCumulatedPct ), BLANK (),
            CurrentCumulatedPct <= 0.7, "A",
            CurrentCumulatedPct <= 0.9, "B",
            "C"
        )
    RETURN
        Result
)
```

## CHAPTER 13

New and returning customers

Download sample files: **https://sql.bi/dax-218**

The New and returning customers pattern helps in understanding how many customers in a period are new, returning, lost, or recovered. There are several variations to this pattern, each with different performance and results depending on the requirements. Moreover, it is a very flexible pattern that allows the identification of new and returning customers, or the computation of these customers' purchase volume – also known as sales amount.

Before using this pattern, you need to clearly define the meaning of new and returning customers, as well as when a customer is lost or recovered. Indeed, depending on the definition you give to these calculations, the formulas are quite different both in their writing and – most important – in performance. Even though you could use the most flexible formula to compute any variation, we would advise you to spend some time experimenting in order to find the best version that fits your needs. The most flexible formula is very expensive from a computational point of view. Therefore, it might be slow even on small datasets.

Introduction

Given a certain time period, you want to compute these formulas:

- **Customers**: the number of customers who made a purchase within that time period.

- **New customers**: the number of customers who made their first purchase within that time period.

- **Returning customers**: the number of customers who have already purchased something in the past, and are returning in that time period.

- **Lost customers**: the number of customers whose last purchase occurred at least 2 months before the start of the current period.

- **Recovered customers:** the number of customers who were considered lost in a previous time period, and then made a purchase in the current period.

The report looks like the one in Figure 13-1.

Calendar Year	# Customers	# New Customers	# Returning Customers	# Lost Customers
⊟ **CY 2007**	**7,999**	**7,999**		**4,425**
January	1,375	1,375		
February	1,153	1,037	116	
March	1,038	900	138	603
April	1,197	960	237	447
May	1,049	774	275	479
June	643	436	207	555
July	823	592	231	609
August	630	423	207	340
September	675	436	239	411
October	489	268	221	295
November	693	397	296	427
December	689	401	288	259
⊟ **CY 2008**	**3,494**	**1,762**	**1,732**	**3,489**
January	327	136	191	391

FIGURE 13-1 The report shows the main calculations of the pattern.

As shown in the report, in January 2007 all customers were new. In February, 116 customers were returning and 1,037 were new, for a total of 1,153 customers. In March, 603 customers were lost.

While the measures computing the number of customers and the number of new customers are easy to describe, calculating the number of lost customers is already complex. In the example, let us look at a customer lost two months after their last purchase. Therefore, the number reported (603) is made up of customers who made their last purchase in January. In other words, out of the 1,375 customers in January 2007, 603 did not buy anything in February, March, and the following months; for this reason, we consider them lost at the end of March.

The definition of lost customers may be different in your business. For example, you might define a customer as lost if they made their last purchase two months ago, even though you already know that they will be making another purchase next month. Imagine a customer who bought something in January and April: are they lost at the end of March or not? The answer leads to different formulations of the same calculation. Indeed, we consider the customer as being temporarily lost at the end of March, because we know the same customer will be recovered later. A report counting the temporarily-lost customers (who did not buy anything for two months, but then made a purchase afterwards) is visible in Figure 13-2.

Calendar Year	# Customers	# Temporarily Lost Customers	# Recovered Customers
⊟ **CY 2007**	**7,999**		
January	1,375		
February	1,153		
March	1,038	1,195	
April	1,197	993	68
May	1,049	900	120
June	643	1,042	110
July	823	984	180
August	630	599	152
September	675	739	163
October	489	560	157
November	693	611	218
December	689	419	236
⊟ **CY 2008**	**3,494**	**963**	**1,334**
January	327	638	148

FIGURE 13-2 The report shows temporarily-lost customers, along with the number of recovered customers.

The number of temporarily-lost customers is higher than the number of lost customers previously shown. The reason is that many of the temporarily-lost customers will buy something in future months. In that case, the report counts them as recovered customers in the month when they make a new purchase.

Another important element to take into account when selecting the right pattern is how you want to look at filters on the report. If the user selects a category of products, how does this filter affect the calculation? Let us say that you filter the Cell Phones category. Do you consider a customer as new the first time they buy a cell phone? If so, then a single customer will be new multiple times, depending on the filter. Otherwise, if you want to consider a customer as new only once, then you need to ignore the filters when computing the number of new customers. Similarly, all the remaining measures might or might not be affected by the filters.

Let us clarify the concept with another example. Figure 13-3 shows the raw data of a reduced version of Contoso with only three customers.

Name	1/3/2007	1/9/2007	2/3/2007	3/14/2007	3/25/2007	4/23/2007	5/15/2007	5/26/2007	6/24/2007	11/12/2007
⊟ **Lal, Dale**										
Cameras and camcorders	977.60							1,222.00		
Games and Toys						8.26			8.88	
⊟ **Mehta, Tammy**										
Games and Toys		18.23								
Home Appliances					239.48					
Music, Movies and Audio Books										7.99
TV and Video			259.47							
⊟ **Suri, Gerald**										
TV and Video				343.20			537.18			

FIGURE 13-3 The report shows three customers along with their purchase history.

Considering the data in Figure 13-3, can you tell when Dale Lal is a new customer, if a user added a filter for Games and Toys? He bought a toy for the first time in April, even though he was already a customer for Cameras and camcorders products. Now focus on Tammy Metha: is she to be considered lost two months after her game purchase in February? She did not buy any other game product, even though she bought products of other categories. Answering these questions is of paramount importance to support your choice of the pattern that will best suit your specific business needs.

Additionally, counting customers is useful, but sometimes you are interested in analyzing the amounts sold to new, returning, and recovered customers. Or you might want to estimate the amount lost because of customer losses, in a report like the one in Figure 13-4. In the report we used the average sales volumes of our lost customers over the last 12 months, as an estimate for lost sales.

Calendar Year	Sales New Customers	Sales Returning Customers	Sales Recovered Customers	Sales Lost Customers (12M)
⊟ CY 2007	**11,309,946.12**			**4,881,363.31**
January	794,248.24			
February	597,699.70	293,436.22		
March	629,295.38	331,993.85		323,602.56
April	650,481.98	477,622.84	60,265.31	379,751.65
May	504,193.23	431,999.51	41,742.72	248,449.35
June	289,031.78	693,272.69	56,006.45	650,953.02
July	415,112.90	507,430.09	60,699.83	508,546.32
August	419,571.13	533,263.45	94,574.46	618,548.73
September	422,136.46	587,732.53	83,103.47	402,645.69
October	225,968.21	688,305.33	109,447.98	473,988.16
November	227,973.12	597,628.75	98,989.41	773,615.50
December	395,243.11	596,305.64	117,619.51	501,262.33
⊟ CY 2008	**7,577,453.30**	**2,350,129.69**	**1,221,855.59**	**6,633,367.25**
January	80,274.19	576,492.50	190,621.39	1,166,756.91

FIGURE 13-4 The report shows the sales amount of new, returning, recovered, and lost customers.

Another important note is to think about how the formulas count the different statuses of a customer inside each time period. For example, if you consider a full year, then it is possible that the same customer is new, temporarily lost, returning, and then permanently lost – all within the same period. On a given day, the status of a customer is well defined. However, throughout longer time frames the same customer can be in different statuses. Our formulas are designed to account for the customer in all their statuses. Figure 13-5 shows a sample report that only filters and shows one customer: Lal Dale.

Month
■ January
■ February
■ March
■ April
■ May
■ June
■ July
■ August
■ September
■ October
■ November
■ December

Calendar Year	# Customers	# New Customers	# Lost Customers	# Returning Customers
⊟ **CY 2007**	1	1	1	
January	1	1		
February				
March				
April	1			1
May	1			1
June	1			1
July				
August			1	
September				
October				
November				
December				
Total	1	1	1	

FIGURE 13-5 The same customer is both new and lost in the same year.

The customer is both new and lost in the same year. Lal Dale was a returning customer for a few months, but not at the year level because he was new during the year. In Figure 13-6 the same report filters out January, thus showing the customer as returning three times within the period, and never showing them as a new customer.

Month ⌄
☐ January
■ February
■ March
■ April
■ May
■ June
■ July
■ August
■ September
■ October
■ November
■ December

Calendar Year	# Customers	# New Customers	# Lost Customers	# Returning Customers
⊟ **CY 2007**	1		1	1
February				
March				
April	1			1
May	1			1
June	1			1
July				
August			1	
September				
October				
November				
December				
Total	1		1	1

FIGURE 13-6 Filtering out January, when the customer was new, the customer now appears as returning in the period.

If we were to describe all the possible combinations of measures in this pattern, this alone would require an entire book. Instead, we show some of the most common patterns, leaving to the reader the task of changing the formulas in case their scenario is different from any of the patterns described.

Finally, the New and returning customers pattern requires heavy calculations. Therefore, we present both a dynamic and a snapshot version of the formulas.

Pattern description

The pattern is based on two types of formulas:

- Internal formulas: their goal is to compute the relevant dates for a given customer.

- External formulas: these are the formulas used in reports. They use the internal formulas to compute the number of customers, the sales amount, or any other measure.

For example, in order to compute the number of new customers, for each customer the internal formula computes the date of their first purchase. The external formula then computes the number of customers whose first purchase happens to fall within the time period currently filtered.

An example is helpful to better understand this technique. Look at Figure 13-7, which shows the reduced dataset we use in order to explain the different formulas.

Name	1/3/2007	1/9/2007	2/3/2007	3/14/2007	3/25/2007	4/23/2007	5/15/2007	5/26/2007	6/24/2007	11/12/2007
Lal, Dale										
Cameras and camcorders	977.60							1,222.00		
Games and Toys						8.26			8.88	
Mehta, Tammy										
Games and Toys		18.23								
Home Appliances					239.48					
Music, Movies and Audio Books										7.99
TV and Video			259.47							
Suri, Gerald										
TV and Video				343.20			537.18			

FIGURE 13-7 The report shows a few customers, along with their purchase history.

Using this data as an example, think about how you can compute the number of new customers in March. The new customers external measure checks how many customers made their first purchase in March. To obtain its result, the external formula queries the internal formulas on a customer-by-customer basis, checking their first purchase. The internal formula returns March 14 for the first purchase of Gerald Suri, whereas the first purchases of the other customers occurred earlier than that. Consequently, the external formula returns 1 as the number of new customers.

Other measures behave the same way, although each comes with peculiarities worthy of a more complete description.

As a first example of code, look at the internal formula that computes the date when a customer must be considered new. Be mindful, each example has different formulas and we provide greater detail on this code in subsequent sections. This first example of DAX is reported here only as an introduction:

Measure (hidden) in the Sales table

```
Date New Customer :=
CALCULATE (
    MIN ( Sales[Order Date] ),
    ALLEXCEPT (
        Sales,
        Sales[CustomerKey],
        Customer
    )
)
```

The internal formula is then used by the external formula, which computes the number of customers who are new in the given period:

Measure in the Sales table

```
# New Customers :=
VAR CustomersWithNewDate =
    CALCULATETABLE (                         -- Prepares a table that
        ADDCOLUMNS (                         -- for each customer contains
            VALUES ( Sales[CustomerKey] ),   -- the date of their first purchase ever
            "@NewCustomerDate", [Date New Customer]
        ),
        ALLSELECTED ( Customer ),            -- Regardless of local filters on customer
        ALLSELECTED ( 'Date' )               -- and on date
    )
VAR CustomersWithLineage =                   -- Here we change the data lineage
    TREATAS (                                -- of the CustomersWithNewDate variable
        CustomersWithNewDate,                -- so that it will filter the
        Customer[CustomerKey],               -- Customer table and the
        'Date'[Date]                         -- Date table
    )
VAR Result =
    CALCULATE (
        DISTINCTCOUNT ( Sales[CustomerKey] ), -- Counts the number of customers only
        KEEPFILTERS ( CustomersWithLineage )  -- if included in @NewCustomerDate variable
    )
RETURN
    Result
```

Using this approach, the pattern is more flexible. Indeed, if you need to change the logic that determines when a customer is to be considered new, lost, or temporarily lost, you only need to update the internal formulas – thus leaving the external formula untouched. Still, we need to raise a big warning for our readers: the formulas shown in this pattern are extremely complex and delicate in the way the filter context is handled. You will certainly need to change them to suit your needs. But do so only after having thoroughly understood their behavior; indeed, each line of DAX in this pattern is the result of hours of thinking and endless tests, as we systematically had to make sure that it was the correct way to write it. In other words, get ready to walk on eggshells with this pattern; we certainly had to!

We organized the patterns in two families: dynamic and snapshot. The dynamic version computes the measures in a dynamic way, considering all the filters of the report. The snapshot version precomputes the values of the internal measures in calculated tables, in order to speed up the calculation of the external measures. Therefore, the snapshot version provides less flexibility, albeit with improved speed.

We also provide three different implementations, depending on how the measure should consider the active filters in the report:

- **Relative**: a customer is considered new the first time they buy one of the products selected in the report.

- **Absolute**: a customer is considered new the first time they buy a product, regardless of any filter present in the report.

- **By category**: a customer is considered new the first time they buy a product from any of the product categories selected in the report. If they buy two products of the same category then they are considered new only once, whereas if they buy two products of different categories then they are considered new twice.

You can find a more complete explanation of the various calculations in the corresponding section of each pattern. Our suggestion is to read the chapter start-to-finish before attempting an implementation on your model. It is better to understand your requirements well before proceeding with the implementation, rather than only finding out at the end that you chose the wrong pattern.

Finally, the demo files of this pattern include two versions: the full version includes the complete database, whereas the base version only includes three customers. The base version is useful to better understand the pattern, because you can easily check the numbers thanks to the limited number of rows in the model. The full version is more useful to evaluate the performance of the different calculations.

Internal measures

There are three internal measures:

- *Date New Customer*: returns the date when the customer is to be considered new.

- *Date Lost Customer*: returns the date when the customer is to be considered permanently lost, checking that there are no sales in following time periods.

- *Date Temporary Lost Customer*: returns the date when the customer might be lost, without checking whether the customer comes back in a following period.

These measures are not intended to be used in reports – they exist only to be used by the external measures. The code of the internal measures is different for each pattern.

External measures

Each pattern defines several measures to count customers and evaluate sales in the various customer states:

- *# New Customers*: counts the number of customers who are new.

- *# Returning Customers*: counts the number of customers who were new in a previous period and made a new purchase within the time period considered.

- *# Lost Customers*: counts the number of customers permanently lost.

- *# Temporarily Lost Customers*: counts the number of customers who are only lost when we look at the current time period, even though they might return in a later period.

- *# Recovered Customers*: counts the number of customers who were temporarily lost and then made a new purchase within the time period considered.

- *Sales New Customers*: returns the value of *Sales Amount* by filtering only the new customers.

- *Sales Returning Customers*: computes the value of *Sales Amount* by filtering only the customers who were new in a previous period and made a new purchase in the period considered.

- *Sales Lost Customers (12M)*: computes the value of *Sales Amount* for 12 months prior to the start of the selected time period, filtering only customers permanently lost in the selected period.

- *Sales Recovered Customers*: returns the value of *Sales Amount* filtering only customers who were previously temporarily lost and who made a new purchase in the period considered.

The code of the external measures is very similar in all the patterns. There are minor variations for some scenarios that are highlighted when we describe the individual patterns.

How to use pattern measures

The formulas presented in the pattern can be grouped into two categories. The measures starting with the # prefix compute the number of unique customers by applying a certain filter. Usually these measures are used as-is and are optimized for this purpose. For example, the following measure returns the number of new customers:

Measure in the Sales table

```
# New Customers :=
VAR CustomersWithNewDate =
    CALCULATETABLE (                           -- Prepares a table that
        ADDCOLUMNS (                           -- for each customer contains
            VALUES ( Sales[CustomerKey] ),     -- the date of their first purchase ever
            "@NewCustomerDate", [Date New Customer]
        ),
        ALLSELECTED ( Customer ),              -- Regardless of any local filters on Customer
        ALLSELECTED ( 'Date' )                 -- and on Date
    )
VAR CustomersWithLineage =                     -- Here we change the data lineage
    TREATAS (                                  -- of the CustomersWithNewDate variable
        CustomersWithNewDate,                  -- so that it filters the
        Customer[CustomerKey],                 -- Customer table and the
        'Date'[Date]                           -- Date table
    )
VAR Result =
    CALCULATE (
        DISTINCTCOUNT ( Sales[CustomerKey] ), -- Counts the number of customers only
        KEEPFILTERS ( CustomersWithLineage )  -- if included ub @NewCustomerDate variable
    )
RETURN
    Result
```

The measures that do not start with the # prefix create a filter of customers that is applied to another measure. For example, the measures with the *Sales* prefix are measures that apply a filter of customers to the *Sales Amount* measure. The following measure can be reused to compute other measures by just changing the *Sales Amount* measure reference in the last CALCULATE function:

Measure in the Sales table

```
Sales New Customers :=
VAR CustomersWithFirstSale =
    CALCULATETABLE (                        -- Prepares a table that
        ADDCOLUMNS (                        -- for each customer contains
            VALUES ( Sales[CustomerKey] ),  -- the date of their first purchase ever
            "@NewCustomerDate", [Date New Customer]
        ),
        ALLSELECTED ( Customer ),           -- Regardless of local filters on Customer
        ALLSELECTED ( 'Date' )              -- and on Date
    )
VAR NewCustomers =
    FILTER (
        CustomersWithFirstSale,             -- Filters the customers
        [@NewCustomerDate]                  -- whose new customer date
            IN VALUES ( 'Date'[Date] )      -- is in the current time period
    )
VAR Result =
    CALCULATE (
        [Sales Amount],                     -- Computes the Sales Amount measure
        KEEPFILTERS ( NewCustomers )        -- by applying the filter for new customers
    )
RETURN
    Result
```

In each pattern we show the two measures (with the # and *Sales* prefixes) when there are differences in the measure structure, even just for performance optimization. If the two measures only differ by the calculation made in the last CALCULATE function, then we only include the # prefix version of the measure.

Dynamic relative

The Dynamic relative pattern takes into account all the filters in the report for the calculation. Therefore, if the report filters one category (Audio, for example), a customer is reported as new the first time they buy a product of the Audio category. Similarly, a customer is considered lost a certain number of days after they last purchased a product of the Audio category. Figure 13-8 is useful to better understand the behavior of this pattern.

Name	# Customers	# New Customers	# Returning Customers	# Temporarily Lost Customers	# Lost Customers
⊟ **Lal, Dale**	1	1			1
⊟ **Cameras and camcorders**	1	1			1
January	1	1			
February					
March				1	
April					
May	1			1	
June					
July				1	1
August					
⊟ **Games and Toys**	1	1			1
February					
March					
April	1	1			
May					
June	1			1	
July					
August				1	1
Total	1	1			1

FIGURE 13-8 The only customer visible (Lal Dale) is considered as new multiple times, for different categories.

The report only takes one customer into account: Lal Dale. He is reported as new in January, when Cameras and camcorders is selected, and he is also considered new in April, for the Games and Toys category. All the other measures behave similarly, by considering the filter where they are evaluated.

Internal measures

The internal measures are the following:

Measure (hidden) in the Sales table

```
Date New Customer :=
CALCULATE (
    MIN ( Sales[Order Date] ),   -- The date of the first sale is the MIN of Order Date
    REMOVEFILTERS ( 'Date' )     -- at any time in the past
)
```

Measure (hidden) in the Sales table

```
Date Lost Customer :=
CALCULATE (                                    -- The last sale occurs two months after
    EOMONTH ( MAX ( Sales[Order Date] ), 2 ), -- the last transaction (end of month)
    REMOVEFILTERS ( 'Date' )                   -- at any time
)
```

Measure (hidden) in the Sales table

```
Date Temporary Lost Customer :=
VAR MaxDate =                      -- The date of the last sale is the MAX of the Order Date
    MAX ( Sales[Order Date] )      -- in the current period (set by the calling measure)
VAR Result =
    IF (
        NOT ISBLANK ( MaxDate ),
        EOMONTH ( MaxDate, 2 )  -- two months later (end of month)
    )
RETURN
    Result
```

New customers

The measure that computes the number of new customers is the following:

Measure in the Sales table

```
# New Customers :=
VAR CustomersWithNewDate =
    CALCULATETABLE (                    -- Prepares a table that
        ADDCOLUMNS (                    -- for each customer contains
            VALUES ( Sales[CustomerKey] ),  -- the date of their first purchase
            "@NewCustomerDate", [Date New Customer]
        ),
        ALLSELECTED ( Customer ),       -- Regardless of local filters on Customer
        ALLSELECTED ( 'Date' )          -- and on Date
    )
VAR CustomersWithLineage =             -- Here we change the data lineage
    TREATAS (                          -- of the CustomersWithNewDate variable
        CustomersWithNewDate,          -- so that it filters the
        Sales[CustomerKey],            -- Customer Key and the
        'Date'[Date]                   -- Date columns in different tables
    )
VAR Result =
    CALCULATE (
        DISTINCTCOUNT ( Sales[CustomerKey] ), -- Counts the number of customers only
        KEEPFILTERS ( CustomersWithLineage )  -- if they appear in their @NewCustomerDate
    )
RETURN
    Result
```

The code computes the date when each customer is new. ALLSELECTED is useful for optimization purposes: it lets the engine reuse the value of the *CustomersWithNewDate* variable in multiple executions of the same expression.

Then, in *CustomersWithLineage* the formula updates the lineage of *CustomersWithNewDate* to let the variable filter *Sales[CustomerKey]* and *Date[Date]*. When used as a filter, *CustomersWithLineage* makes the customers only visible on dates when they are considered new. The final CALCULATE applies the *CustomersWithLineage* filter using KEEPFILTERS to intersect with the current filter context. This way the new filter context ignores customers that are not new in the range of dates considered.

In order to apply the new customers as a filter for another measure like *Sales Amount* we need a slightly different approach, as shown in the following *Sales New Customers* measure:

Measure in the Sales table

```
Sales New Customers :=
VAR CustomersWithFirstSale =
    CALCULATETABLE (                      -- Prepares a table that
        ADDCOLUMNS (                      -- for each customer contains
            VALUES ( Sales[CustomerKey] ),  -- the date of their first purchase ever
            "@NewCustomerDate", [Date New Customer]
        ),
        ALLSELECTED ( Customer ),         -- Regardless of local filters on Customer
        ALLSELECTED ( 'Date' )            -- and on Date
    )
VAR NewCustomers =
    FILTER (
        CustomersWithFirstSale,           -- Filters the customers
        [@NewCustomerDate]                -- where the new customer date
            IN VALUES ( 'Date'[Date] )    -- is in the current time period
    )
VAR Result =
    CALCULATE (
        [Sales Amount],                   -- Evaluates Sales Amount by applying
        KEEPFILTERS ( NewCustomers )      -- the filter for new customers
    )
RETURN
    Result
```

The *NewCustomers* variable holds a list of the values in *Sales[CustomerKey]* corresponding to the new customers, obtained by checking whether the *@NewCustomerDate* is within the filter context of the current evaluation. The *NewCustomers* variable obtained this way is then applied as a filter to compute the *Sales Amount* measure. Even though the variable contains two columns (*Sales[CustomerKey]* and *@ NewCustomerDate*), the only column actively filtering the model is *Sales[CustomerKey]*, because the newly added column does not share the lineage with any other column in the model.

Lost customers

The measure computing the number of lost customers needs to count customers that are not part of the current filter context. Indeed, in March we might lose a customer who made a purchase in January. Therefore, when filtering March the customer is not visible. The formula must look back at January to find that customer. This is the reason why the structure of the code is different from the *New Customers* measure:

Measure in the Sales table

```
# Lost Customers :=
VAR LastDateLost =
    CALCULATE (
        MAX ( 'Date'[Date] ),
        ALLSELECTED ( 'Date' )
    )
VAR CustomersWithLostDate =
    CALCULATETABLE (                         -- Prepares a table that
        ADDCOLUMNS (                         -- for each customer contains
            VALUES ( Sales[CustomerKey] ),   -- the date when they are considered lost
            "@LostCustomerDate", [Date Lost Customer]
        ),
        ALLSELECTED ( Customer ),            -- Regardless of local filters on Customer
        'Date'[Date] <= LastDateLost         -- and on Date
    )
VAR LostCustomers =
    FILTER (
        CustomersWithLostDate,               -- Filters the customers
        [@LostCustomerDate]                  -- whose Lost Customer Date
            IN VALUES ( 'Date'[Date] )       -- falls within the current time period
    )
VAR Result =
    COUNTROWS ( LostCustomers )              -- The count of the lost customers does not
                                             -- use the Sales table (no sales in the period)
RETURN
    Result
```

The *CustomersWithLostDate* variable computes the date of loss for each customer. *LostCustomers* filters out customers whose date of loss is not in the current period. Eventually, the measure computes the number of customers left by counting the rows in *LostCustomers* that correspond to the customers whose date of loss falls within the period visible in the current filter context.

Temporarily-lost customers

The measure computing the number of temporarily-lost customers is a major variation of the measure computing the lost customers. The measure must check that in the current context the customer who is potentially lost did not make a purchase prior to the date when they would have been lost. This is the code that implements this calculation:

Measure in the Sales table

```
# Temporarily Lost Customers :=
VAR MinDate = MIN ( 'Date'[Date] )
VAR CustomersWithLostDateComplete  =
    CALCULATETABLE (                       -- Prepares a table that
        ADDCOLUMNS (                       -- for each customer contains
            VALUES ( Sales[CustomerKey] ), -- the temporarily-lost date
            "@TemporarilyLostCustomerDate", CALCULATE (
                [Date Temporary Lost Customer],
                'Date'[Date] < MinDate
            )
        ),
        ALLSELECTED ( Customer ),          -- Regardless of local filters on Customer
        ALLSELECTED ( 'Date' )             -- and on Date
    )
VAR CustomersWithLostDate =
    FILTER (                               -- Removes the customers without a
        CustomersWithLostDateComplete,     -- temporarily-lost date
        NOT ISBLANK ( [@TemporarilyLostCustomerDate] )
    )
VAR PotentialTemporarilyLostCustomers =
    FILTER (
        CustomersWithLostDate,             -- Filters the customers
        [@TemporarilyLostCustomerDate]     -- whose lost-customer date
            IN VALUES ( 'Date'[Date] )     -- falls within the current period
    )
VAR ActiveCustomers =
    ADDCOLUMNS (                           -- Gets the first order date of
        VALUES ( Sales[CustomerKey] ),     -- customers in the current selection
        "@MinOrderDate", CALCULATE ( MIN ( Sales[Order Date] ) )
    )
VAR TemporarilyLostCustomers =
    FILTER (                               -- Filters the temporarily-lost
        NATURALLEFTOUTERJOIN (             -- customers by combining
            PotentialTemporarilyLostCustomers,-- potential lost customers
            ActiveCustomers                -- and active customers
        ),                                 -- and then comparing dates
        OR (
            ISBLANK ( [@MinOrderDate] ),
            [@MinOrderDate] > [@TemporarilyLostCustomerDate]
        )
    )
VAR Result =
    COUNTROWS ( TemporarilyLostCustomers )
RETURN
    Result
```

The measure first computes the potential date of loss of each customer; it applies a filter on the date so that it only considers transactions made before the start of the current time period. Then, it checks which customers have a loss date that falls within the current period.

The resulting table (*PotentialTemporarilyLostCustomers*) contains the customers that can be potentially lost in the current period. Before returning a result, a final check is required: these customers must not have purchased anything in the current period before the date when they would be considered lost. This validation happens by computing *TemporarilyLostCustomers*, which checks for each customer whether there are sales in the current period before the date when the customer would be considered lost.

Recovered customers

The number of recovered customers is the number of customers that were temporarily lost before a purchase was made in the current period. It is computed by the following measure:

Measure in the Sales table

```
# Recovered Customers :=
VAR MinDate =
    MIN ( 'Date'[Date] )
VAR CustomersWithLostDateComplete =
    CALCULATETABLE (                            -- Prepares a table that
        ADDCOLUMNS (                            -- for each customer contains
            VALUES ( Sales[CustomerKey] ), -- the temporarily-lost date
            "@TemporarilyLostCustomerDate", CALCULATE (
                [Date Temporary Lost Customer],
                'Date'[Date] < MinDate
            )
        ),
        ALLSELECTED ( Customer ),               -- Regardless of local filters on Customer
        ALLSELECTED ( 'Date' )                  -- and on Date
    )
VAR CustomersWithLostDate =
    FILTER (                                    -- Removes the customer without a
        CustomersWithLostDateComplete,          -- temporarily-lost date
        NOT ISBLANK ( [@TemporarilyLostCustomerDate] )
    )
VAR ActiveCustomers =
    ADDCOLUMNS (                                -- Gets the first order date of
        VALUES ( Sales[CustomerKey] ),          -- customers in the current selection
        "@MinOrderDate", CALCULATE ( MIN ( Sales[Order Date] ) )
    )
VAR RecoveredCustomers =
    FILTER (
        NATURALINNERJOIN (                      -- Filters the recovered customers
            ActiveCustomers,                    -- by combining active customers
            CustomersWithLostDate               -- and temporarily-lost customers
        ),                                      -- and then comparing dates
        [@MinOrderDate] > [@TemporarilyLostCustomerDate]
    )
VAR Result =
    COUNTROWS ( RecoveredCustomers )
RETURN
    Result
```

The *CustomersWithLostDateComplete* variable computes the temporarily-lost date for the customers. Out of this list, the *CustomersWithLostDate* variable removes the customers who do not have a temporarily-lost date. The *ActiveCustomers* variable retrieves the first purchase date for the customers in the current selection. The *RecoveredCustomers* variable filters customers that are in both *ActiveCustomers* and *CustomersWithLostDate* lists and have a transaction date greater than the temporarily-lost date.

Finally, the *Result* variable counts the recovered customers.

Returning customers

The last measure in the set of counting measures is # *Returning Customers*:

Measure in the Sales table

```
# Returning Customers :=
VAR MinDate = MIN ( 'Date'[Date] )
VAR CustomersWithNewDate =
    CALCULATETABLE (                         -- Prepares a table that
        ADDCOLUMNS (                         -- for each customer contains
            VALUES ( Sales[CustomerKey] ),   -- their first purchase date
            "@NewCustomerDate", [Date New Customer]
        ),
        ALLSELECTED ( Customer ),            -- Regardless of local filters on Customer
        ALLSELECTED ( 'Date' )               -- and on Date
    )
VAR ExistingCustomers =                      -- To get the existing customers,
    FILTER (                                 -- this filters all customers
        CustomersWithNewDate,                -- and checks that their first purchase took
        [@NewCustomerDate] < MinDate         -- place before the start of the current period
    )
VAR ReturningCustomers =                     -- Obtains the returning customers
    INTERSECT (                              -- as the intersection between
        VALUES ( Sales[CustomerKey] ),       -- the active customers in the selection
        SELECTCOLUMNS (                      -- and the existing customers
            ExistingCustomers,
            "CustomerKey", Sales[CustomerKey]
        )
    )
VAR Result =
    COUNTROWS ( ReturningCustomers )
RETURN
    Result
```

The measure first prepares a table in *CustomersWithNewDate* with the first purchase date for every customer. The *ExistingCustomers* variable filters out all the customers whose date is not strictly earlier than the start of the currently selected period. What remains in *ExistingCustomers* is the set of customers who already purchased products before the current period started. Therefore, if those customers also made purchases within the current period, then they are returning customers. This last condition is obtained by combining *ExistingCustomers* with the customers active in the selected period. The result in the *ReturningCustomers* variable can be used to count the returning customers – as in this measure – or to filter them in a different calculation.

Dynamic absolute

The Dynamic absolute pattern ignores the filters on the report when computing the relevant dates for the customer. Its implementation is a variation of the basic Dynamic relative pattern, with a different set of CALCULATE modifiers to explicitly ignore filters.

The result is an absolute assignment of the status of a customer regardless of report filters, as shown in Figure 13-9: Dale Lal is considered new in January when Games and Toys is selected, even though he purchased cameras and no games.

Name	# Customers	# New Customers	# Returning Customers	# Temporarily Lost Customers	# Lost Customers
⊟ **Lal, Dale**	1	1			1
⊟ **Cameras and camcorders**	1	1			1
January	1	1			
February					
March				1	
April				1	
May	1		1		
June			1		
July					
August				1	1
⊟ **Games and Toys**	1	1			1
January		1			
February					
March				1	
April	1		1		
May			1		
June	1		1		
July					
August				1	1
Total	1	1			1

FIGURE 13-9 Lal Dale is considered new, returning, and lost regardless of the category used in the visual.

The only measure that changes depending on the category is # *Customers*, which shows when Lal Dale purchased products. All the other measures ignore the filter on the product: customers are new only the first time they make a purchase regardless of the report filter.

Internal measures

The internal measures are the following:

Measure (hidden) in the Sales table

```
Date New Customer :=
CALCULATE (                          -- The first sale is
    MIN ( Sales[Order Date] ),       -- the MIN of the order date
    ALLEXCEPT (
        Sales,                       -- ignoring any filter
        Sales[CustomerKey],          -- other than the customer
        Customer
    )
)
```

Measure (hidden) in the Sales table

```
Date Lost Customer :=
VAR MaxDate =
    CALCULATE (                      -- The last sale is the MAX of Order Date
        MAX ( Sales[Order Date] ),   -- in the current period (set by the calling measure)
        ALLEXCEPT (
            Sales,                   -- ignoring any filter
            Sales[CustomerKey],      -- other than Customer
            Customer
        )
    )
VAR Result =
    IF (
        NOT ISBLANK ( MaxDate ),
        EOMONTH ( MaxDate, 2 ) -- two months later (end of month)
    )
RETURN
    Result
```

Measure (hidden) in the Sales table

```
Date Temporary Lost Customer :=
VAR MaxDate =
    CALCULATE (                      -- The last sale is the MAX of Order Date
        MAX ( Sales[Order Date] ),   -- in the current period (set by the calling measure)
        ALLEXCEPT (
            Sales,                   -- ignoring any filter
            'Date',                  -- other than Date
            Sales[CustomerKey],      -- and Customer
            Customer
        )
    )
VAR Result =
    IF (
        NOT ISBLANK ( MaxDate ),
        EOMONTH ( MaxDate, 2 )       -- two months later (end of month)
    )
RETURN
    Result
```

As shown in the previous code, the internal measures are designed to ignore all filters other than the ones on *Customer* – with the noticeable exception of *Date Temporary Lost Customer* which needs to also consider the filters on *Date*.

Please note that the internal measures have been designed to behave properly when called from the external measures. This is the reason why ALLEXCEPT explicitly keeps the filter on *Sales[CustomerKey]* in a somewhat unusual way. If called within an iteration that includes that column, the internal measures do not remove the filter, thereby observing the requirements of the external measure.

New customers

The measure that computes the new customers is the following:

Measure in the Sales table

```
# New Customers :=
VAR CustomersWithNewDate =
    CALCULATETABLE (                         -- Prepares a table that
        ADDCOLUMNS (                         -- for each customer contains
            VALUES ( Sales[CustomerKey] ),   -- the date of their first puchase
            "@NewCustomerDate", [Date New Customer]
        ),
        ALLEXCEPT ( Sales, Customer )
    )
VAR NewCustomers =
    FILTER (
        CustomersWithNewDate,                -- Filters the customers
        [@NewCustomerDate]                   -- whose new customer date
            IN VALUES ( 'Date'[Date] )       -- falls within the current period
    )
VAR Result =                                 -- The count of the new customers
    COUNTROWS ( NewCustomers )               -- does not use the Sales table
RETURN
    Result
```

There are two things to note about this measure. First, the filter in the calculation of *CustomersWithNewDate* uses ALLEXCEPT to ignore any filter apart from the ones on the *Customer* table. Second, in order to check whether a customer is new, the measure filters the content of *CustomersWithNewDate*. It then counts the row in the *NewCustomers* variable, instead of using TREATAS as the corresponding measure in the Dynamic relative pattern. This technique may turn out to be slower than the one used in the Dynamic relative pattern; it is still required because it needs to count a customer even though they might not be visible due to the current filter context.

Lost customers

The measure computing the number of lost customers is the following:

Measure in the Sales table

```
# Lost Customers :=
VAR LastDateLost =
    CALCULATE (
        MAX ( 'Date'[Date] ),
        ALLSELECTED ( 'Date' )
    )
VAR CustomersWithLostDate =
    CALCULATETABLE (                        -- Prepares a table that
        ADDCOLUMNS (                        -- for each customer contains
            VALUES ( Sales[CustomerKey] ),  -- the date when they are considered lost
            "@LostCustomerDate", [Date Lost Customer]
        ),
        ALLEXCEPT ( Sales, Customer ),
        'Date'[Date] <= LastDateLost
    )
VAR LostCustomers =
    FILTER (
        CustomersWithLostDate,              -- Filters the customers
        [@LostCustomerDate]                 -- whose lost customer date
            IN VALUES ( 'Date'[Date] )      -- fall within the current period
    )
VAR Result =
    COUNTROWS ( LostCustomers )             -- The count of the lost customers does not
                                            -- use the Sales table (no sales in the period)
RETURN
    Result
```

Its structure is close to the New Customer measure, the main difference being in the calculation of the *CustomersWithLostDate* variable.

Temporarily-lost customers

The measure computing the number of temporarily-lost customers is a variation of the measure computing the lost customers:

Measure in the Sales table

```
# Temporarily Lost Customers :=
VAR MinDate = MIN ( 'Date'[Date] )
VAR CustomersWithLostDateComplete  =
    CALCULATETABLE (                           -- Prepares a table that
        ADDCOLUMNS (                           -- for each customer contains
            VALUES ( Sales[CustomerKey] ),     -- the temporarily-lost date
            "@TemporarilyLostCustomerDate", CALCULATE (
                [Date Temporary Lost Customer],
                'Date'[Date] < MinDate
            )
        ),                                     -- ignoring any filter
        ALLEXCEPT ( Sales, Customer )          -- other than Customer
    )
VAR CustomersWithLostDate =
    FILTER (                                   -- Removes the customers without a
        CustomersWithLostDateComplete,         -- temporarily-lost date
        NOT ISBLANK ( [@TemporarilyLostCustomerDate] )
    )
VAR PotentialTemporarilyLostCustomers =
    FILTER (
        CustomersWithLostDate,                 -- Filter the customers
        [@TemporarilyLostCustomerDate]         -- where the lost customer date
            IN VALUES ( 'Date'[Date] )         -- falls within the current period
    )
VAR ActiveCustomers =
    CALCULATETABLE (
        ADDCOLUMNS (                           -- Gets the first order date of
            VALUES ( Sales[CustomerKey] ),     -- customers in the current selection
            "@MinOrderDate", CALCULATE ( MIN ( Sales[Order Date] ) )
        ),
        ALLEXCEPT ( Sales, Customer, 'Date' )
    )
VAR TemporarilyLostCustomers =
    FILTER (                                   -- Filters the temporarily-lost
        NATURALLEFTOUTERJOIN (                 -- customers by combining
            PotentialTemporarilyLostCustomers,-- potential lost customers
            ActiveCustomers                    -- and active customers
        ),                                     -- and then by comparing dates
        OR (
            ISBLANK ( [@MinOrderDate] ),
            [@MinOrderDate] > [@TemporarilyLostCustomerDate]
        )
    )
VAR Result =
    COUNTROWS ( TemporarilyLostCustomers )
RETURN
    Result
```

Its behavior is very close to the corresponding measure in the Dynamic relative pattern. The main differences are the use of ALLEXCEPT in the evaluation of *CustomersWithLostDateComplete* and *ActiveCustomers*. In *CustomersWithLostDateComplete* all the filters other than *Customer* are removed, whereas in *ActiveCustomers* the filters are not removed from *Date* and *Customer*.

Recovered customers

The number of recovered customers is the number of customers that were temporarily lost before a purchase made in the current period. It is computed by the following measure:

Measure in the Sales table

```
# Recovered Customers :=
VAR MinDate = MIN ( 'Date'[Date] )
VAR CustomersWithLostDateComplete  =
    CALCULATETABLE (                         -- Prepares a table that
        ADDCOLUMNS (                         -- for each customer contains
            VALUES ( Sales[CustomerKey] ),   -- the temporarily-lost date
            "@TemporarilyLostCustomerDate", CALCULATE (
                [Date Temporary Lost Customer],
                'Date'[Date] < MinDate
            )
        ),                                   -- ignoring any filter
        ALLEXCEPT ( Sales, Customer )        -- other than Customer
    )
VAR CustomersWithLostDate =
    FILTER (                                 -- Removes the customer without a
        CustomersWithLostDateComplete,       -- temporarily-lost date
        NOT ISBLANK ( [@TemporarilyLostCustomerDate] )
    )
VAR ActiveCustomers =
    CALCULATETABLE (
        ADDCOLUMNS (                         -- Gets the first order date of
            VALUES ( Sales[CustomerKey] ),   -- customers in the current selection
            "@MinOrderDate", CALCULATE ( MIN ( Sales[Order Date] ) )
        ),
        ALLEXCEPT ( Sales, Customer, 'Date' )
    )
VAR RecoveredCustomers =
    FILTER (
        NATURALINNERJOIN (                   -- Filters the recovered customers
            ActiveCustomers,                 -- by combining active customers
            CustomersWithLostDate            -- and temporarily-lost customers
        ),                                   -- then by comparing dates
        [@MinOrderDate] > [@TemporarilyLostCustomerDate]
    )
VAR Result =
    COUNTROWS ( RecoveredCustomers )
RETURN
    Result
```

Its behavior is very close to the corresponding measure in the Dynamic relative pattern. The main difference is the use of ALLEXCEPT in the evaluation of the *CustomersWithLostDateComplete* and *ActiveCustomer* variables to correctly set the required filter.

Returning customers

The last measure in the set of counting ones is the # *Returning Customers*:

Measure in the Sales table

```
# Returning Customers :=
VAR MinDate = MIN ( 'Date'[Date] )
VAR CustomersWithNewDate =
    CALCULATETABLE (                         -- Prepares a table that
        ADDCOLUMNS (                         -- for each customer contains
            VALUES ( Sales[CustomerKey] ),   -- their first sale date
            "@NewCustomerDate", [Date New Customer]
        ),                                   -- ignoring any filter
        ALLEXCEPT ( Sales, Customer )        -- other than Customer)
    )
VAR ExistingCustomers =                      -- To compute the existing customers
    FILTER (                                 -- we filter all customers
        CustomersWithNewDate,                -- and check that their
        [@NewCustomerDate] < MinDate         -- first sale happened
                                             -- before the current period
    )
VAR ActiveCustomers =
    CALCULATETABLE (
        VALUES ( Sales[CustomerKey] ),       -- Gets the active customers
        ALLEXCEPT ( Sales, Customer, 'Date' )
    )
VAR ReturningCustomers =                     -- Obtain the returning customers
    INTERSECT (                              -- as the intersection between
        ActiveCustomers,                     -- the active customers in the selection
        SELECTCOLUMNS (                      -- and the existing customers
            ExistingCustomers,
            "CustomerKey", Sales[CustomerKey]
        )
    )
VAR Result =
    COUNTROWS ( ReturningCustomers )
RETURN
    Result
```

Its behavior is very close to the corresponding measure in the Dynamic relative pattern. The main difference is the use of ALLEXCEPT in the evaluation of the *CustomersWithNewDate* and *ActiveCustomers* variables, to accurately set the required filter.

Generic dynamic pattern (dynamic by category)

The generic dynamic pattern is an intermediate level between the absolute and the dynamic patterns. The pattern ignores all the filters from the report except for attributes determined by the business logic. In the examples used in this section, the measures are local to each product category. The result is dynamic for product category and absolute for all the other attributes in the data model. For instance, one customer can be new for a product category and a returning customer for another product category within the same month. The same customers might be considered new multiple times if they buy different categories of products over time. In other words, the analysis of new and returning customers is made by product category. You can customize the pattern by replacing product category with one or more other attributes, so that it fits your business logic.

We purposely avoided excessive optimizations when writing the code of this pattern: the primary goal of this set of measures is to make them easier to update. If you plan on modifying the pattern to fit your needs, this set of measures should be a good starting point.

The rules of this pattern are the following:

- The same customer might be considered a new customer multiple times, one for each combination of dynamic attributes (product category in the example).

- Customers are considered returning customers if they already purchased the same combination of dynamic attributes (product category in the example) they are purchasing in the selected period.

- Customers are temporarily lost if they did not purchase a combination of dynamic attributes (product category in the example) for two months, even though they may have purchased different combinations of dynamic attributes (product category in the example) in the meantime.

- Customers are considered recovered customers if they make a new purchase of products of the very combination of dynamic attributes (product category in the example) for which they were temporarily lost.

It is important to note that the pattern detects the customers, not the combination of dynamic attributes and customers – like customer and product category in the example. Therefore, the measures with the # prefix always return the number of unique customers, whereas the measures with the *Sales* prefix always evaluate the *Sales Amount* measure regardless of the combination of dynamic attributes (product category in the example) for which a customer is considered new/lost/recovered. The difference is visible by filtering two or more combinations of the dynamic attributes. For example, by filtering two product categories, the *Sales* measures for new and returning customers could add up to more than the value of *Sales Amount*; indeed, the same amount can be computed considering the same customer both new and returning, because of their having different states for different categories.

Your requirements might be different from those assumed in this example. In that case, as we already stated in the introduction, you need to very carefully understand the filtering happening in all the measures before implementing any change. These measures are quite complex and easy to break with small changes.

Internal measures

The internal measures are the following:

Measure (hidden) in the Sales table

```
Date New Customer :=
CALCULATE (
    MIN ( Sales[Order Date] ),   -- The first sale is the MIN of Order Date
    ALLEXCEPT (
        Sales,                   -- ignoring filters
        Sales[CustomerKey],      -- other than Customer
        Customer,
        'Product'[Category]      -- and Product Category
    )
)
```

Measure (hidden) in the Sales table

```
Date Lost Customer :=
VAR MaxDate =
    CALCULATE (                      -- The last sale is the MAX of Order Date in the
        MAX ( Sales[Order Date] ),   -- current time period (set by the calling measure)
        ALLEXCEPT (
            Sales,                   -- ignoring any filter
            Sales[CustomerKey],      -- other than Customer
            Customer,
            'Product'[Category]      -- and Product Category
        )
    )
VAR Result =
    IF (
        NOT ISBLANK ( MaxDate ),
        EOMONTH ( MaxDate, 2 )       -- two months later (end of month)
    )
RETURN
    Result
```

Measure (hidden) in the Sales table

```
Date Temporary Lost Customer :=
VAR MaxDate =
    CALCULATE (                     -- The last sale is the MAX of Order Date
        MAX ( Sales[Order Date] ),  -- in the current period (set by the calling measure)
        ALLEXCEPT (
            Sales,                  -- ignoring any filter
            'Date',                 -- other than Date
            Sales[CustomerKey],     -- and Customer
            Customer,
            'Product'[Category]     -- and product category
        )
    )
VAR Result =
    IF (
        NOT ISBLANK ( MaxDate ),
        EOMONTH ( MaxDate, 2 )      -- two months later (end of month)
    )
RETURN
    Result
```

As shown in this code, the internal measures are designed to ignore filters other than the ones on *Customer* and *Product[Category]*.

New customers

The measure that computes the new customers is the following:

Measure in the Sales table

```
# New Customers :=
VAR FilterCategories =
    CALCULATETABLE (
        VALUES ( 'Product'[Category] ),
        ALLSELECTED ( 'Product' )
    )

VAR CustomersWithNewDate =
    CALCULATETABLE (                 -- Prepares a table that contains
        ADDCOLUMNS (                 -- for each customer and category,
            SUMMARIZE (              -- the date of their first purchase
                Sales,
                Sales[CustomerKey],
                'Product'[Category]
            ),
            "@NewCustomerDate", [Date New Customer]
        ),
```

```
        ALLSELECTED ( Customer ),
        FilterCategories,          -- Filter Product Category from ALLSELECTED
        ALLEXCEPT (                -- Removes any filter other than
            Sales,                 -- Customer retrieved by ALLSELECTED so that
            Sales[CustomerKey],    -- the result is unchanged in
            Customer               -- different cells of the report
        )
    )
VAR CustomersCategoryNewDate =
    TREATAS (
        CustomersWithNewDate,      -- Changes the data lineage so that
        Sales[CustomerKey],        -- NewCustomerDate maps Date[Date]
        'Product'[Category],       -- and can be used to join or filter
        'Date'[Date]               -- that same column in the model
    )
VAR ActiveCustomersCategories =
    CALCULATETABLE (
        SUMMARIZE (                -- Retrieves combinations of
            Sales,                 -- Customer, Category, and Date
            Sales[CustomerKey],    -- active in the current selection
            'Product'[Category],
            'Date'[Date]
        ),
        ALLEXCEPT (                -- Removes any filter other than Date and
            Sales,                 -- Customer retrieved by ALLSELECTED so that
            'Date',                -- the result is unchanged in
            Sales[CustomerKey],    -- different cells of the report
            Customer
        ),
        VALUES ( 'Product'[Category] )  -- Restore related Product[Category] filter
    )
VAR ActiveNewCustomers =
    NATURALINNERJOIN (             -- Filters the customers
        CustomersCategoryNewDate,  -- within the current selection
        ActiveCustomersCategories  -- joining Date and Category
    )
VAR NewCustomers =
    DISTINCT (                     -- Gets the list of unique
        SELECTCOLUMNS (            -- new customers
            ActiveNewCustomers,
            "CustomerKey", Sales[CustomerKey]
        )
    )
VAR Result =
    COUNTROWS ( NewCustomers )
RETURN
    Result
```

In this version of the measure, the *CustomersWithNewDate* variable might compute a different date for each product category. Indeed, SUMMARIZE uses the *Product[Category]* column as a group-by condition. Consequently, TREATAS specifies the lineage for the three columns in *CustomersWithNewDate* so that the *@NewCustomerDate* column can be used later to filter or join the *Date[Date]* column.

For performance reasons, the *CustomersWithNewDate* and *CustomersCategoryNewDate* variables are invariant to the filter context of cells in a report, so their result is computed only once for a single visualization. In order to get the actual new customers, it is necessary to filter those combinations that are not visible in the filter context where *# New Customer* is evaluated. This is accomplished by the NATURALINNERJOIN in *ActiveNewCustomers*, which joins the combinations of customer, date, and category visible in the filter context (*ActiveCustomersCategories*) with the combinations in *CustomersCategoryNewDate*.

The *NewCustomers* variable removes the duplicated customers that could be new for different categories in the same period. This way, *NewCustomers* can be used as a filter in following calculations or it can be counted to obtain the number of new customers, as the *# New Customers* measure does.

The *Sales New Customers* measure is similar to *# New Customers*, the only difference is the *Result* variable that uses the *NewCustomersCat* as a filter in CALCULATE instead of just counting the rows of the *NewCustomer* variable. Therefore, we show here only the last part of the code, using ellipsis for the unchanged sections:

Measure in the Sales table

```
Sales New Customers :=
...
VAR NewCustomersCat =
    SELECTCOLUMNS (                         -- new customers/category, remove date
        ActiveNewCustomers,
        "CustomerKey", Sales[CustomerKey],
        "Category", 'Product'[Category]
    )
VAR Result =
    CALCULATE (
        [Sales Amount],                     -- Count the new customers (or sum Sales)
        KEEPFILTERS ( NewCustomersCat )     -- applying the filter for new customers
    )
RETURN
    Result
```

Lost customers

The measure computing the number of lost customers is the following:

Measure in the Sales table

```
# Lost Customers :=
VAR LastDateLost =
    CALCULATE (
        MAX ( 'Date'[Date] ),
        ALLSELECTED ( 'Date' )
    )
VAR CustomersWithLostDate =
    CALCULATETABLE (                        -- Prepares a table that contains
        ADDCOLUMNS (                        -- for each customer and category,
            SUMMARIZE (                     -- the corresponding lost date
                Sales,
                Sales[CustomerKey],
                'Product'[Category]
            ),
            "@LostCustomerDate", [Date Lost Customer]
        ),
        'Date'[Date] <= LastDateLost,
        ALLSELECTED ( Customer ),
        VALUES ( 'Product'[Category] ),
        ALLEXCEPT (                         -- Removes any filter other than
            Sales,                          -- Customer retrieved by ALLSELECTED so that
            Sales[CustomerKey],             -- the result is unchanged in
            Customer                        -- different cells of the report
        )
    )
VAR LostCustomersCategories =
    FILTER (
        CustomersWithLostDate,              -- Filters the customers
        [@LostCustomerDate]                 -- where the lost customer date
            IN VALUES ( 'Date'[Date] )      -- falls within the current period
    )
VAR LostCustomers =
    DISTINCT (                              -- Gets the list of unique
        SELECTCOLUMNS (                     -- lost customers
            LostCustomersCategories,
            "CustomerKey", Sales[CustomerKey]
        )
    )
VAR Result =
    COUNTROWS ( LostCustomers )
RETURN
    Result
```

In this version of the measure, the *CustomersWithLostDate* variable might compute a different date for each product category. The reason is that SUMMARIZE uses the *Product[Category]* column as a group-by condition and that the customer might have different dates of loss – one for each category.

The *LostCustomersCategories* variable only filters the combinations of customers and categories that have a lost date included in the selected time period. Similarly to the *New Customers* measure, the *LostCustomers* variable removes the duplicated customers so it can be used both as a filter and to count the lost customers.

Temporarily-lost customers

The measure computing the number of temporarily-lost customers is a variation of the measure computing the lost customers:

Measure in the Sales table

```
# Temporarily Lost Customers :=
VAR LastDateLost =
    CALCULATE (
        MAX ( 'Date'[Date] ),
        ALLSELECTED ( 'Date' )
    )
VAR MinDate = MIN ( 'Date'[Date] )
VAR FilterCategories =
    CALCULATETABLE (
        VALUES ( 'Product'[Category] ),
        ALLSELECTED ( 'Product' )
    )
VAR CustomersWithLostDateComplete =
    CALCULATETABLE (                    -- Prepares a table that contains
        ADDCOLUMNS (                    -- for each customer and category,
            SUMMARIZE (                 -- the corresponding lost date
                Sales,
                Sales[CustomerKey],
                'Product'[Category]
            ),
            "@TemporarilyLostCustomerDate", CALCULATE (
                [Date Temporary Lost Customer],
                'Date'[Date] < MinDate
            )
        ),
        ALLSELECTED ( Customer ),
        FilterCategories,           -- Filter Product Category from ALLSELECTED
        ALLEXCEPT (                 -- Removes any filter other than
            Sales,                  -- Customer retrieved by ALLSELECTED so that
            Sales[CustomerKey],     -- the result is unchanged in
            Customer                -- different cells of the report
        )
    )
```

```
VAR CustomersWithLostDate =
    FILTER (                                    -- Removes the customer without a
        CustomersWithLostDateComplete,          -- temporarily-lost date
        NOT ISBLANK ( [@TemporarilyLostCustomerDate] )
    )
VAR PotentialTemporarilyLostCustomers =
    FILTER (
        CustomersWithLostDate,                  -- Filter the customers
        [@TemporarilyLostCustomerDate]          -- where the lost customer date
            IN VALUES ( 'Date'[Date] )          -- falls within the current period
    )
VAR ActiveCustomersCategories =
    CALCULATETABLE (
        ADDCOLUMNS (
            SUMMARIZE (                         -- Gets the first order date
                Sales,                          -- for each combination of
                Sales[CustomerKey],             -- customer and category
                'Product'[Category]             -- in the current selection
            ),
            "@MinOrderDate", CALCULATE ( MIN ( Sales[Order Date] ) )
        ),
        ALLEXCEPT (                             -- Removes any filter other than
            Sales,                              -- customer and date
            Sales[CustomerKey],
            Customer,
            'Date'
        ),
        VALUES ( 'Product'[Category] )  -- Restore related Product[Category] filter
    )
VAR TemporarilyLostCustomersCategories =
    FILTER (                                    -- Filters the temporarily-lost
        NATURALLEFTOUTERJOIN (                  -- customers by combining
            PotentialTemporarilyLostCustomers,  -- potential lost customers
            ActiveCustomersCategories           -- and active customers
        ),                                      -- and then comparing dates
        OR (
            ISBLANK ( [@MinOrderDate] ),
            [@MinOrderDate] > [@TemporarilyLostCustomerDate]
        )
    )
VAR TemporarilyLostCustomers =
    DISTINCT (                                  -- Gets the list of unique
        SELECTCOLUMNS (                         -- temporarily-lost customers
            TemporarilyLostCustomersCategories,
            "CustomerKey", Sales[CustomerKey]
        )
    )
VAR Result =
    COUNTROWS ( TemporarilyLostCustomers )
RETURN
    Result
```

The *CustomersWithLostDateComplete* variable needs to enforce the filter on the *Product[Category]* column by using the VALUES function – though the filter might not be directly applied to that column but rather, to other columns cross-filtering *Product[Category]*.

Similarly, the *ActiveCustomersCategories* variable creates a table of combinations of *Sales[CustomerKey]* and *Product[Category]* along with the first purchase date for each combination of customers and product category. This table is then joined to the *PotentialTemporarilyLostCustomers* variable, which contains the content of *CustomersWithLostDate* visible in the current selection. The result of the join filtered by date over the limit of the temporarily-lost date is returned in the *TemporarilyLostCustomersCategories* variable.

Finally, to avoid counting the same customer multiple times, the measure extracts the customer key before finally counting the number of temporarily-lost customers.

Recovered customers

The number of recovered customers is the number of customers that were temporarily lost before a purchase was made in the current period. It is computed by using the following measure:

Measure in the Sales table

```
# Recovered Customers :=
VAR LastDateLost =
    CALCULATE (
        MAX ( 'Date'[Date] ),
        ALLSELECTED ( 'Date' )
    )
VAR MinDate = MIN ( 'Date'[Date] )
VAR FilterCategories =
    CALCULATETABLE (
        VALUES ( 'Product'[Category] ),
        ALLSELECTED ( 'Product' )
    )
VAR CustomersWithLostDateComplete =
    CALCULATETABLE (                         -- Prepares a table that contains
        ADDCOLUMNS (                         -- for each customer and category,
            SUMMARIZE (                      -- the corresponding lost date
                Sales,
                Sales[CustomerKey],
                'Product'[Category]
            ),
            "@TemporarilyLostCustomerDate", CALCULATE (
                [Date Temporary Lost Customer],
                'Date'[Date] < MinDate
            )
        ),
        ALLSELECTED ( Customer ),
        FilterCategories,            -- Filter Product Category from ALLSELECTED
        ALLEXCEPT (                  -- Removes any filter other than
            Sales,                   -- Customer retrieved by ALLSELECTED so that
            Sales[CustomerKey],      -- the result is unchanged in
            Customer                 -- different cells of the report
        )
    )
```

```
VAR CustomersWithLostDate =
    FILTER (                                    -- Removes the customer without a
        CustomersWithLostDateComplete,          -- temporarily-lost date
        NOT ISBLANK ( [@TemporarilyLostCustomerDate] )
    )
VAR ActiveCustomersCategories =
    CALCULATETABLE (
        ADDCOLUMNS (
            SUMMARIZE (                         -- Gets the first order date
                Sales,                          -- for each combination of
                Sales[CustomerKey],             -- customer and category
                'Product'[Category]             -- in the current selection
            ),
            "@MinOrderDate", CALCULATE ( MIN ( Sales[Order Date] ) )
        ),
        ALLEXCEPT (                             -- Removes any filter other than
            Sales,                              -- customer and date
            Sales[CustomerKey],
            Customer,
            'Date'
        ),
        VALUES ( 'Product'[Category] )  -- Restore related Product[Category] filter
    )
VAR RecoveredCustomersCategories =
    FILTER (                                    -- Filters the recovered customers
        NATURALINNERJOIN (                      -- by combining active customers
            ActiveCustomersCategories,          -- and temporarily-lost customers
            CustomersWithLostDate               -- and then by comparing dates
        ),
        [@MinOrderDate] > [@TemporarilyLostCustomerDate]
    )
VAR RecoveredCustomers =
    DISTINCT (                                  -- Gets the list of unique
        SELECTCOLUMNS (                         -- recovered customers
            RecoveredCustomersCategories,
            "CustomerKey", Sales[CustomerKey]
        )
    )
VAR Result =
    COUNTROWS ( RecoveredCustomers )
RETURN
    Result
```

The measure first determines the customers that were temporarily lost before the current date, also summarizing by *Product[Category]*. Because the *Sales[CustomerKey]* and *Product[Category]* columns are part of the tables stored in the *CustomersWithLostDateComplete* and *ActiveCustomers* variables, the join made in *RecoveredCustomersCategories* returns a table that has both columns. This ensures that a customer that was to be considered lost for a given category is recovered only if they buy a product of the same category. The customer might appear multiple times in this table, so duplicated customers are removed in *RecoveredCustomersCategories* in order to count or filter only the unique recovered customers. The *Sales Recovered Customers* measure is similar to *# Recovered Customers*; the only difference is the *Result* variable that uses *RecoveredCustomersCat* as a filter in CALCULATE instead of just counting the rows of the corresponding *RecoveredCustomersCategories* variable in the *# Recovered Customers* measure. Therefore, here we only show the last part of the code, using ellipsis for the identical sections:

Measure in the Sales table

```
Sales Recovered Customers :=
...
VAR RecoveredCustomersCat =
    DISTINCT (                              -- Gets the list of unique
        SELECTCOLUMNS (                     -- recovered customers and categories
            RecoveredCustomersCategories,
            "CustomerKey", Sales[CustomerKey],
            "Category", 'Product'[Category]
        )
    )
VAR Result =
    CALCULATE (
        [Sales Amount],
        KEEPFILTERS ( RecoveredCustomersCat )
    )
RETURN
    Result
```

Returning customers

The last measure in the set of counting measures is *# Returning Customers*:

Measure in the Sales table

```
# Returning Customers :=
VAR MinDate = MIN ( 'Date'[Date] )
VAR FilterCategories =
    CALCULATETABLE (
        VALUES ( 'Product'[Category] ),
        ALLSELECTED ( 'Product' )
    )
VAR CustomersWithNewDate =
    CALCULATETABLE (               -- Prepares a table that contains
        ADDCOLUMNS (               -- for each customer and category,
            SUMMARIZE (            -- the date of their first purchase
                Sales,
                Sales[CustomerKey],
                'Product'[Category]
            ),
            "@NewCustomerDate", [Date New Customer]
        ),         ALLSELECTED ( Customer ),
        FilterCategories,          -- Filter Product Category from ALLSELECTED
        ALLEXCEPT (                -- Removes any filter other than
            Sales,                 -- Customer retrieved by ALLSELECTED so that
            Sales[CustomerKey],    -- the result is unchanged in
            Customer               -- different cells of the report
        )
    )
VAR ExistingCustomers =                        -- To get the existing customers,
    FILTER (                                   -- filters all customers
        CustomersWithNewDate,                  -- and checks that their first purchase
        [@NewCustomerDate] < MinDate           -- took place before the current time period
    )
VAR ActiveCustomersCategories =
    CALCULATETABLE (
        SUMMARIZE (                -- Retrieves combinations of
            Sales,                 -- Customer, Category, and Date
            Sales[CustomerKey],    -- active in the current selection
            'Product'[Category],
            'Date'[Date]
        ),
        ALLEXCEPT (                -- Removes any filter other than Date and
            Sales,                 -- Customer retrieved by ALLSELECTED so that
            'Date',                -- the result is unchanged in
            Sales[CustomerKey],    -- different cells of the report
            Customer
        ),
        VALUES ( 'Product'[Category] )  -- Restore related Product[Category] filter
    )
```

```
VAR ReturningCustomersCategories =
    NATURALINNERJOIN (
        ActiveCustomersCategories,          -- Combines active customers
        ExistingCustomers                   -- and existing customers
    )
VAR ReturningCustomers =
    DISTINCT (                              -- Gets the list of unique
        SELECTCOLUMNS (                     -- recovered customers
            ReturningCustomersCategories,
            "CustomerKey", Sales[CustomerKey]
        )
    )
VAR Result =
    COUNTROWS ( ReturningCustomers )
RETURN
    Result
```

The measure creates a *CustomersWithNewDate* variable which obtains the first sale date for each combination of customer and product category. This result is joined to the combination of customers and product category that is present in the current filter context over *Sales*. The result is the set of returning customers in the *ReturningCustomers* variable that is counted in the *# Returning Customer* measure. The *Sales Returning Customers* measure uses the following *ReturningCustomersCat* variable as a filter instead of the *ReturningCustomers* variable. Here we only write its final lines of code, all the remaining code being identical to the previous formula:

Measure in the Sales table

```
Sales Returning Customers :=
...
VAR ReturningCustomersCat =
    SELECTCOLUMNS (                 -- new customers/category, remove date
        ReturningCustomersCategories,
        "CustomerKey", Sales[CustomerKey],
        "Category", 'Product'[Category]
    )
VAR Result =
    CALCULATE (
        [Sales Amount],                        -- Count the number of customers
        KEEPFILTERS ( ReturningCustomersCat )  -- that are also in ReturningCustomersCat
    )
RETURN
    Result
```

Snapshot absolute

Computing new and returning customers dynamically is a very expensive operation. Therefore, this pattern is oftentimes implemented by using precomputed tables (snapshots) to store the most relevant dates at the desired granularity.

By using precomputed tables, we get a much faster solution albeit with reduced flexibility. In the precalculated absolute pattern, the state of new and returning customers does not depend on the filters applied to the report. The results obtained by using this pattern correspond to those of the Dynamic absolute pattern.

The pattern uses a snapshot table containing the relevant states of each customer (New, Lost, Temporarily lost, and Recovered) shown in Figure 13-10.

CustomerKey	Date	Event
1325	01/03/2007	New
1325	03/31/2007	Temporarily lost
1325	04/23/2007	Recovered
1325	08/31/2007	Lost
1325	08/31/2007	Temporarily lost
1817	01/09/2007	New
1817	01/31/2008	Lost
1817	01/31/2008	Temporarily lost
1817	05/31/2007	Temporarily lost
1817	11/12/2007	Recovered
2618	03/14/2007	New
2618	07/31/2007	Temporarily lost
2618	07/31/2007	Lost

FIGURE 13-10 The snapshot table contains the full history for each customer.

The New and Lost events are unique for each customer, whereas the Temporarily lost and Recovered events can have multiple occurrences over time for each customer.

The resulting table is linked to *Customer* and *Date* through regular relationships. The resulting model is visible in Figure 13-11.

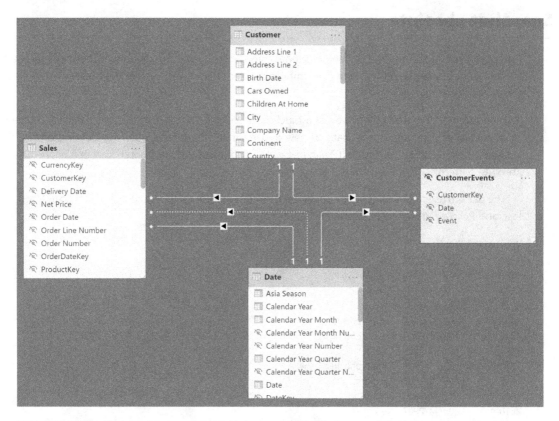

FIGURE 13-11 The *CustomerEvents* snapshot table is connected to *Customer* and *Date*.

Building the *CustomerEvents* table is a critical step. Creating this table as a derived snapshot by using a calculated table in DAX is relatively efficient for the New and Lost states, whereas it can be very expensive for the Temporarily lost and Recovered states. Keep in mind that Temporarily lost is needed in order to compute the Recovered state. In models with hundreds of thousands of customers or with hundreds of millions of sales you should consider preparing this table outside of the data model, and importing it as a simple table.

Once this model is in place, the DAX measures are simple and efficient. Indeed, for this model there is no need to create external and internal measures – the external measures are already simple. The full logic that defines the status of a customer is in the table itself. This is the reason why the resulting DAX code is much simpler.

The only calculation that requires some attention is the # *Returning Customers* measure, because it computes the number of customers dynamically while ignoring any filter other than *Date* and *Customer*. It then subtracts the number of new customers obtained by querying the snapshot table:

Measure in the Sales table

```
# New Customers :=
CALCULATE (
    COUNTROWS ( CustomerEvents ),
    KEEPFILTERS ( CustomerEvents[Event] = "New" )
)
```

Measure in the Sales table

```
# Lost Customers :=
CALCULATE (
    COUNTROWS ( CustomerEvents ),
    KEEPFILTERS ( CustomerEvents[Event] = "Lost" )
)
```

Measure in the Sales table

```
# Temporarily Lost Customers :=
CALCULATE (
    DISTINCTCOUNT ( CustomerEvents[CustomerKey] ),
    KEEPFILTERS ( CustomerEvents[Event] = "Temporarily lost" )
)
```

Measure in the Sales table

```
# Recovered Customers :=
CALCULATE (
    DISTINCTCOUNT ( CustomerEvents[CustomerKey] ),
    KEEPFILTERS ( CustomerEvents[Event] = "Recovered" )
)
```

Measure in the Sales table

```
# Returning Customers :=
VAR NewCustomers = [# New Customers]
VAR NumberOfCustomers =
    CALCULATE (
        [# Customers],
        ALLEXCEPT ( Sales, 'Date', Customer )
    )
VAR ReturningCustomers =
    NumberOfCustomers - NewCustomers
VAR Result =
    IF ( ReturningCustomers <> 0, ReturningCustomers )
RETURN
    Result
```

The measures computing the sales amount for new and returning customers take advantage of the physical relationship between the *CustomerEvents* snapshot table and the *Customer* table, thus reducing the DAX code required and providing higher efficiency:

Measure in the Sales table

```
Sales New Customers :=
CALCULATE (
    [Sales Amount],
    KEEPFILTERS ( CustomerEvents[Event] = "New" ),
    CROSSFILTER (
        CustomerEvents[CustomerKey],
        Customer[CustomerKey],
        BOTH
    )
)
```

Measure in the Sales table

```
Sales Recovered Customers :=
CALCULATE (
    [Sales Amount],
    KEEPFILTERS ( CustomerEvents[Event] = "Recovered" ),
    CROSSFILTER (
        CustomerEvents[CustomerKey],
        Customer[CustomerKey],
        BOTH
    )
)
```

Measure in the Sales table

```
Sales Returning Customers :=
VAR SalesAmount = [Sales Amount]
VAR SalesNewCustomers = [Sales New Customers]
VAR SalesReturningCustomers = SalesAmount - [Sales New Customers]
VAR Result =
    IF (
        SalesReturningCustomers <> 0,
        SalesReturningCustomers
    )
RETURN
    Result
```

Creating the derived snapshot table in DAX

We suggest creating the *CustomerEvents* snapshot table outside of the data model. Indeed, creating it in DAX is an expensive operation that requires large amounts of memory and processing power to refresh the data model. The DAX implementation described in this section works well on models with up to a few thousand customers and up to a few million sales transactions. If your model is larger than that, you can implement a similar business logic using other tools or languages that are more optimized for data preparation.

The complex part of the calculation is the retrieving of the dates when a customer is temporarily lost and then possibly recovered. These events can happen multiple times for each customer. For this reason, for each transaction we compute two dates in two calculated columns in the *Sales* table:

- *TemporarilyLostDate*: this is the date obtained by the *Date Temporary Lost Customer* measure when there are no other transactions between the current row in *Sales* and the date. If the same customer put multiple transactions through on the same date, all of them will have the same value in the *TemporarilyLostDate* column.
- *RecoveredDate*: this is the date of the first purchase made by that same customer after *TemporarilyLostDate*. This column is blank if there are no transactions after *TemporarilyLostDate*.

The code of these calculated columns is the following:

Calculated column in the Sales table

```
TemporarilyLostDates =
VAR TemporarilyLostDate =
    CALCULATE (
        [Date Temporary Lost Customer],
        ALLEXCEPT ( Sales, Sales[Order Date], Sales[CustomerKey] )
    )
VAR CurrentCustomerKey = Sales[CustomerKey]
VAR CurrentDate = Sales[Order Date]
VAR CheckTemporarilyLost =
    ISEMPTY (
        CALCULATETABLE (
            Sales,
            REMOVEFILTERS ( Sales ),
            Sales[CustomerKey] = CurrentCustomerKey,
            Sales[Order Date] > CurrentDate
                && Sales[Order Date] <= TemporarilyLostDate
        )
    )
VAR Result =
    IF ( CheckTemporarilyLost, TemporarilyLostDate )
RETURN
    Result
```

Calculated column in the Sales table

```
RecoveredDates =
VAR TemporarilyLostDate = Sales[TemporarilyLostDate]
VAR Result =
    IF (
        NOT ISBLANK ( TemporarilyLostDate ),
        CALCULATE (
            MIN ( Sales[Order Date] ),
            ALLEXCEPT ( Sales, Sales[CustomerKey] ),
            DATESBETWEEN ( 'Date'[Date], TemporarilyLostDate+1, BLANK() )
        )
    )
RETURN
    Result
```

We then use these calculated columns to obtain two calculated tables as an intermediate step to compute the *CustomerEvents* snapshot table. If you want to leverage an external tool to only compute the Temporarily Lost and Recovered events, you should consider importing these two tables from the data source, where you prepare their content by using dedicated tools for data preparation. The two tables are visible in Figure 13-12 and Figure 13-13.

CustomerKey	TemporarilyLostDate	Event
1325	03/31/2007	Temporarily lost
1325	08/31/2007	Temporarily lost
1817	01/31/2008	Temporarily lost
1817	05/31/2007	Temporarily lost
2618	07/31/2007	Temporarily lost

FIGURE 13-12 The *TempLostDates* table only contains the Temporarily Lost events.

CustomerKey	RecoveredDate	Event
1325	04/23/2007	Recovered
1817	11/12/2007	Recovered

FIGURE 13-13 The *RecoveredDates* table only contains the Recovered events.

Using these intermediate tables, the *CustomerEvents* calculated table is obtained with a final UNION of the four states:

Calculated table

```
CustomerEvents =
VAR CustomerGranularity =
    ALLNOBLANKROW ( Sales[CustomerKey] )
VAR NewDates =
    ADDCOLUMNS (
        CustomerGranularity,
        "Date", [Date New Customer],
        "Event", "New"
    )
VAR LostDates =
    ADDCOLUMNS (
        CustomerGranularity,
        "Date", [Date Lost Customer],
        "Event", "Lost"
    )
VAR Result =
    UNION (
        NewDates,
        LostDates,
        TempLostDates,
        RecoveredDates
    )
RETURN
    Result
```

Splitting the calculation into smaller steps is useful for educational purposes and to provide a guide in case you want to implement part of the calculation outside of the data model. However, if you implement the calculation entirely in DAX then you can skip the intermediate *TempLostDates* and *RecoveredDates* calculated tables. In this case you must pay attention to the CALCULATE functions in order to avoid circular dependencies, by implementing explicit filters obtained by iterating the result of ALLNOBLANKROW. This results in a more verbose definition of the *CustomerEvents* table, proposed here under the name *CustomerEventsSingleTable*:

Calculated table

```
CustomerEventsSingleTable =
VAR CustomerGranularity =
    ALLNOBLANKROW ( Sales[CustomerKey] )
VAR LostDates =
    ADDCOLUMNS (
        CustomerGranularity,
        "Date", [Date New Customer],
        "Event", "New"
    )
```

```
VAR NewDates =
    ADDCOLUMNS (
        CustomerGranularity,
        "Date", [Date Lost Customer],
        "Event", "Lost"
    )
VAR _TempLostDates =
    CALCULATETABLE (
        SUMMARIZE (
            Sales,
            Sales[CustomerKey],
            Sales[TemporarilyLostDate],
            "Event", "Temporarily lost"
        ),
        FILTER (
            ALLNOBLANKROW ( Sales[TemporarilyLostDate] ),
            NOT ISBLANK ( Sales[TemporarilyLostDate] )
        )
    )
VAR _RecoveredDates =
    CALCULATETABLE (
        SUMMARIZE (
            Sales,
            Sales[CustomerKey],
            Sales[RecoveredDate],
            "Event", "Recovered"
        ),
        FILTER (
            ALLNOBLANKROW ( Sales[RecoveredDate] ),
            NOT ISBLANK ( Sales[RecoveredDate] )
        )
    )
VAR Result =
    UNION (
        NewDates,
        LostDates,
        _TempLostDates,
        _RecoveredDates
    )
RETURN
    Result
```

Although the sample file includes a definition of *CustomerEventsSingleTable*, the measures in the report do not use that table. If you want to use this approach, you can replace the definition of *CustomerEvents* with the expression in *CustomerEventsSingleTable* and remove the former expression from the model – you also want to remove the *TempLostDates* and *RecoveredDates* calculated tables that are no longer being used.

Related distinct count

The Related distinct count pattern is useful whenever you have one or more fact tables related to a dimension, and you need to perform the distinct count of column values in a dimension table only considering items related to transactions in the fact table. For demonstration purposes we use the distinct count of the product name in a model with two fact tables: *Sales* and *Receipts*.

Because the product name is not unique – we artificially introduced duplicated names by removing the color description from the product name – a simple distinct count of the product key in the *Sales* or *Receipts* table does not work. Finally, we show how to compute the distinct count of product names that appear in both tables and in at least one of the two.

Pattern description

The *Product[Product Name]* column is not unique in the *Product* table and we need the distinct count of the product names that have related sales transactions. The model contains two tables with transactions related to products: *Sales* and *Receipts*. Figure 14-1 shows this data model.

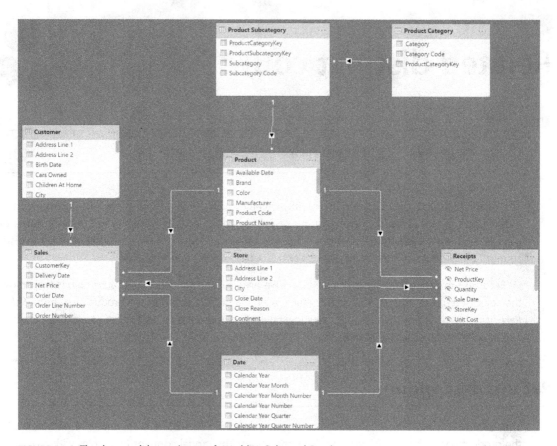

FIGURE 14-1 The data model contains two fact tables: *Sales* and *Receipts*.

Based on this model we want to compute the distinct count of product names appearing:

- In *Sales*.

- In *Receipts*.

- In both the *Sales* and *Receipts* tables.

- In at least one of the *Sales* and *Receipts* tables.

The report is visible in Figure 14-2.

Calendar Year	# Prods from Sales	# Prods from Receipts	# Prods from Both	# Prods from Any
⊟ **CY 2007**	**589**	**679**	**588**	**680**
January	149	479	141	487
February	148	501	143	506
March	172	526	161	537
April	169	561	162	568
May	174	591	169	596
June	156	579	146	589
July	145	575	140	580
August	160	585	152	593
September	173	605	165	613
October	178	605	169	614
November	160	609	157	612
December	184	628	172	640
⊟ **CY 2008**	**689**	**785**	**689**	**785**
January	150	606	144	612
Total	**848**	**880**	**848**	**880**

FIGURE 14-2 The report shows the four measures demonstrated in the pattern.

The code for the first two measures is the following:

Measure in the Sales table

```
# Prods from Sales :=
VAR ProdsFromSales =
    SUMMARIZE ( Sales, 'Product'[Product Name] )
VAR Result =
    SUMX ( ProdsFromSales, 1 )      -- optimization for COUNTROWS ( ProdsFromSales )
RETURN
    Result
```

Measure in the Receipts table

```
# Prods from Receipts :=
VAR ProdsFromReceipts =
    SUMMARIZE ( Receipts, 'Product'[Product Name] )
VAR Result =
    SUMX ( ProdsFromReceipts, 1 )   -- optimization for COUNTROWS ( ProdsFromReceipts )
RETURN
    Result
```

Using SUMMARIZE, the *# Prods from Sales* and *# Prods from Receipts* measures retrieve the distinct product names referenced in the relevant table. SUMX just counts the number of those products and it is used instead of COUNTROWS or DISTINCTCOUNT for performance reasons – more details in the article Analzying the performance of DISTINCTCOUNT in DAX (https://sql.bi/432941).

Despite being longer than a solution using DISTINCTCOUNT and bidirectional cross-filtering, this version of the code is faster in the most frequent case – where the number of products is significantly smaller than the number of transactions.

NOTE The natural syntax to compute the *Result* variable in the *# Prods from Sales* and *# Prods from Receipts* measures should use COUNTROWS. The SUMX version is only suggested for performance reasons in the simple measures. The following measures of this pattern use COUNTROWS because there would be no advantage in using SUMX in more complex expressions.

The formulation using SUMMARIZE and COUNTROWS can be easily extended to accommodate for the next formulas that produce the intersection (*# Prods from Both*) or the union (*# Prods from Any*) of the product names:

Measure in the Receipts table

```
# Prods from Both :=
VAR ProdsFromSales =
    SUMMARIZE ( Sales, 'Product'[Product Name] )
VAR ProdsFromReceipts =
    SUMMARIZE ( Receipts, 'Product'[Product Name] )
VAR ProdsFromBoth =
    INTERSECT ( ProdsFromSales, ProdsFromReceipts )
VAR Result =
    COUNTROWS ( ProdsFromBoth )
RETURN
    Result
```

Measure in the Receipts table

```
# Prods from Any :=
VAR ProdsFromSales =
    SUMMARIZE ( Sales, 'Product'[Product Name] )
VAR ProdsFromReceipts =
    SUMMARIZE ( Receipts, 'Product'[Product Name] )
VAR ProdsFromOne =
    DISTINCT ( UNION ( ProdsFromSales, ProdsFromReceipts ) )
VAR Result =
    COUNTROWS ( ProdsFromOne )
RETURN
    Result
```

We provided the examples for INTERSECT and UNION. But the pattern can easily be adapted to perform more complex calculations. As a further example, the *# Prods in Sales and not in Receipts* measure computes the number of product names that exist in *Sales* but not in *Receipts* by using the set function EXCEPT instead of the INTERSECT or UNION functions used in previous measures:

Measure in the Sales table

```
# Prods in Sales and not in Receipts :=
VAR ProdsFromSales =
    SUMMARIZE ( Sales, 'Product'[Product Name] )
VAR ProdsFromReceipts =
    SUMMARIZE ( Receipts, 'Product'[Product Name] )
VAR ProdsFromSalesAndNotReceipts =
    EXCEPT ( ProdsFromSales, ProdsFromReceipts )
VAR Result =
    COUNTROWS ( ProdsFromSalesAndNotReceipts )
RETURN
    Result
```

The result of the # *Prods in Sales and not in Receipts* measure is visible in Figure 14-3.

Calendar Year	# Prods from Sales	# Prods from Receipts	# Prods in Sales and not in Receipts
⊟ CY 2007	589	679	1
January	149	479	8
February	148	501	5
March	172	526	11
April	169	561	7
May	174	591	5
June	156	579	10
July	145	575	5
August	160	585	8
September	173	605	8
October	178	605	9
November	160	609	3
December	184	628	12
⊟ CY 2008	689	785	
January	150	606	6
Total	848	880	

FIGURE 14-3 The # *Prods in Sales and not in Receipts* measure counts the products present in *Sales* but not in *Receipts*.

The pattern can be extended to compute the distinct count of any column in a table that can be reached through a many-to-one chain of relationships from the fact tables. This is because SUMMARIZE is able to group by any of those columns.

Events in progress

The Events in progress pattern has a broad field of application. It is useful whenever dealing with events with a duration – events that have a start date and an end date. The event is considered to be in progress between the two dates. As an example, we use Contoso orders.

Each order has an order date and a delivery date. The date when the order was placed is considered the start date, and the date when the order was delivered is considered the end date.. An order is considered open when it has been placed but has not yet been delivered. We are interested in counting how many orders are open at a certain date, and what their value is.

As with many of the patterns described, Events in Progress can be handled both dynamically through measures, or statically by using a snapshot table.

Definition of events in progress

You need to compute how many orders are open at a specific time, for Contoso. In Figure 15-1 you can see the result of the calculation at the day level; on each day the number of open orders is the number open orders from the previous day, plus the orders received and minus the orders delivered that day. EOP stands for End Of Period.

Calendar Year	# Orders Received	# Orders Delivered	# Open Orders EOP
⊟ CY 2007	11,703	11,421	282
⊟ January	1,546	1,063	483
01/02/2007	27		27
01/03/2007	80		107
01/04/2007	118		225
01/05/2007	54		279
01/06/2007			279
01/07/2007	41		320
01/08/2007		2	318
01/09/2007	73	3	388
01/10/2007	115	17	486
01/11/2007	40	22	504
01/12/2007	24	33	495
01/13/2007	59	57	497
01/14/2007		49	448
01/15/2007	105	62	491
Total	21,601	21,601	

FIGURE 15-1 The report shows orders received, delivered and open on a daily basis.

However, this way of computing the number of open orders could be ambiguous when we consider a period of several days, such as a month or a year. The ambiguity is explained below. To avoid this ambiguity, it is important to clearly define the desired result. When looking at a single day, the number of orders open is evident, as you can see in Figure 15-2.

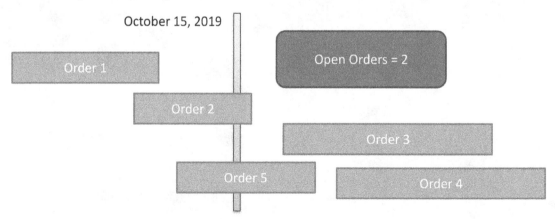

FIGURE 15-2 On October 15, 2019 there are two orders that are open.

In Figure 15-2 only orders number 2 and 5 are open at the date considered (October 15, 2019). Order 1 is already delivered, whereas orders 3 and 4 are yet to be received by Contoso. Therefore, the calculation is clearly defined. Nevertheless, when you report on a larger period of time, like a month, the calculation is harder to define. Look at Figure 15-3 where the time duration is much larger, including the full month of October.

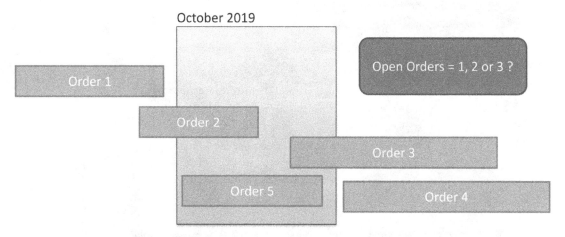

FIGURE 15-3 When looking at October, are there one, two or three open orders?

In Figure 15-3, order 1 is completed before the beginning of October, and order 4 is yet to be received by Contoso after the end of October. Therefore, their status is obvious. However, order 2 is open at the beginning of the month, but it is closed at the end. Order 3 is opened during the month and still open at the end of the month. Order 5 is received and closed during the month. As you see, a calculation that is straightforward on an individual day requires a better definition at an aggregate level.

We do not want to provide an extensive description of every possible option. In this pattern we only consider the following three definitions for the orders in a period longer than one day – each measure is identified with a suffix from the list:

- **ALL**: Returns the orders that were open at any time during the period. For Figure 15-3, we report three orders; we consider order 5 as open because it has been open for some time during the period considered.

- **EOP**: Considers the status of each order at the end of the period. For Figure 15-3, this means reporting only one order (order 3), because all the other orders are either closed or not yet opened at the end of the period.

- **AVG**: Computes the daily average of the orders open in the period. This requires computing the number of open orders day by day, and then averaging it over longer periods.

There might be different definitions of open orders, which usually are slight variations of the three scenarios described above.

Open orders

If the *Orders* table stores data at the correct granularity – storing one row for each order along with order date and delivery date – then the model looks like the one in Figure 15-4.

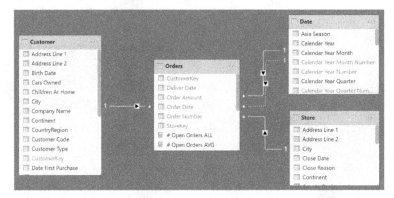

FIGURE 15-4 The data model with an Orders table.

The DAX code computing the open orders for this model is rather simple:

Measure in the Orders table

```
# Open Orders ALL :=
VAR MinDate = MIN ( 'Date'[Date] )
VAR MaxDate = MAX ( 'Date'[Date] )
VAR Result =
    CALCULATE (
        COUNTROWS ( Orders ),
        Orders[Order Date] <= MaxDate,
        Orders[Deliver Date] > MinDate,
        REMOVEFILTERS ( 'Date' )
    )
RETURN
    Result
```

It is worth noting that REMOVEFILTERS is required, in order to remove any report filters that may be affecting the *Date* table.

Based on this measure, you can compute the two variations (end of period and average) using the following formulas:

Measure in the Orders table

```
# Open Orders EOP :=
CALCULATE (
    [# Open Orders ALL],
    LASTDATE ( 'Date'[Date] )
)
```

Measure in the Orders table

```
# Open Orders AVG :=
AVERAGEX (
    'Date',
    [# Open Orders ALL]
)
```

You can see the result of these formulas in Figure 15-5.

Calendar Year	# Orders Received	# Orders Delivered	# Open Orders ALL	# Open Orders EOP	# Open Orders AVG
⊟ **CY 2007**	**11,703**	**11,421**	**11,703**	**282**	**314.2**
January	1,546	1,063	1,546	483	433.9
February	1,278	1,423	1,711	338	480.8
March	1,128	1,152	1,418	314	352.4
April	1,332	1,199	1,601	447	427.6
May	1,144	1,166	1,512	425	355.0
June	723	926	1,097	222	279.0
July	913	880	1,076	255	273.9
August	725	746	955	234	239.5
September	773	824	997	183	266.8
October	582	491	738	274	180.5
November	779	837	1,031	216	268.0
December	780	714	963	282	231.9

FIGURE 15-5 The three measures report different results for numbers of open orders.

The *Orders* table might have more than one row for each order. If the *Orders* table has one row for each line in the order instead of one row for each order, then you should use DISTINCTCOUNT over a column containing a unique identifier for each order – instead of using COUNTROWS over the *Orders* table. This is not the case in our sample model, but in that scenario the *# Open Orders ALL* formula would differ by just one line:

Measure in the Orders table

```
# Open Orders ALL :=
VAR MinDate = MIN ( 'Date'[Date] )
VAR MaxDate = MAX ( 'Date'[Date] )
VAR Result =
    CALCULATE (                                      -- If any order can have several rows
        DISTINCTCOUNT ( Orders[Order Number] ), -- use DISTINCTCOUNT instead of COUNTROWS
        Orders[Order Date] <= MaxDate,
        Orders[Deliver Date] > MinDate,
        REMOVEFILTERS ( 'Date' )
    )
RETURN
    Result
```

If you want to compute the dollar value of the open orders, you use the *Sales Amount* measure instead of the COUNTROWS or DISTINCTCOUNT functions. For example, this is the definition of the *Open Amount*

ALL measure:

Measure in the Orders table

```
Open Amount ALL :=
VAR MinDate = MIN ( 'Date'[Date] )
VAR MaxDate = MAX ( 'Date'[Date] )
VAR Result =
    CALCULATE (
        [Sales Amount],              -- Use Sales Amount instead of DISTINCTCOUNT or COUNTROWS
        Orders[Order Date] <= MaxDate,
        Orders[Deliver Date] > MinDate,
        REMOVEFILTERS ( 'Date' )
    )
RETURN
    Result
```

The other two measures just reference the underlying *Open Amount ALL* measure instead of *# Open Orders ALL*:

Measure in the Orders table

```
Open Amount EOP :=
CALCULATE (
    [Open Amount ALL],
    LASTDATE ( 'Date'[Date] )
)
```

Measure in the Orders table

```
Open Amount AVG :=
AVERAGEX (
    'Date',
    [Open Amount ALL]
)
```

The Figure 15-6 shows the results of the measures defined above.

Calendar Year	Sales Amount	Delivered Amount	Open Amount ALL	Open Amount EOP	Open Amount AVG
⊟ **CY 2007**	**11,309,946.12**	**10,977,203.75**	**11,309,946.12**	**332,742.37**	**336,715.73**
January	794,248.24	578,954.57	794,248.24	215,293.67	244,229.27
February	891,135.91	764,149.38	1,062,037.07	342,280.20	314,930.36
March	961,289.24	1,036,668.02	1,279,111.61	266,901.42	339,674.85
April	1,128,104.82	1,097,388.37	1,379,979.47	297,617.87	405,690.70
May	936,192.74	831,896.19	1,183,655.41	401,914.42	310,091.28
June	982,304.46	978,997.31	1,341,849.56	405,221.58	358,079.60
July	922,542.98	1,135,885.72	1,306,013.92	191,878.84	365,149.51
August	952,834.59	752,205.77	1,130,437.87	392,507.66	318,889.87
September	1,009,868.98	1,053,201.67	1,397,466.29	349,174.97	387,043.26
October	914,273.54	915,091.22	1,237,929.67	348,357.29	338,129.57
November	825,601.87	864,090.04	1,143,645.57	309,869.11	319,769.31
December	991,548.75	968,675.49	1,262,992.31	332,742.37	337,810.46

FIGURE 15-6 The three measures display the value of all open orders compared side by side.

The formulas described in this section work well on small datasets, but they require a big effort from the Formula Engine; this results in reduced performance starting from medium-sized databases and above - think hundreds of thousands of orders. If you need better performance, using a snapshot table is a very good option.

Open orders with snapshot

Building a snapshot simplifies the calculation and speeds up the performance. A daily snapshot contains one row per day and order that is open on that day. Therefore, a single order that has been open for 10 days requires 10 rows in the snapshot.

In Figure 15-7 you can see an excerpt from the snapshot table.

Order Number	Date
200701022CS425	1/2/2007
200701022CS425	1/3/2007
200701022CS425	1/4/2007
200701022CS425	1/5/2007
200701022CS425	1/6/2007
200701022CS425	1/7/2007
200701022CS425	1/8/2007
200701022CS425	1/9/2007
200701022CS425	1/10/2007
200701022CS425	1/11/2007
200701022CS425	1/12/2007
200701022CS425	1/13/2007

FIGURE 15-7 Each order has as many rows as days it has been open.

For large data models where the snapshot requires tens of millions of rows, it is suggested to use specific ETLs or queries in SQL to get the snapshot result. For smaller data models, the snapshot table can be created by using either Power Query or DAX. For example, the snapshot of our sample model can be created using the following definition of the *Open Orders* calculated table:

Calculated table

```
Open Orders =
SELECTCOLUMNS (
    GENERATE (
        Orders,
        DATESBETWEEN (
            'Date'[Date],
            Orders[Order Date],
            Orders[Deliver Date] - 1
        )
    ),
    "StoreKey", Orders[StoreKey],
    "CustomerKey", Orders[CustomerKey],
    "Order Number", Orders[Order Number],
    "Date", 'Date'[Date]
)
```

In Figure 15-8 you can see that the *Open Orders* snapshot has a set of regular relationships with the other tables in the model.

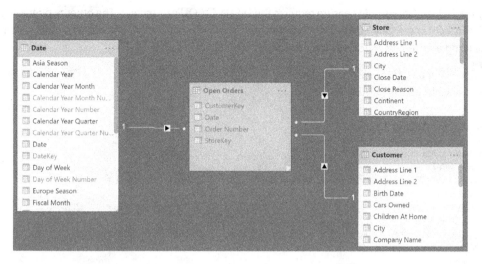

FIGURE 15-8 The snapshot is related to other tables, so to perform slicing and dicing.

Using the snapshot, the formulas that compute the number of open orders are faster and simpler to write:

Measure in the Orders table

```
# Open Orders ALL :=
DISTINCTCOUNT ( 'Open Orders'[Order Number] )
```

Measure (hidden) in the Orders table

```
# Rows Open Orders :=
COUNTROWS ( 'Open Orders' )
```

Measure in the Orders table

```
# Open Orders EOP :=
CALCULATE (
    [# Rows Open Orders],
    LASTDATE ( 'Date'[Date] )
)
```

Measure in the Orders table

```
# Open Orders AVG :=
AVERAGEX (
    'Date',
    [# Rows Open Orders]
)
```

Only the # *Open Orders ALL* measure requires the DISTINCTCOUNT function. The other two measures, # *Open Orders EOP* and # *Open Orders AVG* count the number of open orders one day at a time, which can be done using a faster COUNTROWS over the snapshot table.

The *Open Amount ALL* measure requires you to apply the list of open orders as a filter to the *Orders* table. This is achieved using TREATAS:

Measure in the Orders table

```
Open Amount ALL :=
VAR OpenOrders =
    DISTINCT ( 'Open Orders'[Order Number] )
VAR FilterOpenOrders =
    TREATAS (
        OpenOrders,
        Orders[Order Number]
    )
VAR Result =
    CALCULATE (
        [Sales Amount],
        FilterOpenOrders,
        REMOVEFILTERS ( Orders )
    )
RETURN Result
```

The *Open Amount EOP* and *Open Amount AVG* measures just reference the underlying *Open Amount ALL* measure instead of # *Open Orders ALL*:

Measure in the Orders table

```
Open Amount EOP :=
CALCULATE (
    [Open Amount ALL],
    LASTDATE ( 'Date'[Date] )
)
```

Measure in the Orders table

```
Open Amount AVG :=
AVERAGEX (
    'Date',
    [Open Amount ALL]
)
```

The size of the snapshot depends on the number of orders and on the average duration of an order. If an order typically stays open for a few days, then it is fine to use a daily granularity. If an order is usually active for a much longer period of time (think years) then you should consider moving the snapshot granularity to the month level – one row for each order open in each month.

A possible optimization requires an inactive relationship between *Orders* and *Open Orders*. This is only useful when the *Orders* table has one row per order – the *Orders[Order Number]* column is thus unique and the relationship has a one-to-many cardinality. The inactive relationship should be like the one highlighted in Figure 15-9. Do not use this technique with a many-to-many cardinality because the pure DAX approach based on TREATAS would be similar in performance and simpler to manage.

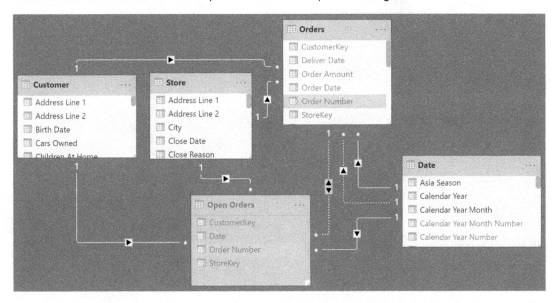

FIGURE 15-9 The inactive one-to-many relationship allows for performance optimization.

Then you should replace the previous *Open Amount ALL* measure with the code of the *Open Amount ALL optimized* measure defined as follows:

Measure in the Orders table

```
Open Amount ALL optimized :=
CALCULATE (
    [Sales Amount],
    USERELATIONSHIP ( 'Open Orders'[Order Number], Orders[Order Number] ),
    CROSSFILTER ( Orders[Order Date], 'Date'[Date], NONE )
)
```

Leveraging the relationship to transfer the filter reduces the workload of the Formula Engine and improves the performance of all the measures based on *Open Amount ALL*. You should just consider the side effects of USERELATIONSHIP in different models, applying the required CROSSFILTER to remove possible ambiguities. Usually it should be enough to disable the relationship between *Orders* and *Date* like in this example, but carefully check the accuracy of the results by comparing the optimized measure with the one based on TREATAS.

Ranking

The ability to rank things is a very common requirement. Finding the best customers, computing the ranking position of products, or detecting the countries with the best sales volumes are among the questions most frequently asked by management.

Ranking can be either static or dynamic. Static ranking assigns to each product a ranking position that is not affected by filters, whereas in dynamic ranking the position is computed every time the user interacts with the report. For example, in dynamic ranking the year selected in the report defines a new calculation of the ranking value.

All the basic ranking calculations are based on the RANKX function, whereas more advanced techniques – like filtering the top 10 products – require the TOPN function and advanced table calculations.

Static ranking

You assign a static ranking to a product by using a calculated column. The calculated column is computed during data refresh. Therefore, the value of the static ranking does not depend on the report filters. For example, in Figure 16-1 the first product is ranked 1 because the LCD HDTV M140 is the top seller among products of any category, whereas the second product (SV 16xDVD M360 Black) shows a product rank equal to 4 instead of 2. The reason is that there are another two products ranked 2 and 3 that are not included in the TV and Video category, which is selected in the Category slicer. Nevertheless, the ranking being static does not consider report filters. It shows the overall ranking of the products visible in the report.

Category	Product Name	Product Rank	Sales Amount
☐ Audio			
☐ Cameras and camcorders	Adventure Works 26" 720p LCD HDTV M140 Silver	1	1,303,983.46
☐ Cell phones	SV 16xDVD M360 Black	4	364,714.41
☐ Computers	Contoso Home Theater System 7.1 Channel M1700 Silver	76	54,620.16
☐ Games and Toys	Litware Home Theater System 5.1 Channel M511 Silver	97	50,104.32
☐ Home Appliances	Contoso Home Theater System 7.1 Channel M1700 White	105	47,917.10
☐ Music, Movies and Audio Books	Contoso Home Theater System 5.1 Channel M1500 Silver	129	42,543.93
■ TV and Video	Contoso Home Theater System 7.1 Channel M1700 Black	143	39,693.85

FIGURE 16-1 The report is showing the overall ranking, even though only a selection of products is visible.

Removing the filter on Category, the overall ranking shows all the products as one would expect. This is shown in the following figure.

Category	Product Name	Product Rank	Sales Amount
☐ Audio			
☐ Cameras and camcorders	Adventure Works 26" 720p LCD HDTV M140 Silver	1	1,303,983.46
☐ Cell phones	A. Datum SLR Camera X137 Grey	2	725,840.28
☐ Computers	Contoso Telephoto Conversion Lens X400 Silver	3	683,779.95
☐ Games and Toys	SV 16xDVD M360 Black	4	364,714.41
☐ Home Appliances	Contoso Projector 1080p X980 White	5	257,154.75
☐ Music, Movies and Audio Books	Contoso Washer & Dryer 21in E210 Pink	6	182,094.12
☐ TV and Video	Fabrikam Independent filmmaker 1/3" 8.5mm X200 White	7	165,594.00

FIGURE 16-2 With no filter on Category, the ranking simply adds one to each row.

To compute the static ranking of a product based on the *Sales Amount* measure we need a calculated column in the *Product* table:

Calculated column in the Product table

```
Product Rank =
RANKX (
    ALL ( 'Product' ),
    [Sales Amount]
)
```

In this code, the ALL function is not needed. However, it clarifies the intention of ranking against all the products which is why we added it; it makes the code easier to read over time.

A similar formula can be used to obtain the ranking over a subset of products. For example, the following calculated column computes the ranking of a product inside its category:

Calculated column in the Product table

```
Rank in Category =
RANKX (
    ALLEXCEPT ( 'Product', 'Product'[Category] ),
    [Sales Amount]
)
```

As shown in the figure below, the fourth row (SV 16xDVD M360 Black) has a *Product Rank* of 4 and a *Rank in Category* of 2, because the latter is the ranking in the TV and Video category.

Product Name	Category	Product Rank	Rank in Category	Sales Amount
Adventure Works 26" 720p LCD HDTV M140 Silver	TV and Video	1	1	1,303,983.46
A. Datum SLR Camera X137 Grey	Cameras and camcorders	2	1	725,840.28
Contoso Telephoto Conversion Lens X400 Silver	Cameras and camcorders	3	2	683,779.95
SV 16xDVD M360 Black	TV and Video	4	2	364,714.41
Contoso Projector 1080p X980 White	Computers	5	1	257,154.75
Contoso Washer & Dryer 21in E210 Pink	Home Appliances	6	1	182,094.12

FIGURE 16-3 *Rank in Category* shows the ranking local to the category of the product.

Dynamic ranking

The Dynamic ranking pattern produces a ranking that changes depending on the report filters. Consequently, it is based on measures instead of calculated columns.

Category		Product Name	Sales Amount	Product Rank
☐ Audio	⌄			
☐ Cameras and camcorders		Adventure Works 26" 720p LCD HDTV M140 Silver	1,303,983.46	1
☐ Cell phones		SV 16xDVD M360 Black	364,714.41	2
☐ Computers		Contoso Home Theater System 7.1 Channel M1700 Silver	54,620.16	3
☐ Games and Toys		Litware Home Theater System 5.1 Channel M511 Silver	50,104.32	4
☐ Home Appliances		Contoso Home Theater System 7.1 Channel M1700 White	47,917.10	5
☐ Music, Movies and Audio Books		Contoso Home Theater System 5.1 Channel M1500 Silver	42,543.93	6
■ TV and Video		Contoso Home Theater System 7.1 Channel M1700 Black	39,693.85	7

FIGURE 16-4 Dynamic ranking ranks products among the ones visible, using the report filters.

The code of the *Product Rank* measure is the following:

Measure in the Product table

```
Product Rank :=
IF (
    ISINSCOPE ( 'Product'[Product Name] ),
    VAR SalesAmountCurrentProduct = [Sales Amount]
    VAR ProductRank =
        RANKX (
            ALLSELECTED ( 'Product' ),
            [Sales Amount]
        )
    VAR Result =
        IF (
            NOT ISBLANK ( SalesAmountCurrentProduct ),
            ProductRank
        )
    RETURN
        Result
)
```

Obtaining different rankings requires modifying the table iterated by RANKX. For example, the following figure shows a *Rank in Category* measure that returns the ranking of a product between the products of the same category, still considering any other filter existing in the report, if any.

Category	Sales Amount	Product Rank	Rank in Category
⊟ **Audio**	**13,805.31**		
Contoso 4GB Portable MP3 Player M450 Yellow	1,247.35	16	5
Contoso 8GB MP3 Player new model M820 Yellow	1,782.20	15	4
NT Bluetooth Stereo Headphones E52 Yellow	385.35	31	6
NT Wireless Bluetooth Stereo Headphones E302 Yellow	1,986.95	12	2
WWI 4GB Video Recording Pen X200 Yellow	6,541.60	4	1
WWI Stereo Bluetooth Headphones New Generation M370 Yellow	1,861.86	13	3
⊟ **Cameras and camcorders**	**2,409.33**		
Contoso Lens Cap Keeper E314 Yellow	329.08	33	2
Contoso USB Cable M250 Yellow	2,080.25	10	1
⊟ **Computers**	**10,379.00**		
Contoso Ultraportable Neoprene Sleeve E30 Yellow	549.12	27	5
SV 40GB USB2.0 Portable Hard Disk E400 Yellow	4,469.73	7	1
SV 4GB Laptop Memory M65 Yellow	3,823.60	8	2
SV 512MB Laptop memory E800 Yellow	842.95	20	3
SV 80GB USB2.0 Portable Hard Disk E500 Yellow	693.60	24	4

FIGURE 16-5 Rank in Category, as a measure, shows the ranking inside the current category.

The definition of the Rank in Category measure is the following:

Measure in the Product table

```
Rank in Category :=
VAR SalesAmountCurrentProduct = [Sales Amount]
VAR ProductsInCategory =
    CALCULATETABLE (
        'Product',
        REMOVEFILTERS ( 'Product'[Product Name] ),
        ALLSELECTED ( 'Product' ),
        VALUES ( 'Product'[Category] )
    )
VAR ProductRank =
    IF (
        ISINSCOPE ( 'Product'[Product Name] ),
        RANKX (
            ProductsInCategory,
            [Sales Amount]
        )
    )
VAR Result =
    IF (
        NOT ISBLANK ( SalesAmountCurrentProduct ),
        ProductRank
    )
RETURN
    Result
```

Showing the top 3 products by category

Ranking is useful to obtain reports that filter products based on their local ranking in a given group. For example, the report below shows how to obtain the top three products for each category. There are two possible solutions to this scenario, depending on whether the product name is part of the report or not.

If the report contains the product name, then we can use the *Rank in Category* measure of the dynamic pattern and rely on Power BI visual filters.

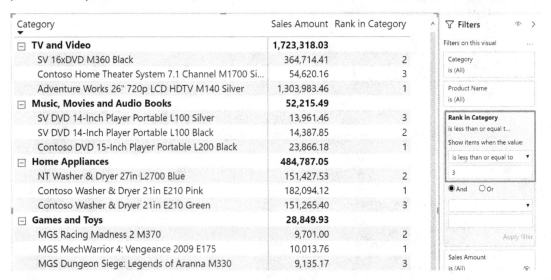

FIGURE 16-6 This report shows the top three products by category, by filtering the *Rank in Category* measure in the visual.

Although this technique is not the most powerful, we show it because it is a very efficient way of filtering the top three products. Besides, it also solves the most common requirement which is to actually show by name the products included in the top three.

Nevertheless, if the product name is not part of the visual, then this technique cannot be used. The reason is that the granularity of the visual is not compatible with the measure and the previous technique no longer works. In the figure below, we removed the product names from the report above.

Category	Sales Amount	Rank in Category
TV and Video	4,392,768.29	
Music, Movies and Audio Books	314,206.74	
Home Appliances	9,600,457.04	
Games and Toys	360,652.81	
Computers	6,741,548.73	
Cell phones	1,604,610.26	
Cameras and camcorders	7,192,581.95	
Audio	384,518.16	
Total	**30,591,343.98**	

Filters panel:

▽ Filters

Filters on this visual

Category
is (All)

Rank in Category
is less than or equal t...

Show items when the value:

is less than or equal to ▼

3

◉ And ○ Or

▼

FIGURE 16-7 *Sales Amount* shows the total for all the products in each category ignoring the filter on the *Rank in Category* measure.

The reason the visual filter is not effective is because it is only applied to the maximum granularity of the visual. Therefore, the visual filter does not necessarily apply to the products. In order to enforce the filter over product names, the measure displaying *Sales Amount* must enforce the computation of the ranking at the correct granularity, determining the products to be included in the calculation and then using those products as a filter. The report must display the amount using the following definition of *Sales Top 3 Products*:

Measure in the Sales table

```
Sales Top 3 Products :=
VAR TopThreeProducts =
    GENERATE (
        ALLSELECTED ( 'Product'[Category] ),      -- For each category
        TOPN (                                     -- retrieve the top
            3,                                     -- three product
            ALLSELECTED ( 'Product'[Product Name] ), -- names based on the
            [Sales Amount]                         -- sales amount
        )
    )
VAR Result =
    CALCULATE (
        [Sales Amount],                            -- Compute sales amount
        KEEPFILTERS ( TopThreeProducts )           -- using TopThreeProducts as a
    )                                              -- further filter
RETURN
    Result
```

The following figure shows the result of *Sales Top 3 Products* side by side with *Sales Amount*. Though the product name is not part of the report, the formula for *Sales Top 3 Products* retrieves sales strictly for the top three products of each category, ignoring all other products. This also applies to the grand total of the report.

Category	Sales Amount	Sales Top 3 Products
TV and Video	4,392,768.29	1,723,318.03
Music, Movies and Audio Books	314,206.74	52,215.49
Home Appliances	9,600,457.04	484,787.05
Games and Toys	360,652.81	28,849.93
Computers	6,741,548.73	561,915.65
Cell phones	1,604,610.26	92,242.59
Cameras and camcorders	7,192,581.95	1,575,214.23
Audio	384,518.16	88,428.16
Total	**30,591,343.98**	**4,606,971.13**

FIGURE 16-8 *Sales Top 3 Products* reports the sales of the top three products for each category.

Performance-wise, the formula used for *Sales Top 3 Products* is slightly slower than the one using the visual-level filter. Therefore, we suggest implementing the first solution, if feasible, and reverting to the full pattern only if strictly necessary or if the client tool does not support visual-level filters.

## CHAPTER 17

Hierarchies

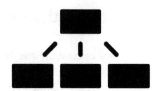

Download sample files: **https://sql.bi/dax-220**

Hierarchies are often created in data models to simplify the browsing of the model by providing users with suggested paths of navigation through attributes. The definition of the hierarchies follows the requirements of the model. For example, the *Date* table usually contains a hierarchy with levels like year, quarter, month, and day. Similarly, the *Product* table usually includes a common hierarchy like *Category*, *Subcategory* and *Product*.

Hierarchies make it possible to insert multiple columns at once in a report, but hierarchies are also useful to drive calculations. For example, a measure can show sales as a percentage over the parent of the current level of the hierarchy. Any other calculation can use the same approach by just customizing the calculation associated to each level of the hierarchy.

Detecting the current level of a hierarchy

Any calculation involving hierarchies requires the DAX code to detect the current level of the hierarchy. Therefore, it is important to understand how to detect the level of a hierarchy where a measure is being evaluated. Figure 17-1 shows the *Product Level* measure whose only goal is to detect the hierarchy level being browsed. The *Product Level* measure is usually hidden in the model because it is only used in other measures and implements a calculation related to the hierarchy level.

Category	Product Level
⊟ **Audio**	**Category**
⊟ **Bluetooth Headphones**	**Subcategory**
NT Bluetooth Active Headphones E202 Black	Product
NT Bluetooth Active Headphones E202 Red	Product
NT Bluetooth Active Headphones E202 Silver	Product
NT Bluetooth Active Headphones E202 White	Product
NT Bluetooth Stereo Headphones E52 Black	Product
NT Bluetooth Stereo Headphones E52 Blue	Product
NT Bluetooth Stereo Headphones E52 Pink	Product
NT Bluetooth Stereo Headphones E52 Yellow	Product
NT Wireless Bluetooth Stereo Headphones E102 Black	Product
NT Wireless Bluetooth Stereo Headphones E102 Blue	Product
NT Wireless Bluetooth Stereo Headphones E102 Silver	Product
Total	**No filter**

FIGURE 17-1 The report shows the level being browsed.

The *Product Level* measure is defined as follows:

Measure (hidden) in the Product table

```
Product Level :=
VAR IsProductInScope = ISINSCOPE ( 'Product'[Product Name] )
VAR IsSubcatInScope = ISINSCOPE ( 'Product'[Subcategory] )
VAR IsCatInScope = ISINSCOPE ( 'Product'[Category] )
VAR Result =
    SWITCH (
        TRUE (),
        IsProductInScope, "Product",
        IsSubcatInScope, "Subcategory",
        IsCatInScope, "Category",
        "No filter"
    )
RETURN
    Result
```

By using ISINSCOPE, the three variables *IsProductInScope*, *IsSubcatInScope*, and *IsCatInScope* check whether each level of the hierarchy is currently being grouped by. In that case, the corresponding column has a single value visible in the filter context.

The SWITCH statement detects the level by looking for the first level visible starting from the more granular one. The order of the conditions in SWITCH is relevant. Indeed, when the product is in scope, both category and subcategory are in scope too. Therefore, the measure must check the most restrictive filter first. The evaluation of the active level must always start from the lowest level of the hierarchy, and move up one step at a time.

The *Product Level* measure is of no use by itself. The technique used in the measure is frequently used to implement a calculation depending on the current level of the hierarchy. We use this measure as a convenient way to detect the hierarchy level in the measures described further in this pattern.

NOTE When ISINSCOPE is not available, ISFILTERED can be used as an alternative technique – this is the case in Excel up to version 2019. However, by using ISFILTERED, the DAX expression operating over hierarchies must assume that the levels beyond the top-level of the hierarchy displayed in a visualization are not filtered outside of the visualization itself – that is, they should not be used in slicers, filters, or selected in other visuals. In order to prevent the user from doing that, if ISINSCOPE is not available it is a best practice to create a hierarchy using only hidden columns – this means duplicating the columns used in levels of a hierarchy so that they are also available as separate filters and slicers without affecting the DAX calculations over the hierarchy itself.

Percentage of parent node

A common hierarchical calculation shows a measure as a percentage over the parent node, as shown in Figure 17-2.

Category	Sales Amount	% Parent
⊟ **Audio**	**102,722.07**	**0.91%**
⊟ **Bluetooth Headphones**	**23,865.91**	**23.23%**
NT Bluetooth Active Headphones E202 Silver	227.70	0.95%
NT Bluetooth Stereo Headphones E52 Blue	20,378.34	85.39%
NT Bluetooth Stereo Headphones E52 Pink	164.42	0.69%
NT Wireless Bluetooth Stereo Headphones E102 Black	388.40	1.63%
NT Wireless Bluetooth Stereo Headphones E102 Silver	287.70	1.21%
NT Wireless Bluetooth Stereo Headphones E102 White	383.60	1.61%
NT Wireless Bluetooth Stereo Headphones E302 Black	275.74	1.16%
NT Wireless Bluetooth Stereo Headphones E302 Pink	324.40	1.36%
WWI Stereo Bluetooth Headphones E1000 Blue	539.20	2.26%
WWI Stereo Bluetooth Headphones E1000 Green	471.80	1.98%
WWI Stereo Bluetooth Headphones E1000 White	424.62	1.78%
⊟ **MP4&MP3**	**60,256.16**	**58.66%**
Contoso 1G MP3 Player E100 White	180.05	0.30%
Contoso 2G MP3 Player E200 Black	129.42	0.21%
Contoso 2G MP3 Player E200 Blue	120.79	0.20%
Contoso 2G MP3 Player E200 Silver	143.44	0.24%
Contoso 4G MP3 Player E400 Green	479.92	0.80%
Contoso 4G MP3 Player E400 Silver	43,366.77	71.97%
Contoso 4GB Flash MP3 Player E401 Blue	901.09	1.50%
Contoso 512MB MP3 Player E51 Blue	81.84	0.14%
Contoso 512MB MP3 Player E51 Silver	184.59	0.31%
Total	**11,309,946.12**	

FIGURE 17-2 The percentage is computed against the parent node in the hierarchy.

The *% Parent* measure detects the level of the hierarchy for the cell being evaluated and uses the value of the parent at the denominator of the ratio:

Measure in the Sales table

```
% Parent :=
VAR AllSelProds =
    ALLSELECTED ( 'Product' )
VAR ProdsInCat =
    CALCULATETABLE (
        'Product',
        AllSelProds,
        VALUES ( 'Product'[Category] )
    )
VAR ProdsInSub =
    CALCULATETABLE (
        'Product',
        ProdsInCat,
        VALUES ( 'Product'[SubCategory] )
    )
VAR Numerator = [Sales Amount]
VAR Denominator =
    SWITCH (
        [Product Level],
        "Category", CALCULATE ( [Sales Amount], AllSelProds ),
        "Subcategory", CALCULATE ( [Sales Amount], ProdsInCat ),
        "Product", CALCULATE ( [Sales Amount], ProdsInSub )
    )
VAR Result =
    DIVIDE (
        Numerator,
        Denominator
    )
RETURN
    Result
```

## CHAPTER 18

Parent-child hierarchies

Download sample files: **https://sql.bi/dax-221**

Parent-child hierarchies are often used to represent charts of accounts, stores, salespersons and such. Parent-child hierarchies have a peculiar way of storing the hierarchy in the sense that they have a variable depth. In this pattern we show how to use parent-child hierarchies to show budget, actual and forecast values in a report using both a chart of accounts and a geographic hierarchy.

Introduction

In the Parent-child pattern the hierarchy is not defined by the presence of columns in the table of the original data source. The hierarchy is based on a structure where each node of the hierarchy is related to the key of its parent node. For example, Figure 18-1 shows the first few rows of a parent-child hierarchy that defines a geographic structure for sales.

EntityKey	ParentEntityKey	EntityName
1		Contoso North America
2		Contoso Europe
3		Contoso Asia
4	1	Contoso United States
5	2	Contoso UK
6	2	Contoso France
7	2	Contoso Italy

FIGURE 18-1 The *Entity* table stores the key of the parent for each entity.

Based on this data structure, we need to display a hierarchy showing Contoso United States under Contoso North America, as shown in Figure 18-2.

Level1	Total
⊞ **Contoso Asia**	27,957,344.35
⊞ **Contoso Europe**	7,857,490.02
⊟ **Contoso North America**	7,110,490.04
⊞ **Contoso Canada**	-164,073.58
⊟ **Contoso United States**	7,274,563.63
⊟ **Contoso Alaska**	-221,591.89
Contoso Anchorage Store	-221,591.89
⊞ **Contoso Catalog Store**	-14,350,470.79
⊞ **Contoso Colorado**	-1,398,224.98
⊞ **Contoso Connecticut**	-46,258.81

FIGURE 18-2 The parent-child hierarchy derives from the parent keys.

The Parent-child pattern implements some sort of self-join of the table containing the entities, which is not supported in Tabular. Because of their nature, parent-child hierarchies may also have a variable depth: the number of levels traversing the hierarchy top to bottom can be different depending on the navigated path. For these reasons, a parent-child hierarchy should be implemented following the technique described in this pattern.

Parent-child hierarchies are often used with charts of accounts. In this case, the nodes also define the sign to use to aggregate a value to its parent. The chart of accounts in Figure 18-3 shows expenses that are subtracted from the total – despite the numbers displayed being all positive – whereas incomes are added.

Level1	Total No Signs
⊟ **Profit and Loss after tax**	**42,925,324.41**
⊟ **Profit and Loss before tax**	**78,729,580.06**
⊟ **Expense**	**273,188,226.99**
⊟ **Cost of Goods Sold**	**154,362,424.28**
⊟ **Selling, General & Administrative Expenses**	**118,825,802.71**
⊟ **Administration Expense**	**13,213,475.64**
⊟ **Human Capital**	**23,697,599.09**
⊟ **IT Cost**	**11,183,230.60**
⊟ **Light, Heat, Communication Cost**	**11,134,446.21**
⊟ **Marketing Cost**	**35,454,610.14**
⊟ **Back-to-School Ad Cost**	**6,646,719.98**
⊟ **Business Ad Cost**	**1,252,331.62**
⊟ **Holiday Ad Cost**	**24,581,461.24**
Internet	8,129,807.30
Other	1,226,664.55
Print	11,775,980.25
Radio & TV	3,449,009.14
⊟ **Spring Ad Cost**	**2,408,139.40**
⊟ **Tax Time / Summer Ad Cost**	**565,957.90**
⊟ **Other Expenses**	**2,471,889.07**
⊟ **Property Costs**	**21,670,551.96**
⊟ **Income**	**351,917,807.05**
⊟ **Sale Revenue**	**351,917,807.05**
⊟ **Taxation**	**35,804,255.64**
Total	**42,925,324.41**

FIGURE 18-3 A parent-child hierarchy used with charts of accounts may define the sign to use to aggregate values.

The DAX expressions aggregating data over a parent-child hierarchy must consider the sign used to aggregate data at lower level of a hierarchy node.

Basic Parent-child pattern

Neither hierarchies of variable depth nor self-joins are directly supported in a Tabular model. The first step in handling parent-child hierarchies is to flatten the hierarchical structure to a regular hierarchy made up of one column for each possible level of the hierarchy. We must move from the data structure of Figure 18-4 to that of Figure 18-5. In Figure 18-4 we only have the three columns required to define a parent-child hierarchy.

EntityKey	ParentEntityKey	EntityName
1		Contoso North America
2		Contoso Europe
3		Contoso Asia
4	1	Contoso United States
5	2	Contoso UK
6	2	Contoso France
7	2	Contoso Italy

FIGURE 18-4 The parent-child hierarchy shows a row for each node of the hierarchy and a single column with the name, regardless of the number of levels in the hierarchy.

The full expansion of the parent-child hierarchy in this example requires four levels. Figure 18-5 shows that there is one column for each level of the hierarchy, named *Level1* to *Level4*. The number of columns required depends on the data, so it is possible to add additional levels to accommodate for future changes in the data.

EntityName	Level1	Level2	Level3	Level4
Contoso Ahal Province	Contoso Asia	Contoso Turkmenistan	Contoso Ahal Province	
Contoso Alaska	Contoso North America	Contoso United States	Contoso Alaska	
Contoso Albany Store	Contoso North America	Contoso United States	Contoso New York	Contoso Albany Store
Contoso Alberta	Contoso North America	Contoso Canada	Contoso Alberta	
Contoso Alexandria Store	Contoso North America	Contoso United States	Contoso Virginia	Contoso Alexandria Store
Contoso Alsace	Contoso Europe	Contoso France	Contoso Alsace	
Contoso Amsterdam Store	Contoso Europe	Contoso the Netherlands	Contoso North Holland	Contoso Amsterdam Store
Contoso Anchorage Store	Contoso North America	Contoso United States	Contoso Alaska	Contoso Anchorage Store
Contoso Annapolis Store	Contoso North America	Contoso United States	Contoso Maryland	Contoso Annapolis Store
Contoso Appleton Store	Contoso North America	Contoso United States	Contoso Wisconsin	Contoso Appleton Store
Contoso Arlington Store	Contoso North America	Contoso United States	Contoso Texas	Contoso Arlington Store
Contoso Armenia	Contoso Asia	Contoso Australia	Contoso Armenia	
Contoso Ashgabat No.2 Store	Contoso Asia	Contoso Turkmenistan	Contoso Ahal Province	Contoso Ashgabat No.2 Store
Contoso Ashgabat No.1 Store	Contoso Asia	Contoso Turkmenistan	Contoso Ahal Province	Contoso Ashgabat No.1 Store
Contoso Asia	Contoso Asia			

FIGURE 18-5 Flattened hierarchy where each level of the original parent-child hierarchy is stored in a separate column.

The first step is to create a technical column called *EntityPath* by using the PATH function:

Calculated column in the Entity table

```
EntityPath =
PATH ( Entity[EntityKey], Entity[ParentEntityKey] )
```

The *EntityPath* column contains the full path to reach the node corresponding to the row of the table, as shown in Figure 18-6. This technical column is useful to define the *Level* columns.

EntityKey	ParentEntityKey	EntityName	EntityPath
1		Contoso North America	1
2		Contoso Europe	2
3		Contoso Asia	3
4	1	Contoso United States	1|4
5	2	Contoso UK	2|5
6	2	Contoso France	2|6
7	2	Contoso Italy	2|7
8	2	Contoso Germany	2|8
9	2	Contoso the Netherlands	2|9
10	2	Contoso Denmark	2|10
11	2	Contoso Sweden	2|11

FIGURE 18-6 The *EntityPath* technical column contains the traversal path to reach the node from the root level.

The code for all the *Level* columns is similar, and only differs in the value assigned to the *LevelNumber* variable. This is the code for the *Level1* column:

Calculated column in the Entity table

```
Level1 =
VAR LevelNumber = 1
VAR LevelKey = PATHITEM ( Entity[EntityPath], LevelNumber, INTEGER )
VAR LevelName = LOOKUPVALUE ( Entity[EntityName], Entity[EntityKey], LevelKey )
VAR Result = LevelName
RETURN
    Result
```

The other columns have a different name and a different value assigned to *LevelNumber*, corresponding to the relative position of their level in the hierarchy. Once all the *Level* columns are defined, we hide them and create a regular hierarchy in the table that includes all of them – all the *Level* columns. Only exposing these columns through a hierarchy is important in order to make sure they are used in properly by the user navigating a report.

If used straight in a report, the hierarchy still does not provide an optimal result. Indeed, all the levels are always shown, even though they might contain no value. Figure 18-7 shows a blank row under Contoso Asia Online Store, even though the *Level4* column for that node is blank - thus meaning that the node can be expanded only three levels, not four.

Level1	Amount
⊟ **Contoso Asia**	**183,201,917.25**
⊞ **Contoso Australia**	**11,187,797.24**
⊞ **Contoso Bhutan**	**3,069,521.49**
⊟ **Contoso China**	**109,024,911.19**
⊟ **Contoso Asia Online Store**	**69,969,056.93**
	69,969,056.93
⊟ **Contoso Asia Reseller**	**23,267,326.65**
	23,267,326.65
⊟ **Contoso Beijing**	**3,726,108.03**
Contoso Beijing Store	3,726,108.03

FIGURE 18-7 Rows with blank names should be hidden, but this does not happen by default.

To hide the unwanted rows, for each row we must check whether the current level is available by the visited node. This can be accomplished by checking the depth of each node. We need a calculated column in the hierarchy table containing the depth of the node defined by each row:

Calculated column in the Entity table

```
Depth =
PATHLENGTH ( Entity[EntityPath] )
```

We need two measures: *EntityRowDepth* returns the maximum depth of the current node, whereas *EntityBrowseDepth* returns the current depth of the matrix by leveraging the ISINSCOPE function:

Measure in the Entity table

```
EntityRowDepth :=
MAX ( Entity[Depth] )
```

Measure in the Entity table

```
EntityBrowseDepth :=
    ISINSCOPE ( Entity[Level1] )
    + ISINSCOPE ( Entity[Level2] )
    + ISINSCOPE ( Entity[Level3] )
    + ISINSCOPE ( Entity[Level4] )
```

Finally, we use these two measures to blank out the result if the *EntityRowDepth* is greater than the browsing depth:

Measure in the StrategyPlan table

```
Sum Amount :=
SUM ( StrategyPlan[Amount] )
```

Measure in the StrategyPlan table

```
Total Base :=
VAR Val = [Sum Amount]
VAR EntityShowRow =
    [EntityBrowseDepth] <= [EntityRowDepth]
VAR Result =
    IF ( EntityShowRow, Val )
RETURN
    Result
```

The report obtained by using the *Total Base* measure no longer contains rows with an empty description, as shown in Figure 18-8.

Level1	Total Base
⊟ **Contoso Asia**	183,201,917.25
⊞ **Contoso Australia**	11,187,797.24
⊞ **Contoso Bhutan**	3,069,521.49
⊟ **Contoso China**	109,024,911.19
⊟ **Contoso Asia Online Store**	69,969,056.93
⊟ **Contoso Asia Reseller**	23,267,326.65
⊟ **Contoso Beijing**	3,726,108.03
Contoso Beijing Store	3,726,108.03

FIGURE 18-8 The rows with a blank name have disappeared because *Total Base* also returns blank in those cases.

The same pattern must be applied to any measure that could be reported by using the parent-child hierarchy.

Chart of accounts hierarchy

The Chart of accounts pattern is a variation of the basic Parent-child hierarchy pattern, where the hierarchy is also used to drive the calculations. Each row in the hierarchy is tagged as either Income, Expense or Taxation. Incomes need to be summed, whereas expenses and taxation must be subtracted from the total. The Figure 18-9 shows the content of the table containing the hierarchy items.

AccountKey	ParentAccountKey	AccountName	AccountType
1		Profit and Loss after tax	
2	24	Income	Income
3	24	Expense	Expense
4	2	Sale Revenue	Income
5	3	Cost of Goods Sold	Expense
6	3	Selling, General & Administrative Expenses	Expense
7	6	Administration Expense	Expense
8	6	IT Cost	Expense
9	6	Human Capital	Expense
10	6	Light, Heat, Communication Cost	Expense
11	6	Property Costs	Expense
12	6	Other Expenses	Expense
13	6	Marketing Cost	Expense
14	13	Holiday Ad Cost	Expense
15	13	Spring Ad Cost	Expense
16	13	Back-to-School Ad Cost	Expense
17	13	Business Ad Cost	Expense
18	13	Tax Time / Summer Ad Cost	Expense
19	1	Taxation	Taxation
20	14	Radio & TV	Expense
21	14	Print	Expense
22	14	Internet	Expense
23	14	Other	Expense
24	1	Profit and Loss before tax	

FIGURE 18-9 Each row in the hierarchy defines an *AccountType* that drives the calculations.

The implementation is similar to the Parent-child pattern, grouping the calculation by *AccountType* and applying the proper sign to the calculation depending on the value of *AccountType*:

Measure in the StrategyPlan table

```
Total :=
VAR Val =
    SUMX (
        SUMMARIZE ( StrategyPlan, Account[AccountType] ),
        VAR SignToUse =
            IF ( Account[AccountType] = "Income", +1, -1 )
        VAR Amount = [Sum Amount]
        RETURN
            Amount * SignToUse
    )
VAR AccountShowRow = [AccountBrowseDepth] <= [AccountRowDepth]
VAR EntityShowRow = [EntityBrowseDepth] <= [EntityRowDepth]
VAR Result =
    IF ( AccountShowRow && EntityShowRow, Val )
RETURN
    Result
```

The *Total* measure can use both parent-child hierarchies: the hierarchy defined in the *Entity* table – shown in the previous example – and the hierarchy defined in the *Account* table, which is the subject of this section.

The formula in *Total* returns the right result for each node of the hierarchy. However, in these types of reports it is commonly requested that the numbers be shown as positive despite being expenses. The requirement can be fulfilled by changing the sign of the result at the report level. The following *Total No Signs* measure implements the calculation this way: It first determines the sign to use for the report, and then it changes the sign of the result in order to show expenses as positive numbers, even though they are internally managed as negative numbers:

Measure in the StrategyPlan table

```
Total No Signs :=
VAR BrowseLevel = [AccountBrowseDepth]
VAR AccountName =
    SWITCH (
        BrowseLevel,
        1, SELECTEDVALUE ( Account[Level1] ),
        2, SELECTEDVALUE ( Account[Level2] ),
        3, SELECTEDVALUE ( Account[Level3] ),
        4, SELECTEDVALUE ( Account[Level4] ),
        5, SELECTEDVALUE ( Account[Level5] ),
        6, SELECTEDVALUE ( Account[Level6] ),
        7, SELECTEDVALUE ( Account[Level7] )
    )
VAR AccountType =
    LOOKUPVALUE ( Account[AccountType], Account[AccountName], AccountName )
VAR ValueToShow = [Total]
VAR Result =
    IF ( AccountType = "Income", +1, -1 ) * ValueToShow
RETURN
    Result
```

The report obtained using *Total No Signs* is visible in Figure 18-10.

Level1	Total No Signs
⊟ **Profit and Loss after tax**	**42,925,324.41**
⊟ **Profit and Loss before tax**	**78,729,580.06**
⊟ **Expense**	**273,188,226.99**
⊟ **Cost of Goods Sold**	**154,362,424.28**
⊟ **Selling, General & Administrative Expenses**	**118,825,802.71**
⊟ **Administration Expense**	**13,213,475.64**
⊟ **Human Capital**	**23,697,599.09**
⊟ **IT Cost**	**11,183,230.60**
⊟ **Light, Heat, Communication Cost**	**11,134,446.21**
⊟ **Marketing Cost**	**35,454,610.14**
⊟ **Back-to-School Ad Cost**	**6,646,719.98**
⊟ **Business Ad Cost**	**1,252,331.62**
⊟ **Holiday Ad Cost**	**24,581,461.24**
Internet	8,129,807.30
Other	1,226,664.55
Print	11,775,980.25
Radio & TV	3,449,009.14
⊟ **Spring Ad Cost**	**2,408,139.40**
⊟ **Tax Time / Summer Ad Cost**	**565,957.90**
⊟ **Other Expenses**	**2,471,889.07**
⊟ **Property Costs**	**21,670,551.96**
⊟ **Income**	**351,917,807.05**
⊟ **Sale Revenue**	**351,917,807.05**
⊟ **Taxation**	**35,804,255.64**
Total	**42,925,324.41**

FIGURE 18-10 The result of the parent-child hierarchy using the *Total No Signs* measure.

The pattern shown above works fine if the chart of accounts contains the *AccountType* column, which defines each item as being either an income or an expense. Sometimes the chart of accounts has a different way of defining the sign to use. For example, there could be a column defining the sign to use when aggregating an account to its parent. This is the case of the *Operator* column shown in Figure 18-11.

AccountKey	ParentAccountKey	AccountName	Operator
1		Profit and Loss after tax	
2	24	Income	+
3	24	Expense	-
4	2	Sale Revenue	+
5	3	Cost of Goods Sold	+
6	3	Selling, General & Administrative Expenses	+
7	6	Administration Expense	+
8	6	IT Cost	+
9	6	Human Capital	+
10	6	Light, Heat, Communication Cost	+
11	6	Property Costs	+
12	6	Other Expenses	+
13	6	Marketing Cost	+
14	13	Holiday Ad Cost	+
15	13	Spring Ad Cost	+
16	13	Back-to-School Ad Cost	+
17	13	Business Ad Cost	+
18	13	Tax Time / Summer Ad Cost	+
19	1	Taxation	-
20	14	Radio & TV	+
21	14	Print	+
22	14	Internet	+
23	14	Other	+
24	1	Profit and Loss before tax	+

FIGURE 18-11 The operator column indicates the sign to use to aggregate one account to its parent.

In this case, the code to author is more complex. We need one column for each level of the hierarchy, stating how that account needs to be shown when aggregated at any given level of the hierarchy. A single account can be aggregated at one level with a plus, but at a different level with a minus.

These columns need to be built from the bottom of the hierarchy. In this example we need seven columns because there are seven levels. The column indicates the sign to use when aggregating that specific item of the hierarchy at the desired level. Figure 18-12 shows the result of the seven columns in this example.

AccountKey	ParentAccountKey	AccountName	Depth	Operator	S L1	S L2	S L3	S L4	S L5	S L6	S L7
1		Profit and Loss after tax	1		1						
2	24	Income	3	+	1	1	1				
3	24	Expense	3	-	-1	-1	-1				
4	2	Sale Revenue	4	+	1	1	1	1			
5	3	Cost of Goods Sold	4	+	-1	-1	-1	1			
6	3	Selling, General & Administrative Expenses	4	+	-1	-1	-1	1			
7	6	Administration Expense	5	+	-1	-1	-1	1	1		
8	6	IT Cost	5	+	-1	-1	-1	1	1		
9	6	Human Capital	5	+	-1	-1	-1	1	1		
10	6	Light, Heat, Communication Cost	5	+	-1	-1	-1	1	1		
11	6	Property Costs	5	+	-1	-1	-1	1	1		
12	6	Other Expenses	5	+	-1	-1	-1	1	1		
13	6	Marketing Cost	5	+	-1	-1	-1	1	1		
14	13	Holiday Ad Cost	6	+	-1	-1	-1	1	1	1	
15	13	Spring Ad Cost	6	+	-1	-1	-1	1	1	1	
16	13	Back-to-School Ad Cost	6	+	-1	-1	-1	1	1	1	
17	13	Business Ad Cost	6	+	-1	-1	-1	1	1	1	
18	13	Tax Time / Summer Ad Cost	6	+	-1	-1	-1	1	1	1	
19	1	Taxation	2	-	-1	-1					
20	14	Radio & TV	7	+	-1	-1	-1	1	1	1	1
21	14	Print	7	+	-1	-1	-1	1	1	1	1
22	14	Internet	7	+	-1	-1	-1	1	1	1	1
23	14	Other	7	+	-1	-1	-1	1	1	1	1
24	1	Profit and Loss before tax	2	+	1	1					

FIGURE 18-12 The columns from *S L1* to *S L7* show the sign required when aggregating the account at the correspondent hierarchical level.

For instance, examine the rows with *AccountKey* 4 and 5: account 4 (Sale Revenue) must be summed when aggregated at levels 1, 2, 3 and 4, whereas it is not visible at other levels. Account 5 (Cost of Goods Sold) must be summed when aggregated at level 4, but it must be subtracted when aggregated at levels 1, 2, and 3.

The DAX formula computing the sign at each level starts from the most granular level – level 7 in our example. At this most granular level, the sign to use is just the operator converted into +1 or -1, for convenience in further calculations:

Calculated column in the Account table

```
SignToLevel7 =
VAR LevelNumber = 7
VAR Depth = Account[Depth]
RETURN
    IF ( LevelNumber = Depth, IF ( Account[Operator] = "-", -1, +1 ) )
```

All the other columns (from level 1 to level 6) follow a similar pattern, though for each level the DAX expression must consider the sign at the more granular, adjacent level (stored in the *PrevSign* variable) and invert the result when that level shows a "-" sign, as shown in the column for level 6:

Calculated column in the Account table

```
SignToLevel6 =
VAR LevelNumber = 6
VAR PrevSign = Account[SignToLevel7]
VAR Depth = Account[Depth]
VAR LevelKey =
    PATHITEM ( Account[AccountPath], LevelNumber, INTEGER )
VAR LevelSign =
    LOOKUPVALUE ( Account[Operator], Account[AccountKey], LevelKey )
RETURN
    IF (
        LevelNumber = Depth,
        IF ( Account[Operator] = "-", -1, +1 ),
        IF ( LevelNumber < Depth, IF ( LevelSign = "-", -1, +1 ) * PrevSign )
    )
```

Once the level columns are ready, the *Signed Total* measure computing the total with custom signs is the following:

Measure in the StrategyPlan table

```
Signed Total :=
VAR BrowseDepth =
    MAX ( [AccountBrowseDepth], 1 )
VAR AccountShowRow = [AccountBrowseDepth] <= [AccountRowDepth]
VAR EntityShowRow = [EntityBrowseDepth] <= [EntityRowDepth]
VAR Result =
    IF (
        AccountShowRow && EntityShowRow,
        SWITCH (
            BrowseDepth,
            1, SUMX (
                VALUES ( Account[SignToLevel1] ),
                [Sum Amount] * Account[SignToLevel1]
            ),
            2, SUMX (
                VALUES ( Account[SignToLevel2] ),
                [Sum Amount] * Account[SignToLevel2]
            ),
            3, SUMX (
                VALUES ( Account[SignToLevel3] ),
                [Sum Amount] * Account[SignToLevel3]
            ),
            4, SUMX (
                VALUES ( Account[SignToLevel4] ),
                [Sum Amount] * Account[SignToLevel4]
            ),
            5, SUMX (
                VALUES ( Account[SignToLevel5] ),
                [Sum Amount] * Account[SignToLevel5]
            ),
            6, SUMX (
                VALUES ( Account[SignToLevel6] ),
                [Sum Amount] * Account[SignToLevel6]
            ),
            7, SUMX (
                VALUES ( Account[SignToLevel7] ),
                [Sum Amount] * Account[SignToLevel7]
            )
        )
    )
RETURN
    Result
```

We can compare the result of this last *Signed Total* measure with that of the previous *Total* measure in Figure 18-13.

Level1	Total	Signed Total
⊟ **Profit and Loss after tax**	**42,925,324.41**	**42,925,324.41**
⊟ **Profit and Loss before tax**	**78,729,580.06**	**78,729,580.06**
⊟ **Expense**	**-273,188,226.99**	**-273,188,226.99**
⊟ **Cost of Goods Sold**	**-154,362,424.28**	**154,362,424.28**
⊟ **Selling, General & Administrative Expenses**	**-118,825,802.71**	**118,825,802.71**
⊟ **Administration Expense**	**-13,213,475.64**	**13,213,475.64**
⊟ **Human Capital**	**-23,697,599.09**	**23,697,599.09**
⊟ **IT Cost**	**-11,183,230.60**	**11,183,230.60**
⊟ **Light, Heat, Communication Cost**	**-11,134,446.21**	**11,134,446.21**
⊟ **Marketing Cost**	**-35,454,610.14**	**35,454,610.14**
⊟ **Back-to-School Ad Cost**	**-6,646,719.98**	**6,646,719.98**
⊟ **Business Ad Cost**	**-1,252,331.62**	**1,252,331.62**
⊟ **Holiday Ad Cost**	**-24,581,461.24**	**24,581,461.24**
Internet	-8,129,807.30	8,129,807.30
Other	-1,226,664.55	1,226,664.55
Print	-11,775,980.25	11,775,980.25
Radio & TV	-3,449,009.14	3,449,009.14
⊟ **Spring Ad Cost**	**-2,408,139.40**	**2,408,139.40**
⊟ **Tax Time / Summer Ad Cost**	**-565,957.90**	**565,957.90**
⊟ **Other Expenses**	**-2,471,889.07**	**2,471,889.07**
⊟ **Property Costs**	**-21,670,551.96**	**21,670,551.96**
⊟ **Income**	**351,917,807.05**	**351,917,807.05**
⊟ **Sale Revenue**	**351,917,807.05**	**351,917,807.05**
⊟ **Taxation**	**-35,804,255.64**	**-35,804,255.64**
Total	**42,925,324.41**	**42,925,324.41**

FIGURE 18-13 The two formulas return a different sign for the same node in the hierarchy.

The amount for "Internet" is negative in *Total*, because it is an expense. However, in *Signed Total* the same row holds a positive number and it becomes negative only when it traverses the Expense node, which is aggregated to the parent with a minus sign.

Security pattern for a parent-child hierarchy

A common security requirement for parent-child hierarchies is to restrict the visibility to a node (or a set of nodes) including all of its children. In that scenario, the PATHCONTAINS function is useful.

By applying the following expression to a security role on the *Account* table, we limit the visibility to the node provided in the second argument of PATHCONTAINS. This way, all the children of the node are made visible to the user, because the node requested (2, corresponding to Income) is also part of the *AccountPath* value of all the children nodes:

```
PATHCONTAINS (
    Account[AccountPath],
    2  -- Key of Income
)
```

If we used the *AccountKey* column to limit the visibility, we would end up limiting the visibility to only one row and the user would not see the children nodes. By leveraging the path column, we can easily select multiple rows by including all the nodes that can be reached when traversing a path that includes the filtered node.

When the security role is active, the user can only see the nodes (and the values) included in the tree starting from the Income node, as shown in Figure 18-14.

Level1	Total
⊟ **Profit and Loss after tax**	**351,917,807.05**
⊟ **Profit and Loss before tax**	**351,917,807.05**
⊟ **Income**	**351,917,807.05**
⊟ **Sale Revenue**	**351,917,807.05**
Total	**351,917,807.05**

FIGURE 18-14 The hierarchy is limited to the node that is visible for the active security role.

The nodes above the Income node (*Level3*) no longer consider other children nodes in the *Total* measure. In case this is misleading in the report, consider removing the initial levels from the report (in this case *Level1* and *Level2*) or using different descriptions of the nodes in Level1 and Level2 in order to better explain the result.

It is worth noting that the security role defined by using PATHCONTAINS may slow down the performance if used with a hierarchy with thousands of nodes. The expression in the role security must be evaluated for every node of the hierarchy when the end user opens a connection, and PATHCONTAINS can be expensive if it is applied to thousands of rows or more.

Like-for-like comparison

The like-for-like sales comparison is an adjusted metric that compares two time periods, restricting the comparison to products or stores with the same characteristics. In this example, we use the like-for-like technique to compare the sales of Contoso stores that had sales in all the time periods considered. The stores are continuously updated: new stores are opened, other stores are closed or renovated. The like-for-like comparison only evaluates those stores that were open in all the periods considered. This way, the report does not show a store that seems to be underperforming simply because it was closed during the period analyzed.

As is the case with many other patterns, like-for-like can be computed statically or dynamically. The choice is both in terms of performance and in terms of business requirements. The variations of the "Same store sales" measure described in the following paragraphs are examples of like-for-like sales comparisons.

Introduction

If you analyze sales figures without considering whether stores were open or closed within the time period you are analyzing, looking at the following report might mislead you into thinking that there were issues in 2009 because of the dramatic drop in sales.

CountryRegion	Brand	CY 2007	CY 2008	CY 2009
Canada ⌄	A. Datum	111,650.79	95,652.05	39,326.78
	Adventure Works	91,005.43	151,783.52	81,406.38
	Contoso	368,183.96	314,781.48	143,651.54
	Fabrikam	254,605.79	365,726.91	103,550.61
	Litware	176,079.29	138,174.87	78,944.87
	Northwind Traders	44,105.39	61,465.21	13,191.43
	Proseware	129,118.19	230,146.25	42,887.68
	Southridge Video	68,326.69	56,096.06	37,126.83
	Tailspin Toys	2,178.28	1,484.96	
	The Phone Company	94,575.60	116,545.75	48,045.60
	Wide World Importers	91,764.94	206,801.72	32,737.94
	Total	**1,431,594.35**	**1,738,658.77**	**620,869.65**

FIGURE 19-1 Sales in 2009 dropped significantly.

In 2009 many stores were closed. Therefore, the numbers reflect a substantial drop in sales due to the lower number of open stores, as you can see in the following report that shows which stores were open in different years. A blank cell means that the store was closed in that particular year.

CountryRegion	Store Name	CY 2007	CY 2008	CY 2009
Canada ⌄	Contoso Calgary Store	Open	Open	
	Contoso Montreal No.1 Store	Open	Open	Open
	Contoso Montreal No.2 Store		Open	Open
	Contoso Ottawa No.1 Store	Open	Open	Open
	Contoso Ottawa No.2 Store		Open	
	Contoso Toronto No.1 Store		Open	
	Contoso Toronto No.2 Store	Open	Open	
	Contoso Toronto No.3 Store	Open	Open	
	Contoso Vancouver No.1 Store		Open	Open
	Contoso Vancouver No.2 Store	Open	Open	
	Contoso Westminster Store	Open	Open	Open

FIGURE 19-2 Not all the stores are open every year.

In the "same store sales" measure, you must compute the sales amount just for the stores that were open during the entire time period (2007-2009), namely three stores.

Store Name	CY 2007	CY 2008	CY 2009
Contoso Montreal No.1 Store	168,746.53	153,915.08	127,914.90
Contoso Ottawa No.1 Store	213,596.88	156,587.95	124,981.59
Contoso Westminster Store	202,966.73	149,906.79	113,587.59
Total	**585,310.15**	**460,409.83**	**366,484.08**

FIGURE 19-3 Only three stores were open during the entire three-year period.

The measure must compute the correct value even when sliced by different attributes, as shown in Figure 19-4.

CountryRegi... ⌄

Canada ⌄

Brand	CY 2007	CY 2008	CY 2009
A. Datum	48,847.03	33,992.65	11,366.88
Adventure Works	51,484.26	30,234.99	32,699.33
Contoso	145,742.12	86,563.32	104,033.14
Fabrikam	105,102.41	93,027.33	50,545.71
Litware	64,186.71	23,884.22	58,501.79
Northwind Traders	18,583.98	21,613.96	
Proseware	54,689.01	44,616.72	30,628.83
Southridge Video	15,365.10	19,001.24	29,862.20
Tailspin Toys	323.64		
The Phone Company	39,310.60	31,625.65	21,183.00
Wide World Importers	41,675.29	75,849.76	27,663.20
Total	**585,310.15**	**460,409.83**	**366,484.08**

FIGURE 19-4 The measure totals the same numbers also when sliced by other attributes.

Same store sales with snapshot

The best method to solve the same store sales scenario is to use a snapshot table to manage store statuses. Later in this pattern we also demonstrate how to compute same store sales in a dynamic way without a snapshot table. Nevertheless, the snapshot table is the best option for both performance and manageability.

The snapshot table must contain all the stores and years, with an additional column indicating the status.

Store Name	Calendar Year Number	Status
Contoso Calgary Store	2007	Open
Contoso Calgary Store	2008	Open
Contoso Calgary Store	2009	Closed
Contoso Montreal No.1 Store	2007	Open
Contoso Montreal No.1 Store	2008	Open
Contoso Montreal No.1 Store	2009	Open
Contoso Montreal No.2 Store	2007	Closed
Contoso Montreal No.2 Store	2008	Open
Contoso Montreal No.2 Store	2009	Open

FIGURE 19-5 The snapshot table *StoreStatus* indicates the status of each store in different years.

The *StoreStatus* snapshot table can be created with the following calculated table:

Calculated table

```
StoreStatus =
VAR AllStores =
    CROSSJOIN (
        FILTER (
            ALLNOBLANKROW ( 'Date'[Calendar Year Number] ),
            'Date'[Calendar Year Number] IN { 2007, 2008, 2009 }
        ),
        ALLNOBLANKROW ( Store[StoreKey] )
    )
VAR OpenStores =
    SUMMARIZE (
        Receipts,
        'Date'[Calendar Year Number],
        Receipts[StoreKey]
    )
VAR Result =
    UNION (
        ADDCOLUMNS ( OpenStores, "Status", "Open" ),
        ADDCOLUMNS ( EXCEPT ( AllStores, OpenStores ), "Status", "Closed" )
    )
RETURN
    Result
```

The *StoreStatus* snapshot table has a granularity by store and year. Therefore, it has a regular strong relationship with the *Store* table and a weak Many-Many-Relationship (MMR) with the *Date* table. If weak relationships are not available in your tool - like in Power Pivot - then you must transfer the filter from *Date* to *Store* in DAX using TREATAS or INTERSECT.

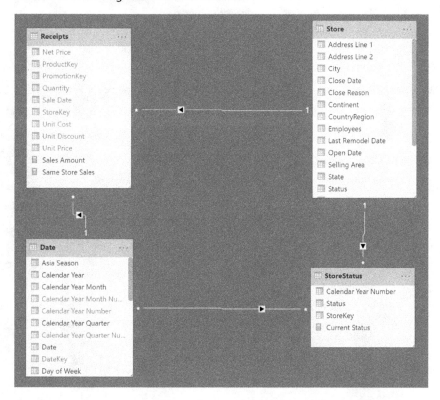

FIGURE 19-6 The data model requires a weak MMR relationship between *Date* and *StoreStatus*.

The *Same Store Sales* measure checks the stores whose status is always "Open" during the entire selected period. If a store is "Closed" at any point, then SELECTEDVALUE returns either blank or "Closed", filtering out that store:

Measure in the Receipts table

```
Same Store Sales :=
VAR OpenStores =
    CALCULATETABLE (
        FILTER (
            ALLSELECTED ( StoreStatus[StoreKey] ),      -- Filter the stores
            CALCULATE (                                 -- where the Status is
                SELECTEDVALUE ( StoreStatus[Status] )   -- always OPEN
            ) = "Open"                                  --
        ),                                              --
        ALLSELECTED ( 'Date' )                          -- Over all selected years
    )
VAR FilterOpenStores =
    TREATAS (                   -- Use OpenStores to filter
        OpenStores,             -- Store[StoreKey]
        Store[StoreKey]         -- by changing its data lineage
    )
VAR Result =
    CALCULATE (
        [Sales Amount],
        KEEPFILTERS ( FilterOpenStores )
    )
RETURN
    Result
```

The formula requires the snapshot table to contain the rows for all the years and stores. If you store in the snapshot table only the years when a store was open, then the code no longer works.

Same store sales without snapshot

In case you do not have the option of building a snapshot table, same store sales can be computed in a more dynamic way using only DAX code.

If the snapshot table is not available, then you must compute the number of years of the report dynamically, and then filter all the stores that have sales in all the years. In other words, if the report is showing three years, then only the stores that have sales in all three years should survive the filter. If a store does not have sales in any one of the selected years, then that store will not be considered for the calculation:

Measure in the Receipts table

```
Same Store Sales Dynamic :=
VAR NumberOfYears =
    CALCULATE (
        DISTINCTCOUNT ( 'Date'[Calendar Year] ),
        CROSSFILTER ( Receipts[Sale Date], 'Date'[Date], BOTH ),
        ALLSELECTED ( )
    )
VAR StoresAndYears =
    CALCULATETABLE (
        SUMMARIZE (                         -- Group the Receipts table
            Receipts,                       -- by store and year
            Store[StoreKey],                -- in order to count how
            'Date'[Calendar Year]           -- many years a store is present in
        ),                                  --
        ALLSELECTED ( )                     -- Over all selected years and stores
    )
VAR StoresAndYearCount =
    GROUPBY (
        StoresAndYears,
        Store[StoreKey],
        "@Years", SUMX ( CURRENTGROUP (), 1 )
    )
VAR OpenStores =
    FILTER (
        StoresAndYearCount,
        [@Years] = NumberOfYears
    )
VAR Result =
    CALCULATE (
        [Sales Amount],
        KEEPFILTERS ( OpenStores )          -- Filters Store[StoreKey]
    )
RETURN
    Result
```

From a computation perspective, this formula is much more expensive than the one using the snapshot. Besides, the entire logic to determine whether a store is open or closed lies inside the formula. In our experience, such business logic is better handled outside of DAX, possibly stored in the data source.

Therefore, if you do not have that information available in the data source we suggest the implementation using the snapshot - even for smaller data models.

The *Same Store Sales Dynamic* measure shows three stores that were open in Canada for the entire time period (2007-2009).

Store Name	CY 2007	CY 2008	CY 2009
Contoso Montreal No.1 Store	168,746.53	153,915.08	127,914.90
Contoso Ottawa No.1 Store	213,596.88	156,587.95	124,981.59
Contoso Westminster Store	202,966.73	149,906.79	113,587.59
Total	**585,310.15**	**460,409.83**	**366,484.08**

FIGURE 19-7 Only three stores were open in Canada during the entire three-year period.

Transition matrix

The Transition matrix pattern analyzes changes in an attribute assigned to an entity at regular intervals. For example, customers might receive a ranking evaluation every month, or products might have a rating score measured every week. Measuring the changes in rating between two points in time might require the evaluation of how many items moved from one rating to another within the considered interval. The transition matrix enables the end user to make this kind of analysis by just manipulating filters in a report and without having to write any custom query.

Introduction

Each product is assigned a monthly rating based on the comparison between the percentage of sales in the current month and in the previous month. The configuration is depicted in Figure 20-1.

Rating	Min Growth	Max Growth
Decreasing	0.00%	80.00%
Stable	80.00%	120.00%
Increasing	120.00%	99999900.00%

FIGURE 20-1 The configuration table for ratings is based on growth percentage.

A simple implementation of the dynamic segmentation lets you analyze how many products fall under each rating every month, like in Figure 20-2.

Calendar Year	Decreasing	Stable	Increasing	Total
⊟ **CY 2008**	**2,223**	**1,301**	**1,622**	**2,223**
January	601	123	289	**1,013**
February	735	113	245	**1,093**
March	695	163	227	**1,085**
April	786	149	279	**1,214**
May	751	188	257	**1,196**
June	725	266	187	**1,178**
July	704	239	236	**1,179**
August	779	208	191	**1,178**
September	756	193	200	**1,149**
October	832	177	210	**1,219**
November	781	143	229	**1,153**
December	780	156	236	**1,172**

FIGURE 20-2 Counting the number of products in each rating is possible using the dynamic segmentation.

As you can imagine, one same product might be assigned different ratings over time. The same matrix in Figure 20-3, focusing on a single product, shows the situation for A. Datum SLR Camera.

Product Name

A. Datum SLR Camera X136 Silver⌄

Calendar Year	Decreasing	Stable	Increasing
⊟ **CY 2007**	**1**	**1**	**1**
January	1		
February		1	
March			1
May	1		
July	1		
August			1
September		1	
November	1		

FIGURE 20-3 The same camera is assigned different ratings over time.

From a broader point of view, an interesting analysis is: taking all the products that had a given rating in a starting month, how did they evolve over time? Has their rating improved or worsened in the following months? You can see the result in Figure 20-4.

Calendar Year	Decreasing	Stable	Increasing	Total
⊟ **CY 2007**	**36**	**36**	**32**	**36**
January	26			**26**
February	21	9	6	**36**
March		36		**36**
April	8	10	13	**31**
May	11	6	9	**26**
June	20	5	3	**28**
July	7	8	9	**24**
August	14	6	4	**24**
September	9	5	10	**24**
October	13	4	5	**22**
November	14	5	3	**22**
December	19	3	6	**28**

Starting Month

March 2007 ∨

Starting Rating

Stable ∨

Brand

Contoso ∨

FIGURE 20-4 The report shows the rating evolution of the 36 products ranked Stable in March 2007.

The report is showing that there are 36 products rated Stable in March 2007. The rating for that same set of products changes in different months, and a product only has a rating for months when there are sales. The number of products with a rating might thus change over time. In April for example, 8 out of the 36 products have a lower rating, 10 have the same rating, and 13 have a higher rating. 5 of the original 36 products have no rating in April 2007, because there were no sales for those 5 products. The products considered in April are only products with a rating in March 2007, the only change is their monthly rating and the 5 products without sales in April are not included because they have no rating in that month. The same reasoning applies to all the other months, always based on the 36 products that are Stable in March.

There are multiple ways of generating the transition matrix; here, we outline two possible solutions. The first solution is based on a snapshot table, generating a very fast static transition matrix. The second solution is based on pure DAX code, resulting in a slower but more flexible dynamic transition matrix.

Both patterns share some of the data modeling requirements. Therefore, we first explain the easier static transition matrix. Later on, we dive into more details with the dynamic transition matrix. In the dynamic transition matrix section, we will not repeat some of the details explained in the static transition matrix. Therefore, if you need to implement the dynamic transition matrix pattern, please review the static pattern first, in order to gather the required information on how to setup your model.

Static transition matrix

The static transition matrix uses a snapshot table containing the rating assigned to each product on a monthly basis. In the example provided, we generated this snapshot through a DAX calculated table. In your scenario, you might have the same information already provided in the data source. The important thing is that the table must contain the month, the product, and the rating assigned. In Figure 20-5 you can see an excerpt of the *Monthly Ratings* snapshot table.

Calendar Year Month Number	Calendar Year Month	ProductKey	Product Name	Product Rating
200702	February 2007	457	WWI Desktop PC1.60 E1600 White	Decreasing
200702	February 2007	459	WWI Desktop PC1.80 E1801 White	Increasing
200702	February 2007	469	Proseware LCD17 E200 Black	Decreasing
200702	February 2007	472	Proseware CRT19 E201 Black	Stable
200702	February 2007	473	Proseware CRT17 E104 Black	Stable
200702	February 2007	474	Proseware CRT15 E10 Black	Decreasing
200702	February 2007	483	Proseware LCD17 E200 White	Increasing
200702	February 2007	484	Proseware LCD17W E202 White	Increasing
200702	February 2007	485	Proseware LCD15 E103 White	Stable
200702	February 2007	486	Proseware CRT19 E201 White	Decreasing
200702	February 2007	487	Proseware CRT17 E104 White	Decreasing

FIGURE 20-5 The snapshot contains the month, the product, and the product ratings for every month.

The snapshot table is not enough to solve the scenario. We need two additional tables to enable the user to select a starting month and a starting rating. The user interface provided to the user is visible in Figure 20-6.

Calendar Year	Decreasing	Stable	Increasing	**Total**
CY 2007	**125**	**125**	**109**	**125**
January	79			**79**
February	82	23	20	**125**
March		125		**125**
April	27	23	42	**92**
May	42	19	28	**89**
June	57	19	18	**94**
July	35	16	27	**78**
August	51	18	10	**79**
September	43	13	21	**77**

Starting Month: March 2007 ①

Starting Rating: Stable ②

Brand: All

FIGURE 20-6 There needs to be four independent columns in the model to let the user create this report.

The slicer for Starting Month (1) cannot be based on the *Date[Calendar Year Month]* column. Indeed, the *Date* table is already used in the rows of the matrix (3). Therefore, the *Date* table cannot be filtered by an external slicer in order to show – for example – September 2007 even though the starting month is March 2007. Similarly, the slicer with the Starting Rating (2) cannot use the same snapshot rating attribute applied to the columns of the matrix (4). The columns of the matrix and the slicer must be fed by different tables.

We need two calculated tables for the slicers that we call *Starting Month* and *Starting Rating:*

Calculated table

```
Starting Month =
SELECTCOLUMNS (
    SUMMARIZE ( Sales, 'Date'[Calendar Year Month], 'Date'[Calendar Year Month Number] ),
    "Starting Month", 'Date'[Calendar Year Month],
    "Starting Month Sort", 'Date'[Calendar Year Month Number]
)
```

Calculated table

```
Starting Rating =
SELECTCOLUMNS (
    SUMMARIZE ( Rating, Rating[Rating], Rating[RatingKey] ),
    "Starting Rating", Rating[Rating],
    "Starting Rating Sort", Rating[RatingKey]
)
```

These two slicer tables are not linked with any of the other tables in the model. Only the DAX code will read their selection and use it to compute the result of the measures.

However, the snapshot tables must be linked with the remaining part of the model through appropriate relationships. In this example we use a weak many-to-many relationship with *Date* based on the *Calendar Year Month Number* column, and a simple one-to-many strong relationship with *Product* based on the *ProductKey* column. The diagram is visible in Figure 20-7.

FIGURE 20-7 The snapshot table must have relationships with the other entities in the model.

Once the model is set, the DAX code must read the current selection on the two slicer tables and use the information to determine the list of products that – in the selected month – are in the selected status.

Once the list of products is computed, it is used as a filter over the snapshot table in order to restrict the calculation strictly to the relevant products:

Measure in Sales table

```
# Products Matrix :=
VAR SelectedStartingMonths =
    TREATAS (
        VALUES ( 'Starting Month'[Starting Month] ),
        'Date'[Calendar Year Month]
    )
VAR SelectedStartingRatings =
    TREATAS (
        VALUES ( 'Starting Rating'[Starting Rating] ),
        'Monthly Ratings'[Product Rating]
    )
VAR StartingProducts =
    CALCULATETABLE (
        VALUES ( 'Monthly Ratings'[ProductKey] ),
        SelectedStartingRatings,
        SelectedStartingMonths,
        REMOVEFILTERS ( 'Monthly Ratings'[Product Rating Sort] ),
        REMOVEFILTERS ( 'Date' )
    )
VAR Result =
    CALCULATE (
        DISTINCTCOUNT ( 'Monthly Ratings'[ProductKey] ),
        KEEPFILTERS ( StartingProducts )
    )
RETURN
    Result
```

Because the static transition matrix is based on a calculated table, its results are not dynamic. This means that if the user filters the customers in a specific country, the numbers in the transition matrix will not change. The only tables that affect the result are the ones linked through physical relationships with the snapshot. In this example these tables are *Date* and *Product*.

If you need a dynamic transition matrix that recomputes its result every time based on the current selection across the entire data model, then you need to implement the more powerful (albeit slower) dynamic transition matrix.

Dynamic transition matrix

The dynamic transition matrix solves the same scenario as the static transition matrix, with the noticeable difference that it does not require the snapshot table. Instead, it computes the result every time the measure is evaluated, resulting in a dynamic calculation.

The data model is the same as the static transition matrix, but no snapshot table is required this time. The result is visible in Figure 20-8, where we added a slicer filtering one continent – the same slicer would have no effect on a static transition matrix.

Starting Month	Calendar Year	Decreasing	Stable	Increasing	Total
March 2007 ⌄	⊟ **CY 2007**	64	64	30	64
	January	32			**32**
Starting Rating	February	35	10	19	**64**
	March		64		**64**
Stable ⌄	April	2	15	5	**22**
	May	19	6	1	**26**
Continent	June	15	3	2	**20**
	July	15	3	2	**20**
Europe ⌄	August	16		1	**17**
	September	17	2	1	**20**
	October	18	2	2	**22**
	November	11	2	3	**16**
	December	18	2	3	**23**

FIGURE 20-8 The dynamic transition matrix responds to any filter in the report.

Because the pattern requires computing the ranking of a product multiple times, this time we created a measure to return the rating of a product in a given month:

Measure in the Sales table

```
Status :=
CALCULATE (
    DISTINCT ( Rating[Rating] ),
    FILTER (
        ALLNOBLANKROW ( Rating ),
        VAR CurrentValue = [% Of Previous Month]
        VAR LowerBoundary = Rating[Min Growth]
        VAR UpperBoundary = Rating[Max Growth]
        RETURN
            AND ( CurrentValue >= LowerBoundary, CurrentValue < UpperBoundary )
    )
)
```

The final measure is quite intricate. It is divided into two separate steps:

1. Compute the list of the products that are in one of the selected states and months, chosen by the user with the slicers. To perform this operation – since the ranking of each product is unknown at the beginning – the formula computes the ranking of each product and then filters out the ones that are not selected.

2. Compute the status of the products computed earlier, this time in the current filter context. This second step is very similar to the previous one; the only important difference is in the filtering of dates and products, as better outlined in the code comments:

Measure in Sales table

```
# Products Matrix Dynamic :=
VAR SelectedStartingMonths =                      -- First we save the
    TREATAS (                                     -- selected starting month
        VALUES ( 'Starting Month'[Starting Month] ),  -- as a Date column to make
        'Date'[Calendar Year Month]               -- it filter Date, later on
    )
VAR SelectedStartingRatings =                     -- Save the currently selected
    VALUES ( 'Starting Rating'[Starting Rating] ) -- rating as the starting point
VAR CurrentRatings -                              -- Save the ratings of the current filter
    VALUES ( Rating[Rating] )                     -- context (not the starting, the current ones)

VAR StartingProdsAndMonths =                      -- We store the products and months
    CALCULATETABLE (                              -- of the starting time period in a variable
        SUMMARIZE (
            'Sales',
            'Product'[ProductKey],
            'Date'[Calendar Year Month]           -- Beware that the report is filtering
        ),                                        -- a different period. For this reason we
        SelectedStartingMonths,                   -- need to remove the outer filter on date
        REMOVEFILTERS ( 'Date' )                  -- and replace it with the starting month
    )
VAR StartingProdAndStatus =                       -- Here we compute the Status assigned to
    CALCULATETABLE (                              -- the products in the starting months,
        FILTER (                                  -- only keeping the products whose status
            StartingProdsAndMonths,               -- is among the selected starting ratings
            [Status] IN SelectedStartingRatings
        ),
        REMOVEFILTERS ( 'Date' )                  -- Required to get rid of the original filter
    )
VAR StartingProductsInStatus =                    -- Finally, we are only interested in the
    DISTINCT (                                    -- product keys, so we remove other columns
        SELECTCOLUMNS (                           -- from the previous table
            StartingProdAndStatus,                -- This variable will only filter Product
            "ProductKey", 'Product'[ProductKey]
        )
    )
```

```
--
-- At this point, we determined the products that were in the given status
-- in the starting month. The next step is to use the current filter context
-- created by the matrix to check where those products are in the target period.
--
-- The code is very similar to the previous code, this time using StartingProductsInStatus
-- as a filter over Sales, so to restrict the analysis
--
VAR CurrentProdsAndMonths =              -- Determines the products and months
    CALCULATETABLE (                     -- in the current time period
        SUMMARIZE (
            'Sales',
            'Product'[ProductKey],
            'Date'[Calendar Year Month]
        ),                               -- Restricting the products visible to the ones
        StartingProductsInStatus         -- determined in the previous steps
    )
VAR CurrentProdAndStatus =
    CALCULATETABLE (                     -- Here we compute the Status assigned to
        FILTER (                         -- each product, for each month in the current period
            CurrentProdsAndMonths,
            [Status] IN CurrentRatings
        ),
        REMOVEFILTERS ( 'Date' )
    )
VAR CurrentProducts =                    -- We want to count products, therefore we remove
    DISTINCT (                           -- all other columns and only keep the unique
        SELECTCOLUMNS (                  -- values in ProductKey
            CurrentProdAndStatus,
            "ProductKey", 'Product'[ProductKey]
        )
    )
VAR Result =
    COUNTROWS ( CurrentProducts )
RETURN
    Result
```

As you see, this code is not trivial at all. Changing it to make it fit your specific needs requires a deep understanding of its inner workings.

The dynamic transition matrix, albeit very powerful, is extremely demanding on CPU and RAM. Its speed mainly depends on the number of products. In data models with hundreds of thousands of products, it is unlikely to be usable. On the other hand, on smaller models it works just fine, though the static transition matrix displays much better performance.

Survey

The Survey pattern uses a data model to analyze correlations between different events related to the same entity, such as customer answers to survey questions. For example, in healthcare organizations the Survey pattern can be used to analyze data about patient status, diagnoses, and medicine prescribed.

Pattern description

You have a model that stores answers to questions. Therefore, consider a *Questions* table containing questions and possible answers shown in Figure 21-1.

Question	Answer
Gender	Female
Gender	Male
Job	Consultant
Job	IT Pro
Job	Teacher
Movie Preferences	Cartoons
Movie Preferences	Comedy
Movie Preferences	Horror

FIGURE 21-1 Every question has several possible answers.

The answers are stored in an *Answers* table containing in each row the survey target (the *Customer* in this case), one question and one answer. There are multiple rows in case the same customer provides multiple answers to the same question. The real model would store information with integer keys; In Figure 21-2 we are using strings to clarify the concept.

Customer	Question	Answer
Allen Cortez	Job	IT Pro
Allen Cortez	Job	Teacher
Alvin Benton	Gender	Male
Alvin Benton	Movie Preferences	Cartoons
Alvin Benton	Movie Preferences	Horror
Ana Carlson	Gender	Female
Ana Carlson	Job	IT Pro
Ana Carlson	Movie Preferences	Cartoons
Ann Hood	Gender	Female

FIGURE 21-2 Every row in the *Answers* table contains the answer of a customer to one specific question.

By using a DAX formula, we can answer a request like, "How many customers enjoy cartoons, broken down by job and gender?" Consider Figure 21-3 as an example. In this table, totals are not strict totals. This is explained later.

Question 1 ⌄
☐ Gender
☐ Job
■ Movie Preferences
☐ Sport Practiced
☐ Yearly Net Income

Question 2 ⌄
■ Gender
■ Job
☐ Movie Preferences
☐ Sport Practiced
☐ Yearly Net Income

Question 2	Cartoons	Comedy	Horror	**Total**
⊟ **Gender**	**25**	**19**	**28**	**52**
Female	9	9	13	25
Male	16	10	15	27
⊟ **Job**	**31**	**28**	**32**	**70**
Consultant	14	11	15	30
IT Pro	19	11	19	36
Teacher	15	14	18	36
Total	**38**	**36**	**43**	**89**

FIGURE 21-3 Every cell shows the number of customers who like one kind of movie and provided different answers to the job and gender questions.

The report includes two slicers to select the questions to intersect in the report. The columns in the matrix have the answers to the question selected in the Question 1 slicer, whereas the rows of the matrix provide the details of questions and answers corresponding to the selection made in the Question 2 slicer. The highlighted cell shows that 9 customers who answered Cartoons to the Movie Preferences question also answered Female to the Gender question.

In order to implement this pattern, you need to load the *Questions* table twice. This way you can use two slicers for the questions to analyze. Moreover, the relationship between the two copies of the questions must be inactive. Because we use the tables as filters, we named them *Filter1* and *Filter2*. You can see the resulting diagram in Figure 21-4.

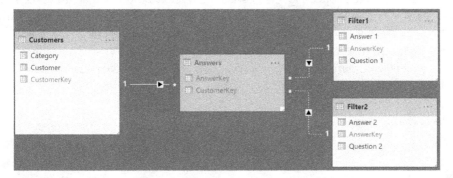

FIGURE 21-4 The Survey data model includes inactive relationships between the *Filter* and *Answers* tables.

To compute the number of customers who answered Q1 (the question filtered by *Filter1*) and Q2 (the question filtered by *Filter2*) you can use the following formula:

Measure in the Customers table

```
CustomersQ1andQ2 :=
VAR CustomersQ1 =
    CALCULATETABLE (
        VALUES ( Answers[CustomerKey] ),
        USERELATIONSHIP ( Answers[AnswerKey], Filter1[AnswerKey] )
    )
VAR CustomersQ2 =
    CALCULATETABLE (
        VALUES ( Answers[CustomerKey] ),
        USERELATIONSHIP ( Answers[AnswerKey], Filter2[AnswerKey] )
    )
RETURN
    CALCULATE (
        COUNTROWS ( Customers ),
        CROSSFILTER ( Answers[CustomerKey], Customers[CustomerKey], BOTH ),
        CustomersQ1,
        CustomersQ2
    )
```

The formula activates the correct relationship when computing *CustomersQ1* and *CustomersQ2*. It then uses the two variables as filters for the *Answers* table, which filters the customers through the CROSSFILTER modifier.

You can compute any calculation using the previous formula - provided that the CROSSFILTER modifier makes the *Answers* table filter the table you are basing your code on. Therefore, you can replace COUNTROWS (*Customer*) with any expression involving the *Customers* table. For example, the *RevenueQ1andQ2* measure provides the total revenue made off of the customers included in the selection; The only difference with the *CustomersQ1andQ2* measure is the *Revenue Amount* measure reference that replaces the previous COUNTROWS (*Customer*) expression:

Measure in the Customers table

```
RevenueQ1andQ2 :=
VAR CustomersQ1 =
    CALCULATETABLE (
        VALUES ( Answers[CustomerKey] ),
        USERELATIONSHIP ( Answers[AnswerKey], Filter1[AnswerKey] )
    )
VAR CustomersQ2 =
    CALCULATETABLE (
        VALUES ( Answers[CustomerKey] ),
        USERELATIONSHIP ( Answers[AnswerKey], Filter2[AnswerKey] )
    )
RETURN
    CALCULATE (
        [Revenue Amount],
        CROSSFILTER ( Answers[CustomerKey], Customers[CustomerKey], BOTH ),
        CustomersQ1,
        CustomersQ2
    )
```

The result of the *RevenueQ1andQ2* measure is visible in Figure 21-5.

Question 2	Cartoons	Comedy	Horror	Total
⊟ **Gender**	**1,441,200.00**	**1,085,100.00**	**1,162,800.00**	**2,725,000.00**
Female	648,000.00	512,100.00	661,700.00	**1,460,500.00**
Male	793,200.00	573,000.00	501,100.00	**1,264,500.00**
⊟ **Job**	**1,537,200.00**	**1,347,200.00**	**1,378,500.00**	**3,323,700.00**
Consultant	718,200.00	469,200.00	816,100.00	**1,510,700.00**
IT Pro	654,900.00	558,900.00	648,200.00	**1,361,800.00**
Teacher	844,900.00	640,900.00	725,600.00	**1,756,600.00**
Total	**1,986,000.00**	**1,852,500.00**	**1,852,900.00**	**4,407,000.00**

FIGURE 21-5 Every cell shows the revenue made off of customers who like one kind of movie and provided different answers to the job and gender questions.

If you only count the number of customers, then the previous code can be simplified and sped up by using the following variation:

Measure in the Customers table

```
CustomersQ1andQ2optimized :=
VAR CustomersQ1 =
    CALCULATETABLE (
        VALUES ( Answers[CustomerKey] ),
        USERELATIONSHIP ( Answers[AnswerKey], Filter1[AnswerKey] )
    )
VAR CustomersQ2 =
    CALCULATETABLE (
        VALUES ( Answers[CustomerKey] ),
        USERELATIONSHIP ( Answers[AnswerKey], Filter2[AnswerKey] )
    )
RETURN
    CALCULATE (
        DISTINCTCOUNT ( Answers[CustomerKey] ),
        CustomersQ1,
        CustomersQ2
    )
```

It is important to understand the condition computed in each cell. We use Figure 21-6 to explain this further, where we labeled a few cells from A to E.

Question 1		Question 2	Cartoons	Comedy	Horror	**Total**
☐ Gender	⌄	⊟ **Gender**	Ⓑ 25	19	28 Ⓓ 52	
☐ Job		Female	Ⓐ 9	9	13	25
■ Movie Preferences		Male	16	10	15	27
☐ Sport Practiced		⊟ **Job**	31	28	32	70
☐ Yearly Net Income		Consultant	14	11	15	30
		IT Pro	19	11	19	36
Question 2	⌄	Teacher	15	14	18	36
■ Gender		**Total**	Ⓒ 38	36	43 Ⓔ 89	
■ Job						
☐ Movie Preferences						
☐ Sport Practiced						
☐ Yearly Net Income						

FIGURE 21-6 Each cell computes a different number, the explanation is in the text below.

Here is what is computed in each cell:

A	Female AND prefers Cartoons
B	(Female OR Male) AND prefers Cartoons
C	(Female OR Male OR Consultant OR IT Pro OR Teacher) AND prefers Cartoons
D	(Female OR Male) AND prefers (Cartoons OR Comedy OR Horror)
E	(Female OR Male OR Consultant OR IT Pro OR Teacher) AND prefers (Cartoons OR Comedy OR Horror)

The formula uses an AND condition for the intersection between questions selected in Question 1 and Question 2, whereas it uses an OR condition for the answers provided to one same question. Remember that the OR condition means "any combination" (do not confuse it with an "exclusive or") and the OR condition also implies a non-additive behavior of the measure.

Basket analysis

The Basket analysis pattern builds on a specific application of the Survey pattern. The goal of Basket analysis is to analyze relationships between events. A typical example is to analyze which products are frequently purchased together. This means they are in the same "basket", hence the name of this pattern.

Two products are related when they are present in the same basket. In other words, the event granularity is the purchase of a product. The basket can be the most intuitive, like a sales order; but the basket can also be a customer; In that case, products are related if they are purchased by the same customer, albeit across different orders.

Because the pattern is about checking when there is a relationship between two products, the data model contains two copies of the same table of products. The two copies are named *Product* and *And Product*. The user chooses a set of products from the *Product* table; the measures show how likely it is that products in the *And Product* table are associated to the original selection.

We included in this pattern additional association rules metrics: *support*, *confidence*, and *lift*. These measures make it easier to understand the results and they extract richer insights from the pattern.

Defining association rules metrics

The pattern contains several measures, which we describe in detail in this section. In order to provide the definitions, we examine the orders containing at least a product of the Cameras and camcorders category and one product of the Computers category, as shown in Figure 22-1.

Category		And Category	
Cameras and camcorders ⌄		Computers	

2,361		**2,933**	**21,601**
# Orders		# Orders And	# Orders Total

400	**1.85%**	**16.94%**	**1.25**
# Orders Both	% Orders Support	% Orders Confidence	Orders Lift

FIGURE 22-1 Analysis of the orders with "Cameras and camcorders" products that also contain "Computers" products.

The report in Figure 22-1 uses two slicers: The Category slicer shows a selection of the *Product[Category]* column, whereas the And Category slicer shows a selection of the *'And Product'[And Category]* column. The *# Orders* measure shows you how many orders contain at least one product of the "Cameras and camcorders" category, whereas the *# Orders And* measure shows how many orders contain at least one product of both the "Cameras and camcorders" **and** "Computers" categories. We describe the other measures later. First, we need to make an important note: by inverting the selection between Category and And Category, the results are different by design. Most measures provide the same result (*# Orders Both*, *% Orders Support*, *Orders Lift*), whereas confidence (*% Orders Confidence*) depends on the order of the selection. In Figure 22-2 you can see the report from Figure 22-1, with the difference that the selections were inverted between the Category and And Category slicers.

Category		And Category	
Computers		Cameras and camcorders	

2,933		**2,361**	**21,601**
# Orders		# Orders And	# Orders Total

400	**1.85%**	**13.64%**	**1.25**
# Orders Both	% Orders Support	% Orders Confidence	Orders Lift

FIGURE 22-2 Analysis of the orders with "Computers" products that also contain "Cameras and camcorders" products.

Next, you find the definition of all the measures used in the pattern. There are two versions of all the measures: one considering the order as a basket, the other using the customer as a basket. For example, the description of *# And* applies to both *# Orders And* and *# Customers And*.

# #

 # Orders and *# Customers* return the number of unique baskets in the current filter context. Figure 22-1 shows 2,361 orders containing one product from the "Cameras and camcorders" category, whereas Figure 22-2 shows 2,933 orders containing at least one product from the "Computers" category.

And

 # Orders And and *# Customers And* return the number of unique baskets containing products of the *And Product* selection in the current filter context. These measures ignore the *Product* selection. Figure 22-1 shows 2,933 orders containing at least one product from the "Computers" category.

Total

 # Orders Total and *# Customers Total* return the total number of baskets and ignore any filter over *Product* and *And Product*. Both Figure 22-1 and Figure 22-2 report 21,601 orders. Be mindful that the filter on *And Product* is ignored by default because the relationship is not active; the only filter being explicitly ignored in the measure is the filter on *Product*. If there were a filter over *Date*, the measure would report only the baskets in the selected time period, and still ignore the filter over *Product*.

Both

 # Orders Both and *# Customer Both* return the number of unique baskets containing products from both the categories selected with the slicers. Figure 22-1 shows that 400 orders contain products from both categories: "Cameras and camcorders" **and** "Computers".

% Support

% Orders Support and *% Customers Support* return the support of the association rule. *Support* is the ratio between *# Both* and *# Total*. Figure 22-1 shows that 1.85% of the orders contain products from both categories: "Cameras and camcorders" **and** "Computers".

% Confidence

% Orders Confidence and *% Customers Confidence* return the confidence of the association rule. *Confidence* is the ratio between *# Both* and *#*. Figure 22-1 shows that out of all the orders containing "Cameras and camcorders", 16.94% also contain "Computers" products.

Lift

Orders Lift and *Customers Lift* return the ratio of confidence to the probability of the selection in *And Product*.

$$Lift = \frac{\%\ Confidence}{\left(\dfrac{\#\ And}{\#\ Total}\right)}$$

A lift greater than 1 indicates an association rule which is good enough to predict events. The greater the lift, the stronger the association. Figure 22-1 reports that the association rule between "Cameras and camcorders" and "Computers" is 1.25, obtained by dividing the % Confidence (16.94%) by the probability of # *Orders And* over # *Orders Total* (2933/21601 = 13.58%).

Sample reports

This section describes several reports generated on our sample model. These reports are useful to better understand the capabilities of the pattern.

The report in Figure 22-3 shows the products that are more likely to be present in orders containing "Contoso Optical USB Mouse M45 White".

Category

| Computers | ∨ |

Product Name

| Contoso Optical USB Mouse M45 White | ∨ |

Basket Analysis by Order

And Category	# Orders Both	% Orders Support	% Orders Confidence	Orders Lift	# Orders And	# Orders
⊟ **Computers**						
SV Keyboard E90 White	720	3.33%	99.45%	29.67	724	724
Contoso Education Essentials Bundle M300 Grey	1	0.00%	0.14%	1.24	24	724
Proseware CRT17 E104 White	1	0.00%	0.14%	9.95	3	724
Proseware LCD17W E202 White	1	0.00%	0.14%	2.13	14	724
⊟ **Games and Toys**						
SV Hand Games women M40 Black	5	0.02%	0.69%	0.67	224	724
MGS Flight Simulator 2002 M360	2	0.01%	0.28%	1.22	49	724
MGS Zoo Tycoon 2: Extinct Animals M210	1	0.00%	0.14%	1.15	26	724
⊟ **Audio**						
Contoso 4G MP3 Player E400 Silver	3	0.01%	0.41%	0.16	568	724
NT Bluetooth Stereo Headphones E52 Blue	3	0.01%	0.41%	0.15	586	724
⊟ **Cell phones**						
Contoso Single-line phones E10 Black	1	0.00%	0.14%	3.32	9	724
⊟ **Home Appliances**						
Contoso Washer & Dryer 21in E210 White	1	0.00%	0.14%	1.19	25	724

FIGURE 22-3 Basket analysis between products grouped by category.

"SV Keyboard E90 White" is present in 99.45% (confidence) of the orders that contain the selected mouse. The support of 3.33% indicates that the orders with this combination of products represent 3.33% of the total number of orders (21,601 as shown in Figure 22-1). The high lift value (29.67) is also a good indicator of the quality of the association rule between these two products.

The report in Figure 22-4 shows the pairs of products that are most likely to be in the same order, sorted by confidence.

All Products by Order

Product Name	And Product	# Orders Both	% Orders Support	% Orders Confidence	Orders Lift
A. Datum SLR Camera X137 Grey	Contoso Telephoto Conversion Lens X400 Silver	880	4.07%	99.89%	24.49
Contoso Telephoto Conversion Lens X400 Silver	A. Datum SLR Camera X137 Grey	880	4.07%	99.89%	24.49
Contoso Optical USB Mouse M45 White	SV Keyboard E90 White	720	3.33%	99.45%	29.67
SV Keyboard E90 White	Contoso Optical USB Mouse M45 White	720	3.33%	99.45%	29.67
Adventure Works 26" 720p LCD HDTV M140 Silver	SV 16xDVD M360 Black	2,160	10.00%	99.40%	9.82
SV 16xDVD M360 Black	Adventure Works 26" 720p LCD HDTV M140 Silver	2,160	10.00%	98.77%	9.82
SV 40GB USB2.0 Portable Hard Disk E400 Silver	Contoso USB Cable M250 White	400	1.85%	98.77%	50.20
Contoso 4G MP3 Player E400 Silver	NT Bluetooth Stereo Headphones E52 Blue	560	2.59%	98.59%	36.34
NT Bluetooth Stereo Headphones E52 Blue	Contoso 4G MP3 Player E400 Silver	560	2.59%	95.56%	36.34
Contoso USB Cable M250 White	SV 40GB USB2.0 Portable Hard Disk E400 Silver	400	1.85%	94.12%	50.20
Contoso 4G MP3 Player E400 Silver	A. Datum SLR Camera X137 Grey	33	0.15%	5.81%	1.42
Contoso 4G MP3 Player E400 Silver	Contoso Telephoto Conversion Lens X400 Silver	33	0.15%	5.81%	1.42
NT Bluetooth Stereo Headphones E52 Blue	A. Datum SLR Camera X137 Grey	33	0.15%	5.63%	1.38
NT Bluetooth Stereo Headphones E52 Blue	Contoso Telephoto Conversion Lens X400 Silver	33	0.15%	5.63%	1.38
A. Datum SLR Camera X137 Grey	Contoso 4G MP3 Player E400 Silver	33	0.15%	3.75%	1.42
A. Datum SLR Camera X137 Grey	NT Bluetooth Stereo Headphones E52 Blue	33	0.15%	3.75%	1.38
Contoso Telephoto Conversion Lens X400 Silver	Contoso 4G MP3 Player E400 Silver	33	0.15%	3.75%	1.42
Contoso Telephoto Conversion Lens X400 Silver	NT Bluetooth Stereo Headphones E52 Blue	33	0.15%	3.75%	1.38

FIGURE 22-4 Basket analysis between products.

The dataset used in this example returns somewhat similar confidence values when the order of the two products is reversed. However, this is not common. Focus on the highlighted lines: when "Contoso USB Cable M250 White" is in the first column the confidence of an association with "SV 40GB USB2.0 Portable Hard Disk E400 Silver" is slightly smaller than the other way around. In real datasets, these differences are usually bigger. Even though support and lift are identical, the order matters for confidence.

The same pattern can use the customer as a basket instead of the order. By using the customer, there are many more products in each basket. With more data, it is possible to perform an analysis by category of product instead of by individual product. For example, the report in Figure 22-5 shows what the associations are between categories in the customers' purchase history.

% Customers Confidence

Category	Audio	Cameras and camcorders	Cell phones	Computers	Games and Toys	Home Appliances	Music, Movies and Audio Books	TV and Video
Audio		22.87%	11.23%	20.46%	31.59%	17.95%	7.22%	24.77%
Cameras and camcorders	12.17%		12.44%	39.72%	34.92%	22.74%	7.63%	23.22%
Cell phones	20.29%	42.21%		48.19%	24.09%	46.38%	21.92%	40.58%
Computers	9.77%	35.63%	12.74%		32.95%	20.31%	6.99%	22.13%
Games and Toys	5.45%	11.31%	2.30%	11.89%		10.82%	2.09%	20.69%
Home Appliances	9.20%	21.89%	13.16%	21.79%	32.17%		8.02%	27.65%
Music, Movies and Audio Books	19.10%	37.93%	32.10%	38.73%	32.10%	41.38%		38.99%
TV and Video	7.22%	12.72%	6.55%	13.50%	34.99%	15.73%	4.30%	

FIGURE 22-5 Basket analysis between categories.

Customers buying "Cell phones" are likely to buy "Computers" too (confidence is 48.19%), whereas only 12.74% of customers buying "Computers" also buy "Cell phones".

Basic pattern example

The model requires a copy of the *Product* table, needed to select the *And Product* in a report. The *And Product* table can be created as a calculated table using the following definition:

Calculated table

```
And Product =
SELECTCOLUMNS (
    'Product',
    "And Category", 'Product'[Category],
    "And Subcategory", 'Product'[Subcategory],
    "And Product", 'Product'[Product Name],
    "And ProductKey", 'Product'[ProductKey]
)
```

There is an inactive relationship between the *And Product* table and *Sales*, connecting the *Sales[ProductKey]* column used in the relationship between *Product* and *Sales*. The relationship must be inactive because it is only used in the measures of this pattern and should not affect other measures in the model. Figure 22-6 shows the relationships between *Product*, *And Product*, and *Sales*.

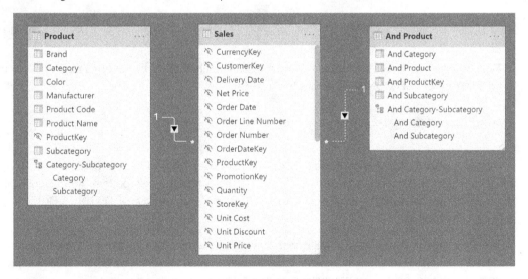

FIGURE 22-6 Relationships between *Product*, *And Product*, and *Sales*.

We use two baskets: orders and customers. An order is identified by *Sales[Order Number]*, whereas a customer is identified by *Sales[CustomerKey]*. From now on, we show only the measures for orders, because the measures for the customers are a basic variation – obtained by replacing *Sales[Order Number]* with *Sales[CustomerKey]*. The curious reader can find the customer measures in the sample files.

The first measure counts the number of unique orders in the current filter context:

Measure in the Sales table

```
# Orders :=
SUMX ( SUMMARIZE ( Sales, Sales[Order Number] ), 1 )
```

Before we describe the remaining measures in the pattern, a small digression is required. The # *Orders* measure is actually a DISTINCTCOUNT over *Sales[Order Number]*. We used an alternative implementation for both flexibility and performance reasons. Let us elaborate on the rationale of this choice.

The # *Orders* measure could have been written using the following formula with DISTINCTCOUNT:

```
DISTINCTCOUNT ( Sales[Order Number] )
```

In DAX this is a shorter way to perform a COUNTROWS over DISTINCT:

```
COUNTROWS ( DISTINCT ( Sales[Order Number] ) )
```

You can replace DISTINCT with SUMMARIZE this way:

```
COUNTROWS ( SUMMARIZE ( Sales, Sales[Order Number] ) )
```

The last three versions of the formula return the same result in terms of performance and query plan. Using SUMX instead of COUNTROWS leads to the same result:

```
SUMX ( SUMMARIZE ( Sales, Sales[Order Number] ), 1 )
```

Usually, replacing COUNTROWS with SUMX produces a query plan with lower performance. However, the specifics of Basket analysis make this alternative much faster in this pattern. More details about this optimization are available in this article: Analizing the performance of DISTINCTCOUNT in DAX (https://sql.bi/432941).

The advantage of using SUMMARIZE is that we can replace the second argument with a column that represents the basket even if it is in another table, as long as the table is related to *Sales*. For example, the measure computing the number of unique customer cities can be written this way:

```
SUMX ( SUMMARIZE ( Sales, Customer[City] ), 1 )
```

The first argument of SUMMARIZE needs to be the table containing the transactions, like *Sales*. If the second argument is a column in *Customer*, then you have no choice: you must use that column. For example, for the city of the customer you specify *Customer[City]*. In case you use the column that defines the relationship, like *CustomerKey* for *Customer*, then you can choose to use either *Sales[CustomerKey]* or *Customer[CustomerKey]*. Whenever possible, it is better to use the column available in *Sales* to avoid traversing the relationship. This is why instead of using *Customer[CustomerKey]* to identify the customer as a basket, we used *Sales[CustomerKey]*:

```
SUMX ( SUMMARIZE ( Sales, Sales[CustomerKey] ), 1 )
```

Now that we have explained why we use SUMMARIZE instead of DISTINCT to identify the basket attribute, we can move forward with the other measures of the pattern.

Orders And computes the number of orders by using the selection made in *And Product*. It activates the inactive relationship between *Sales* and *And Product*:

Measure in the Sales table

```
# Orders And :=
CALCULATE (
    [# Orders],
    REMOVEFILTERS ( 'Product' ),
    USERELATIONSHIP ( Sales[ProductKey], 'And Product'[And ProductKey] )
)
```

Orders Total returns the number of orders, while ignoring any selection in *Product*:

Measure in the Sales table

```
# Orders Total :=
CALCULATE (
    [# Orders],
    REMOVEFILTERS ( 'Product' )
)
```

Orders Both (Internal) is a hidden measure used to compute the number of orders including **at least** one item of *Product* and one item of *And Product*:

Measure in the Sales table

```
# Orders Both (Internal) :=
VAR OrdersWithAndProducts =
    CALCULATETABLE (
        SUMMARIZE ( Sales, Sales[Order Number] ),
        REMOVEFILTERS ( 'Product' ),
        REMOVEFILTERS ( Sales[ProductKey] ),
        USERELATIONSHIP ( Sales[ProductKey], 'And Product'[And ProductKey] )
    )
VAR Result =
    CALCULATE (
        [# Orders],
        KEEPFILTERS ( OrdersWithAndProducts )
    )
RETURN
    Result
```

This hidden measure is useful to compute *# Orders Both* and other calculations described later in the optimized version of the pattern. *# Orders Both* adds a check to return blank in case the selection in *Product* and *And Product* contains at least one identical product. This is required to prevent the report from showing associations between a product and itself:

Measure in the Sales table

```
# Orders Both :=
IF (
    ISEMPTY (
        INTERSECT (
            DISTINCT ( 'Product'[ProductKey] ),
            DISTINCT ( 'And Product'[And ProductKey] )
        )
    ),
    [# Orders Both (Internal)]
)
```

% Orders Support is the ratio of *# Orders Both* to *# Orders Total*:

Measure in the Sales table

```
% Orders Support :=
DIVIDE ( [# Orders Both], [# Orders Total] )
```

% Orders Confidence is the ratio of *# Orders Both* to *# Orders*:

Measure in the Sales table

```
% Orders Confidence :=
DIVIDE ( [# Orders Both], [# Orders] )
```

Orders Lift is the result of the division of *% Orders Confidence* by the ratio of *# Orders And* to *# Orders Total*, as per the formula we had introduced earlier:

$$Lift = \frac{\% \ Confidence}{\left(\dfrac{\# \ And}{\# \ Total}\right)}$$

Measure in the Sales table

```
Orders Lift :=
DIVIDE (
    [% Orders Confidence],
    DIVIDE (
        [# Orders And],
        [# Orders Total]
    )
)
```

The code described in this section works. Yet, the measures might display performance issues in case there are more than a few thousand products. The optimized pattern provides a faster solution, but at the same time it requires additional calculated tables and relationships to improve the performance.

Optimized pattern example

The optimized pattern reduces the effort required at query time to find the best combinations of products to consider. The performance improvement is obtained by creating calculated tables that pre-compute the existing combinations of products in the available baskets. Because we consider orders and customers as baskets, we created two calculated tables that are related to *Product*, as shown in Figure 22-7.

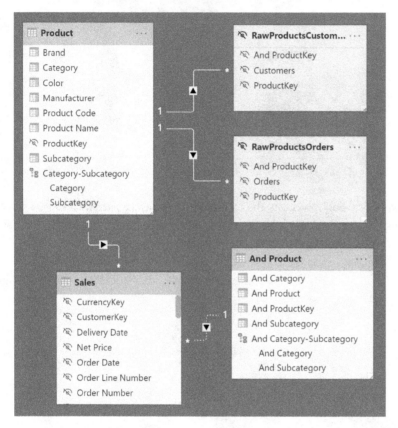

FIGURE 22-7 Relationships between *Product*, *RawProductsCustomers*, *RawProductsOrders*, *And Product*, and *Sales*.

The *RawProductsOrders* and *RawProductsCustomers* tables contain in each row, a combination of two product keys alongside the number of baskets containing both products. The rows that would combine identical products are excluded:

Calculated table

```
RawProductsOrders =
FILTER (
    SUMMARIZECOLUMNS (
        'Sales'[ProductKey],
        'And Product'[And ProductKey],
        "Orders", [# Orders Both (Internal)]
    ),
    NOT ISBLANK ( [Orders] ) && 'And Product'[And ProductKey] <> 'Sales'[ProductKey]
)
```

Calculated table

```
RawProductsCustomers =
FILTER (
    SUMMARIZECOLUMNS (
        'Sales'[ProductKey],
        'And Product'[And ProductKey],
        "Customers", [# Customers Both (Internal)]
    ),
    NOT ISBLANK ( [Customers] ) && 'And Product'[And ProductKey] <> 'Sales'[ProductKey]
)
```

The filter from *Product* automatically propagates to the two *RawProducts* tables. Only the filter from *And Product* must be moved through a DAX expression in the *# Orders Both* measure. Indeed, *# Orders Both* is the only measure that differs from the ones in the basic pattern:

Measure in the Sales table

```
# Orders Both :=
VAR ExistingAndProductKey =
    CALCULATETABLE (
        DISTINCT ( RawProductsOrders[And ProductKey] ),
        TREATAS (
            DISTINCT ( 'And Product'[And ProductKey] ),
            RawProductsOrders[And ProductKey]
        )
    )
VAR FilterAndProducts =
    TREATAS (
        EXCEPT (
            ExistingAndProductKey,
            DISTINCT ( 'Product'[ProductKey] )
        ),
        Sales[ProductKey]
    )
VAR OrdersWithAndProducts =
    CALCULATETABLE (
        SUMMARIZE ( Sales, Sales[Order Number] ),
        REMOVEFILTERS ( 'Product' ),
        FilterAndProducts
    )
VAR Result =
    CALCULATE (
        [# Orders],
        KEEPFILTERS ( OrdersWithAndProducts )
    )
RETURN
    Result
```

 # Orders Both cannot use the *# Orders Both (Internal)* implementation because of the way it applies the filters. *# Orders Both* transfers the filter from *And Product* to *RawProductsOrders* and then to *Sales* in order to retrieve the orders that include any of the items in *Any Product*. This technique is somewhat complex, but it is useful in order to reduce the workload in the formula engine. All this results in better performance at query time.

Currency conversion

Currency conversion is a complex scenario where both the data model and the quality of the DAX code play an important role. There are two kinds of currencies: the currency used to collect orders and the currency used to produce the report. Indeed, you might collect orders in multiple currencies, but need to report on those orders using only one currency, so to be able to compare all the values with the same unit of measure. Alternatively, you might collect (or store) orders in a single currency, but need to report the values using different currencies. Finally, you might have both orders that are collected in different currencies and reports that need to show many different currencies.

In this pattern, we cover three different scenarios where we simplified the description by only using EUR and USD:

- **Multiple sources, single target**: orders are in both EUR and USD, but the report must convert all currencies into USD.

- **Single source, multiple targets**: orders are only in USD, but the user can choose to see the report in either EUR or USD.

- **Multiple sources, multiple targets**: orders are in both EUR and USD, but the user can choose to see the report in either EUR or USD.

The formulas depend on the currency conversion table available. The requirement is often to perform the currency conversion for each day of the year. Sometimes it is only possible to perform the currency conversion at a different granularity, for example at the month level. The differences in managing these different cases are minimal, and we highlight them when showing the DAX code.

For demo purposes, we created models with both the daily and the monthly currency conversions. Therefore, you find both formulas and models in the same demo file, though you should only use one of the two exchange rate granularities for a specific implementation.

We created the daily currency conversion tables by tweaking the data available in Contoso. Therefore, these examples contain imaginary currency conversion rates with the sole purpose of showing a technique – and no guarantee of accuracy at all.

Multiple source currencies, single reporting currency

In this scenario, the source data contains orders in different currencies, and the report converts values into a single currency. For example, orders are in EUR, USD, and other currencies; the report must convert the order currency to USD.

The first thing to analyze is the model shown in Figure 23-1.

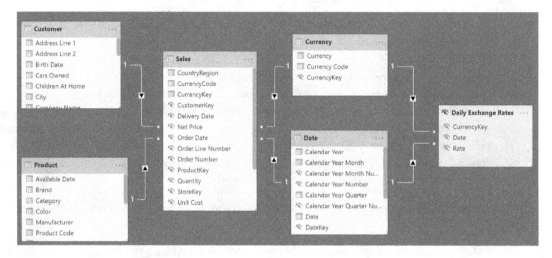

FIGURE 23-1 The model shows how to link Sales with the Daily Exchange Rates, through Date and Currency.

The *Sales* table stores the transaction value with the local currency. Every column that contains a monetary amount uses the local currency, like *Net Price*, *Unit Price*, and *Unit Discount*. The *Sales* table has a relationship with the *Currency* table that depends on the currency of the transaction.

A simple measure computing the sales amount would only work if sliced by the source currency; indeed, it is not possible to aggregate values in different currencies without performing a currency conversion first. For this reason, we called the measure doing this calculation *Sales (Internal)*, and we also hide this measure from the user:

```
Sales (Internal) := SUMX ( Sales, Sales[Quantity] * Sales[Net Price] )
```

As shown in Figure 23-2, *Sales (Internal)* produces a meaningless total, because it is summing values in different source currencies. Instead, the two measures *Sales USD (Monthly)* and *Sales USD (Daily)* produce a result that make sense, because they convert the *Sales (Internal)* value to USD. The differences in the report between the *Sales USD (Monthly)* and *Sales USD (Daily)* measures are due to the fluctuation of the currency exchange rates within each month.

Currency	Sales (Internal)	Sales USD (Monthly)	Sales USD (Daily)
Australian Dollar	9,450,623.49	7,933,488.34	8,139,714.02
British Pound	1,912,319.96	3,600,158.51	3,687,092.41
Canadian Dollar	910,355.97	853,860.13	874,937.42
EURO	2,544,568.45	3,536,014.77	3,618,749.70
Indian Rupee	4,702,011.45	97,149.69	97,767.82
Japanese Yen	5,412,928.66	56,871.57	58,309.90
South Korean Won	76,603,112.92	60,845.21	61,387.63
US Dollar	9,557,875.85	9,557,875.85	9,557,875.85
Total	**111,093,796.76**	**25,696,264.06**	**26,095,834.75**

FIGURE 23-2 The sum of *Sales (Internal)* across different currencies produces a meaningless result.

To perform an efficient currency conversion, we aggregate *Sales (Internal)* at the granularity of the exchange rate for each currency, and then we apply the conversion rate. For example, the *Sales USD (Daily)* measure implements the calculation at a day granularity by iterating with a SUMX the result of a table that has one row for each date and currency:

Measure in the Sales table

```
Sales USD (Daily) :=
VAR AggregatedSalesInCurrency =
    ADDCOLUMNS (
        SUMMARIZE (
            Sales,
            'Date'[Date],                    -- Day granularity
            'Currency'[Currency]
        ),
        "@SalesAmountInCurrency", [Sales (Internal)],
        "@Rate", CALCULATE (
            SELECTEDVALUE ( 'Daily Exchange Rates'[Rate] )
        )
    )
VAR Result =
    SUMX (
        AggregatedSalesInCurrency,
        [@SalesAmountInCurrency] / [@Rate]
    )
RETURN
    Result
```

To achieve optimal performance, it is essential to reduce the number of iterations to retrieve the currency exchange rate. Performing the currency exchange rate for every transaction would be time-consuming because all the transactions made on the same day with the same currency have the same currency exchange rate. SUMMARIZE over *Sales* significantly reduces the granularity of the entire formula. In case the currency exchange rates are available at the month level, the formula must reduce the granularity to the month level, like *Sales USD (Monthly)*:

Measure in the Sales table

```
Sales USD (Monthly) :=
VAR AggregatedSalesInCurrency =
    ADDCOLUMNS (
        SUMMARIZE (
            Sales,
            'Date'[Calendar Year Month],  -- Month granularity
            'Currency'[Currency]
        ),
        "@SalesAmountInCurrency", [Sales (Internal)],
        "@Rate", CALCULATE (
            SELECTEDVALUE ( 'Monthly Exchange Rates'[Rate] )
        )
    )
VAR Result =
    SUMX (
        AggregatedSalesInCurrency,
        [@SalesAmountInCurrency] / [@Rate]
    )
RETURN
    Result
```

The measures used in this example do not check whether a currency exchange rate is available or not because the operation being performed is a division – which results in a division by zero error in case a rate is missing. An alternative approach is to use the conditional statement in the following examples, which controls the error message displayed if a currency exchange rate is missing. You should use either one of the two techniques that raise an error in case a rate is missing, otherwise the report would show inaccurate numbers without any warning to the user.

Single source currency, multiple reporting currencies

In this scenario, the source data contains orders in a single currency (USD in our example), and the user changes the currency to use in the report through a slicer. The report converts the original amount according to the date of the transaction and to the currency selected by the user.

The model shown in Figure 23-3 does not show any direct relationship between the *Sales* and *Currency* tables. Indeed, all the sales transactions are in USD, and the *Currency* table allows the user to select the desired report currency.

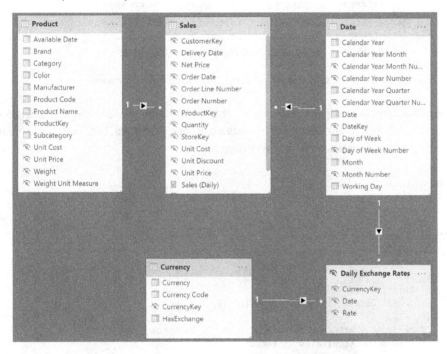

FIGURE 23-3 There is no direct relationship between *Sales* and *Currency*.

The user can either choose the desired currency with a slicer, or use the *Currency[Currency]* column in a matrix as shown in Figure 23-4, which performs the conversion using the monthly currency exchange rates.

Brand	US Dollar	EURO	Swiss Franc	Japanese Yen
A. Datum	1,876,700.93	1,349,641.55	2,188,060.92	207,131,483.49
Adventure Works	3,487,205.96	2,502,060.56	4,062,967.87	385,565,761.33
Contoso	6,373,833.45	4,525,161.41	7,267,013.90	678,207,396.28
Fabrikam	4,550,734.83	3,215,644.06	5,154,600.03	475,927,753.05
Litware	2,805,103.65	1,959,499.34	3,131,210.26	288,508,223.27
Northwind Traders	929,007.20	651,631.42	1,056,457.09	99,082,749.82
Proseware	2,094,389.36	1,492,048.49	2,394,307.59	220,829,404.98
Southridge Video	1,185,827.04	853,425.81	1,376,666.12	130,044,881.12
Tailspin Toys	247,577.19	174,871.49	278,909.35	25,575,107.97
The Phone Company	994,610.67	706,391.99	1,131,215.32	104,353,077.46
Wide World Importers	1,544,506.69	1,096,004.63	1,749,311.25	161,069,948.85
Total	**26,089,496.96**	**18,526,380.74**	**29,790,719.70**	**2,776,295,787.61**

FIGURE 23-4 The report shows the same sales amount by product brand in different currencies.

The structure of the formula to obtain the desired result is similar to the previous example, even though its implementation is slightly different because of the data model being different. The *Sales (Daily)* measure applies a different currency conversion rate for every day:

Measure in the Sales table

```
Sales (Daily) :=
IF (
    HASONEVALUE ( 'Currency'[Currency] ),
    VAR AggregatedSalesInUSD =
        ADDCOLUMNS (
            SUMMARIZE (
                Sales,
                'Date'[Date]        -- Day granularity
            ),
            "@Rate", CALCULATE ( SELECTEDVALUE ( 'Daily Exchange Rates'[Rate] ) ),
            "@USDSalesAmount", [Sales (internal)]
        )
    VAR Result =
        SUMX (
            AggregatedSalesInUSD,
            IF (
                NOT ( ISBLANK ( [@Rate] ) ),
                [@USDSalesAmount] * [@Rate],
                ERROR ( "Missing conversion rate" )
            )
        )
    RETURN
        Result
)
```

The initial test with HASONEVALUE ensures that only one currency is visible in the current filter context. The *AggregatedSalesInUSD* variable stores a table with the sales amount in USD and the corresponding currency exchange rate at the day granularity. The *@Rate* column retrieves the proper exchange rate thanks to the existing filter over *Currency[Currency]* and the context transition from *Date[Date]* aggregated by SUMMARIZE. The *Result* variable gets the final result by summing the result of the product of *@Rate* by *@USDSalesAmount*, or raises an error in case *@Rate* is not available. This breaks the report with an error message that describes the data quality issue (Missing conversion rate).

If the currency exchange rate is only available at the month level, *Sales (Monthly)* only differs from *Sales (Daily)* by the argument of SUMMARIZE:

Measure in the Sales table

```
Sales (Monthly) :=
IF (
    HASONEVALUE ( 'Currency'[Currency] ),
    VAR AggregatedSalesInUSD =
        ADDCOLUMNS (
            SUMMARIZE (
                Sales,
                'Date'[Calendar Year Month Number]  -- Month granularity
            ),
            "@Rate", CALCULATE ( SELECTEDVALUE ( 'Monthly Exchange Rates'[Rate] ) ),
            "@USDSalesAmount", [Sales (internal)]
        )
    VAR Result =
        SUMX (
            AggregatedSalesInUSD,
            IF (
                NOT ( ISBLANK ( [@Rate] ) ),
                [@USDSalesAmount] * [@Rate],
                ERROR ( "Missing conversion rate" )
            )
        )
    RETURN
        Result
)
```

Multiple source currencies, multiple reporting currencies

This scenario is a combination of the previous two. The source data contains orders in different currencies, and the user changes the currency to use in the report through a slicer. The report converts the original amount according to the date of the transaction, the original currency, and the reporting currency selected by the user.

There are two currency tables in the data model: *Source Currency* and *Target Currency*. The *Source Currency* table has a relationship with *Sales* and represents the currency of the transaction. The *Target Currency* table allows the user to select the desired currency for the report. The model is visible in Figure 23-5.

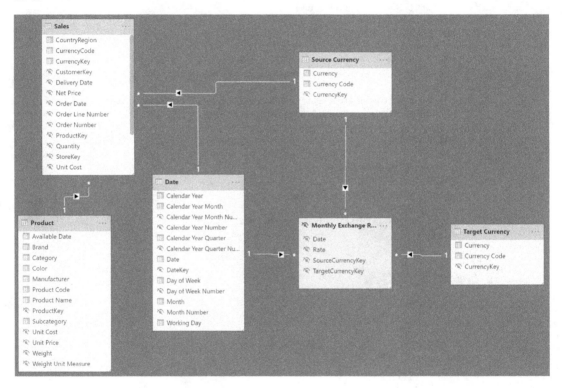

FIGURE 23-5 In this model there are two currencies: the source linked to Sales, and the target for the user to select.

This model enables the conversion of any source currency into any target currency. Figure 23-6 shows orders collected in different currencies from several countries using the monthly currency exchange rates. The report converts the original amount into the currency displayed in the column of the matrix.

Currency	US Dollar	EURO	Swiss Franc	Japanese Yen
Australian Dollar	**7,933,488.34**	**5,527,565.12**	**8,991,966.71**	**855,377,050.84**
Australia	7,933,488.34	5,527,565.12	8,991,966.71	855,377,050.84
British Pound	**3,600,158.51**	**2,510,508.10**	**4,089,163.38**	**381,055,228.14**
United Kingdom	3,600,158.51	2,510,508.10	4,089,163.38	381,055,228.14
Canadian Dollar	**853,860.13**	**608,319.24**	**989,280.76**	**94,774,145.95**
Canada	853,860.13	608,319.24	989,280.76	94,774,145.95
EURO	**3,340,064.92**	**2,395,524.83**	**3,887,251.92**	**369,306,897.75**
France	985,051.43	714,129.44	1,151,301.91	107,510,881.06
Germany	2,180,279.87	1,557,234.24	2,547,349.09	245,249,618.39
Portugal	174,733.61	124,161.15	188,600.92	16,546,398.29
Indian Rupee	**97,149.69**	**69,082.51**	**104,958.68**	**9,188,362.62**
India	97,149.69	69,082.51	104,958.68	9,188,362.62
Japanese Yen	**56,871.57**	**40,585.82**	**61,611.01**	**5,412,928.66**
Japan	56,871.57	40,585.82	61,611.01	5,412,928.66
Total	**15,881,593.14**	**11,151,585.61**	**18,124,232.45**	**1,715,114,613.95**

FIGURE 23-6 The model converts any source currency into any target currency.

The formula of the measure – like the model – is a mix of the two previous ones. The HASONEVALUE function checks that only one target currency is selected. The *AggregatedSalesInCurrency* variable contains a table with the sales amount aggregated at the available granularity of the currency exchange rate, also including the source currency. The *@Rate* column fetches the proper exchange rate thanks to the existing filter over *'Target Currency'[Currency]*, and thanks to the context transition from *Date[Date]* and *'Source Currency'[Currency]* aggregated by SUMMARIZE. The *Result* variable obtains the final result by summing the result of the product of *@Rate* by *@SalesAmount*, or raising an error in case *@Rate* is not available:

Measure in the Sales table

```
Sales (Daily) :=
IF (
    HASONEVALUE ( 'Target Currency'[Currency] ),
    VAR AggregatedSalesInCurrency =
        ADDCOLUMNS (
            SUMMARIZE (
                Sales,
                'Date'[Date],                  -- Day granularity
                'Source Currency'[Currency]
            ),
            "@SalesAmount", [Sales (Internal)],
            "@Rate", CALCULATE ( SELECTEDVALUE ( 'Daily Exchange Rates'[Rate] ) )
        )
    VAR Result =
        SUMX (
            AggregatedSalesInCurrency,
            IF (
                NOT ( ISBLANK ( [@Rate] ) ),
                [@SalesAmount] * [@Rate],
                ERROR ( "Missing conversion rate" )
            )
        )
    RETURN
        Result
)
```

As with the previous examples, it is important to use the granularity of the currency exchange table. If the currency exchange rate is only available at the month level, the *Sales (Monthly)* measure only differs from *Sales (Daily)* by the argument of SUMMARIZE:

Measure in the Sales table

```
Sales (Monthly) :=
IF (
    HASONEVALUE ( 'Target Currency'[Currency] ),
    VAR AggregatedSalesInCurrency =
        ADDCOLUMNS (
            SUMMARIZE (
                Sales,
                'Date'[Calendar Year Month],    -- Month granularity
                'Source Currency'[Currency]
            ),
            "@SalesAmount", [Sales (Internal)],
            "@Rate", CALCULATE ( SELECTEDVALUE ( 'Monthly Exchange Rates'[Rate] ) )
        )
    VAR Result =
        SUMX (
            AggregatedSalesInCurrency,
            IF (
                NOT ( ISBLANK ( [@Rate] ) ),
                [@SalesAmount] * [@Rate],
                ERROR ( "Missing conversion rate" )
            )
        )
    RETURN
        Result
)
```

Budget

This pattern includes several coding techniques you may find useful for budgeting scenarios. The techniques do not apply only to budgeting. We use the budget as an example to show how to reallocate a measure at a different granularity, and how to combine measures coming from tables with different granularities into the same chart.

Besides, each company has its own approach for creating and managing a budget. This pattern is just an example of what can be done. You must adapt the measures and the techniques shown in this pattern to your specific business.

Introduction

The initial table used for the budget contains forecasts of sales at a certain granularity. In our example, this table contains forecasts of sales by store country, product category, and year. There are three forecasts named Low, Medium, and High. Figure 24-1 shows the full dataset.

CountryRegion Scenario	China CY 2008	CY 2009	CY 2010	Germany CY 2008	CY 2009	CY 2010	United States CY 2008	CY 2009	CY 2010
⊟ High									
Audio	22,741.98	32,652.58	79,149.63	48,840.18	53,187.05	53,256.31	49,183.10	41,832.44	80,901.46
Cameras and camcorders	1,014,379.01	940,003.97	836,707.90	1,371,666.05	628,004.48	565,460.90	1,434,119.79	1,091,740.03	676,593.36
Cell phones	186,172.07	207,453.03	294,348.65	214,064.20	162,933.66	225,682.32	170,028.64	197,756.05	283,919.17
Computers	1,392,080.19	823,375.85	851,143.90	808,569.14	756,248.25	691,700.09	948,909.45	968,075.04	806,608.26
Games and Toys	31,921.31	41,629.25	83,603.77	33,259.50	28,700.71	72,718.12	41,645.50	57,473.35	40,535.82
Home Appliances	962,636.14	2,065,497.67	1,446,198.48	878,675.11	931,151.82	1,223,877.35	1,040,724.86	1,829,195.83	1,316,539.49
Music, Movies and Audio Books	52,890.66	39,882.87	34,968.37	23,098.24	40,263.07	51,497.48	30,647.14	61,848.20	41,273.14
TV and Video	570,624.32	435,158.50	513,254.38	861,068.50	263,013.84	359,939.03	1,245,888.53	409,893.88	571,128.22
⊟ Low									
Audio	16,076.23	22,299.32	48,905.46	33,975.77	36,483.68	35,195.47	32,924.23	28,236.90	49,330.16
Cameras and camcorders	718,518.46	564,002.38	532,450.48	922,327.17	416,953.79	399,722.36	1,010,119.16	688,071.45	454,759.47
Cell phones	129,851.11	136,089.19	197,802.29	134,453.55	113,110.97	147,184.12	115,273.65	134,538.95	193,158.13
Computers	959,248.53	522,140.78	614,303.86	516,397.10	500,099.65	455,221.43	640,716.64	661,124.42	581,031.37
Games and Toys	20,313.56	28,576.01	57,164.97	23,394.39	19,057.27	46,876.14	29,645.95	38,473.90	27,470.55
Home Appliances	582,239.60	1,382,550.86	976,183.98	598,089.78	623,466.87	832,236.60	624,434.91	1,159,977.84	851,878.50
Music, Movies and Audio Books	35,402.62	27,787.24	23,603.65	15,591.31	28,114.73	33,782.35	19,998.55	44,786.63	27,162.66
TV and Video	406,879.95	285,229.94	362,817.75	538,167.81	170,185.43	248,738.35	823,553.43	263,265.17	379,191.69
⊟ Medium									
Audio	19,605.16	25,484.94	60,488.34	41,620.32	47,033.18	43,994.34	42,679.55	34,860.37	65,773.55
Cameras and camcorders	845,315.84	736,963.11	663,834.37	1,229,769.56	519,905.35	448,468.99	1,284,472.51	899,080.02	593,405.65
Cell phones	156,447.12	159,323.93	244,898.08	160,990.43	122,536.89	192,320.58	145,532.99	173,441.79	235,047.84
Computers	1,123,022.67	656,023.03	777,131.38	706,648.66	561,087.41	597,108.63	770,482.03	794,923.40	683,566.32
Games and Toys	25,589.81	32,809.49	72,885.34	27,058.58	22,960.57	58,895.67	34,586.94	49,398.58	34,170.69
Home Appliances	745,266.69	1,699,038.40	1,084,648.86	679,311.85	777,309.35	949,728.83	765,973.49	1,412,793.53	1,205,905.92
Music, Movies and Audio Books	43,933.37	31,056.33	30,888.72	19,441.02	35,403.73	37,078.18	26,491.59	54,916.93	37,392.76
TV and Video	486,271.16	347,395.44	451,309.88	652,976.94	214,389.43	286,780.69	1,140,304.75	313,252.23	435,368.24

FIGURE 24-1 The forecast dataset contains data for store country, product category, year, and scenario.

Based on this dataset, we work with the following requirements:

- Allocating the forecast at a different granularity. For example, computing the monthly forecast based on the sales in the previous year.

- Combining actuals and forecasts in the same report, using the actual values for the past months and the forecasts for the future months of the current year.

- Correcting the forecast of future months based on how far they are from the actuals in past months of the current year.

Additionally, we want to keep in mind new products that might be introduced throughout the years, as well as discontinued products for which the forecast should not be computed. For this purpose, we use a table called *Override* that states when a product was introduced, along with the sales forecast for the first year. The same *Override* table also includes the dismission date of the discontinued products that are not used in order to allocate the forecast. The allocation of the new products by store country must be based on past sales of other products.

The data model

Before diving into the details of the calculations, it is important to make some considerations about the data model.

The scenario we are analyzing is a top-down forecasting scenario. Therefore, the source data contains a forecast of sales for different scenarios at a low granularity. Low granularity means that the information provided is at a very high level: year, store country, and product category. There are no details about individual products, months or stores. Consequently, the *Forecast* table is linked with the relevant tables using weak Many-Many-Relationships (MMR) and it has a Single-Many-Relationship (SMR) only with the *Scenario* table, as depicted in the diagram in Figure 24-2.

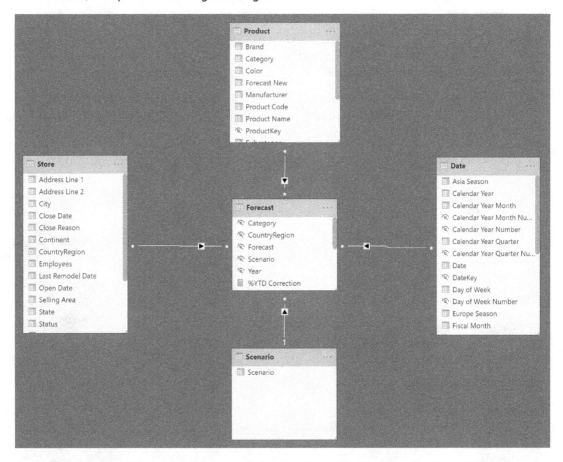

FIGURE 24-2 The relationships between Forecast and other dimensions (other than Scenario) are weak MMR relationships.

The following relationships start off of the *Forecast* table:

- MMR with *Store* based on the *CountryRegion* column.
- MMR with *Product* based on the *Category* column.
- MMR with *Date* based on the *Year* column.
- SMR with *Scenario* based on the *Scenario* column.

All the MMRs are weak relationships; they only filter at the granularity of the relationship. At a more detailed (higher) granularity, they just repeat the total at the supported grain.

NOTE The use of MMR and SMR is required to avoid confusion with other definitions of many-to-many relationships. A complete description of the MMR and SMR relationships in Power BI is available in the article, Relationships in Power BI and Tabular models (https://sql.bi/649118).

The *Scenario* table implements the best practice of always using dimension tables to slice and dice, instead of using columns in the fact table (*Forecast* in this case) for slicers and filters.

The forecast information of this pattern comes from an Excel file. The same Excel file includes another table called *Override*, which contains information about new and dismissed products. The relevant columns in the *Override* table are:

- **Year New**: the year a new product was introduced.

- **Year Del**: the year a product was (or will be) dismissed.

- **Amount**: the forecast sales over all countries for the first year.

Because the *Override* table has the same granularity as the *Product* table, we used Power Query to merge these three columns directly in the *Product* table. Figure 24-3 shows the content of these three columns imported in *Product* from the *Override* table.

Category	Subcategory	Product Name	Year New	Year Del	Forecast New
Computers	Laptops	Microsoft Surface azure	2010		25,000.00
Computers	Laptops	Microsoft Surface black	2010		25,000.00
Computers	Laptops	Microsoft Surface gray	2010		55,000.00
Clothes	Shirts	Power BI T-shirt black	2010		5,000.00
Clothes	Shirts	Power BI T-shirt blue	2010		6,000.00
Clothes	Shirts	Power BI T-shirt gray	2010		7,000.00
Audio	Recording Pen	WWI 1GB Digital Voice Recorder Pen E100 Pink		2010	0.00
Audio	Recording Pen	WWI 2GB Pulse Smart pen M100 White		2010	0.00

FIGURE 24-3 For each new or dismissed product, the relevant information is stored in the *Product* table itself.

This is not necessarily an optimal model. We designed it to show you the DAX code, but different requirements might justify using a different model. You should update the calculations to reflect your specific requirements and data model.

Business choices

As with the model, we needed to set some business choices in order to author the DAX code. The following sections describe the business rules implemented in this pattern.

Allocation based on the previous year

When the forecast needs to be reallocated, we consider the sales in the previous year as an allocation factor. In other words, in order to show the forecast of a subcategory, we reallocate the budget defined at the category level by the percentage of sales of the given subcategory against the corresponding category in the previous year.

This is better depicted in Figure 24-4.

CountryRegion	Sales PY	% Sales PY (BG)	Forecast Amount
⊟ **China**	**235,478.92**	**100.00%**	**197,802.29**
⊟ **Cell phones**	**235,478.92**	**100.00%**	**197,802.29**
Cell phones Accessories	64,544.86	27.41%	54,217.68
Home & Office Phones	12,223.51	5.19%	10,267.75
Smart phones & PDAs	69,460.60	29.50%	58,346.90
Touch Screen Phones	89,249.95	37.90%	74,969.96
⊟ **Germany**	**196,245.49**	**100.00%**	**147,184.12**
⊟ **Cell phones**	**196,245.49**	**100.00%**	**147,184.12**
Cell phones Accessories	49,266.84	25.10%	36,950.13
Home & Office Phones	7,816.40	3.98%	5,862.30
Smart phones & PDAs	87,579.85	44.63%	65,684.89
Touch Screen Phones	51,582.40	26.28%	38,686.80
⊟ **United States**	**232,720.63**	**100.00%**	**193,158.13**
⊟ **Cell phones**	**232,720.63**	**100.00%**	**193,158.13**
Cell phones Accessories	60,502.83	26.00%	50,217.35
Home & Office Phones	11,179.50	4.80%	9,278.99
Smart phones & PDAs	100,769.80	43.30%	83,638.93
Touch Screen Phones	60,268.50	25.90%	50,022.86
Total	**664,445.05**	**100.00%**	**538,144.54**

FIGURE 24-4 The forecast is allocated to subcategories based on the sales of the previous year.

Consequently, a previously existing product that had no sales in one year, will have a forecast of zero in the following year.

Dismissed products do not contribute to the allocation

If a product is dismissed, its forecast for the new year is zero since the product is no longer available for sale. Consequently, the forecast for the new year does not include dismissed products. If we ignored this condition, the allocation would produce undesired results.

For example, think about what would happen if all the products in the category Cell Phones Accessories were dismissed. In the United States, they contribute for 26% of sales, as shown in Figure 24-4. Because the products of this category are dismissed, the forecast for the next year does not include their sales. The allocation formula must take this into account, by increasing the percentages of other subcategories to compensate for the absence of a certain category. If not, the total allocated forecast would only add up to 74% of the total forecast, hiding the 26% that are no longer being allocated to dismissed products.

In summary, if a product is dismissed one year, its sales in the previous year are not considered for the forecast allocation.

New products have their own forecast amount

This is not really a business decision, but rather a choice to simplify the model. If a product is being introduced as new, then its sales in the previous year are at zero. As we stated earlier, this would translate into an empty forecast for the following year. Still, the product being new is expected to have no sales in the previous year.

For this reason, every new product has a forecast amount associated to it for the year when it is being introduced. This is a single value, which is allocated in different store countries depending on the distribution percentage of all the other products over the store countries.

As with other options, this is not necessarily the best choice; but we must make a choice in order to write working code. In other scenarios, there could be a table containing more detailed forecasts, or the issue could be ignored for a specific business. Therefore, consider this as an optional implementation option and not as a mandatory requirement.

Products can be dismissed or introduced on a yearly basis

In order to keep the model simple enough, we introduced this artificial limitation: a product is introduced at the beginning of a year (therefore it starts selling in January) and dismissed at the end of a year (no more sales in the new year).

Handling the introduction of products at different points in time introduces a new level of complexity around time. Indeed, when computing the forecast for the new products, the amount should be allocated only starting at a given point in time. Dismissed products present a similar issue. We decided not to handle this complexity in order to focus more on the allocation algorithm. Specific and more detailed business requirements might require some adjustment to the proposed formulas.

Forecast allocation

The allocation of forecast uses sales in the previous year to determine the percentage of the total forecast that must be allocated to the current selection. The formula is composed of two main sections: the allocation of the forecast and the computation of the value for new products.

Figure 24-5 helps us better understand the calculation by showing the *Forecast Amount* and the *% Sales PY (BG)* measures side by side. *% Sales PY (BG)* is the allocation percentage at the budget granularity that is internally computed in *Forecast Amount*. The sample file includes a separate definition of *% Sales PY (BG)* just to display this intermediate calculation that is not relevant to the pattern.

CountryRegion	Sales PY	% Sales PY (BG)	Forecast Amount
China	**235,478.92**	**100.00%**	**204,498.39**
Cell phones	**235,478.92**	**100.00%**	**197,802.29**
Cell phones Accessories	64,544.86	27.41%	54,217.68
Home & Office Phones	12,223.51	5.19%	10,267.75
Smart phones & PDAs	69,460.60	29.50%	58,346.90
Touch Screen Phones	89,249.95	37.90%	74,969.96
Clothes			**6,696.10**
Shirts			6,696.10
Germany	**196,245.49**	**100.00%**	**152,368.79**
Cell phones	**196,245.49**	**100.00%**	**147,184.12**
Cell phones Accessories	49,266.84	25.10%	36,950.13
Home & Office Phones	7,816.40	3.98%	5,862.30
Smart phones & PDAs	87,579.85	44.63%	65,684.89
Touch Screen Phones	51,582.40	26.28%	38,686.80
Clothes			**5,184.67**
Shirts			5,184.67

FIGURE 24-5 The figure shows the relevant parts of the forecast allocation by product.

There are two categories selected in the report: Cell phones and Clothes. Clothes is a new category, that was not present in the previous year. The full forecast for each store country (China and Germany are visible in Figure 24-5) includes the allocated forecast for the selected country, plus the amount assigned to new products through the *Forecast New* column imported from the *Amount* column in the *Override* table of the Excel file.

The model is designed in a way that there is a single forecast amount for each product for the entire year. This number must be allocated by store country based on the sales of the previous year for that country, as shown by *% Sales PY by Store* in Figure 24-6. This time, the allocation is made only by store country – no other columns are involved.

CountryRegion	Sales PY	% Sales PY by Store
China	235,478.92	35.44%
Germany	196,245.49	29.54%
United States	232,720.63	35.02%
Total	**664,445.05**	**100.00%**

FIGURE 24-6 The figure shows the relevant parts of the forecast allocation by country.

This is the definition of the *Forecast Amount* measure:

Measure in the Forecast table

```
Forecast Amount :=
IF (
    HASONEVALUE( 'Date'[Calendar Year Number] ),
    VAR SelectedScenario = SELECTEDVALUE ( Scenario[Scenario], "Medium" )
    VAR Categories = VALUES ( 'Product'[Category] )
    VAR Countries = VALUES ( Store[CountryRegion] )
    VAR CurrentYear = VALUES ( 'Date'[Calendar Year Number] )

    -- Here we compute the PY sales amount at the forecast granularity,
    -- that is Category, CountryRegion, and Year. We do this by removing
    -- any filter on the granularity tables and then by restoring only
    -- the filters corresponding to the forecast granularity.
    VAR PYSalesAmountAtGrain =
        CALCULATE (
            [Sales PY],
            REMOVEFILTERS ( 'Product' ),
            REMOVEFILTERS ( 'Store' ),
            REMOVEFILTERS ( 'Date' ),
            Categories,
            Countries,
            CurrentYear,
            KEEPFILTERS ( 'Product'[Year Del] < CurrentYear )
        )

    -- No special treatment for the forecast amount, as it is already at the
    -- Category, CountryRegion, and Year granularity despite any further filter.
    VAR CurrentForecastedAmount =
        CALCULATE (
            SUM ( Forecast[Forecast] ),
            Scenario[Scenario] = SelectedScenario
        )
    VAR CategoriesCountries =
        CROSSJOIN ( Categories, Countries )

    -- To compute the forecast value we iterate over categories and countries (note
    -- that there is always a single year selected, no need to iterate on that),
    -- we compute the sales amount at the Category/Country level. Then, we divide
    -- the result by the sales amount at the forecast granularity to obtain the
    -- percentage to allocate the forecast.
    -- The filter on Product[Year Del] guarantees that products removed before
    -- the current year are not being considered, as they will have no forecast amount.
```

```
    VAR ForecastValue =
        CALCULATE (
            SUMX (
                KEEPFILTERS ( CategoriesCountries ),
                VAR PYSalesAmount =  [Sales PY]
                VAR AllocationFactor = DIVIDE ( PYSalesAmount,  PYSalesAmountAtGrain )
                RETURN AllocationFactor * CurrentForecastedAmount
            ),
            KEEPFILTERS ( 'Product'[Year Del] < CurrentYear )
        )
    -- Now we determine the amount of new products, which must be allocated
    -- by country using the sales of any product in the same period in the
    -- previous year.
    VAR NewProductsAmount =
        CALCULATE (
            SUM ( 'Product'[Forecast New] ),
            KEEPFILTERS ( 'Product'[Year New] = CurrentYear )
        )

    -- Here we compute the PY sales at the forecast granularity, regardless of
    -- any product and country, because the forecast for a new product is specified
    -- as a single number that sums sales in all the countries.
    VAR PYSalesAmountAtGrainAnyProduct =
        CALCULATE (
            [Sales PY],
            REMOVEFILTERS ( 'Product' ),
            REMOVEFILTERS ( 'Store' ),
            REMOVEFILTERS ( 'Date' ),
            CurrentYear
        )

    -- Similarly to what we did with the forecast, we allocate the new value.
    -- This time we need to iterate only on Countries, as there is only one year
    -- and categories should not be part of the iteration
    VAR NewValue =
        SUMX (
            KEEPFILTERS ( Countries ),
            VAR PYSalesAmountAnyProduct =
                CALCULATE (
                    [Sales PY],
                    REMOVEFILTERS ( 'Product' )
                )
            VAR AllocationFactor =
                DIVIDE ( PYSalesAmountAnyProduct, PYSalesAmountAtGrainAnyProduct )
            RETURN
                AllocationFactor * NewProductsAmount
        )
    --
    -- The result is the forecast value plus the value of new products, both reallocated
    -- according to different business requirements.
    --
    VAR Result =
        ForecastValue + NewValue
    RETURN
        Result
)
```

The formula works with a single year selected and it also produces correct results with a reduced set of dates within one year. It is also possible to implement time intelligence calculations over the *Forecast Amount* measures, like the year-to-date in the *YTD Forecast* measure:

Measure in the Forecast table

```
YTD Forecast :=
CALCULATE (
    [Forecast Amount],
    DATESYTD ( 'Date'[Date] )
)
```

Showing actuals and forecasts on the same chart

A common requirement is to show both actual and forecast measures in the same chart. This type of requests might end up in producing reports that are not very useful, like the one visible in Figure 24-7. The *YTD Sales (not filtered)* measure displays the year-to-date of *Sales Amount*: because the *Sales* table contains data until August 14, 2010, the year-to-date is a flat line from August to December.

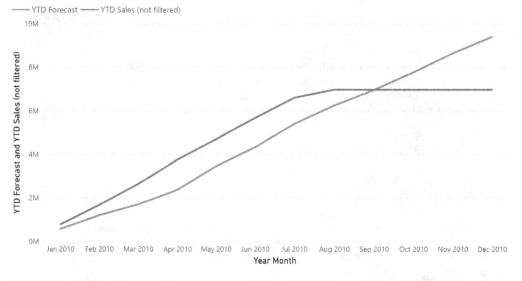

FIGURE 24-7 Actual and forecast sales are represented in the same line chart, relying on the projection measures.

A better visualization in these cases shows the actual sales amount up to the last day of sales available, and then it uses the forecast for the following days to complete the chart for the future months. Figure 24-8 shows this type of report through a line chart.

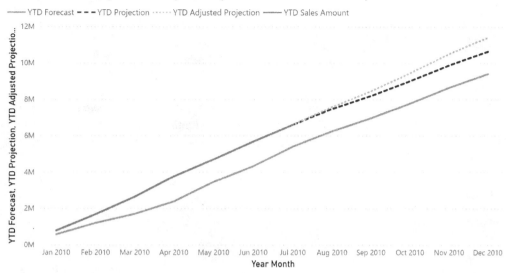

YTD Forecast, YTD Projection, YTD Adjusted Projection and YTD Sales Amount by Year Month

—— YTD Forecast — — YTD Projection ······ YTD Adjusted Projection —— YTD Sales Amount

FIGURE 24-8 Actual and forecast sales are represented in the same line chart using the projection measures.

The last complete month showing data for the *YTD Sales Amount* measure is July 2010. The following months are not displayed thanks to the date check in the following implementation:

Measure in the Sales table

```
YTD Sales Amount :=
VAR LastAvailableDate =
    CALCULATE (
        MAX ( Sales[Order Date] ),
        REMOVEFILTERS ( 'Date' )
    )
VAR LastVisibleDate =
    MAX ( 'Date'[Date] )
VAR Result =
    IF (
        LastVisibleDate <= LastAvailableDate,
        CALCULATE ( [Sales Amount], DATESYTD ( 'Date'[Date] ) )
    )
RETURN
    Result
```

The *YTD Forecast* measure is only used to display the complete forecast in the line chart; It just computes the year-to-date of *Forecast Amount* defined in the previous section:

Measure in the Forecast table

```
YTD Forecast :=
CALCULATE (
    [Forecast Amount],
    DATESYTD ( 'Date'[Date] )
)
```

The *YTD Projection* measure computes the year-to-date of the *Projection Amount* measure. The latter uses *Sales Amount* for the dates available in the *Sales* table (until August 14, 2010 in this example) and *Forecast Amount* for the dates following the last date available in *Sales* (dates greater than August 14, 2010 in this example):

Measure in the Forecast table

```
YTD Projection :=
CALCULATE (
    [Projection Amount],
    DATESYTD ( 'Date'[Date] )
)
```

Measure in the Forecast table

```
Projection Amount :=
VAR LastAvailableDate =
    CALCULATE (
        MAX ( Sales[Order Date] ),
        REMOVEFILTERS ( 'Date' )
    )
VAR ActualSalesAmount = [Sales Amount]
VAR ForecastedAmount =
    CALCULATE (
        [Forecast Amount],
        KEEPFILTERS ( 'Date'[Date] > LastAvailableDate )
    )
VAR Result =
    ActualSalesAmount + ForecastedAmount
RETURN
    Result
```

The *YTD Adjusted Projection* measure is like *YTD Projection;* however, it applies an adjustment factor to the *Forecast Amount* based on the comparison between available transactions and the corresponding forecast:

Measure in the Forecast table

```
YTD Adjusted Projection :=
CALCULATE (
    [Adjusted Projection Amount],
    DATESYTD ( 'Date'[Date] )
)
```

Measure in the Forecast table

```
Adjusted Projection Amount :=
VAR LastAvailableDate =
    CALCULATE (
        MAX ( Sales[Order Date] ),
        REMOVEFILTERS ( 'Date' )
    )
VAR ActualSalesAmount = [Sales Amount]
VAR AdjustmentFactor = [% Adjustment]
VAR ForecastAmount =
    CALCULATE (
        [Forecast Amount] * AdjustmentFactor,
        KEEPFILTERS ( 'Date'[Date] > LastAvailableDate )
    )
VAR Result =
    ActualSalesAmount + ForecastAmount
RETURN
    Result
```

The adjustment factor computed by the *% Adjustment* measure could have many different implementations, depending on specific business requirements. In this example we use the ratio between *Sales Amount* and *Forecast Amount* for the dates available in the *Sales* table:

Measure in the Forecast table

```
% Adjustment :=
VAR LastAvailableDate =
    CALCULATE (
        MAX ( Sales[Order Date] ),
        REMOVEFILTERS ( 'Date' )
    )
VAR CurrentYear =
    SELECTEDVALUE ( 'Date'[Calendar Year] )
VAR Result =
    CALCULATE (
        DIVIDE (
            [Sales Amount],
            [Forecast Amount]
        ),
        'Date'[Date] <= LastAvailableDate,
        'Date'[Calendar Year] = CurrentYear
    )
RETURN
    Result
```

Index

A

ABC, 217-229, 391

ADDCOLUMNS, 51, 179, 183, 196, 198-199, 220, 222, 227, 229, 237, 240-241, 243-248, 251-255, 258, 261-265, 267, 275-276, 328, 365-366, 368-369, 372-373, 391

ALLEXCEPT, 86-87, 91-95, 97, 100, 102, 106, 108, 110, 112-113, 116, 118-119, 121, 123-124, 130, 133-136, 138, 140, 148, 150-151, 153, 156-157, 159, 161, 163-165, 167-168, 177, 206, 216, 237, 250-255, 257-259, 261-265, 267, 271, 273-274, 297, 391

ALLNOBLANKROW, 207, 275-276, 328, 339, 391

allocation, 169, 171, 376, 379-382, 391

ALLSELECTED, 192, 210-211, 214, 216, 227, 229, 237, 240-241, 243-248, 252, 258-259, 261-262, 264, 267, 298-299, 301, 307, 330-331, 391

ambiguity, 284, 293, 391

association, 349-354, 358, 391

AVERAGEX, 43-45, 79-80, 121, 123-124, 165, 167-168, 287-288, 291-292, 391

AVG, 42-45, 78-80, 120-121, 123-124, 164-165, 167-168, 285, 287-288, 291-292, 391

B

basket, xvii, 349, 351, 353-354, 356-357, 391

benchmark, 32, 71, 111, 155, 391

best-selling, 217, 391

bidirectional, 224, 280, 391

BLANK, 204, 229, 274, 391

BOTH, 272, 331, 345-346, 391

budget, 309, 375, 379, 381, 391

C

CALCULATETABLE, 7, 20-23, 27-29, 31, 43-45, 97, 100, 102, 121, 123-124, 140, 165, 167-168, 171-172, 179, 183, 204, 206, 237, 240-241, 243-248, 251-255, 258-259, 261-265, 267, 273, 276, 299, 307, 330-331, 338, 340-341, 345-347, 358, 362, 391

calendar, 1-5, 8-10, 14, 50-51, 53, 57, 81-84, 86, 96, 103-104, 117-118, 125-130, 139, 210-211, 214, 216, 222-225, 328, 331, 336-338, 340-341, 366, 369, 373, 382, 388, 391

CALENDARAUTO, 9

cardinality, 49, 293, 391

circular, 204, 275, 391

classification, 86, 129, 209, 217-218, 221, 225-226, 228, 391

CLOSINGBALANCEYEAR, 182, 391

CONVERT, 7, 127, 391

correlation, 343, 391

COUNTROWS, 79-80, 140, 150, 153, 172, 204, 206, 210, 214, 245-248, 251-255, 259, 261, 263, 265, 268, 271, 279-281, 286-288, 291-292, 341, 345-346, 356, 391

CROSSFILTER, 272, 293, 331, 345-346, 391

SUMX, 97, 100, 102, 127, 140, 194-196, 198, 211, 219-220, 222, 227, 229, 279-280, 317, 322, 331, 356-357, 364-366, 368-369, 372-373, 383, 394

survey, 343-345, 349, 394

SWITCH, 25, 66, 103-104, 145-146, 219-220, 222, 229, 304-305, 307, 317, 322, 394

T

target, 341, 344, 363, 370-373, 394

taxation, 316, 394

temporarily-lost, 232-233, 245-248, 252-254, 262-265, 395

time-intelligence, 50, 395

time-related, xv, xvii, 1-5, 8, 11, 49, 53-54, 83, 88, 125-126, 131, 395

time-shift, 128, 395

to-date, 26, 32, 67, 71, 105, 111, 147, 155, 395

TOPN, 199-200, 295, 301, 395

TOTAL, 13, 395

TOTALMTD, 17-18, 395

TOTALQTD, 16, 395

TOTALYTD, 13, 15, 395

TREATAS, 179, 183, 223-224, 237, 240, 243, 251, 259, 292-293, 329-330, 338, 340, 362, 395

U

UNION, 275-276, 280, 328, 395

USERELATIONSHIP, 171-172, 293, 345-347, 357-358, 395

W

weak, 329, 337, 377-378, 395

week, 2-4, 8-10, 46-50, 83-87, 91, 93-97, 100-104, 106, 108-110, 112-113, 115-121, 123-125, 127-130, 133-134, 136, 138-140, 148, 150-151, 153, 156-157, 159-161, 163-165, 167-168, 189-190, 333, 395

week-based, 2-3, 83-84, 117, 125, 395

WEEKDAY, 3, 9, 46, 95, 127, 395

weekly, 3, 395

week-over-week, 101-103, 395

week-related, 2-4, 8, 49, 83-84, 125, 395

week-to-date, 90, 95, 109, 115, 395

Y

YEAR, 6, 9, 20, 27, 32, 39, 41, 45, 51, 126-127, 395

year-over-year, 19, 24, 59-60, 65, 96-97, 101, 103, 109, 138, 141, 145, 213, 395

year-to-date, 1, 5, 10-11, 13-14, 26, 32, 38, 46, 49, 55-56, 58, 67, 71, 75, 83, 87-88, 90, 93-95, 105, 111, 117, 125, 130, 132-133, 136-137, 147, 155, 160, 384-386, 395

Alberto Ferrari and **Marco Russo** co-founded SQLBI, where they publish frequent articles about DAX and other Microsoft tools.

They are regular speakers at major international conferences such as Microsoft Ignite, PASS Summit, and SQLBits. Both currently teach, consult, and mentor on Microsoft Business Intelligence technologies.

www.sqlbi.com

Latest books

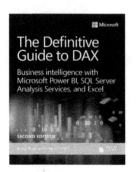

The Definitive Guide to DAX, Second Edition

Microsoft Press

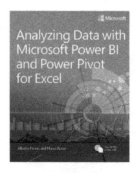

Analyzing Data with Microsoft Power BI and Power Pivot for Excel

Microsoft Press

CPSIA information can be obtained
at www.ICGtesting.com
Printed in the USA
BVHW011919070422
633691BV00007B/30

9 781735 365206